A HISTORY OF JERUSALEM

BY THE SAME AUTHOR

The KRT Text in the Literature of Ras Shamra

The Legacy of Canaan

Archaeology and the Old Testament World

I and II Kings: a Commentary

The Canaanites (Ancient Peoples and Places series)

Joshua, Judges and Ruth (Century Bible series)

A HISTORY OF JERUSALEM

JOHN GRAY

Illustrated
and with maps and plans

FREDERICK A. PRAEGER, *Publishers*

New York · Washington

BOOKS THAT MATTER

Published in the United States of America in 1969
by Frederick A. Praeger, Inc., *Publishers*
111 Fourth Avenue, New York, N.Y. 10003

Library of Congress Catalog Card Number: 72–90412

PRINTED IN GREAT BRITAIN

CONTENTS

ILLUSTRATIONS

The illustrations reproduced in this book were supplied by the following: École Biblique, 1, 2, 3, 5, 8, 9, 23, 24, 30; Camera Press, 4; Paul Popper, 6, 7, 25, 26, 32; Radio Times Hulton Picture Library, 10, 12; Willem van de Poll, 11, 21, 27, 28, 29, 31; the Israel Museum, 13, 14, 15, 16, 17, 18; British School of Archaeology in Jerusalem, 19, 20; the author, 22.

MAPS AND PLANS

PREFACE

The lack of political cohesion in Palestine and Syria has always been notorious, so that it is simpler to write a history of individual cities in this region than of the land and its people. As the capital of the first considerable national state in the land, where the worship of Israel was first concentrated in Solomon's Temple, Jerusalem is the focus of important interests and ideologies, which invest it with quite a peculiar significance among all cities of its age, and redeem its history from the merely local.

The increasing interest in, and indeed intelligent knowledge of, Jerusalem and its history and topography, now that the city has become, perhaps more than ever before, the objective of Christian pilgrimage, has encouraged us to enter in some detail into the vexed questions of topography and the controversial points in the history of the city, in which we have endeavoured to provide argument and documentation to satisfy the more critical pilgrims and to be of some value to scholars. It is hoped that the argumentation on topographical details in the first chapter will not deter the more general reader from entering into the narrative of the sequel. In the more familiar Hebrew period much detail has had to be sacrificed to the presentation of larger issues in just perspective as an introduction to ideological issues in the history of the city in later chapters of the book. We hope that the sacrifice is found to be in the interests of general clarity.

The writer has indulged his own interest in the Arab and Crusading periods, but he hopes that the less familiar facts of those phases will be welcomed for their own sake and add enlightenment to general interest. The same hope is expressed in the case of the rather obscure and dull Turkish period, which we have endeavoured to relieve by giving a factual introduction to the present Arab-Jewish controversy in which it is hoped that prejudices may be counteracted by facts in a situation where, nevertheless, heartburning is inevitable.

I should like to take this opportunity to express my gratitude to all who have helped in the production of this book, to all whose help with maps and plans is acknowledged in another place, and to my colleagues in Aberdeen whom I have personally consulted, to Mrs. Heather Lyall, M.A., and her assistants, Cartographers in the University of Aberdeen Geography Department, and James Somerville, A.R.I.B.A., and to Professor Armel H. Diverres, M.A., L.ès L., D. de l'Univ., (Paris) Professor of French in the University of Aberdeen, who kindly assisted me with Medieval French chronicles of the Crusades, and to Miss Margaret Finnegan, B.Sc. Econ., Warden at Royal Holloway College, University of London, to whose judgement I have been happy to defer in the difficult matter of the presentation of this history of the Ottoman period. In the reading of proofs I am again deeply indebted to my assistant the Rev. William Johnstone, M.A., B.D., who has done his work with characteristic patience and thoroughness. Finally I thank Miss Valerie J. Green and the editorial staff of Robert Hale & Company for their kindness and helpful co-operation and their compositors, for their expert presentation of my work.

JOHN GRAY

King's College,
University of Aberdeen,
Christmas, 1967

I

THE SITUATION AND DEVELOPMENT OF THE CITY

The mountains are round about Jerusalem (Psalm cxxv. 2)

Few cities in the world are so immediately evocative of a long and colourful history as Jerusalem. Its massive battlemented Turkish wall with its fortified gateways, the Damascus Gate (Pl. 11), the Stephen Gate (Pl. 30), the Golden Gate in the towering eastern wall (Pl. 21), which is also the boundary wall of the Muslim Sacred Precinct, the Dung Gate, the Zion Gate and the Jaffa Gate by the strong Turkish Citadel, proclaim the fortress and evoke its long history. As colourful are the Arabic names of these main gates, respectively *bāb al-ʻamūd* ('the Gate of the Pillar'), *bāb al-'asbāṭ* ('the Gate of the Tribes'), *bāb aḍ-ḍahireh* ('the Gate of the Height; the Herod Gate'), *bāb- al maghārib* ('The Gate of the Moors'), *bāb an-nabi da'ūd* ('the Gate of the Prophet David') and *bāb al-khalīl* ('the Gate of the Friend', i.e. Hebron, so called through its association with Abraham the Friend of God). Within the walls spire, dome and minaret, cross and crescent, bell-chime and muezzin proclaim the interest of Christianity and Islam, and, if the traditional synagogue is less spectacular, the solemn note of the ram's horn may still be distinguished in the multifarious jangle of an Oriental city. Within the walls Jerusalem still has its Muslim, Christian and Armenian quarters, and until 1947–48 had its Jewish quarter, sundered from the precinct of the former Temple by the famous Wailing Wall.

The very stones of Jerusalem are eloquent. Great marginal-drafted blocks in the lower courses of the Wailing Wall (Pl. 7) and elsewhere are the hall-mark of the work of Herod the Great, and the lions from the arms of the Mamlūk Sultan Baybars at the Stephen Gate (Pl. 30) stir memories of the last struggles of the Crusaders, the memory of whose irruption into Jerusalem attaches to the adjacent *burj abī-laqlaq* ('the Tower of the Stork') at the north-east corner of the Turkish wall

(Pls. 28 and 29), which in the north of Jerusalem runs along a rock-scarp fronted by a rock-cut fosse. This has been the northern limit of the city since it was rebuilt by Hadrian in A.D. 135 and possibly since the Jewish revolt of A.D. 66–70. Southwards beyond the Turkish wall and immediately south of the Sacred Precinct the stones of the south-east hill still testify to the history of Jerusalem from the eighteenth century B.C. to the second century B.C. Here are the recently discovered city wall of David and his predecessors low down the eastern slope, and the walls of the successors of Judas the Maccabee in 'the day of small things' on the crest of the south-east hill, the water tunnel and shaft from the spring of Giḥon (fig. on pp. 26–27) and the tunnel and pool of Siloam with the inscription from Hezekiah's time. Beyond the Qidron, clinging precariously to the hill-side, the village of Silwān perpetuates the name of Siloam. And under the name *wādī 'n-nār* the Qidron ravine leads to the great arid gulf of the Judaean wilderness past the desert monastery of Mar Saba (Pl. 23), where life has scarcely moved out of the Byzantine era, over the scorched cliffs to the great sink of the Dead Sea, the refuge of the saints of the New Covenant at Qumran and the last stronghold of resurgent Judaism after the fall of Jerusalem in A.D. 70 and in A.D. 135. Westwards from Jerusalem lie the cultivable lands of the ancient city in the Plain of the Repha'im, the scene of David's decisive victory over the Philistines.[1] Here the rude flint artifacts of man of the Old Stone Age have been found, and above the small plain the western skyline is broken by a line of large tumuli, great drystone cairns on platforms, which were certainly associated with sacrifices in the Jewish monarchy, but in what strange unorthodox cult is still a mystery.[2] Eastwards over the Qidron ravine on the slopes of the Mount of Olives, associated in Jewish and Muslim tradition with the last judgement, is the traditional cemetery of the Jews including the ornate tombs of noble and priestly families and multitudes of prone grave-slabs extending high up the slopes of the Mount of Olives, registering the pious wish that the soul might be 'bound up in the bundle of life'. As if symbolically there soar from the summit the spire and minaret of the Church and the Mosque of the Ascension of Him who is the Resurrection and the Life. And in living witness of the permanence of the ideal of Jerusalem and the extraordinary vitality of the Jews, the capital of the new Israel with its Parliament buildings, law-courts and administrative buildings, modern university, schools and great synagogue, 'the Temple of Solomon', modern multi-storey flats, shops and cinemas, sprawls like a precocious giant northwards and westwards beyond the walls of the Old City and the orthodox Jewish ghettos of the Mea Sheārīm and the Bukhāra quarters. Nor have the Arabs

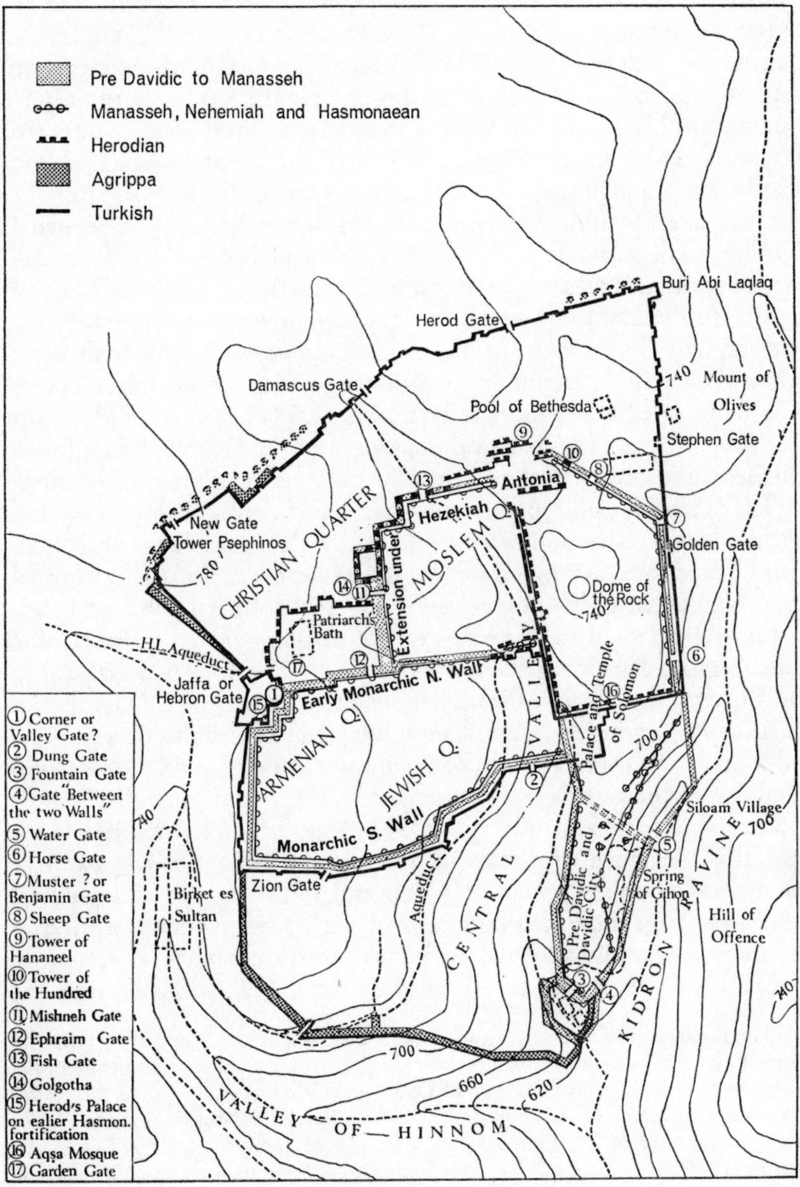

Fig 1. DEVELOPMENT OF ANCIENT JERUSALEM. (*Heather Smith*, now Lyall)

2

of Jordan been slow to follow this northward and modern trend.

Jerusalem is renowned as the capital of the kingdom of David and his house; the site of the Temple of Solomon and the Second Temple; the focus of the faith of Jews in Palestine and abroad, of Christendom, and of Islam, which holds the place of the Temple lesser in sanctity only to Medina and Mecca. Its walls have echoed the clash of arms of imperial Assyrians, Babylonians, Greeks, Romans, Franks and Saracens, and latterly Arab and Jew in louder but less spectacular contest. But the city has a reputation for which it was never naturally designed.* Remote, some 2,500 feet above sea-level, and isolated by deep and rugged ravines, it was not a natural station on the highways of trade or empire. Just east of the watershed of the mountains of Judah, where the land rapidly deteriorates in the rain-shadow, with little cultivable land and only two perennial springs, both so deep in the Qidron ravine as to be useless for extensive irrigation, Jerusalem seemed destined for obscurity. In the settlement and expansion of the Hebrew tribes Judah and Benjamin occupied the cultivable land north and west of the city,[3] but left the local people in possession of the fortress on the south-east hill and evidently of the south-west hill, which they may have cultivated. This isolated fortress was selected by David for the capital of his national state. Neither in Judah nor belonging to the northern tribes of Israel, it was well adapted to serve as the seat of one who was to essay the difficult task of welding the autonomous tribes into a national unity, and this was the origin of Jerusalem as the metropolis of Judaism and Christianity. Two generations later it relapsed to the status of a provincial capital after the disruption of Solomon's kingdom and the secession of all the northern tribes except Benjamin. But by this time the Temple had been built and a mystic dynastic ideology had been created, which held the allegiance of Judah to Jerusalem. Again the comparative remoteness of the hill-state of Judah and the economic and political weakness of the truncated kingdom preserved her from absorption in the Assyrian Empire and enabled her to survive the northern kingdom of Israel for over a century. From this time, and especially after the

* The reputation of Jerusalem misled even archaeologists in the early days, who assumed that Jerusalem was much more extensive than it actually was, including the whole south-west hill from the time of David and even earlier. A. Alt set the matter in proper perspective in two important articles ('Jerusalems Aufstieg', *Zeitschrift der deutschen morgenländischen Gesellschaft* LXXIX, 1925, pp. 1–19; 'Das Taltor von Jerusalem', *Palästinajahrbuch* XXIV, 1928, pp. 74–98), pointing out that the inclusion of the south-west hill as an annexe to the fortified area on the south-east hill before the time of David would have resulted in a settlement many times larger than the normal Palestinian city of the time and would have weakened the defences of the south-east hill.

Babylonian Exile in 586, Jerusalem became the ideal focus of the faith of Judaism, which was expressed seventy years later in traditional form in the rebuilding of the Temple and as it was to be expressed under the Jewish princes of the House of Hashmon and Herod the Great, when it became the capital of a state which compared favourably with that of Solomon. But from the end of the first great Jewish revolt against Rome (A.D. 66–70) to the present day Jerusalem enjoyed capital status only in the century of the Frankish Kingdom of Jerusalem (1099–1187), until under the British Mandate (1921–1947) the sentiment of Christianity prevailed in the elevation of Jerusalem to the administrative capital. More recently Zionism struggled to drive a narrow salient through the mountains to include the new Jewish city outside the Turkish walls as the capital of the State of Israel. This last event is an admirable illustration of the compelling force of Jerusalem as a symbol in faith and politics, which contrasts so strongly with the practical significance of the city in the historical situation.

Just as the Temple saved Jerusalem from relapsing to the status of a mere provincial capital at the disruption of Solomon's kingdom, when it might more practicably have been supplanted by an administrative capital better corresponding to political realities such as Bethlehem or Hebron, so under Roman administration under Hadrian, when the administrative capital of Palestine was Caesarea, Jerusalem held its significance as the capital of Christendom. Under the Arabs, when it was included in a province the capital of which was Ramleh on the eastern edge of the coastal plain, Jerusalem had a peculiar significance for the Muslims, whose Prophet Muḥammad had been considerably stimulated by Judaism. The status of the city in Islam is indicated by the Arabic names *bayt al-maqdaś* ('the sanctuary') and *al-qudś* ('sanctity'). This status was maintained under the Turks after the Crusading interlude, when, though Jerusalem was the capital only of a *sandjak*, or minor province, the city round the Sacred Precinct retained its ecclesiastical significance.

Thus for the Jews Jerusalem had the mystical significance of a national capital, invested with associations with David and his House and with the more sanguine hopes in his Messianic successor. It was the home and fortress of the faith of Judaism, Christianity and Islam. Withdrawn from the beaten track of the culture and politics of the world, from which it was defended by its steep mountain barrier in the west, and on the edge of the eastern wilderness, it was indeed a fastness of ancient values, combating new ideas and defending the old with the fierce fervour of fanaticism, stoning its prophets, crucifying the Lord Jesus, and until recently the bulwark of Arab nationalism and Islam, outfacing Zionism from the Turkish battlements of the Old City.

To the traveller or invader from the west who passed northwards or southwards along the trunk highway through the coastal plain Judah was a hard mountain core of some thirty miles from north to south by about fifteen miles from east to west.[4] Her outward defences were the steep western limestone slopes, precipitous and broken and covered with harsh scrub. On the east the way from the Jordan Valley by Jericho winds upwards some three thousand feet in fifteen miles through a tangle of powdery desolate hills unrelieved by verdure except for a faint green covering briefly at the end of winter. At aḍ-Ḍaharīyeh south of Hebron some twenty-five miles south of Jerusalem the hills of Judah descend abruptly, barring easy access from Beersheba some twenty miles to the south.

Near the height of this massif, but lower than Hebron to the south and Bethel eleven miles to the north, stood ancient Jerusalem overshadowed by higher ridges in all directions but isolated from them all except on the north, her vulnerable side. The outer defences of Jerusalem, however, though formidable, were not impregnable. The mountain wall was penetrated from the west by five wadis, or winter watercourses, all of which gave access to the narrow plateau on which Jerusalem, Bethlehem and Hebron stood, and three of which penetrated almost to Jerusalem itself. These will be largely the key to the history of Jerusalem.

The southernmost pass, covered to the south by the fortress-city of Lachish, perhaps the second city of the Kingdom of Judah under the descendants of Solomon, was the Wādī 'l-Afranj, the Wadi of the Franks, or Crusaders. This was immediately commanded by the city of Marisha as it debouched from the central mountains of Judah by the large village of Bayt Jibrīn, Israeli Bēth Guvrīn, which the Crusaders wrongly identified with Beersheba. This avenue became particularly significant in the defence of Judah when the disruption of Solomon's kingdom left the reduced Kingdom of Judah vulnerable to Egypt and the Philistines in the south, and at this time both Lachish and Marisha were fortified strongly by Rehoboam the son of Solomon.[5] It was important too in the period of the Latin Kingdom of Jerusalem so long as Askalon remained a Saracen bridgehead in Palestine (until 1153), from which the Wādī 'l-Afranj presumably acquired its present name.

Six miles farther north the mountain barrier is pierced by the Wādī 's-Sanṭ, covered where it debouches on to the coastal plain by the Crusading fortress of Blanchegarde, the Arab Tell aṣ-Ṣāfī ('The Gleaming Mound'), conspicuous on a high limestone bluff south of the wadi.* Further east before the north-south trough between the central massif and the low foothills is crossed by the wadi stood the fortress of Azekah, Arab Tell az-Zakārīyeh, and just before the wadi breaks from the central mountains the approach was covered by Socoh, Khirbet 'Abbūd near Tell ash-Shuweikeh. All three points were fortified by Rehoboam.[6] This was the historic Vale of Elah, where David fought Goliath.[7] On that occasion the Philistine invaders from the coastal plain had encamped between Azekah and Socoh and Saul and the Israelites, not strong enough to meet them in battle, were defending the interior and lay on the slope where the wadi forks right to just north of Hebron and left, giving access to the narrow plateau just south of Bethlehem, intent on harassing their march. The top of the former pass was covered by Bethṣūr, fortified by Rehoboam,[8] near the conspicuous ruin of a medieval fortress Khirbet Burj aṣ-Ṣūr four miles north of Hebron. This was the southern bastion of the Jewish patriots under Judas Maccabaeus and his brothers after they occupied Jerusalem. The head of the latter pass was covered by Etam, another of Rehoboam's fortresses,[9] the name of which is conserved in 'Ain 'Aṭān near Khirbet al-Khōkh by the so-called Pools of Solomon at Wādī Urṭas about two miles south-west of Bethlehem which was also fortified by Rehoboam.[10] This is but seven miles from Jerusalem, without serious obstacle except the ravines which isolated the city itself on three sides.

The next avenue of approach is the Wādī 'ṣ-Ṣurār, the Vale of Sorek, associated with Samson and his heroic exploits in love and war with the Philistines and the home of Delilah, who betrayed him.[11] The entrance to the central mountains here was commanded on the south by Bethshemesh and on the north by another of Rehoboam's fortresses at Ṣor'ah, the former Arab village of Ṣar'ah, the home of Samson.[12] This wadi and a tributary give access to the heart of the hill-country by the village of al-'Inab, also called Abū Ghōsh, near ancient Qiryath-jearim, where the ark came on its return from the Philistines by way of Bethshemesh.[13] The main Wādī 'ṣ-Ṣurār leads directly to the very heart of the central plateau north of Jerusalem by Qulūniyeh. The strategic significance of this point was appreciated by the Romans after the suppression of the Jewish revolt of A.D. 66–70 since they established a colony of veterans here, whence the name of the former Arab village Qulūniyeh (Colonia), and posted a garrison at al-'Inab. The strategic significance of the Wādī 'ṣ-Ṣurār and its tributary by al-'Inab is also indicated by the fortress of the Hospitallers and the Church at the latter place and by the fortress of al-Qasṭal commanding the height

* This, I believe, was Gath of the Old Testament, but I believe that it was also called Libnah ('White').

above the two valleys. This was a key point in the struggle between Arabs and Jews for access to Jerusalem in the war of 1947–48, in which an important factor was the remarkable pro-Jewish attitude of the inhabitants of al-'Inab. The Wādī 'ṣ-Ṣurār leads eventually past the Arab village of Lifta, Biblical Nephtoaḥ[14] on the north-west outskirts of modern Jerusalem, to the plateau just north of the city, from which an attack could be mounted on the city's most vulnerable side. In November of 1917 one column of the Allied forces attacked by the upper part of this valley, when they succeeded in capturing the commanding height crowned by the village of Nabī Samwīl ('the Prophet Samuel'), ancient Miṣpah of I Samuel vii, with its conspicuous minaret, which is a notable landmark for Jerusalem.

The most northerly pass was the famous Ascent of Beth-ḥōrōn from the Valley of Aijalon, where the town of Aijalon, Arab Yālū, was fortified by Rehoboam.[15] From this place and Bayt Nūbā, Betenoble of the Crusading Chronicles, the Wādi Salmān gives access to al-Jīb, Biblical Gibeon, commanded to the north by Beth-ḥōrōn the Nether, which was fortified by Solomon.[16] This pass is first mentioned in Israel's national verse epic* celebrating Joshua's victory over the King of Jerusalem and his Amorite allies in the Battle of Gibeon:

> Sun, stand thou still at Gibeon,
> And thou, moon, in the Valley of Aijalon.
> And the sun stood still and the moon stayed
> Until the people took vengeance on their enemies.[17]

Here significantly Jerusalem was immediately involved since Gibeon, which had made its peace with the Israelites, was but six miles from the city on its vulnerable north side. It was by this way too that the Pharaoh Sheshonk came on his raid through Palestine on the disruption of Solomon's kingdom in 926 B.C., and it was probably at Gibeon that Rehoboam met him and bought him off with the treasure of Solomon's

* From this citation and from David's lament for Saul and Jonathan, which is also cited from the Book of Yashar (II Samuel i. 18), it appears that this work was devoted to warlike exploits, particularly the activity of Yahweh the God of Israel for his people, hence it may be identical with the book of the Wars of Yahweh, Yashar ('upright, proper, legitimate') possibly being the first word of the epic, by which a book was often known, e.g., 'In the beginning', 'And these are the names' etc. for Genesis, Exodus and the other books of the Pentateuch. The poetic citation concerning the building of the Temple in I Kings viii. 12–13 is from 'the Book of the Song' according to the Septuagint Greek translation, which, by the transposition of two consonants in the Hebrew original may be a scribal corruption of 'the Book of Yashar'. If this is so, the Book of Yashar culminated in the foundation of the Temple in the fourth year of Solomon's reign.

Temple.[18]* This was the direct line of march in the campaigns of the Greek (Seleucid) rulers of Syria against the Jewish rebels under Judas Maccabaeus, and it was at Adasa at the head of the pass that Judas won his first notable victory, and, fighting his last desperate action against hopeless odds, fell with his face to the foe. By the same way the Roman legions under the over-confident Cestius Gallus fled in unaccustomed confusion in the early days of the Jewish revolt in A.D. 66. Failure of the power occupying Jerusalem to prevent an assailant occupying the central plateau on its weakest side generally boded the city's doom, as when the army of the First Crusade advanced unopposed by the Wādī Salmān to Jerusalem in two days, and the occupation of the plateau by the Allies in 1917 forced the Turco-German forces to abandon Jerusalem, though they contested every inch of the Allied advance and actually held the higher ground to the north of the Allied lines for two more months.

So far we have considered Jerusalem mainly as a mountain fastness, the objective of the advance of hostile armies, and have noted the formidable mountain barrier on the west and the weary ascent from the Jordan Valley. Not only is the latter a steep and barren escarpment of gleaming white limestone and marl, which in its lower reaches is an ancient sea-bottom, but it involves a long toilsome climb. One is always conscious of the great void between Jerusalem and the Dead Sea, and from the Mount of Olives east of the city the impression is particularly striking. Actually Jerusalem lies east of the watershed of the hills of Judah. Her water-courses, the Qidron ravine and the Valley of Hinnom, unite in the Wādī 'n-Nār, 'the Valley of Fire' which carries the flash winter-torrents through the Desert of Judah and eventually, in a series of towering waterfalls, over the cliffs to the Dead Sea south of the monastic settlement of the Sect of the New Covenant at Qumran. This arid, rugged wilderness at the back-door of Jerusalem relates intimately to the history of the city, not only as a barrier to the invader but as the chief of these 'areas of refuge'[19] with which the land is so well furnished. This must be emphasized particularly in view of three significant phases in the history of Jerusalem, the secession of the Sect of the New Covenant, the last desperate stand of the insurgents in the Jewish revolt of A.D. 66–70 and the last great Jewish revolt under Simon bar Kokhba, which was suppressed in 135. It was also an area of refuge, both actual and potential, for Herod the Great, who had no illusions

* From the fact that there is no mention of Jerusalem in Sheshonk's itinerary on the wall of the temple of Amon at Karnak it may fairly be deduced that he received the submission and tribute of Rehoboam here, B. Mazar, 'The Campaign of the Pharaoh Sheshonk to Palestine', *VT Supplement* IV, 1957, pp. 57–66.

about his popularity as an Idumaean by descent and as a vassal of Rome, and it was the retreat of solitaries when Jerusalem was the Christian metropolis in the Byzantine age.

Having now cleared the approaches, we may consider the city more nearly. A point of vantage would be the station 'about two stadia [furlongs] from the wall near its angle opposite the Tower Psephinus'[20] from which Titus launched his first attack in the revolt of A.D. 66–70. This would roughly coincide with the modern Russian compound with its hospice, hospital and cathedral.

From here ancient Jerusalem deploys to the south and south-east within the Turkish wall and beyond. It is dominated from a distance by our point of vantage in the north-west, and from the north-east by the ridge of Mount Scopus and its southern extensions the Mount of Olives and Jebel Baṭn al-Hawa, 'the Mountain of the Belly of Hell', called in Christian times 'the Mount of Offence', which was probably the site of the alien cults which Solomon established for his harem.[21] From the west also Jerusalem was overlooked by the ridge which rises southwards to the Hill of Evil Counsel and to the summit crowned by Government House of the British Mandate, now the headquarters of the United Nations Organization. Those are the mountains which 'are round about Jerusalem',[22] which also included the south-west hill by the present Citadel.

The city on which Titus looked from his headquarters on Mount Scopus, or from his assault base, stretched southwards on two ridges divided by a central valley, 'the Cheese-makers' Valley' of Josephus, which is probably the misunderstanding of a Hebrew or Aramaic term meaning 'the Central Valley'. The western half comprises the Christian quarter of the Turkish Old City in the north-west as far south as the Turkish Citadel on the site of Herod's palace, and beyond it lies the Armenian quarter as far as the Southern city-wall. Beyond the wall is 'the Hill of Zion' of Christian and later Jewish tradition, which is here quite unreliable. On this side the city is bounded on the west and south by a deep valley-bottom, the Wādī 'r-Rabābī, the Valley of Hinnom in the Old Testament and Gehenna in Aramaic, notorious in Scripture in its southern part as the scene of human sacrifice under Ahaz and Manasseh. The eastern slope of this ridge towards the Central Valley is occupied in the north by part of the Muslim quarter and in the south by the former Jewish quarter, which abutted on the south part of the western wall of the Muslim Sacred Precinct, the famous Wailing Wall. The eastern ridge descends from the north wall in three stages. The Muslim quarter extends to the north limit of the Sacred Precinct, which encloses the Dome of the Rock, the Aqṣa Mosque (fig. I [16]) and related buildings. This was the suburb of Bezetha, enclosed in the walled area of the city on the outbreak of the Jewish revolt of A.D. 66–70.[23] The name signifies, according to the feasible suggestion of Dalman, 'the Fragment' (Aramaic *biṣ'ᵃthā*), an apt description of this odd outlying eminence so lately incorporated in the city. The next stage, slightly lower and separated by a depression, is the hill occupied by the Muslim Sacred Precinct, an artificial platform since its southern extension was constructed as an esplanade by Herod the Great in his rebuilding of the Temple. This was the site of the Temple of Solomon and the Second Temple. Beyond the south wall of the Sacred Precinct, which coincides here with the Turkish city-wall, the east ridge descends in a narrow tongue between the ravine of the Qidron on the east and the lower part of the Central Valley, both formerly much more precipitous before the accumulation of debris over three thousand years. This termination of the east ridge, now quite unspectacular and occupied by isolated houses and vegetable plots, was the Jebusite city occupied by David.

As 'the mountains are round about Jerusalem' within the Turkish wall, Jebusite Jerusalem, or as we may call it, the city of David, was overtopped by the hill to the north, on which Solomon built the Temple, to which the devotees thus literally 'went up', and by the hill over the Central Valley to the west, on which Herod the Great built his palace-fort on the site of the present Turkish Citadel by the Jaffa, or Hebron, Gate (fig. I [15]). The least impressive hill in Jerusalem, this narrow ridge, the flat top of which measures only some four hundred yards by just over a hundred yards at the widest, surprises us by its limited extent. But we remember that it was primarily a citadel rather than a city, and a closer consideration reveals obvious advantages to this purpose. Bounded to the east and west respectively by the deep ravines of the Qidron torrent and the Central Valley, which joined at the south tip, and contracting in the north to a very narrow saddle, it enjoyed the advantage of the only perennial spring accessible to a defensive position in the whole vicinity. Though the whole of Jerusalem within the Turkish wall is honey-combed by rock-hewn cisterns for rain-water, there are but two sources of perennial water in the vicinity, the Spring of Giḥon ('the Gusher') in the Qidron Valley east of the north part of the south-east hill, known to Christians as the Spring of the Lady Mary ('Ain Sitti Miriam) and to local Arabs as the Spring of the Mother of the Steps' ('Ain Umm ad-Darāj), and Job's Well (Bīr 'Ayyūb, probably 'Ain Rogel, about seven hundred yards down the Qidron ravine below the confluence with the Valley of Hinnom (Wādī 'r-Rabābī). The former determined the site of the citadel of Jerusalem.

The first phase of the city's history as a fortified settlement like that

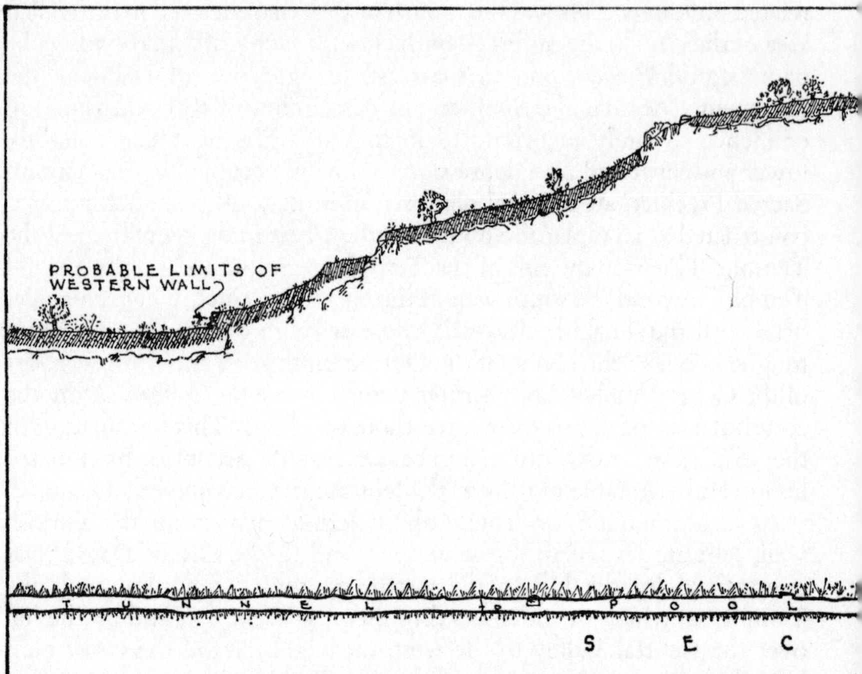

Fig II. Water Tunnel and Shaft from the Spring of Gihon—eas
(*J. L. Somerville after L. H. Vincent and M. A*

of many of the inland settlements of Palestine was associated with the sedentarization of Amorite tribesmen towards the end of the third millennium, though pottery from the end of the fourth millennium and from the third millennium indicates that the site had been already settled. The tribal autonomy of the Amorite settlers, which limited political cohesion, made them very sensitive to the advantages of defensible positions, in which a primary consideration was water, here the Spring of Giḥon. In course of time, probably by the end of the thirteenth century, this source was tapped by tunnel and shaft from the slope of the hill (fig. II above), and, as has been demonstrated by recent excavations of the French and British Schools of Archaeology in Jerusalem, this shaft was actually within the wall, which was much lower down the east slope than was previously supposed (fig. II). After the water was thus made accessible within the wall the source could be walled over and effectively concealed. Doubtless the west hill and the

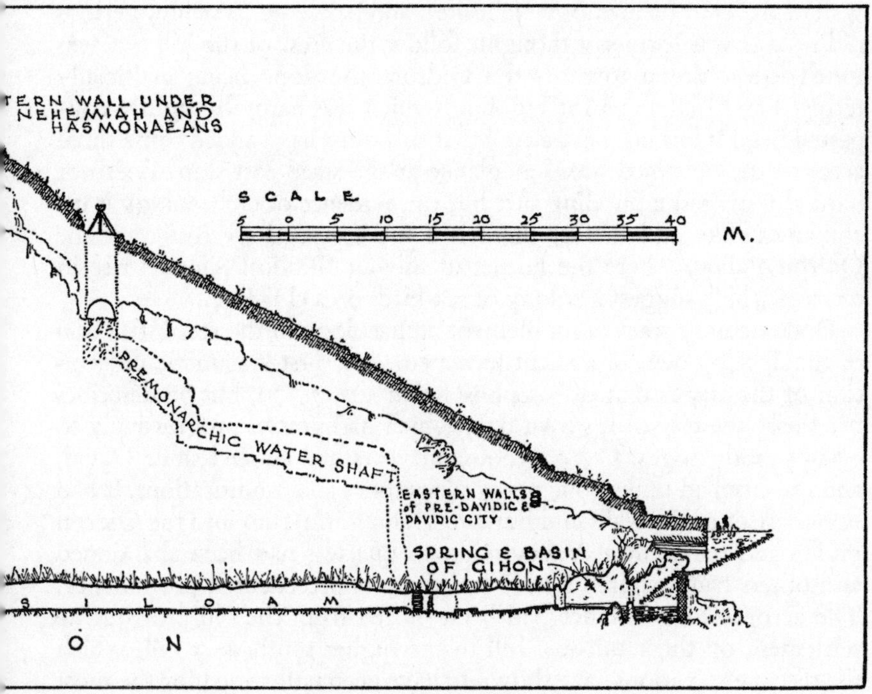

n of the north-east of ancient Jerusalem on the south-east hill.
alem de l'Ancien Testament 1 *and* 2)

whole area of modern Jerusalem was occupied and worked by peasants from the end of the third millennium, but the concentration of settlement was within the citadel on the south-east hill above the Spring of Giḥon, which had evidently a sacred significance, since Solomon was anointed king here.[24]

The area of the top of the south-east hill extends to some fifteen acres. This of itself, though it does not impress, would not be surprising, roughly corresponding to the size of other settlements of the Bronze Age excavated in Palestine even at sites not naturally so limited as the south-east hill of Jerusalem.* The recent excavations, however, on the east slope of the hill above the Spring of Giḥon have revealed that the

* The occupation on the following tells (ruin-mounds) is as follows: Gezer, Tell ad-Duweir (Lachish), 18 acres; Megiddo, Samaria, 15; Tell en-Naṣbeh (Miṣpah of II Kings xxv. 23 ff.; Jeremiah xl. 6 ff.), Tell ar-Rumeileh (Bethshemesh), 7–8. Hazor in N. Galilee is quite exceptional, comprising 170 acres, the citadel amounting to 25.

wall of the Late Bronze Age (Jebusite), and Iron Age (Israelite) periods did not, as was formerly thought, follow the crest of the hill but was much lower down towards the Qidron, the slope being artificially terraced and buttressed for building, which was naturally tightly congested here. It has been estimated that this must have added some three acres to the occupied site.[25] A glance at the steep east slope does not naturally suggest a building site, but the evidence of archaeology is incontrovertible, and in fact there is a modern analogy just over the Qidron Valley, where the houses of Silwān (Biblical Siloam) rise in terraces which suggest a colony of sea-birds on a cliff-face.

Documentary sources supplement archaeology in the reconstruction of the development of ancient Jerusalem. The first systematic description of the city is that of Josephus[26] *circa* A.D. 75–79, but he describes primarily the city of his own day, which had grown progressively to occupy both ridges. Over a thousand years had elapsed since David, and the city had undergone many vicissitudes and modifications. It had been destroyed, its walls and buildings falling into ruin into the Qidron ravine and the Central Valley. Certain quarters had been abandoned and others had acquired a new and quite unprecedented prominence. The acropolis for instance had been shifted from the old pre-Israelite settlement on the south-east hill to the higher south-west hill, which the recent excavations have shown to have been unfortified for the most part and not intensively occupied before the Hellenistic Age. However reliable Josephus may be on the Jerusalem of his own time and near his time, he is unreliable on the earlier periods, as is indicated by his reference to the south-west hill as 'the city of David', which has been the source of many errors concerning the fortified area of Jerusalem under the House of David. In Jerusalem of Josephus' time in fact the city of the Old Testament was unrecognizable.

Apart from Josephus' description of Jerusalem with its limitations for the periods more remote from his own time, Nehemiah's memoirs of his work as Provincial Governor of Judah in the second half of the fifth century B.C. give the fullest description of the wall and gates of Jerusalem, which he partly repaired and partly rebuilt. This is particularly valuable since it gives a threefold account of the south-west and south-east sections in Nehemiah's nocturnal inspection,[27] of the actual building,[28] and the festal procession round the completed wall.[29] This of course is relevant to the earlier periods since Nehemiah's work was largely restoration. From sporadic references to local topography in the books of II Samuel, I and II Kings and Chronicles, Isaiah, Jeremiah, Zephaniah and Zechariah the walls of earlier Jerusalem may be reconstructed from Nehemiah's description. There is still a fair measure of conjecture, but this may be considerably reduced by archaeology, particularly since the recent work of the British and French Schools of Archaeology in Jerusalem on the slope of the south-east hill and on the south-west hill.

The position of the east wall of Jerusalem in the pre-Israelite period and under the House of David has been located at least in certain short sections well down the slope towards the Qidron ravine (pl. 2). The west wall of this settlement on the south-east hill is still a problem, but from the line of a rock-scarp on the west slope of this hill parallel to the Central Valley its situation may be fairly conjectured. The construction of a partly open conduit, mainly for irrigation, from the Spring of Giḥon along the east side of the hill used to be associated with a thick wall with buttresses across the mouth of the Central Valley, which was thought to serve as a barrage as well as a city wall (fig. III). The partial exposure of the conduit suggested that it must be a work of peacetime, being impracticable after the time of Solomon. The wall across the mouth of the Central Valley naturally suggested an extension of the fortifications to the west of the Central Valley, which would seem to be imperative after the construction of the Siloam tunnel and pool, which is feasibly dated in the time of Hezekiah (715–686) (fig. III), and the line of such a wall on the lower slope of the south-west hill was conjectured by a rock-scarp. No trace of a wall itself, however, has been detected, nor does the debris in the Central Valley indicate an occupation of the lower slopes of the south-west hill during the Hebrew monarchy, though this might be explained if the assumed wall here was strictly round the Pool of Siloam and the lower pool (Birket al-Ḥamrā). The wall below the latter pool, blocking the mouth of the Central Valley, which used to be regarded as part of the city wall under the monarchy, is now demonstrated to be from the first century A.D., probably part of the fortification of Jerusalem under Agrippa I (A.D. 40–44) like the wall round the south part of the south-west hill and the gate at the south-east tip of that hill, which Bliss and Dickie regarded as the wall of Jerusalem under the House of David. The lack of archaeological evidence for a wall west of the pools has prompted Dr. Kenyon's suggestion that the vital Pool of Siloam may have been rather a vast cistern covered with the native rock,[30] and actually *outside* the city wall, but this is surely precluded by the reference to 'the pool [of Siloam] between the two walls'[31] in Hezekiah's time.

As is well known, the north-east hill was unoccupied until David acquired the threshing-floor of Araunah the Jebusite for a sanctuary.[32] The south-east hill was 'the city of David'. His sepulchre and those of his descendants were towards the south apex according to Nehemiah's

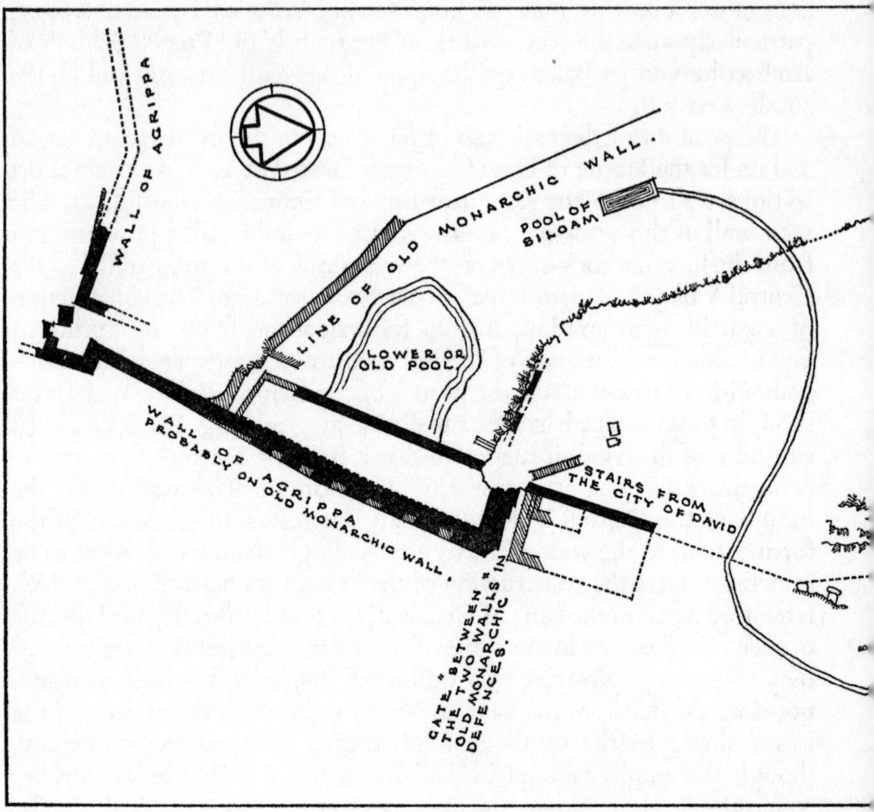

Fig III. The Course of the Siloam Tunnel
(*J. L. Somerville after L. H. Vincent and M*

reference to a section of the wall 'over against the sepulchres of David, and to the pool which was made',[33] but the tombs of the kings of Judah have almost wholly disappeared through quarrying in the Roman period. The fortress of this ancient settlement, which would also be the palace, would naturally command the Spring of Giḥon and the narrow saddle at the north end of the hill, which was dominated by the hill to the north, and since Solomon's palace immediately adjoined the Temple it must have been an extension of the palace of David. It is Solomon's extension of the palace-complex here that complicates the problem of the north wall of David's city and the earlier settlement, which doubtless ran across the hill here. The city expanded beyond the south-east hill with Solomon's extension of the palace and his building of the

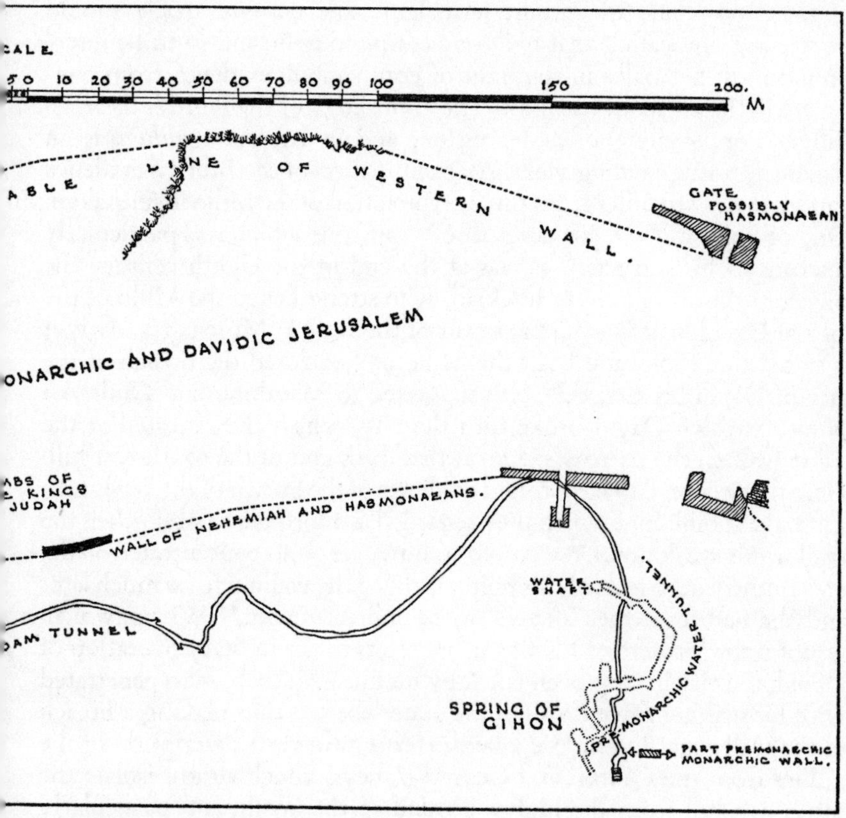

:ions on the south-east hill of Jerusalem.
:usalem de l'Ancien Testament I *and* 2)

Temple, and this extension occasioned other significant adjustments. In connection with the Temple, the walls may have been extended northwards above the Qidron Valley and north of the Temple and west to include a new area, the Second Quarter (Mishneh), which eventually came to be associated with the priests and government officials.[34] The line of such a wall, however, which probably did not extend beyond the north limit of the Muslim Sacred Precinct of the present day, is purely conjectural, and the direction and extent of the north wall of ancient Jerusalem under the Davidic kings is problematical even in later descriptions which are more specific than for Solomon's time.

A notable feature associated with Solomon was the Millo. The location and nature of this feature constitutes one of the outstanding problems in the topography of ancient Jerusalem. The definite article should be stressed, indicating that *millô'* is a common noun and so to be interpreted most naturally in the light of comparative evidence from elsewhere in the ancient Near East. The etymology of the word indicates a 'filling', or levelling of a depression, and in Assyria a *milu* was an esplanade with retaining walls. An examination of the Biblical evidence shows no need to differ from this interpretation of the Millo in Jerusalem. One of Solomon's major enterprises[35]* and one which was particularly onerous to his subjects,[36] it was at the end of the eighth century the object of the attention of Hezekiah, who strengthened the Millo of the city of David *in addition to* the repair of the walls.[37] More particularly it is stated that 'Solomon built the Millo and enclosed the breach of the city of David his father'.[38] This suggested to Macalister and Duncan a point at which David broke into the city, which they located at the short wall on the narrow saddle at the north end of the south-east hill. Here they claimed to have found evidence of the breach of the wall and a subsequent building, which they regarded as a fortress, to strengthen the wall at this weak point.[39] Crowfoot, however, who concentrated on the area immediately west of this point, showed the walling to be much later and the nature of the 'fortress' to be indeterminate.[40] We may well doubt if the 'breach' of I Kings xi. 27 refers to the military operation of David, the city having been taken by his kinsman Joab, who penetrated with his striking force through the water-shaft,[41] thus making a breach in the wall superfluous. We take the term rather as a description of the gullies from the Qidron and Central Valleys, which almost isolate the south-east hill from the higher ground to the north, and particularly of the depression in the Qidron side between the south-east hill and the Ophel, or 'bulge'. The location of the Millo suggested by Macalister and Duncan is precluded by the fact that the Millo is noted as part of Hezekiah's fortifications,[42] which completely enclosed the north-east hill north of the saddle of the south-east hill, and Weill's view that the Millo was the filling of the saddle between the south-east hill and Solomon's palace at the south end of the north-east hill[43] is open to the

* II Samuel v. 9, referring to David's building, or rebuilding, of the wall of the pre-Israelite city 'from the Millo inwards' need not signify that the Millo was a feature of pre-Israelite Jerusalem, but simply that David's work extended from where the Millo was at the time of the writer, who certainly post-dated Solomon, with whom the Millo was specifically associated. If the Millo, however, denotes the terracing and buttressing of the slope of the south-east hill towards its north end, the discovery of the pre-Israelite wall low down the slope makes it possible that the Millo originated in pre-Israelite times. Considering the steepness of the slope and the violence of the winter rains at Jerusalem such a work would need constant maintenance and even occasionally major reconstruction.

same objection. Here the Alexandrine Greek (Septuagint) version of II Chronicles xxxii. 5 is helpful, rendering *millô'* by *analēmma* ('raised work'). According to the latest opinion of Vincent, terrace and buttress work strengthening the west flank of Solomon's palace was denoted, where the sharp eastward bend of the Central Valley cut into the south-east hill at its northern extremity.[44] This is possible, but in view of the grievous public burden involved we think of a larger work of the same nature in the deep depression east of the north end of the south-east hill, where such an esplanade in the time of Solomon, before the city had spread westwards over the Central Valley, was imperative to provide for his increased buildings south of the Temple and palace. According to the most obvious etymology the Millo was indeed the 'filling' of the gulf between the City of David on the south-east hill and the Ophel, or 'bulge' to the north-east. This feature immediately east of the palace of Solomon and his successors was probably the site of the barracks for the professional soldiers on whom the Davidic dynasty so largely depended, and may have been 'the house of the Millo' at which Joash was assassinated by two of his retainers.[45] At this particular point there have been no excavations to support this conjecture, but the general conception of a *millô'*, or terraced embankment, is almost certainly attested by the system of terraces supported by massive retaining walls and buttresses to hold buildings on the steep slope of the south-east hill immediately north of the Spring of Giḥon revealed by the excavations of the British and French Schools of Archaeology in Jerusalem.[46] It may well be that this work, apparently first undertaken in the fourteenth century and maintained until the destruction of the city by Nebuchadrezzar in 586, was itself the Millo.[47] Strained by the tremendous out-thrust of the terrace-filling and the superstructures, and vulnerable on the steep slope to weather and earthquake, those substructures demanded constant attention, and might well be a grievous public burden, as noted in Solomon's administration.[48] Apart from regular maintenance, Solomon's special attention to the Millo, if this indeed denotes those terraces and buttresses, might be explained by much more extensive building in his reign on the terraces thus prepared.

In the history of the Davidic monarchy in the Books of Samuel, Kings and Chronicles there is surprisingly little data for a reconstruction of Jerusalem under the House of David, apart from the waterworks, which with the aid of archaeology we may reconstruct from the time of David (fl. 1000) to Hezekiah (715–686). In the account of the defeat of Amaziah (795–767) there is mention of two gates, the Ephraim Gate and the Corner Gate, between which Jehoash of Israel (796–781) demolished 400 cubits, or about two hundred yards.[49] The

Ephraim Gate would naturally be situated in the north wall, that part of the fortification which Amaziah's northern neighbour would naturally demolish, but the position is not further specified, and of course the statement that Jehoash demolished two hundred yards of wall between the Ephraim Gate and the Corner Gate does not necessarily mean that this was the actual distance between the two gates. More precisely Nehemiah xii. 39 (cf. viii. 16)* locates the Ephraim Gate in the north wall of the monarchic period after David (Josephus' first north wall) just west of Hezekiah's north extension (fig. I [12]).

The Corner Gate is mentioned again in a text referring to Jerusalem before 586, Jeremiah xxxi. 38, from immediately after that date, declaring that 'the city shall be built to the Lord from the Tower of Hananeel and to the Gate of the Corner'. Also from the post-Exilic period, probably before Nehemiah's reconstruction just after the middle of the fifth century, and visualizing the city before the disaster of 586, Zechariah xiv. 10 describes its extent 'from the Benjamin Gate unto the place of the First Gate, unto the Corner Gate, and from the Tower of Hananeel unto the king's wine-presses'. Whether 'the king's wine-presses' is accepted as genuine, referring to the rock-hewn presses by the King's Garden, which was just beyond the mouth of the Central Valley, or, as has been suggested,[50] 'the royal tombs' should be read with slight emendation, the south extremity of Jerusalem is indicated, which indicates the Tower of Hananeel (fig. I [9]) as the north extremity. This suggests that the Benjamin Gate of Zechariah xiv. 10 was the east extremity of the city (fig. I [7]), possibly identical with the Sheep Gate or 'the Prison Gate' (better the Inspection, or Muster, Gate) of Nehemiah xii. 39. The fact that the Tower of Hananeel with the Sheep Gate and the Tower of the Hundred (A. V. 'Meah') (fig. I [10]) were built and sanctified by the priests in Nehemiah's reconstruction[51] indicates that it adjoined the Temple area. Hence the Corner Gate is to be located in the west, being the extremity of the city in that direction, where it is located by Simons at the site of the present Citadel by the Jaffa, or Hebron, Gate (fig. I [1]).[52] This to be sure would accord with Josephus' classical description of the earliest north wall of Jerusalem, which, like the fortification of the south-west hill (which he mistakenly regards as Zion), he ascribes to David.[53] Excavations in the Turkish Citadel by C. N. Johns, while not revealing any building which might be dated before the Hellenistic period, to which he was the first to ascribe the wall round the south-west hill which Bliss and Dickie had dated to the Davidic monarchy, revealed quantities of pottery of the seventh-century

* See below, p. 42.

B.C. More was found by Dr. Kenyon in the filling of what was apparently the fosse of a wall running east from the vicinity of the Citadel to the Muslim Sacred Precinct, like the wall described by Josephus as the earliest north wall of Israelite Jerusalem.* Here there is a distinctive cross valley running from the west to join the north-south Central Valley, and it might fairly be argued that the south bank of this would be the natural line of fortification on the north of Jerusalem. Indeed if Josephus' statement that the strength of the first wall was increased by the valleys refers inclusively to the north wall this must have been so. With the reservation that the seventh-century pottery found out of stratification in the Citadel and in Dr. Kenyon's soundings in the Muristan may denote only open settlements and that a wall of the monarchic period along the south bank of the cross valley is yet not proved by archaeology, and probably never will be, we may tentatively accept Josephus' north wall here as strategically feasible, though later than the time of David and even Solomon. In Zechariah xiv. 10, which describes the extent of the city from east to west as from the Benjamin Gate to the Corner Gate, 'the place of the First Gate', which lies between, probably denotes rather 'the Principal Gate' in the north wall, or the Ephraim Gate.

This north wall, probably built after Solomon, from the site of the Citadel to the south-west of the north-east hill presupposes a wall running south from the Citadel and then east. Here the natural line southwards would be that of the present west wall of the Old City. Here also Dr. Kenyon has excavated in 1964 in the grounds of the Armenian patriarchate and has found sufficient masonry and pottery from the Hebrew monarchy to make it feasible that the south wall on the south-west hill enclosed the summit, perhaps running eventually north-east probably to join the west wall of the city of the Jebusites and David at the north-west of the south-east hill, where Crowfoot discovered a Maccabaean gate. The west and south wall on the south-west hill would thus roughly correspond to the direction, and perhaps even nearly to the location, of the present Turkish wall. Actually the south wall of the extension to the south-west hill seems to be indicated in II Chronicles xxvi. 9, which states that 'Uzziah built towers in Jerusalem at the Corner Gate and at the Valley Gate and at the turning of the wall'. The 'turning of the wall' may indicate a point south-east of the Corner Gate by the Turkish Citadel where the wall turned north-east to link up with the north-west angle of the fortifications of the City

* Vincent discusses fragments of ancient walling along this line (*Jérusalem de l'Ancien Testament* I, 1954, pp. 52–64), but only one, with affinities with masonry from the acropolis of Samaria in Ahab's time (early ninth century) (*op. cit.*, fig. 13), is conceivably from the Davidic dynasty.

of David on the south-east hill. This is the only text where the Corner Gate and the Valley Gate are mentioned together, and we suspect that the conjunction has the explicative force ('the Corner Gate, that is to say the Valley Gate'), the two being identical. Nehemiah iii. 15, in the enumeration of the gates in a counterclockwise direction, states that a thousand cubits were repaired between the Valley Gate and the Dung Gate. This does not necessarily indicate the precise distance between the two gates, but it does indicate the direction and position of the Dung Gate roughly on the site of the present Dung Gate, or Gate of the Moors on the slope of the south-west hill just west of the Central Valley (fig. I [2]). It is possible, however, that the Dung Gate was on the site of the Maccabaean gate discovered by Crowfoot at the north-west corner of the south-east hill, though to be sure no work earlier than the Hellenistic age was discovered here.

Hezekiah's construction of the famous tunnel from Giḥon through the south-east hill to the Pool of Siloam (fig. III on p. 30) would seem at first sight to demand an extension of the city wall westwards to the lower slopes of the south-west hill, but as has been pointed out there is no trace here of an actual wall or of occupation from the Davidic monarchy, though seventh-century debris under the wall across the mouth of the valley may suggest that there was a wall earlier than the present work of the first century A.D. The mention of the pool for the waters of the old pool (i.e. for the water which formerly flowed into the old pool, Birket al-Ḥamrā, round the east contour of the south-east hill) between the two walls[54] makes unavoidable the conclusion that both pools were enclosed by walls to the south and west. Here the writer may take the opportunity to withdraw an earlier conjecture on the location of the Upper Pool in Isaiah vii. 3, which he formerly suggested might be a pool fed from the depression beyond the Damascus Gate by the Central Valley.[55] Vincent[56] is certainly correct in taking the Upper Pool as the basin for collecting the water in the rock-chamber at Giḥon, to be brought down the conduit in the east side of the hill in the time of Ahaz and then in face of invasion diverted into the depression, later the Pool of Siloam, instead of being allowed to flow on to Birket al-Ḥamrā. This expedient in times of stress probably suggested to Ahaz' son Hezekiah the construction of the Siloam tunnel and pool, and a rock-hewn pit may have been already in existence as a receptacle for water at such times before the tunnel was hewn. An alternative view is proposed by Dr. Kenyon[57] who suggests that Hezekiah's tunnel to a pool in a rock-roofed cavern at the Pool of Siloam was continued to carry the outflow under the south escarpment of the city to the Qidron valley. This might account for the absence of any vestige of walling west of the pool. The inscription on the wall of the tunnel just before the present pool, however, suggests that this was the terminal of the tunnel.

Manasseh the son of Hezekiah is specifically mentioned in connection with the extension to the fortifications of Jerusalem.[58] He apparently extended the old wall on the lower slope of the south-east hill northwards to include the north-east hill, which until then may have been considered well enough protected by the precipitous slope and by the temenos wall of the Temple. Manasseh's fortification was continued to the north and westwards, where it eventually joined the north wall at the Fish Gate, which was just east or just west of the Central Valley (fig. I [13]. In this extension of the city in the north-east the Tower of Hananeel (fig. I [9]), first mentioned about a century later in Jeremiah xxxi. 37 (A.V. 38) and in Zechariah xiv. 10, was built together with other features in the north-east sector of the wall mentioned in Nehemiah's restoration such as the Benjamin Gate (probably the same as the Inspection, or Muster, Gate,[59]) the Tower of the Hundred and the Sheep Gate. The line of Manasseh's north wall may have been suggested by the depression which runs north-west to south-east at the north-east angle of the present Muslim Sacred Precinct, his wall possibly running along above the south bank of this depression, culminating in the high ground about the site of the later fortress Antonia north-west of the Sacred Precinct. We note a new feature, the Fish Gate, which is given apparently as the point at which Manasseh's extension in the north joined an older fortification. This may have been in a northern extension built by Hezekiah when he repaired the damage which Jehoash had done in the north wall[60] since it is stated that 'he built up the wall that was broken and raised it up to the towers, *and another wall without. . . .*' This was dictated no doubt by the expansion of the residential quarter to the north-west. The Fish Gate was evidently in the north wall, so called probably from the sale of salt fish from the coast by such as the Tyrian traders in Nehemiah's time.[61] Since this was between the north-west of the Temple area and the Ephraim Gate it may have been just east or just west of the Central Valley or even on the line of the valley south of the present Damascus Gate, which would suggest that the Ephraim Gate in the earlier north wall was further west than the Central Valley. Nehemiah's work was a reconstruction of Manasseh's work except on the east side of the south-east hill. Here the massive terraces and buttresses which the steep slope demanded to support buildings in the pre-Israelite period and during the Davidic monarchy had been destroyed, and their reconstruction was beyond the resources of the struggling community in the fifth century, as indicated by recent excavations, nor was the community sufficiently numerous to require the additional living-space which the terraces had provided. Nor in the fragmentation of provinces under the Persian Empire was there any need of defensive fortifications as in the capital of a sovereign state. So here the wall followed the east crest of the hill, and the old wall low down on the slope and the terraces and buttresses were never restored.

Nehemiah's celebrated inspection of the walls and gates of Jerusalem by night three days after his arrival was evidently confined to the south part of the city, probably because he was already familiar with the state of the wall in the north by the Temple. He rode out by the Valley Gate. Since the Corner Gate, according to Jeremiah xxxi. 38 and Zechariah xiv. 10 can hardly but be located by the Tower of the Furnaces in the description of Nehemiah's restoration,[62] probably on the site of the Turkish Citadel, the Valley Gate probably coincides with the Corner Gate, which is not explicitly mentioned in Nehemiah and is never mentioned together with the Valley Gate except in II Chronicles xxvi. 9, where the names may be alternatives. One gate in this position might be expected, giving access to the city from the road along the ridge of the hills of Judah from Bethlehem and Hebron, as the Hebron, or Jaffa, Gate did until 1948. The valley by which the gate is named is the upper part of the Valley of Hinnom. The Dragon (*tannīn*) Well, to which this gate is orientated in Nehemiah iii. 13 raises a problem, since no spring is known here. Here indeed Josephus[63] specifically mentions 'the Serpent's Pool', which he locates by Herod's tombs', i.e. the reputed tombs of Herod's wife Mariammē and members of his family, which are known on the crest of the slope west of the valley opposite the south-west corner of the Turkish wall, and actually above the winter catchment pool Birket as-Sulṭān. It may be noted that Josephus refers not to a spring but a pool, such as was familiar there since the twelfth century (the Pool of Germanus) (fig. I), later repaired by the Mamlūk Sultan Barquq, hence its modern name. At the present time this is a winter catchment only, but in Josephus' time it may well have been fed by a sluice from the low-level aqueduct from 'Ain al-'Arrūb nine miles south of Bethlehem to the Temple area, which was associated with Pilate.[64] Vincent[65] indeed considers this work, at least from the reservoirs in the Wādī Urṭas, the reputed Pools of Solomon, to have been the work of Solomon since the work in this section is markedly cruder than the rest of the canal, and to be sure it was a similar work to the canal from Giḥon along the east of the south-east hill to Birket al-Ḥamrā, which is usually associated with Solomon, though of course on a much larger scale, to which, however, the resources of Solomon's kingdom and his administration were certainly adequate. Vincent goes on to suggest that the name Dragon Well reflected the resemblance of this long tortuous canal to a serpentine water-monster, *tannīn*, known as one of the monsters of Chaos in Canaanite and Hebrew mythology. While this is feasible, the mythological associations of *tannīn* are, we think, significant, and the winter catchment which dried in summer might well have suggested the mythological theme of a defeated dragon, cf. the association of water-monsters like Leviathan and the 'dragons' (*tannīnīm*) with the dried-up streams, the vanquished enemies of God in his conflict and triumph as King in Psalm lxxiv. 13–15, and the monster of the Nile (*tannīn*) dragged out of its element and left high and dry in Ezekiel xxix. 3–5.

The next point, the Dung Gate, might best be located about the Dung Gate, or Gate of the Moors, in the present south Turkish wall (fig. I [2]).

Nehemiah went on to the Fountain Gate by the King's Pool.[66] This is usually identified with the postern with stairway in the south-east angle of the fortifications on the south-east hill (fig. IV on p. 40) but the enumeration of the Fountain Gate, the wall of the pool of the conduit (A.V. 'the Pool of Shiloah') for the King's Garden and 'unto the stairs that go down from the city of David'[67] (fig. IV on p. 40) indicates that the Fountain Gate was at the south-west angle of the fortifications on the south-east hill, giving direct access to the Pool of Siloam. This of course is conjectural, since neither gate nor wall has been traced by archaeology, and Vincent assumes that the note on the Fountain Gate, which he locates at the south-east angle of the wall round the south-east hill, has been misplaced,[68] but the correctness of the Hebrew text is indicated by the mention of the Fountain Gate in association with other features in the same order also at Nehemiah iii. 15 and xii. 37. The wall of the pool of the conduit for the King's Garden is the wall above the south scarp of the south-east hill, so named because of the notable feature, still to be noticed in spite of the destruction of the conduit which fed the Lower Pool (Birket al-Ḥamra) (Pl. 1). The third of those points, 'the stairs that go down from the city of David', was the most striking of Weill's discoveries on the south-east hill,[69] and is a cardinal point in the vexed problem of the fortifications of the City of David. This corridor from out of the postern in the south-east angle of the city (fig. IV on p. 40) was surely 'the gate between the two walls'[70] by which Zedekiah, the last king of Judah, escaped by night when the Babylonians took the city in 586 B.C. Nehemiah passed on up the Qidron wadi and from an indefinite point he turned back and re-entered the city by the Valley Gate.

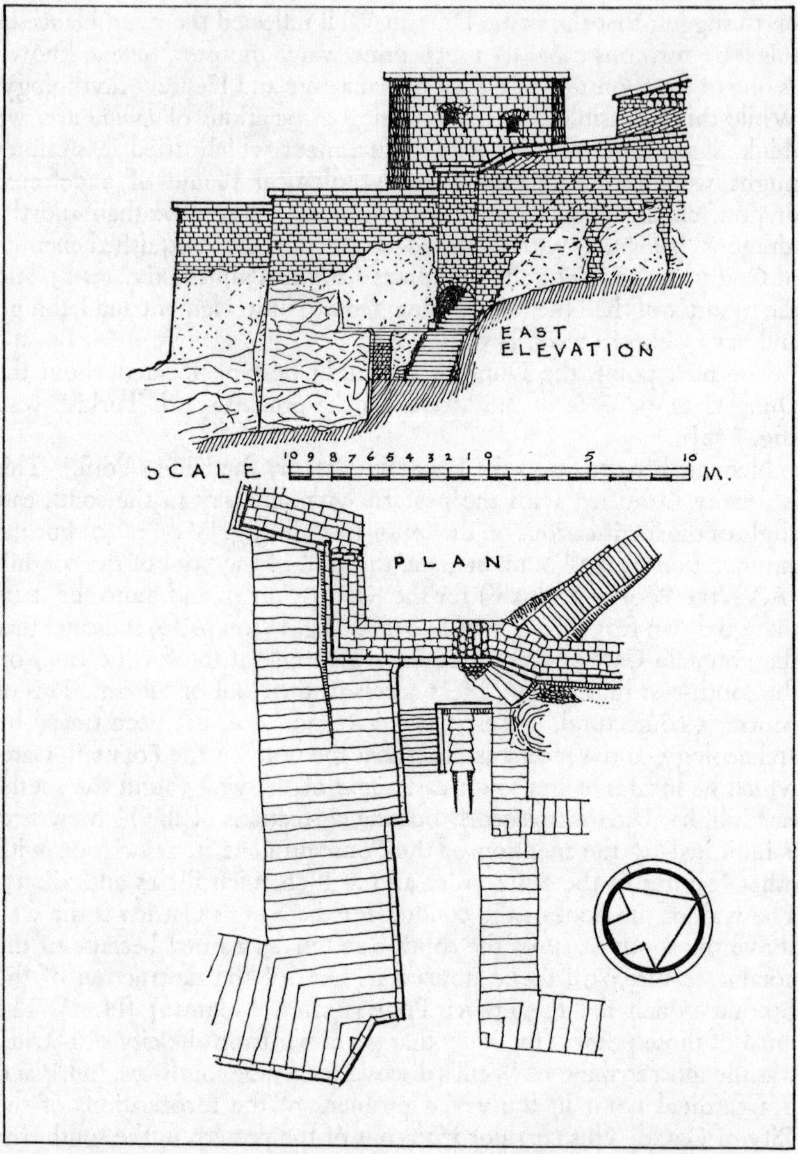

Fig. IV. THE DEFENCES OF PRE-ISRAELITE AND ISRAELITE JERUSALEM.
This shows the south point of the city on the south-east hill, with the 'stairs of the city of David' and the 'gate between the two walls'.
(*J. L. Somerville after Raymond Weill* La Cité de David)

This section is described again in the account of Nehemiah's reconstruction in Nehemiah iii, in the same direction and sequence, the Valley Gate to the Dung Gate (Nehemiah iii. 13) and the Fountain Gate (Nehemiah iii. 15), the wall of the pool of the conduit by (better 'for') the King's Garden and 'the stairs that go down from the city of David' (Nehemiah iii. 15). The work on the south-east wall is next located 'over against the sepulchres of David', which are thus located near the south apex of the south-east hill (Pl. 3), and 'to the pool that was made' (Nehemiah iii. 16). The last feature is either an irrigation pool filled from one of the lateral sluices in the conduit from Giḥon along the east and south of the south-east hill or the artificially enlarged basin of the Spring of Giḥon. The next point, 'the house of the mighty' (Nehemiah iii. 16) is naturally located by the palace of the House of David at the north part of the south-east hill, where 'the armoury at the turning of the wall' (Nehemiah iii. 19) is also naturally located. Here 'the turning of the wall' is vague, but if it is borne in mind that the wall of Nehemiah, like that of the later Hasmonaeans, ran along the crest of the south-east hill* it is more specific, referring to the change of direction from north to north-east occasioned by the depression in the east side of the hill between the south-east hill and the eastward bulge of the Ophel, where again the east wall turns due north (fig. I). The reconstruction of the wall is described in a northerly direction, the next reference being to 'the house of Eliashib the high priest' (Nehemiah iii. 20) which must have been by, or in, the Temple precinct. In the same vicinity, though apparently out of sequence in the text, is 'the tower which lies out from the king's high house' (Nehemiah iii. 25). This feature is mentioned again in Nehemiah iii. 26 in the note on the settlement of Temple servants (Nethīnīm), which is apparently a redactional gloss. Here the settlement of the Temple-servants is given as Ophel ('the bulge'), which is obviously located between the outlying tower and the Water Gate, which obviously related to the Spring of Giḥon. In this vicinity too, probably in the court of Solomon's palace where it abutted on the Temple precinct, lay the Horse Gate (fig. I [6]).[71] From here the wall probably coincided with the east temenos wall of the Temple, since the work is ascribed to the priests in sections adjoining their houses (Nehemiah iii. 28). The next point is the Inspection, or Muster, Gate (A. V. 'Miphqad'), which was probably also called the Benjamin Gate (fig. I [7]),[72] which is given as the east extremity of the city in Zechariah xiv. 10. The wall apparently turned west or north-west north of this point according to the reference in

* There is so far no definite trace of a wall of this period along the crest, but neither is there any trace of wall or occupation down the slope.

Nehemiah iii. 31 to 'the going up of the corner', probably following Manasseh's wall along the south bank of the wadi which runs south-east towards the Qidron. Still apparently in a north-west direction and before the Tower of Hananeel, which was the north extremity of the city (fig. I [9]),[73] was the Sheep Gate,[74] with which the pool by the sheep market was[75] probably associated (fig. I [8]). The connection of the Sheep Gate with the precinct of the Temple is suggested by the fact that it was repaired and consecrated by the High Priest and the Temple staff, who also took responsibility for the Tower of the Hundred (fig. I [10]) (A.V. 'Meah') and the Tower of Hananeel (Nehemiah iii. 1). With the Fish Gate, which is next mentioned (Nehemiah iii. 3), the wall probably descended to the Central Valley. The next gate to be mentioned is termed in the standard Hebrew text *sha'ar hayyᵉshānā*, rendered in A.V. as 'the Old Gate'. The grammar is suspect, however, on two counts, and the text may be a corruption of *sha'ar hammishneh*, the Mishneh Gate, or Gate of the Second Quarter (fig. I [11]),[76] which like the Fish Gate was probably part of Hezekiah's extension.[77] The next point west or south-west of this point is 'the Broad wall' *ḥômā hārᵉḥābhā*). The ungrammatical Hebrew text here may be emended after the Septuagint to *ḥômath hārᵉḥōbh*, 'the wall of the square, or public place', such as is commonly found by main city gates. This might denote the vicinity of the Ephraim Gate, which is not named in this passage but is mentioned between 'the Broad Wall' (A.V.), or 'the wall of the square' and 'the Old Gate', or Mishneh Gate, in the account of the dedication of the walls in Nehemiah xii. 38–9. In this connection it may be noted that at the memorable Feast of Tabernacles in Nehemiah viii the booths, or bivouacs, were erected in the square, or public place, by the Ephraim Gate. Here the old monarchic north wall before Hezekiah's northward extension has been reached and the last point is the Tower of the Furnaces or Baking Ovens or perhaps Limekilns (Nehemiah iii. 11), which can hardly be other than part of the Corner Gate at the west extremity of the city by the Turkish citadel.[78] This picture of Nehemiah's restoration is confirmed by the description of the festal procession in the dedication of the restored wall (Nehemiah vii. 27–40). Unfortunately it is not amplified except in the inclusion of the Ephraim Gate, which was probably in the old east-west wall just west of the junction with the second north-south wall, and in the detail that the procession from the Fountain Gate went over (A.V. 'up by') 'the stairs of the city of David'. This means that the procession entered the city by the Fountain Gate at the south-west corner by the Pool of Siloam and, mounting the wall, literally passed over the stairway, which, as Weill's excavation has demonstrated, descended through a postern in the wall at the south-east corner of the south-east hill (fig. IV on p. 40). At first glance the extent of the wall described seems too great to have been completed in fifty-two days (Nehemiah vi. 15), but in many cases it simply involved repair, as the Hebrew verb (literally 'strengthened') clearly indicates, and a similar work had probably been undertaken quite recently (see below p. 110). Moreover, considering the provincial status of Jerusalem in the Persian Empire, Nehemiah's restoration of the walls was symbolic rather than effective against any but robber bands, as suggested by the taunt of his neighbours 'Even that which they build, if a fox go up he shall break down their stone wall' (Nehemiah iv. 3). This exhausts our knowledge of the development and extent of Jerusalem in the Old Testament.

The city had many vicissitudes in the Hellenistic period (333–63 B.C.), particularly under the Greek rulers of the Syrian House of Seleucus and the Jewish patriots and native rulers of the House of Hashmon, but in this period archaeological evidence is scanty and the documentary sources, I Maccabees and Josephus, as scanty and ambiguous. Antiochus IV (Epiphanes) first fortified part of the city as a citadel, or *akra* in 175 B.C. (I Maccabees i. 33), which was more than a mere citadel, being in fact a Syrian cantonment, which gave shelter also to the more liberal and moderate Jews who were prepared to collaborate. The fact that the *akra* denoted both the citadel of Antiochus and the part of the city that it commanded has been one of the main sources of confusion in the interpretation of the data of I Maccabees and Josephus.

In this debated point the evidence of the sources must be cited and distinctly considered.

In the account of the intensification of Syrian pressure on Judah I Maccabees i. 33–6 states:

> And they built the city of David with a great and strong wall, and with strong towers, and it became unto them a citadel (*akra*) and they put there a sinful nation, transgressors of the law, and they strengthened themselves therein. And they stored up arms and victuals, and gathered together the spoils of Jerusalem, and they laid them up there, and they became a sore snare; and it became a place to lie in wait against the sanctuary. . . .

At first sight the reference to 'the city of David' seems conclusive, the historical city of David being on the south-east hill, and the *akra* has been located there by several authorities, particularly, and most recently, J. Simons,[79] who regards the whole south-east hill as the *akra*, not without some justification as we shall argue. But we have already seen that Josephus retains an uncritical tradition that the south-west hill was the city of David, and it may be that the writer of I Maccabees held the same view, the source of which was doubtless the incorporation of the summit of the south-west hill in the early Hebrew monarchy, though not actually under David. If this were so, a site between the more populous part of the city, now on the south-west hill, and the Temple would be the most normal site for the citadel proper. Here the site of the later Hasmonaean palace and of the Ṣephardi and Ashkenazi synagogues in the Jewish quarter of the city till 1947 on the north-east spur of the south-west hill, which is actually thirty feet above the rock-surface of the Temple area and about a hundred and fifty yards distant, has been suggested by F. M. Abel[80] and L. H. Vincent.[81] This is a very apt site for a fortress, or citadel, which would not only command access to the Temple from the Upper City but would effectively guard the settlement on the lower south-east hill, where the Jewish collaborators could live safely under Syrian tutelage. A fortification of the south-east hill may also be visualized in I Maccabees i. 33–6.

I Maccabees xii. 35 ff. goes on to state that Jonathan the brother of Judas Maccabaeus, having occupied Jerusalem but being unable to reduce the *akra*, raised a high barricade between the *akra* and the city, isolating it so that the garrison had no longer any access to the market in the city and were reduced to starvation (I Maccabees xiii. 21). The isolation of the actual citadel of the Syrian garrison would be more practicable if it were actually in the city, where Abel and Vincent locate it, than if it were on the south-east hill, in which case the garrison would probably have been able to make sorties to the villages for food. Simons on the other hand rightly observes that the blockading of the *akra* would have been much simpler if the citadel proper had been at the north end of the south-east hill. Simons' observation too that the garrison would be better isolated here from the actual settlement within the main part of the city is not without its point and has a modern analogy in the quartering of British garrison troops during the Mandate in the Allenby Barracks by the German Colony in the south-west suburbs of Jerusalem.

I Maccabees xii. 37 next describes building operations, mentioning the collapse of a wall 'towards the wadi' and the repair of 'what was called Caphenatha'. It is not certain if this was part of the circumvallation of the *akra* ('the Famine, or Starvation, Wall'?) or if it was part of the general repair of the city wall, or if 'the wadi' was, as we should normally expect, the Qidron ravine or, as is possible, the lower, steeper part of the Central Valley. Caphenatha also is quite uncertain. Etymologically the word may suggest 'famine' (Aramaic) or possibly an Aramaic form of a Hebrew root *kāphāl*, 'double'[82] and may refer to the wall enclosing the Second Quarter of the City as Simons[83] and Vincent[84] suggest. Alternatively we might suggest that it refers to the secondary incorporation of the summit of the south-west hill before the northward extension to include the Second Quarter. In this case it might refer to the north and south walls, the 'double' fortifications roughly on the line of the present Turkish south wall and the oldest monarchic north wall on the south-west hill, Josephus' first north wall, which ran just north and south of the spur on which Abel and Vincent would locate the *akra*.* Here it would require only a north-south cross wall of about four hundred yards west of the spur to isolate the feature and less than half of that length on the east to isolate it from the south-east hill, which we regard as the *akra* in the wider sense, and where access to the Spring of Giḥon was of great importance to the Syrian garrison.

Under Simon, the successor of Jonathan, I Maccabees xiv. 37 states that the *akra* was now occupied by a Jewish garrison. Here a complication is introduced by Josephus, who states that the *akra* was demolished by Simon to bring it down below the level of the Temple, which it had formerly dominated, an operation which occupied three years.[85] This gives some semblance of feasibility to the view that the *akra* proper was on the site of Solomon's palace on the south-east hill, which is apparently visualized as the *akra* in Josephus' famous description of Jerusalem,[86] a point to which we will revert. If Josephus is visualizing the actual fortress here he is hazarding an explanation of the palpable fact that the site in question was much lower than the site of the Temple. But it is significant that the writer of I Maccabees, writing only about twenty years after Simon's occupation of the *akra*, does not mention such a demolition, which to be sure would have had no point since Simon's purpose was to use the *akra* as a fortification. The eminence on which Abel and Vincent locate the *akra* proper is still about thirty feet higher than the rock-level of the Temple area, but this is not an insuperable difficulty in view of the fact that Josephus was writing in Rome after some ten years' absence from Palestine. Actually in his information on the demolition of the *akra* he is unreliable. It was in fact not destroyed by Simon since it was still standing in the reign of

* I propose another alternative that Caphenatha may mean 'the linking wall' from the south-west hill over the ravine of the Central Valley connecting the fortifications of the south-west hill to the old wall round the south-east hill, in which case 'the wadi' would be the lower part of the Central Valley.

Antiochus VII (139–128 B.C.).[87] Josephus knew this site as the palace of the Hasmonaean princes, first mentioned under Alexandra the widow of Alexander Jannaeus.[88] If this was indeed the site of the *akra*, Josephus' reference to the reduction of the hill on which it stood probably refers rather to the dismantling of the earlier fortress and the levelling of the site for the palace and its grounds long after the time of Simon, and probably to a construction from the debris of the citadel of a ramp over the Central Valley to connect the main part of the city with the Temple hill, as they were connected by Herod by a bridge. This seems to be visualized by Josephus in *War* V. iv. 1. In Josephus' statement about the reduction of the hill on which the *akra* stood to bring it lower than the Temple, we must remember that he was visualizing the Temple in its esplanade within its battlemented precinct wall opposite the eminence to the south-west, now crowned no longer by the fortress of the *akra*, but by the palace of the Hasmonaeans, which would not be such an imposing building. This was still higher than the Temple courts in the first century A.D. since King Herod Agrippa II was able to watch the Temple service from his dining-room window.[89] The general impression, however, in the time of Josephus was of a feature no longer dominating the Temple, an impression increased by the filling in of the Central Valley. Considering that Josephus wrote his history of the Revolt a decade after he left Jerusalem and his *Antiquities* somewhat later it is not surprising that he should not have remembered that the site of *akra* on the north-east spur of the south-west hill over against the Temple[90] was actually still thirty feet higher than the highest part of the rock-surface under the Temple.

In his account of the Hasmonaean period Josephus, except for his erroneous attribution of the demolition of the *akra* to Simon[91] and the hyperbolic statement that this operation occupied the whole population three years, adds nothing to the information in I Maccabees, his main source, except the consistent statement that the feature was in the Lower City.[92] Thus the evidence of I Maccabees and Josephus so far supports the location of the *akra* on the north-east spur of the south-west hill, or at least does not contradict it, provided that we understand 'the city of David' in I Maccabees i. 33–6 as referring to the north part of the south-west hill, which was incorporated in the defences of the city in the Davidic monarchy though not by David, and the Lower City as referring to the lower slopes of the west ridge towards the Central Valley rather than strictly to the old settlement on the south-east hill, to which indeed the *akra* in the wider sense also refers.

With these points in view we may consider Josephus' celebrated description of Jerusalem of his day in *War* V. iv. 1:

> The city was built upon two hills, which are opposite to one another, and have a valley to divide them asunder. . . . Of these hills, that which contains the Upper City is much higher, and in length more direct. Accordingly it was called the Citadel by King David; . . . but it is called by us the Upper Market-place. But the other hill, which was called Akra, and sustains the Lower City, is of the shape of the moon when she is horned; over against this was a third hill, but naturally lower than Akra, and partly formed from the other by a broad valley. However, in those times when the Hasmonaeans reigned, they filled up that valley with earth, and had a mind to join the city to the Temple. They then took off part of the height of the Akra, and reduced it to a less elevation than it was before, that the Temple might be superior to it. Now the Valley of the Cheese-mongers (Tyropoeon) . . . distinguished the hill of the Upper City from that of the Lower.

Here the *akra*, again associated with the Lower City, is quite definitely located on the south-east hill, which is described as crescent-shaped, probably referring to its shape between the curved, roughly parallel valleys of the Qidron and the Central Valley. This is the text built upon by those who support a location of the *akra*, citadel as well as city-quarter, upon the south-east hill. If this location were correct the third hill naturally lower than the *akra* and parted formerly from the other by a broad valley, filled up with debris from the demolition of the *akra* might indicate that the fortress proper was on the site of Solomon's palace or even higher up nearer the Temple before its reconstruction by Herod.[93] In this case the third hill would be the south-east hill south of the saddle at the narrowest point of the south-east hill at the north, where the depression between the eastward bend of the Central Valley and the westward bend of the Qidron might conceivably give the impression of a valley filled in. But the difficulty remains that this site was not less than sixty feet lower than the Temple site and would not so effectively control communications between the Temple and the more populous Upper City, though dominating the Lower City on the south-east hill. At any rate it is clear from Josephus' description that *akra* has two senses for him, the whole of the south-east hill, the Lower City, to which alone 'crescent-shaped' applies, and the fortress proper as distinct from a lower hill, which we take to be the south-east hill. In so far as he visualizes the fortress in the Lower City Josephus may be thinking of the lower slopes of the city on the western ridge. In this case the 'broad valley', which once separated the *akra* from the third, lower, or south-east hill, would be the broader part of the Central Valley before its narrowing and steep descent about the south-west corner of the present Muslim Sacred Precinct, where a ramp crossed the valley under the Hasmonaeans to join the main city with the Temple, where the same purpose was effected under Herod the Great by a bridge, traces of which remain in the Wilson Arch to the south part of the west wall of the Ḥaram, which here coincides with Herod's precinct wall. Thus in spite of difficulties owing to the fact that Josephus wrote in Rome after an absence of over a decade and at a remove of over two centuries from the Hasmonaean period he describes, when the city was greatly different from the Herodian city he knew, there is sufficient evidence to locate the *akra* after Abel and Vincent on the site of the Maccabaean palace on the north-east spur of the south-west hill.

As the Jewish patriots under Judas Maccabaeus and his brothers won limited successes they fortified the Temple area over against the Syrian *akra*, which was first occupied by Simon when they had won independence, and later demolished either under John Hyrcanus (134–104 B.C.) or Alexander Jannaeus (103–76 B.C.), to be replaced by the palace of the Hasmonaean princes, which is first mentioned under Alexandra-Salome, the widow of Alexander Jannaeus and his secular heir. The demolition of the *akra* was probably connected with the fortification of the high point of vantage north-west of the Temple area, the Baris (Aramaic *bir*ᵉ*thā*, 'the Fortress'),[94] which was probably a development of the Tower of Hananeel[95] and was itself developed by Herod the Great as Antonia. The Hasmonaean princes evidently developed the Upper City probably within the walls of Hezekiah and Manasseh, though in the congestion of the continuous occupation of this area nothing distinctively Hasmonaean may be identified except in the foundations of the wall at the Turkish Citadel. On the south-east hill, however, the Hasmonaean wall on the crest of the hill may be partly traced, including the well-known buttress above the Spring of Giḥon, formerly exhibited as part of the Jebusite fortification.

Herod the Great (37–4 B.C.) next developed the city, his most conspicuous monuments being his palace-fort by the Turkish Citadel with its three great towers Hippicus, Phasael and Mariammē (fig. I [15] on p. 17), the Temple (Pl. 6), the precinct of which was greatly enlarged, particularly towards the south, by great substructures and a tremendous outer wall, the lower courses of which may be partly seen today in the south and west, or Wailing, Wall (Pl. 7) (see further pp. 162, 192), and the Antonia.

Josephus' description of Herod's palace on the summit of the south-west hill with its gardens with 'groves of trees and long walls through them, with deep canals and cisterns',[96] implies a regular supply of water at a higher level than the aqueduct from the Wādī 'Urṭas which ran round the upper part of the Wādī 'r-Rabābī and the south-west hill to the Temple. Herod's palace and gardens in fact must have been supplied by an aqueduct from a higher point in the west ridge north of the palace. Here the ancient cistern known as the Patriarch's Bath was probably the reservoir for this aqueduct, being fed by the aqueduct through the Wādī 'l-Meiseh from the Mamilla Pool about eight hundred yards north-west of the Patriarch's Bath. The name Mamilla in fact may be a corruption of 'the filler' (*mᵉmallē*),[97] though that is uncertain.* The Mamilla Pool in turn may have been fed by the high-level aqueduct from 'Ainal-'Arrūb and south-west of the Wādī 'Urṭas past Bethlehem to just north of the present railway station at Jerusalem, though from this point north to the Mamilla Pool considerable deviation and siphonage would have been necessary. According to Vincent's feasible reconstruction[98] an earlier, cruder canal from the springs in the Wādī 'Urṭas to Jerusalem (the low-level aqueduct) was supplemented by Herod for the use of his palace-fort the Herodium south-east of Bethlehem and for irrigation there[99] by tapping the source of 'Ainal-'Arrūb and adding one, or perhaps two, of the three 'Pools of Solomon' in the Wādī 'Urṭas. It is not certain whether this or the low-level aqueduct was the one repaired by Pontius Pilate, but it was certainly later repaired by the tenth legion, stamps of which appear on the clay pipes in the excavations at Herod's palace in the Citadel. The excavator C. N. Johns suggests that this may have been the work of the tenth legion when it organized its camp on the south-west hill of Jerusalem after A.D. 70, but the work may be that of the same legion about the end of the second century.

Guarding the Temple at the north-west angle of the sacred precinct and also keeping watch on the movement of Herod's restive subjects at their national festivals, the Antonia was a fortress worthy of Herod the Great. Described by Josephus[100] as a fortress in strength and extent capable of holding a permanent garrison of a Roman cohort, not less than six hundred, and a palace in splendour, it was a great self-contained complex with porticoes, baths and great paved courts (fig. V on pp. 50–51), part of which, with a large double cistern below, may still be seen under the Church and Convent of Our Lady of Zion. It was a great rectangle with four great corner towers, the highest, that at the north-east angle, being forty feet high. It stood on a rock platform

* Albright's proposal that the word is a corruption of Arabic *ma'manu 'llah* ('the place under the security of Allah', i.e. a cemetery, which is a feature of the site,) is not feasible, since the name Mamilla is attested in Byzantine sources long before the place was appropriated as a burial-ground for distinguished Muslim families, as Vincent (*op. cit.* I, p. 302) n., points out.

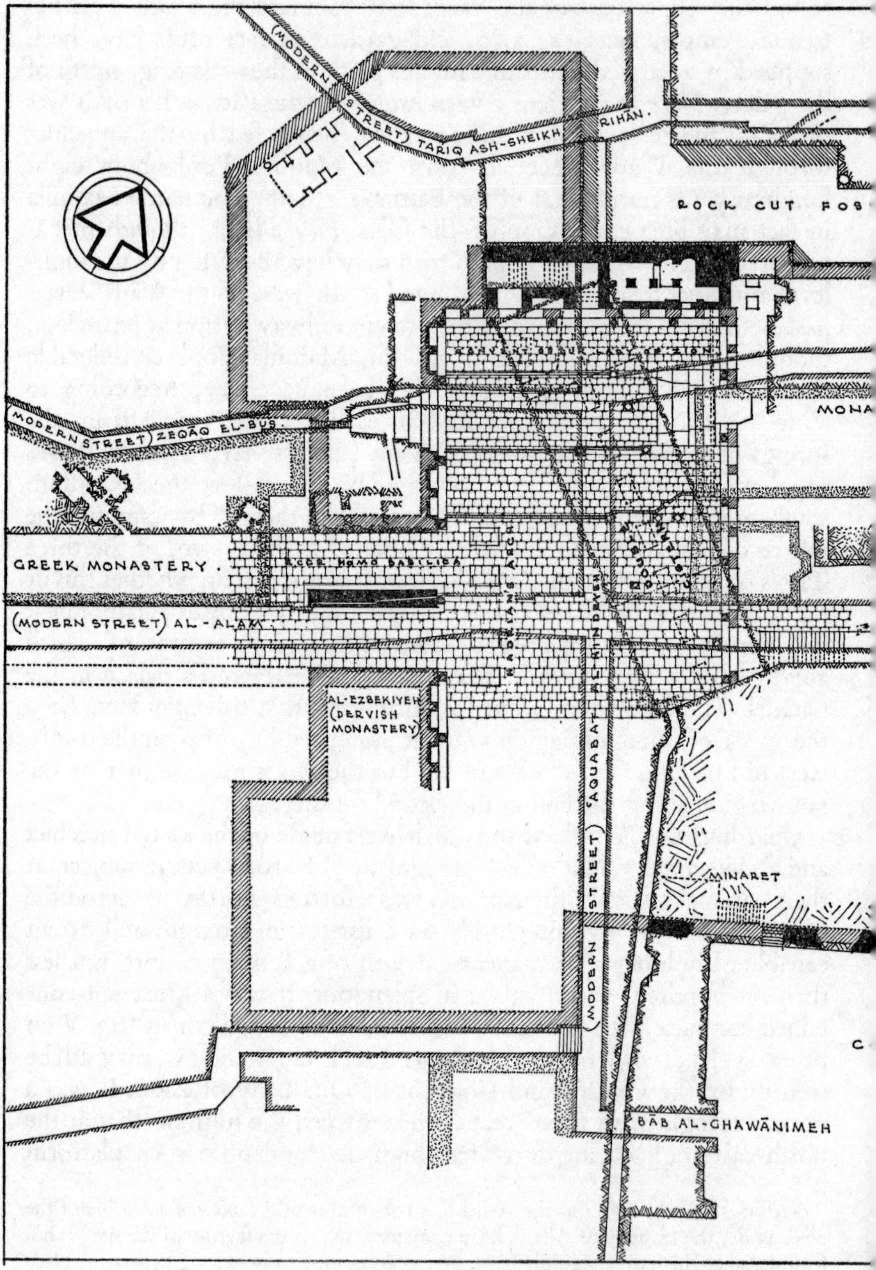

Fig. V. SITE AND PLAN OF THE ANTONIA. (*J. L. Somerville after L*

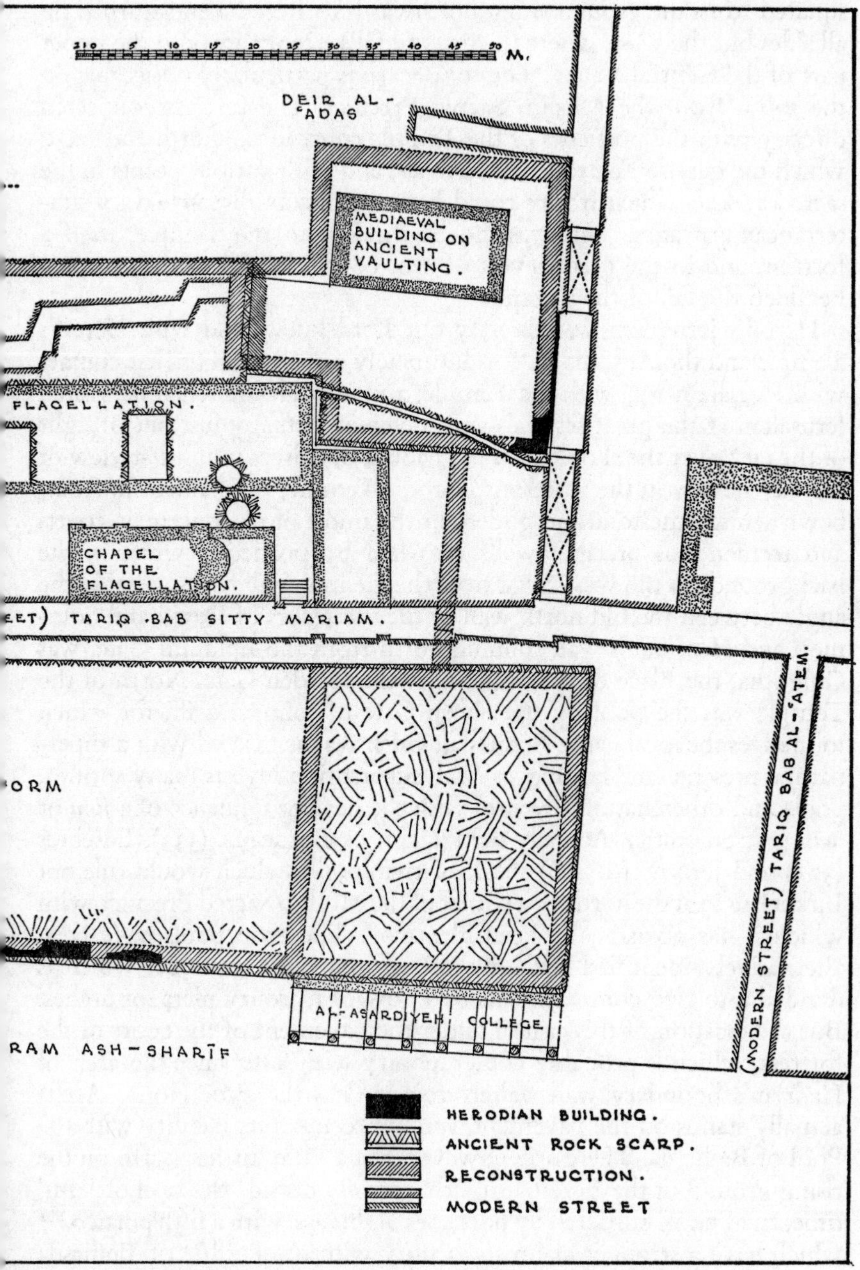

and M. A. Stève Jérusalem de l'Ancien Testament)

squared from the ground rising northwards to Bezetha and scarped on all sides but the west, where the ground falls steeply away to the upper part of the Central Valley. The rock-scarp is particularly noticeable on the south from the Muslim Sacred Precinct. The fortress connected directly with the porticoes of the Temple court in the north and west, which the garrison patrolled at festivals, and with various points in the sacred area to which troops could be immediately dispatched by subterranean passages. This was indeed the key to the Temple, itself a fortress, and in the great revolt of A.D. 66–70 the fall of the Antonia heralded the fall of the Temple.

Herod's Jerusalem was the city our Lord knew, and with Herod's Temple and the Antonia he was intimately associated. His first contact with Jerusalem was with the Temple, and in adult life when he visited Jerusalem at the great festivals and stayed at Bethany just out of sight of the city over the shoulder of the Mount of Olives in his first view of the city he saw in the forefront Herod's Temple, resplendent in fresh-hewn white limestone and gilded, in the midst of its concentric courts and tremendous precinct walls crowned by porticoes, while in the background on the west ridge over the Central Valley just outside the angle between the old north wall of the successors of David and Solomon and Hezekiah's wall running north from the Ephraim Gate, was Golgotha, the Place of the Skull, now the Garden Gate. North of the Temple was the pool by the Sheep Gate of John v. 2 ff., for which John gives the local name Bethesda, which was associated with a supernatural presence and healing, as Arab superstition invests many springs, pools and other natural features with the healing influence of a *jinn* or *wālī* (patron-spirit). Actually the Pilgrim of Bordeaux (333), Eusebius (323) and Jerome (fl. 400) speak of twin pools, which would rule out Birket Isra'in at the north-east corner of the Muslim Sacred Precinct, with which it has occasionally been identified. The twin pools have been alternatively identified with the cistern under the Antonia, which is divided into two compartments by a row of masonry piers for arches. But the location of this cistern under the pavement of the court of the fortress, which is probably contemporary with Jesus since the arch of Hadrian's boundary wall (falsely regarded as the Ecce Homo Arch) actually stands on the pavement, surely precludes its identity with the Pool of Bethesda. There are, however, just a little further north on the rising ground of the Bezetha suburb, actually outside the wall of Jesus' time, twin pools bordered by porticoes of this age with a fifth portico,[101] which have a stronger claim to identity with the Pool(s) of Bethesda (fig. I).[102] This feature may be referred to in the famous copper scroll from Qumran, which purports to be an inventory of Temple vessels and treasure with a note on the locations of the several caches. One of these places is Betheshuḥayin (the Place of the Two Pools) or possibly Betheshdathayin.[103] The similarity of the latter with Bethesda is striking, and the dual form of the name will be noted. Etymologically Bethesda may mean 'the Place of Up-welling', from a root attested in Aramaic and in North-Canaanitish (Ugaritic), and may be a reference to the disturbance of the water to which John v. 4 refers, if indeed this is not a secondary gloss prompted by the intermittent flow of the Spring of Giḥon into the Pool of Siloam, which was also associated with healing in the Gospel.[104] If Betheshdathayin is the correct reading in the copper scroll, as may well be, it would confirm the explanation we have suggested of Bethesda, which has alternatively been explained as 'the Place of Mercy' (*bēyth ḥasdā*).

On the lower slopes of the Mount of Olives before the Qidron ravine lay Gethsemane ('the Winepress') (Pl. 32), where the olives from the terraced slopes of the Mount of Olives and the valley-bottom of the upper Qidron were crushed, and it is interesting to note that the scene of the Last Supper was located here[105] until it was located in the end of the sixth century on the present traditional site south of Herod's palace and its grounds on the summit of the south-west hill. Indeed the first to locate it on the south-west hill was Alexander, a pilgrim from Cyprus, the tradition being already established when Sophronius mourns the fall of Jerusalem to the Muslims (638).

The house of the High Priest Caiaphas is shown at the Church of St. Peter of the Cock-crow on the east slopes of the south part of the south-west hill in the villa with its private mill and rock-hewn cells, which are claimed as places of detention, including the cell in which our Lord was detained the night that he was convicted by the High Priest's Council until the morning, so that the conviction might be legalized before the Sanhedrin, which met either in the south-west corner of the Sacred Precinct or in the Council House, which, according to Josephus[106], lay just west of that point, so near the Wailing Wall. This location of the House of Caiaphas at the Church of St. Peter of the Cock-crow (*gallicantus*), though accepted in the Crusading period, is relatively late, the earliest clear reference being in Epiphanius Hagiopolitā (750–800). Josephus' mention in *War* II. xvii. 6 of the house of Ananias the High Priest in the Jewish revolt being burnt by the extremists, who held the lower city, indicates a location on the south-west hill, where Theodosius[107] locates it fifty Roman paces (about eighty yards) from where he locates 'the mother of all the churches' just south of the summit of the south-west hill and apparently to the north, since he locates the Praetorium of Pilate, obviously visualizing

Herod's palace by the Citadel, a hundred Roman paces (about 160 yards) beyond,[108] and indeed the Armenians have claimed the site at the Church of the Holy Redeemer.

From the Sanhedrin Jesus was taken to Pilate's headquarters (*praetorium*). It will always be debated whether the scene of Jesus' sentence by Pilate was the Antonia or Herod's great palace-fort on the site of the Turkish Citadel. In favour of the latter is the fact that at that time, when there was no native ruler in Judaea, the palace of Herod would be the more natural residence of the Roman procurator, up from his headquarters in Caesarea for the occasion of Passover. Indeed it is mentioned in this connection by Josephus as the temporary headquarters of the Roman commander Sabinus in 4 B.C.[109] and of the procurator Gessius Florus (A.D. 64–66),[110] and by Philo of Alexandria, who states that Herod's palace was occupied by the procurators, mentioning specifically an incident associated with Pilate there.[111] The former location, which incidentally was also Herod's palace before the other was built, is supported by the Pilgrim of Bordeaux (333)[112] and Jerome's account of the pilgrimage of St. Paula (404)[113] among the early pilgrims, and notably by Père L. H. Vincent among recent authorities; the site at the Citadel was accepted by Epiphanius (390) and Theodosius (530) and among modern scholars by Dalman, Benoit and Kopp.[114] The term *praetorium* of course is quite indeterminate, meaning simply 'headquarters', originally referring to a general's headquarters, however temporary, and then to the headquarters of a provincial governor, as for instance in Caesarea.[115] Now notwithstanding Josephus' and Philo's references to Herod's palace, even if they did refer to Herod's later palace, as the headquarters of Roman procurators, in view of the mood of the Jews in the office of Pontius Pilate, exacerbated at the Passover festival and so liable to explode, it would not be strange if Pilate's headquarters on that occasion were the Antonia, where the situation in the Sacred Precinct might be kept under close observation, as so often in the experience of foreign powers occupying Jerusalem. While on general grounds either the Antonia or Herod's palace might be the *praetorium* on this occasion, the mention of the *lithostrōton* in John xix. 13, where the Aramaic name *gabbᵉthā* is also given, is obviously specific. *Lithostrōton* by itself might mean any stone pavement, but the fact that the local name is also cited particularizes it as *the* Stone Pavement,[116] that in fact bedded in Roman cement in the rock-cut groundlevel of the Antonia, which antedates the time of Hadrian since the triple arch of his boundary wall of the city is a later construction, and which measures about 2,500 square yards.[117] The most probable connotation of *gabbᵉthā* is 'raised ground', probably referring to the higher ground on which the Antonia was built, the higher elevation being clearly discernible from the rock-scarp at the north-west corner of the Muslim Sacred Precinct. The reference may be more specifically to the rock of the Antonia rising to Bezetha as the 'very high mountain' (*har gābhôah me'ôdh*) from which in Ezekiel xl. 2 the angel showed Ezekiel the Temple.[118]

Pilate heard Jesus' statement within his headquarters, the Jews meanwhile crowding the outer courts as near as they might to avoid ceremonial pollution in anticipation of the Passover, and, finding no sufficient grounds for a capital charge, seized the opportunity of Jesus' being a Galilean to send him to Herod the Tetrarch of Galilee, who was up for the festival.[119] Jesus was thus sent to the Hasmonaean palace on the north-east spur of the south-west hill over against the south-west of the Temple area, and as he would go under an escort of Roman soldiers the party would go by the city roughly along the Central Valley and not by the west portico of the Temple court, and by the same way Herod sent Jesus back again. As a last resort Pilate endeavoured to satisfy the Jews by scourging Jesus, which must also have taken place in the Antonia, where the Franciscans show a Chapel of the Flagellation, though the precise location of this episode is uncertain. Finally along the line roughly of the *via dolorosa*, which cannot validly be proved nor disproved, Jesus bore the cross to Golgotha ('the Place of the Skull'), probably passing out of the city by the Mishneh Gate (see above p. 42) in the wall of Hezekiah's northward extension, to the traditional site of the Crucifixion, which there is no good reason to doubt (see below pp. 198–200).

Josephus describes in *War* V. iv. 2 the fortifications of Jerusalem on the eve of the Jewish revolt in A.D. 66, and in his account of the three north walls of the city recapitulates on earlier fortifications. Beginning at the Turkish Citadel, where the western tower Hippicus was evidently a key point in the outer wall, he describes the wall very summarily 'through a place called Bethso to the Gate of the Essenes', then southwards. Here the southward stretch, with a 'bending above the Pool of Siloam', may refer to the west wall of the south-east hill with a westward extension to include the pool and the Lower, or Solomon's, Pool, as he describes it (Birket al-Ḥamrā). The fact that only two places, Bethso and the Gate of the Essenes, are mentioned between Hippicus and this southward stretch of the wall and that both points except for this passage are quite unknown is not conducive to clarity, but there seems nevertheless a solution to the problem. After Dalman[120] we propose that Bethso means 'the Place of Excrement' (*bēyth ṣô'āh*), alluding possibly to a rubbish dump or sewer from the palace to the

Valley of Hinnom, and that the Gate of the Essenes is identical with the Dung Gate, which Josephus does not mention by its usual name, and not with the Valley Gate as is usually supposed. The Gate of the Essenes may refer to an Essene settlement on the more sparsely occupied south-west hill outside the city walls of that time or to the Essene settlements in the Wilderness of Judah down the Qidron Valley such as Qumrān. On our assumption that the Gate of the Essenes was the Dung Gate and not the Valley Gate, we may account for Josephus' omission of any reference to the Valley Gate on the grounds that it was so near the Tower of Hippicus as to require no mention along with the latter. While we have explained the note on the turning of the wall in the south 'above the Pool of Siloam' as referring to an extension of the wall to include the pool and the Lower Pool, it is still possible that the reference is to a wall along the west side of the south-west hill which turned eastwards at the high scarp above the pool to the east. The mention of a further bend towards the east, at Solomon's Pool (Birket al-Ḥamrā), however, is more intelligible on the assumption of an extension from the wall along the west side of the south-east hill to include the Pool of Siloam continuing south-east to include the Lower Pool before running north as Josephus describes to the Ophel, or 'Bulge' north-east of the south-east hill, where the wall joined the east precinct of the Temple, which, as in the present Turkish fortifications of the Old City, probably coincided with the city wall as far as the north-east corner of the city in Herod's time. As distinct from those parts of the wall, which did not substantially vary between the time of Manasseh and Herod except for the contraction to the east crest of the south-east hill, the north wall underwent developments. The first north wall, which Josephus dates to the Davidic monarchy, though wrongly ascribing it to David himself, ran between Hippicus to the west cloister of Herod's Temple by a feature known as the *Xystus*, or Polished Pavement and the Council House of the Jewish Sanhedrin, joining the west precinct wall of the Temple probably just north of the Wailing Wall about the present Gate of the Chain (*Bāb aś-Śilśileh*). We have already considered the limited amount of archaeological evidence from the Citadel and from more recent work in the Muristan which may substantiate Josephus' statement that the wall in the Davidic monarchy ran on this line, which, Josephus implies, ran above the south bank of the cross valley just south of David Street, which was thus utilized as a natural fosse. The west part of this wall as far as the Ephraim Gate was retained by Hezekiah in his repair and extension of the north wall,[121] with which Manasseh's extension from the north-east of the south-east hill and north of the Temple linked up at the Fish Gate,[122] where Hezekiah's wall probably crossed the Central Valley to link up with the north-west precinct wall of the Temple. As in his description of other sections Josephus omits certain features, such as the Ephraim Gate, the Mishneh Gate and the Fish Gate in Hezekiah's wall, nor does he mention the next part in Manasseh's wall to the Tower of Hananeel in the north-east, which was developed in the Baris of the Hasmonaeans and the Antonia of Herod, which Josephus mentions. We consider it not unlikely that the Gennath, or Garden, Gate, from which the second wall ran northwards, or rather north-westwards from the first wall, may be a contemporary name for the Ephraim Gate,* the name of which may have lost its significance after the northward extension of the city.

The third wall described by Josephus ran northwards, or rather northwestwards, roughly along the line of the present Turkish wall from the Tower Hippicus to the Tower Psephinus, of which a fragment survives under the Collège des Frères at the north-west angle of the Turkish wall (Pl. 9). Josephus then describes its eastward course, descending 'till it came over against the monuments of Helena', continuing through 'the royal caverns'† to join the east wall above the Qidron Valley.[123] 'The monuments, or monumental tombs, of Helena' can hardly have been other than the well-known Tombs of Helena and her family, who were proselytes to Judaism from the Aramaean royal house of Adiabene in North Mesopotamia, which are situated about 750 yards north of the Damascus Gate in the present Turkish wall of the Old City. Now traces of the lower courses of a wall including immense stones 450 yards north of the Damascus Gate and 250 yards south of the Tombs of the Kings, as Helena's tombs are called, known best through the excavations of E. L. Sukenik and L. Mayer in 1925–27, seem at first sight to suggest Josephus' third north wall. Such a vast extension, which was certainly far beyond immediate needs to enclose the settled area, which had now expanded to include Bezetha north of the Temple area, would be quite unprecedented in the development of Jerusalem. Josephus states that the third wall was begun by Herod Agrippa I (41–44) at a time when tension was rising which was to culminate

* This is the same conclusion as that of Simons (*op. cit.*, p. 234) reached independently. Simons rightly in our opinion locates the Gate west of the junction of the north extension of the wall and the first wall, and notes the significance of the name 'the Garden Gate' with reference to the tradition that Jesus was buried in a garden. Quite independently of the name, however, we regard the site of the Church of the Holy Sepulchre as outside Josephus' second wall.

† Josephus' statement that the third wall actually ran 'through the royal caverns' is substantiated by the fact that the present north wall of the Old City is built at one point over 'Solomon's quarries', the roof of which at a certain place has actually subsided under the wall.

in the Jewish revolt. The apparent disuniform state of the wall seems to support Josephus' statement that Agrippa's work was interrupted, probably by Roman intervention[124] and was later completed on the outbreak of the war. There are, however, serious objections to this view. Vincent, a determined opponent of the view, emphasized the poor work, which does not agree with Josephus' praise of Agrippa's work. The wall, though containing some huge blocks, is not founded in rock-trenches and would be easily mined; it has an ill-articulated core and often thin sides and is of an uneven thickness. Moreover Josephus' description of the tombs of Helena's family as 'distant more than three furlongs from the city'[125] corresponds rather to the distance from the north Turkish wall (about 750 yards) than to the 250 yards which the tombs are distant from the Mayer-Sukenik wall. Furthermore the statement that the third wall ran 'through the royal caverns' (not 'sepulchres') seems certainly to visualize the third wall as roughly in line with the present Turkish wall of Sulaymān the Magnificent (fl. 1537) (Pl. 8), and certain rock-cuttings just in front of the Turkish wall between the north-west angle and the Damascus Gate seem to indicate the line of Josephus' third wall. The Mayer-Sukenik wall still remains a problem. From certain superstructures which antedate the Byzantine period it may, as Vincent suggested,[126] have been constructed during the revolt of Simon bar Kokhba in A.D. 132–135. Dr. Kenyon, however, who has recently devoted special attention to the wall, maintains that it faces south, which would seem to exclude it as a defensive wall for Jerusalem. Coins of the Roman procurators between A.D. 54 and 59 in the fill behind the north face indicate a later date than Agrippa,[127] and indeed the marginal drafted blocks suggest the re-use of materials of Agrippa. This might seem to rule out the possibility that the wall is the circumvallation of the Romans before Jerusalem fell to Titus in A.D. 70. But the blocks may have come from Agrippa's quarries in the vicinity of the wall, being rejected in favour of smaller blocks after Agrippa's work had been interrupted and later hastily completed by the rebels. In view of the great length of over four hundred yards from the summit of the north-west hill to the Qidron Valley this seems a more likely view than that proposed by Dr. Kenyon that the wall enclosed the temporary headquarters of the Roman garrison after A.D. 70 before the permanent legionary camp was laid out on the south-west hill. Coins and pottery from after the first century A.D., which Dr. Kenyon also attests outside the north face of the wall,[128] leave open the possibility that the wall was connected with the revolt of Simon bar Kokhba, but in this case, if indeed the wall faces south, it would be Roman rather than Jewish work, to contain the insurgents after the Romans had evacuated Jerusalem.

Though Josephus does not mention it, Agrippa also extended the wall on the south-west hill to encompass a greater area of the summit than ever before. C. N. Johns, who distinguished building of the first and second centuries B.C. in his excavation of the Citadel, related these phases under the later Hasmonaeans and Herod the Great to the wall round the south-west hill,[129] which Bliss and Dickie had related to the Hebrew Monarchy.[130] Now Johns' view must be modified in the light of excavations since 1961, which demonstrate the wall in question and the gateway at the south tip of the south-west hill to be from the time of Agrippa.[131] Pottery evidence from the lower east slopes of the south-west hill indicates that there was now, perhaps for the first time, a considerable occupation of the south part of the hill, including the rather pretentious villa with its private mill, traces of which are shown in the Church of St. Peter of the Cock-crow as the residence of Caiaphas the High Priest before whom Jesus was condemned. This settlement was probably connected with the economic development under Herod the Great and Herod Agrippa I, under whom the settlement had already overflowed to the south-west and north-east, and more immediately with the migration of a number of Jews to the capital from the provinces as feeling between nationalism and Roman domination under the procurators intensified. Part of this wall of Agrippa was probably revealed in the great squared blocks with marginal drafting found *in situ* in the towers flanking the Damascus Gate in the excavations of R. W. Hamilton in 1937–38[132] and in others re-used in the present Turkish wall.

After the suppression of the Jewish revolt of A.D. 66–70 the city was destroyed, the wall south of Herod's palace being retained as a fortification of the camp of the Tenth Legion Fretensis, which occupied the south-west hill, possibly defended on the north by Josephus' first north wall, from the later Hebrew monarchy, with the Cross Valley as a natural fosse. Gradually the site of Jerusalem was re-occupied by camp-followers and traders, and by Jewish insurgents under Simon bar Kokhba in the last great Jewish revolt in A.D. 132–135, to which the Mayer-Sukenik wall in the north has been feasibly dated.

After this interlude the city was rebuilt under Hadrian as Aelia Capitolina in honour of himself, Publius Aelius Hadrianus, and Jupiter of the Roman Capitol. It was apparently an open town, though perhaps defined by walls, but for delimitation rather than defence, and with triumphal arches rather than fortified gates. Its north limit was probably the line of the Turkish north wall, as suggested by a memorial inscription to the Emperor and his successor by the present Damascus

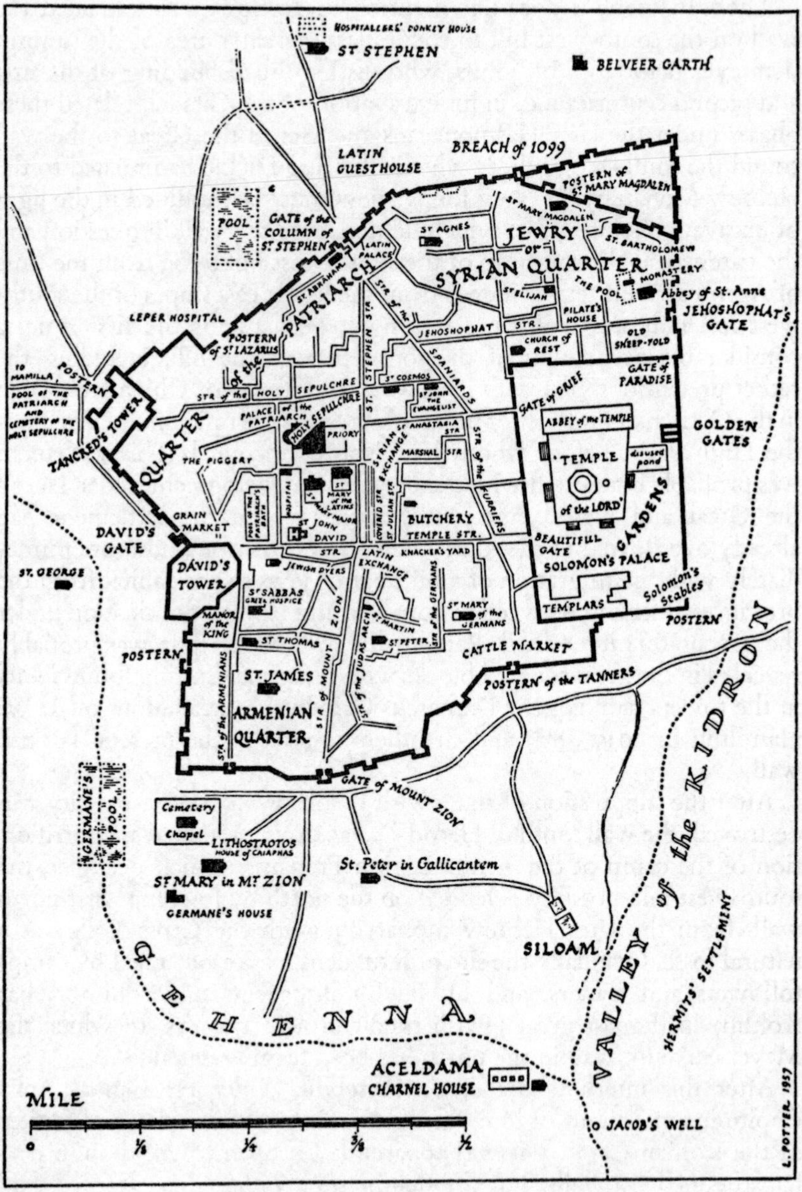

Fig. VI. PLAN OF FRANKISH JERUSALEM. (*Courtesy of the École Biblique and Elek Books Ltd.*)

Gate (Pl. 11). This may be the pillar inside the main north gate depicted as standing at the head of the main north-south street (*cardo maximus*) of Jerusalem in the representation of the city in the famous mosaic in the floor of the orthodox Church at Madaba (sixth century). The gateway of Aelia Capitolina has now been recovered by the excavations of J. B. Hennessy for the Jordanian Department of Antiquities under the Damascus Gate in the Turkish wall. From this time Jerusalem was an open city until the fifth century, when the city was fortified again under Byzantine administration on the line of the present Turkish wall in the north, north-east and north-west,* with a refortification under the Empress Eudocia on the line of the wall of Herod Agrippa I round the southern part of the western ridge and on the eastern edge of the crest of the south-eastern hill above the Qidron ravine, which was later abandoned under the Muslims. It is uncertain whether Byzantine remains on the lower east slope of the hill indicate secular settlement or simply ecclesiastical settlements on holy sites, such as the church of the Empress Eudocia above the Pool of Siloam. The present old city within the Turkish wall represents roughly the extent and general plan of Jerusalem under the Muslims, Franks (Pl. 29, fig. VI) and Turks, when Sulayman the Magnificent built the present wall of the Old City in the sixteenth century, which was largely a restoration of the Byzantine, Frankish and Mamluke fortifications. From this time, and probably from a long time before, the bulk of the south-west and south-east hills were outside the walls and were largely residential with garden-plots as they are at the present time, when the trend of development of modern Jerusalem beyond the walls is north and west to an extent which dwarfs the ancient city.

* This is suggested by the map of Frankish Jerusalem in the MS of Cambrai in the middle of the twelfth century and by the fact that in the siege of the city in 1099 Raymond of Toulouse besieged the wall by the site of the present Zion Gate, and that wall had not appreciably altered since the fifth century, as indicated by the mosaic map of Madaba in the sixth century A.D.

NOTES FOR CHAPTER I

1 II Samuel v. 18 ff.

2 R. Amiran, 'The Tumuli West of Jerusalem: Summary and Excavations 1953', *Israel Exploration Journal* VIII, 1958, pp. 205–29

3 Joshua xv. 8, 63; xviii. 16

4 A. D. Baly, *The Geography of the Bible*, 1957, p. 163. The distance from Geba to aḍ-Ḍaharīyeh is 30 miles and from Qiryath-jearim to the Dead Sea is 18 miles

5 II Chronicles xi. 8–9

6 II Chronicles xi. 7 ff.

7 I Samuel xvii. 1–2

8 II Chronicles xi. 7

9 II Chronicles xi. 6

10 II Chronicles xi. 6

11 Judges xiii. 2; xvi. 4

12 Judges xiii. 2

13 I Samuel v. 10 ff.

14 Cf. the Waters of Nephtoaḥ (*mê nephtôaḥ*) of Joshua xv. 9, which is possibly 'the Wells of Meneptah which is in the mountain range' in a thirteenth-century Egyptian papyrus (J. A. Wilson in *Ancient Near Eastern Texts relating to the Old Testament*, ed. J. B. Pritchard, 1950, p. 258)

15 II Chronicles xi. 10

16 I Kings ix. 17; I Chronicles xii. 24

17 Joshua x. 12–13

18 I Kings xiv. 25–6

19 The felicitous phrase of A. D. Baly, *op. cit.*

20 Josephus, *War* V. iii. 5

21 I Kings xi. 7; II Kings xxiii. 13

22 Psalm cxxv. 2

23 Josephus, *War* V. iv. 2

24 I Kings i. 45

25 This is based on the estimate of K. M. Kenyon (*Palestine Exploration Quarterly*, 1963, p. 9) that the eastern wall is about 161 feet lower down the slope than the crest of the hill

26 *War* V. iv

27 Nehemiah ii. 2 ff.

28 Nehemiah iii

29 Nehemiah xii. 31 ff.

30 K. M. Kenyon, *Palestine Exploration Quarterly*, 1965, p. 15

31 Isaiah xxii. 11

32 II Samuel xxiv. 18–25

33 Nehemiah iii. 16

34 II Kings xxii. 14

35 I Kings ix. 15, 24

36 I Kings xi. 27–8

37 II Chronicles xxxii. 5

38 I Kings xi. 27

39 R. A. S. Macalister and J. G. Duncan, *Excavation on the Hill of Ophel 1923–1925* (*Palestine Exploration Fund Annual IV*), 1926, pp. 45 ff.

40 J. W. Crowfoot, *Palestine Exploration Quarterly*, 1945, p. 7 *n.*

41 II Samuel v. 8

42 II Chronicles xxxii. 5

43 R. Weill, *La Cité de David, Compte rendu des fouilles exécutées à Jérusalem sur le site de la ville primitive, Campagne de 1923–24*, 1947, pp. 31 ff. fig.

44 L. H. Vincent, *Jérusalem de l'Ancien Testament* II, 1956, pp. 635–6

45 II Kings xii. 21, EVV 20

46 K. M. Kenyon, 'Excavations in Jerusalem 1961', *Palestine Exploration Quarterly*, 1962, p. 82, Pl. XXII, 1963, pp. 12–14

47 K. M. Kenyon, *Palestine Exploration Quarterly*, 1963, p. 14

48 I Kings xi. 27–8

49 II Kings xiv. 13=II Chronicles xxv. 23

50 J. Simons, *Jerusalem in the Old Testament*, 1952, p. 208, *n.* 2

51 Nehemiah iii. 1

52 Simons, *op. cit.*, p. 233

53 *War* V. iv

54 Isaiah xxii. 11

55 J. Gray, *I and II Kings: a Commentary*, 1963, pp. 616–18

56 Vincent, *op. cit.* I, 1954, p. 290

57 K. M. Kenyon, *Jerusalem*, 1967, pp. 170–71, 178

58 II Chronicles xxxiii. 14

59 Simons, *op. cit.*, p. 452; Vincent, *op. cit.* II, 1956, p. 604 *n.*

60 II Chronicles xxxii.

61 Nehemiah xiii. 16

62 Nehemiah iii. 11

63 *War* V. iii. 2

64 Josephus, *Antiquities* II, ix. 4

65 Vincent, *op. cit.* I, p. 309

66 Nehemiah ii. 14

67 Nehemiah iii. 15

68 Vincent, *op. cit.* I, p. 244

69 R. Weill, *op. cit.*, pp. 36–9, 40 ff.

70 II Kings xxv. 4

71 II Kings xi. 16; II Chronicles xxiii. 15; Jeremiah xxxi. 40; Nehemiah iii. 28

72 So Simons, *op. cit.*, p. 452

73 Zechariah xiv. 10

74 Nehemiah iii. 32

75 John v. 2

76 Simons, *op. cit.*, p. 453; Vincent, *op. cit.* I, pp. 240, 243

77 II Chronicles xxxii. 5

78 Simons, *op. cit.*, p. 233. The limekilns may be associated with quarrying which K. M. Kenyon attests just north of the Citadel and south of the Holy Sepulchre

79 Simons, *op. cit.*, pp. 144–57. J. Wellhausen, *Israelitische und jüdische Geschichte*, 2nd ed., 1895, p. 261. G. A. Smith (*Jerusalem*, I, 1907, p. 160), though inclining to rely on Josephus and Wellhausen in locating the *akra* on the south-east hill, is well aware of the difficulties, and is otherwise non-committal

80 F. M. Abel, *La Revue Biblique* XXXV, 1926, pp. 520 ff.

81 Vincent, *La Revue Biblique* XLII 1934, pp. 205 ff.; *Jérusalem de l'Ancien Testament* I, 1954, pp. 7 ff., 17–21

82 G. Dalman, *Palästinajahrbuch* XIV, 1918, p. 64

83 Simons, *op. cit.* I, pp. 155–6

84 Vincent, *op. cit.* I, p. 179

85 *Antiquities* XIII. vi. 7; *War* V. iv. 1

86 *War* V. iv. 1

87 I Maccabees xv. 28

88 *Antiquities* XIII. xvi. 2

89 *Antiquities* XX. viii. 11

90 I Maccabees xiii. 52

91 *Antiquities* XIII. vi. 7; *War* I. ii. 2

92 *Antiquities* XII. v. 4; *War* I. i. 4

93 Vincent (*op. cit.* I, pp. 11–13) regards the 'third hill' as the Temple hill and 'the Broad Valley' as the Central Valley (*op. cit.*, pp. 13–16)

94 Josephus, *Antiquities* XV. xi. 4

95 Jeremiah xxxi. 33; Zechariah xiv. 10; Nehemiah iii. 1; xii. 39

96 *War* V. iv. 4 cf. V. vii. 3

97 Cf. G. Dalman, *op. cit.*, p. 202 *n.* 3

98 Vincent, *op. cit.* I, pp. 307–12

99 Josephus, *War* I. xxi. 10; *Antiquities* XV. ix. 4

100 *War* X. v. 8

101 Cf. John v. 2

102 J. Jeremias, *Die Wiederentdeckung von Bethesda*, 1949, pp. 5 ff.

103 J. M. Allegro (*The Treasure of the Copper Scroll*, 1960, pp. 53, 165–6) considers both readings, but prefers the former

104 John ix. 7

105 Theodosius, ed. Tobler, XI

106 *War* V. iv. 2

107 Ed. Tobler, VI

108 *Ibidem* VII

109 *Antiquities* XVII. x. 12

110 *War* II. xiv. 8

111 *Legatio ad Gaium* VI. 175 ff.

112 Ed. Tobler, p. 18

113 Ed. Tobler, p. 32

114 G. Dalman, *Sacred Sites and Ways*, ET., P. Levertoff, 1935, pp. 335–337; P. Benoit, 'Prétoire, Lithostroton et Gabbatha', *La Revue Biblique* LIX, 1952, pp. 531–50, a particularly valuable contribution as coming from a Dominican colleague of Père Vincent; and C. Kopp, *The Holy Places of the Gospel*, 1963, pp. 365–73

115 Acts xxiii. 35

116 W. F. Albright, *The Archaeology of Palestine*, 1949, p. 245

117 L. H. Vincent, *La Revue Biblique* XLII, pp. 110–13

118 Vincent, *Jérusalem de l'Ancien Testament*, I, 1954, p. 218

119 Luke xxiii. 6

120 *Jerusalem und seine Geländer*, 1930, p. 86

121 II Chronicles xxxii. 5

122 II Chronicles xxxiii. 14

123 Josephus, *War* V. iv. 2

124 Josephus, *War* V. iv. 2

125 *War* V. iv. 2

126 L. H. Vincent, *La Revue Biblique* LIV, 1947, pp. 120 ff.

127 K. M. Kenyon, *Palestine Exploration Quarterly*, 1966, p. 87

128 *Ibidem*, p. 88

129 C. N. Johns, 'The Citadel, Jerusalem', *Quarterly of the Department of Antiquities in Palestine* XIV, 1950, pp. 139–47

130 F. J. Bliss and A. C. Dickie, *Excavations at Jerusalem* (Palestine Exploration Fund Publication), 1898

131 K. M. Kenyon, *Palestine Exploration Quarterly*, 1962, p. 84

132 R. W. Hamilton, *Quarterly of the Department of Antiquities in Palestine* X, 1940, pp. 1–26

II

AN AMORITE CITY STATE

Thy father was an Amorite and thy mother a Hittite (Ezekiel xvi. 3)

To judge from debris from the south-east hill, concentrated settlement at Jerusalem probably developed from the end of the fourth millennium parallel to the urban development throughout Syria and Palestine at defensible sites favoured by soil and water.[1] The history of Jerusalem, however, in the two millennia until David's time remains poorly documented and illustrated only by unstratified debris from the south-east hill.*

Just after the beginning of the second millennium, however, the veil is lifted to give a brief, though illuminating, glimpse into Jerusalem's obscurity. From that time a number of texts was recovered at Luxor in Upper Egypt belonging, according to their stylized hieroglyphic (hieratic) script, to the middle of the nineteenth century B.C.[2] These are fragmentary, naming enemies of the Pharaoh and their localities, and were written on pots, which were then broken as part of a rite of execration. Among chiefs of localities in Syria and Palestine two chiefs are named in connection with *Urushalimmu*, the name of Jerusalem which is used in Egyptian political correspondence five centuries later. This is the first mention of the city in written records, and scanty as it is it permits substantial deductions.

The names of the chiefs, Yaqir-'ammu ('The Uncle, or Patron-god of the Tribe, is Noble') and Shayzanu ('Cleaver'), like the other names of Palestinian and Syrian chiefs in these Execration Texts, are Semitic and of a common Amorite type in vogue at the end of the third millennium and the beginning of the second, to which the names of the

* In 1867 Warren reported Early Bronze Age tombs on the slopes of the Mount of Olives. More of these have just been found with pottery dating from the transition from the Early Bronze Age to the Middle Bronze Age (*c*. 2300–1900 B.C.), K. M. Kenyon, *Palestine Exploration Quarterly*, 1966, pp. 74–5.

Hebrew patriarchs also conform. Those names commonly mention one of the gods worshipped, the other part of the name being a predicate in a short sentence, like Abraham, and occasionally the predicate only may appear, the divine name being omitted or understood, as in the names of the Hebrew patriarchs Isaac and Jacob. Thus these are not merely names of obscure individuals, but give insight into ethnic affinities, thanks to comparative material from elsewhere in Syria and Mesopotamia, and into the gods worshipped, and from the predicates indicate the nature of these gods and the relationship of their worshippers to them. Here Yaqir-ʿammu denotes the god as *ʿammu*, which in Arabic means 'paternal uncle', but is also a term of respect for an elder, who is not necessarily a kinsman.* More specifically, however, in Arabic it denotes the common ancestor of a tribe and its various branches, in whom the tribe and its social ethic find cohesion. The *ʿamm* in fact is often regarded as tantamount to an intercessory saint, with a decided moral authority over the tribesmen. Among the Amorites in Palestine named in the Execration Texts the kinship relation is often the predicate of the gods, which denotes a stage of political development when tribal conditions, with the paramount importance of social relations, were not yet remote. Such conditions may be further indicated by the fact that certain of the localities mentioned in those texts are associated, like Jerusalem, with more than one chief, Askalon, for instance, having three.†

The name of the city in the Execration Texts is no less interesting, being also compounded with the name of the god Shālim, now known as an Amorite god, particularly from a mythological text from Rās Shamrā which describes the birth of Shachar and Shālim, the twin-gods manifest in the Venus-star, which heralded the Dawn and Evening.‡ The name Jerusalem has been explained as 'Shālim has founded', the verbal element being taken as cognate with a South Arabian root with this sense, and while this is not certain, there is no doubt that early in the second millennium the god Shālim was particularly associated with Jerusalem. This association may underly the personification of *shālôm*

* In Starkey's team of about 400 Palestinian workmen at Tell ad-Duweir the Egyptian foreman of great experience was known to all as *ʿamm Sultan*.

† This may explain the name Qiryath 'Arbaʿ ('Fortress of Four'), the alternative name for Hebron. The texts from Saqqara about half a century after the Luxor Texts associate only one chief with each locality, hence Albright (*Journal of the Palestine Oriental Society* VIII, 1928, pp. 223–56), Vincent (*Vivre et Penser* II, 1942, p. 207) and Alt (*Kleine Schriften zum Alten Testament* III, 1953, pp. 68–71) see evidence of the process of political consolidation between *c.* 1850 and *c.* 1800. Posener (*op. cit.*) attaches less significance to the plurality of names.

‡ *Shālim* means etymologically 'he who completes (sc. the day)'.

('peace', or better, 'concord') in the Psalmist's declaration that Righteousness and Peace will kiss each other[3] (Psalm lxxxv, 10, Hebrew text 11).

Some time in this period the incident involving Abraham and Melchiṣedeq 'the King of Salem'[4] is probably to be dated, if indeed the historicity of that tradition may be pressed, which, at least in all its context and details, we consider doubtful. Here, somewhat adventitiously, Melchiṣedeq King of Salem and priest of the most high God (*'El 'elyôn*) is introduced as meeting Abraham and entertaining him with bread and wine, and blessing him in the name of El Elyon the Creator (A.V. 'possessor') of Heaven and Earth. The incident closes with Abraham's payment to Melchiṣedeq of 'tithes of all'.* The significance of the incident, which is probably out of context, is uncertain, and it probably served a particular purpose of the compiler at the time of David or Solomon. This has been thought to be the authentication of David's adoption of the local cult of El Elyon at Jerusalem† and the local priest, once also the king, with whom, it is suggested, Ṣadoq, who supplanted Abimelech of the House of Eli under Solomon, was identified.[5] The situation is complicated by the doubt and obscurity in Scripture regarding the lineage of Ṣadoq.[6] This in itself rather supports the theory of the non-Israelite origin of Ṣadoq. In this connection it is interesting that, apart from Abdi-Khipa in the fourteenth century, the only two kings of Jerusalem before David who are known to us include the element ṢDQ in their names, namely Melchiṣedeq and Adoniṣedeq. Thus if ṢDQ was not the name of a god in pre-Israelite Jerusalem‡ the conception of *ṣedeq*, either in the sense of 'right' or 'righteous', was already associated with the cult of the god of Jerusalem, which would facilitate the assimilation of the cult to that of the God of Israel.

However this may be, the passage casts some light on the cult in pre-Israelite Palestine and on the priestly function of the ancient Canaanite king. Both subjects are admirably elucidated by the Rās Shamrā Tablets. There El, the senior god of the Canaanite pantheon, is the supreme authority in nature and in human relations, particularly associated with moral issues, hence not substantially different from the God (also El) worshipped by the Hebrew patriarchs, and one to whose cult that of Yahweh, the God militant on behalf of the tribal

* This incident interrupts Abraham's recovery of the prisoners and spoils of Sodom and neighbouring cities apparently both north and south of the Dead Sea, and the association is unlikely to be original.

† It has been suggested that in an Aramaic inscription from Sefireh near Aleppo (P. Ronzevalle, *Mélanges de l'Université de St. Joseph* XV, 1931, pp. 237–60) which mentions 'El and Elyon' two deities were denoted, but the conjunction here may be explicative, 'El even Elyon'.

‡ Philo of Byblos (fl. A.D. 100) attests a Canaanite god Ṣuduq.

confederacy of Israel, with his interest in historical relationships and the destiny of his people and in the moral principles of the Law, could without difficulty be assimilated. The legends of the ancient kings Keret and Dan'el from Rās Shamrā also indicate that the ancient Canaanite king in an age roughly contemporary with Melchiṣedeq was also priest, the channel of divine blessing in nature to the community.[7] He stood also in a peculiar relation to El, which is expressed in the Keret text from Rās Shamrā as the relation of father to son,[8] and his rule is the visible guarantee of the rule of the Divine King, which is the conception underlying Psalm ii. It was by eventually adopting, and, we must emphasize, adapting, this mystique of royalty according to the distinctive ethos of Israel that David was able to found a dynasty in Jerusalem, which, by contrast to Saul's monarchy which perished with him, lasted, with a brief interlude of six years under the usurping Queen-mother Athaliah,[9] until the destruction of throne, Temple and State by the Babylonians in 586, and was to set the pattern for the Messianic hope in Israel.

In the latter part of the Middle Bronze Age (eighteenth to sixteenth century B.C.) there were ethnic disturbances from the highlands of Iran to South Anatolia and Syria, probably connected with the westward movement of the Aryans and the subsequent displacement of Anatolian elements such as the Hurrians, whose distinctive names are well attested in documents from the fifteenth and fourteenth centuries from North Syria to Palestine. Many of these, most indeed in Palestine, were of the new military class in the feudal system which the breeding of horses and the new chariot tactics of the Aryans involved. These Hurrians are doubtless the Horites of the Old Testament and may be referred to also in loose usage as 'Hittites' in the stereotyped enumeration of peoples in Palestine before Israel. Jerusalem almost certainly felt the impact of the new ethnic elements and new techniques in the second part of the Middle Bronze Age, the Hyksos period, remains of which have been found in caves in the Wādī Khareitūn south-east of Bethlehem, and it may reasonably be inferred that the political, social and cultural development in Jerusalem was parallel to that of the rest of Syria and Palestine at this time, when a feudal system based on the horse and light war-chariot was firmly established and eventually adopted and modified as the basis of David's power as king of Israel in Jerusalem *c.* 1000 B.C.

When Egypt revived under the native Eighteenth Dynasty and expelled the foreign Hyksos from the Lower Nile and from South Palestine and swept on to 'the inverted river',* the Euphrates, the

* As distinct from the northward-flowing Nile.

Pharaohs organized Palestine as a sphere of influence under native rulers, confirming the rule of loyal native magnates and supplanting others by Egyptian nominees, often from the new class of military specialists, a kind of feudal aristocracy established throughout Syria and Palestine in the Hyksos period. When Jerusalem next emerges in history in the correspondence on cuneiform tablets of various local chiefs of Palestine and Syria with their Egyptian suzerain, which were recovered from the Egyptian chancellory in the middle of the fourteenth century at Tell el-Amarna 190 miles south of Cairo, one of these, Abdi-Khipa, was ruler of Jerusalem. His origin seems to be indicated by his name 'the worshipper of Khipa', who was a Hurrian goddess well known and worshipped also by the Hittites in Anatolia. Thus there may be more than the exaggeration of invective in Ezekiel's taunt to Jerusalem, 'Thy father was an Amorite and they mother a Hittite',[10] though Ezekiel may never have heard of Abdi-Khipa.

Jerusalem at this time was one of many vassal-states in Palestine, which, lying next to Egypt, was much more strictly under Egyptian control than the larger and more wealthy states of North Syria, where the urgent menace of the Hittites occasioned a more cautious policy on the part of Egypt and a greater degree of local autonomy. The actual status of Abdi-Khipa is not explicitly stated in his correspondence, where he claims that he is an Egyptian official, but an *u-i-u* (Egyptian *we'u*)* rather than a *khazanu* (provincial overseer). He states: 'Neither my father nor my mother has set me in this place; the strong hand of the king has installed me in my father's house.'[11] This suggests that he was hereditary king of Jerusalem, but had to be confirmed in office by the Pharaoh. Doubtless where Egypt found the petty kings of the city-states of Palestine loyal they confirmed them in office; otherwise a new king would be installed by the Pharaoh, or a fief might be ruled by a commandant without royal status. It is not possible to define the status of those provincial rulers more precisely since they refer to themselves in the Amarna correspondence as 'the man of X' or 'the man of Y'.

The correspondence of Abdi-Khipa and his contemporaries witnesses to the decline of Egyptian power in the fourteenth century under Akhnaten, who was apparently too much preoccupied with his monotheistic reformation in his new capital at Tell al-Amarna and too fondly optimistic about the possibility of attaching his vassals in Palestine and Syria to Egyptian politics by a policy of enlightened toleration to appreciate the realities of the situation. The result was that, though the

* This may derive from a verbal root meaning 'to be distant' and refer to a foreign ruler.

native principalities like Jerusalem were supervised by Egyptian resident officers, apparently stationed in the south of the coastal plain, and had small Egyptian garrisons of provincial and mercenary troops, they were able to engage rather freely in privateering enterprises, especially in the hill country, to which evidently the Egyptian officers paid little attention. Thus Abdi-Khipa is accused by Shuwardata, probably the ruler of Ki-il-ti, or Biblical Qeilah north-west of Hebron, of seeking to expand his realm by force and intrigue with the subjects of Ki-il-ti[12] in which he was evidently but too successful. Abdi-Khipa for his part protests his loyalty to Egypt, claims that he is slandered,[13] and counters the accusations of his neighbours by alleging similar aggression against his own and neighbouring territory by Shuwardata and Milkilu, the ruler possibly of Aijalon in the foothills west of Jerusalem. The town of Bit-Ninib, possibly Bethlehem,[14] in the territory of Jerusalem has been annexed to Ki-il-ti[15] and Rubute, possibly hārabbah of Joshua xv. 60, a few miles west of Jerusalem, has likewise been seized. The activities of Khabiru in Palestine are also a ready pretext for the activities of local rulers like Abdi-Khiba, which might otherwise have attracted the attention of the Egyptian commissioners.

When the Amarna Tablets were first deciphered the Khabiru, whose name in this its Akkadian form or in the Egyptian form ʿApirw immediately suggests the Hebrews (*ʿibhrīm*), were once assumed to be the Hebrew invaders generally associated with Joshua, an assumption which long vitiated the interpretation of archaeological evidence, notably at Jericho, which was traditionally associated with the Hebrew settlement. A fuller and more objective study of archaeological evidence of the vicissitudes of Palestinian settlements in the Late Bronze Age (*c.* 1500–1200 B.C.) and a more critical consideration of Biblical evidence on the settlement of Israel in Palestine reveal a highly complex situation, and, so far as one may speak of a Hebrew invasion, the main phase of the settlement of Israel in Palestine must be dated more than a century after the Amarna correspondence. The Khabiru of Abdi-Khipa's correspondence and the rest of the Amarna Tablets, or as they are called in ideogram SA–GAZ, are a much larger group than the Biblical Hebrews, being attested in documents from the second millennium to the twelfth century and from Mesopotamia to Egypt, where they are called ʿApirw.[16] They are thus not the Hebrews who effected the decisive settlement as Israel in Palestine, though the Hebrews of Scripture were Khabiru. The Khabiru are displaced persons, aliens of miscellaneous origin, settled in their own quarters in the various states, where they might, if the state were sufficiently strong, be controlled and recruited for labour or for mercenary service. Since most states had this 'border fringe' they were a ready source of recruitment in any private enterprise of the local rulers like Abdi-Khipa, who might exploit the Khabiru of his own territory or that of his neighbours, to attack his rivals or, as possibly in the case of Ki-il-ti,[17] to subvert the rule of the rival ruler. These allies were the more useful in that their employer might disclaim responsibility and allege that the general confusion wrought by the Khabiru in the Egyptian province had demanded his intervention when other rulers had not been able to control them. The comparative remoteness of Jerusalem behind its mountain barriers and the security of the fortress on the south-east hill behind its wall on the lower east slope of the hill just above the Spring of Giḥon encouraged the privateering raids of Abdi-Khipa without much fear of reprisals. Yet he was, though apparently a king, an Egyptian vassal. Schaeffer's brilliant discoveries in the city and palace of Rās Shamrā (ancient Ugarit) in North Syria have familiarized us with a Canaanite city state under a dynasty of native kings and a feudal order where he was absolute save for his nominal allegiance to Egypt and, more effectively from *c.* 1350 to the beginning of the twelfth century, to the Hittites. But Jerusalem was not Ugarit, the strategic position and ubiquitous commercial relations of which made her unique among Canaanite city states, as is indicated by the fact that the palace far exceeds in size and splendour any such building outside Mesopotamia. Palestine was both culturally and politically much more provincial than Syria. So now in Jerusalem the royal power of Abdi-Khipa was severely limited by Egypt. Egyptian officers were resident in Palestine and at least theoretically liable to visit and investigate the local situation. Tribute was paid, including in the correspondence of Abdi-Khipa human-kind of both sexes as slaves,[18] and local rulers including Abdi-Khipa had to furnish porters and escorts for Egyptian caravans.[19] In one passage Abdi-Khipa refers to his having put a ship on the sea,[20] but since the context refers to an Egyptian expedition to North Mesopotamia the reference may be to tribute to fit out a troop transport and perhaps to man the vessel. In view of the appeal of Abdi-Khipa and contemporary provincial rulers for an increase of their garrison troops for protection against their neighbours and the Khabiru it seems unlikely that they were allowed to retain standing armies. In this case, with a skeleton of a feudal retinue as a relic of former times, they probably engaged on their adventures at the expense of their neighbours by suborning the alien Khabiru.* The Egyptian garrisons in the land were relatively small and

* This may explain Abdi-Khipa's charge against Labaya, probably of Shechem, and Milkilu, probably of Aijalon, that they had handed over their land to the Khabiru (Knudtzon 287, 29–31).

consisted of mercenaries, Shardanu from the Mediterranean and Sudanese (Kashi). Abdi-Khipa had some of the latter, who evidently treated his property and even his person with little respect.[21] Indeed these garrisons were probably not to stiffen local armed forces but rather to maintain the Egyptian vassals in office and at the same time to limit their local activity. No doubt the Egyptian garrison in Jerusalem was as embarrassing to Abdi-Khipa as the British Police to Ḥāj Amīn al-Ḥuseini, whom the Mandatory power installed as Grand Mufti in Jerusalem after the First World War, and who became the nationalist leader when the implications of the Balfour Declaration became apparent during the Mandate.

After Abdi-Khipa until the main phase of the Israelite occupation of the Central Highlands Jerusalem relapses into obscurity. Its kings were probably more strictly controlled under the militant Pharaohs Seti I and Ramses II of the Nineteenth Dynasty throughout the thirteenth century, who were repeatedly active through Palestine against the Hittites in central Syria and such native princes as succumbed to Hittite intrigues or saw in the embarrassment of Egypt the chance of independence. Possibly the House of Abdi-Khipa was among the local rulers or 'brothers of rulers' whom the Egyptian records of the time note as deported to Egypt, for the next king of Jerusalem to be named bears not a Hurrian name but the good Amorite name of Adoniṣedeq. There is no mention of Jerusalem at this time in Egyptian records, but the place-name 'the Spring of the Waters of Nephtoaḥ',[22] which is Lifta on the upper course of the Wādī 'ṣ-Ṣurār just north-west of the modern Jewish city of Jerusalem, is probably 'the wells of (the Pharaoh) Meneptah, which is in the mountain range' in an Egyptian papyrus from the thirteenth century (see above, p. 22), and would thus indicate that the district of Jerusalem was well known to Egyptian armies, patrols and caravans until *c.* 1225 B.C.

In the last quarter of the thirteenth century the power of Egypt rapidly declined, and she was not able to prevent the influx of tribes from the desert. Soon she was obliged to reach a compromise too with the 'Sea-peoples' including the Philistines, who were settled now in the south part of the coastal plain in their five great baronies of Ekron, Ashdod, Gath, Askalon and Gaza. Among the former were the militant elements of Israel, the nucleus of the tribal confederacy whose basis was the religious experience of the Great Deliverance from Egypt and the Covenant with Yahweh the God of Israel at Sinai.

The conventional view is that all Israel invaded under Joshua via the Jordan by Jericho and the pass by Ai and Bethel to defeat an Amorite coalition under Adoniṣedeq the Amorite king of Jerusalem and overrun the whole of South Palestine.[23] But a more critical study of the source of this presentation of the 'conquest', and especially comparison with the view of a much slower and sporadic settlement in the Book of Judges, indicates that this is a highly schematized view of Israel's settlement, which is actually a theological prelude to the philosophy of history from the settlement of Israel until the fall of Jerusalem to Babylon in the historical work Joshua-Judges-Samuel-Kings rather than a sober presentation of history. Here Israel's settlement is assumed from the viewpoint of a time when her supremacy in the land after David and Solomon was unquestioned. For our present purpose we may safely isolate as the historical nucleus the account of events leading to the Amorite coalition and the Battle of Gibeon in Joshua x. 1–14, the more so as this alone is relevant to the history of Jerusalem, whose king Adoniṣedeq was the moving spirit in the coalition.*

In the reconstruction of this campaign further literary analysis is necessary. After the defeat and pursuit of the defeated enemy from Gibeon down the Pass of Beth-ḥoron, the Wādī Salmān just south of Bayt 'Ur (see above p. 22), to Azekah and Maqqedah in the valley which runs north to south, separating the foothills of Judah from the higher hills of the interior,[24] the compiler goes back and quotes verses from the poetic national saga of Israel, the Book of Yashar (see above, p. 22, n.).

> Sun, be thou still over Gibeon,
> And thou, moon, in the Valley of Aijalon.
> And the sun was still, and the moon stayed
> Until the people had avenged themselves upon their enemies.
>
> (Joshua x. 12b–13b)

This is followed (vv. 13c–14) by the prose statement:

* In the account of the settlement of South Palestine in Joshua iii –x most of the action is located at, or about, the shrine of Gilgal or on the way there from Bethel and the north. Much again consists of independent local legends explaining notable features on the way, such as the ruin-mound and name of Ai ('the Ruin'), the tree there where the king of Ai was stated to have been hanged by Joshua, the stone-heap of Achan and the Hill of Foreskins, where the connection with the Hebrew conquest was the result of pilgrim tradition, perhaps fostered by the priests of the cult of Gilgal. Local explanatory legend concerning natural features by the Cave of Makkedah (Joshua x. 17–27) has similarly associated them with the sequel to Israel's defeat of the Amorite coalition at Gibeon (Joshua x). The traditions associated with Gilgal (Joshua iii. 8), which are really developments of the cult-legend of that central shrine, are probably separate from that of the campaign against the Amorites at Gibeon (Joshua x), which is the tradition of an actual historical event, apart from the sequel (Joshua x. 16–27), which is explanatory legend associating local topographical features about the Cave of Maqqedah with the defeat of the Amorite kings and the tradition of the sweeping conquest of the south of Palestine.

> So the sun stood still in the midst of the sky and hasted not to go down about a whole day, and there was no day like that before or after it, that the Lord hearkened unto the voice of a man, for the Lord fought for Israel.

Here the prose paraphrase misinterprets the poetic quotation, which is a prayer by Joshua that the sun should not rise until he should surprise the enemy after a night march,[25] as verse 9 explicitly states, though wrongly in our opinion stating that Joshua came from Gilgal, an addendum which betrays the influence of the cult-legend of the central shrine at Gilgal. Now the mention of the Valley of Aijalon in Joshua's *advance* indicates a separate tradition from that in Joshua iii–viii and may indicate that the campaign was really occasioned by the expansion of Joshua's tribe of Ephraim southwards towards Jerusalem.[26] Here it may be noted that Joshua's home at Timnath-heres is probably to be located at Khirbet at-Tibneh about fifteen miles north of Gibeon (al-Jib).

We may now proceed with our reconstruction of the incidents in Joshua ix–x so far as they concern the history of Jerusalem. The various elements of the Hebrew kinship, which the Egyptian inscriptions of the fifteenth century attest as Joseph-el and Jacob-el settled about Shechem in the Central Highlands, and others had been drawn into a tribal confederacy by younger, more aggressive elements, who had penetrated Palestine about 1225 B.C., and had realized solidarity with the others on the basis of sacramental experience of the Great Deliverance from Egypt and the Covenant with Yahweh God of Israel at Sinai. This bond, effected and regularly renewed at the central shrine of the confederacy at Shechem[27], strengthened all members, and the tribe of Ephraim under Joshua, who probably already had an authority in the tribal confederacy, had begun to expand southwards in the direction of Jerusalem. Eventually they and possibly also the neighbouring tribe of Benjamin had made an alliance with Gibeon, Chephirah, Qiryath-jearim and Beeroth, Bīreh just south-west of Bethel[28], which formed a coalition for their common safety under their elders.[29] The ruling class of these places is given in the Old Testament as 'Hivite', but the Septuagint Greek translation of this ethnic term is often 'Hurrian', so that here we have probably an alien Anatolian element in the population, a relic of the Egyptian administration.* Now the consolidation of the tribal confederacy of Israel was sufficient to rouse the Amorites in

* Among the cylinder seals found in Palestine the most common type is that from Mitanni in north Mesopotamia, where an Aryan aristocracy ruled over a Hurrian subject people in the fifteenth and fourteenth centuries, as observed by B. Parker in her study of such seals in Palestine, *Iraq* IX, 1949, pp. 1–42.

the Central Highlands to a defensive alliance, but when the Israelites pressed southwards and made an alliance with the Hurrians on the plateau seven miles north of Jerusalem the king of Jerusalem called up his allies from the Southern Highlands and marched on Gibeon.[30] Here the identity of the allies in the south-west is confused by the association of the local explanatory legend of the Cave of Maqqedah, but quite apart from this doubt there is no reason to doubt the initiative and leading role of the king of Jerusalem, who was most immediately threatened by the activity of the Israelites at Gibeon. The result was a defeat, but Jerusalem within its Bronze Age wall round the south-east hill remained intact. The apprehension of the king of Jerusalem at the Israelite penetration of Palestine and the growth of the tribal confederacy may have occasioned the security measure of the first tunnel from the Spring of Giḥon and the shaft of access from within the city wall (see above p.26).

In the somewhat exaggerated account of Joshua's occupation of the south of Palestine after the Battle of Gibeon (Joshua x. 28–43) there is no mention of the reduction of Jerusalem, and in fact it is stated in Joshua xv. 8, 63 that even when the territory of the city state was occupied the city itself remained in possession of its pre-Israelite inhabitants, being only reduced under David.[31] In apparent contradiction to these passages it is stated in Judges i. 8 that 'the children of Judah had fought against Jerusalem and had taken it, and smitten it with the edge of the sword, and set the city on fire'.* We note particularly that this is said to have been the exploit, not of Joshua and all Israel, but of the tribe of Judah independently. The source of the tradition in Judges i. 8 may be the destruction of the villages in the vicinity of Jerusalem, notably in the cultivable Plain of the Repha'im west of the city beyond the Valley of Hinnom, which was occupied by Judah when the city itself still defied the Israelites.[32]† The Plain of the Repha'im, the only considerable extent of cultivable land about Jerusalem, would obviously not have been ceded without a struggle. Hence the defeat of the

* Possibly the incident, if really historical, may relate to the destruction of some outpost or watchtower on the south-west hill of Jerusalem, which at that time was outside the walled settlement. But even if that were so the south-west hill was not permanently occupied by the Israelites since Joshua xv. 8 describes the boundary west of the Valley of Hinnom, which certainly excludes the south-west hill, and though the territory assigned, possibly ideally, to Benjamin in Joshua xviii. 16 includes Jerusalem it is stated that the city continued to defy them (Judges i. 21).

† A similar conclusion as to the nature of the Hebrew settlement is reached by Alt (*Kleine Schriften zum Alten Testament* I, 1953, p. 200) from the fact that at Tappuah south of Shechem the settlement fell to Ephraim but the land to Manasseh (Joshua xvii. 8).

king of Jerusalem and his Amorite allies about Gibeon may have been an opportune occasion for the encroachment of Judah from Bethlehem, which had probably been occupied long before by independent penetration by Judah from the south, or by connubium, or intermarriage, as the incident of Judah and the Canaanite Tamar near Hebron[33] and their descendants in Bethlehem[34] suggest. There is no reason, however, to doubt the tradition that the pre-Israelite inhabitants of Jerusalem, always described as Jebusites, continued to occupy the fortress on the south-east hill for another two centuries or so until the beginning of David's reign. They could hardly survive so long without cultivable land, and this suggests that the Israelite occupation, which Judges represents as being sporadic and piecemeal as the result of independent action by the various elements of Israel, must in this case have involved a *modus vivendi* with the people of Jerusalem, which, however, did not exclude incidents such as the destruction mentioned in Judges i. 8, though not involving the destruction of the fortress on the south-east hill.

The inhabitants of Jerusalem immediately before David's men took the city are always referred to as Jebusites. Their ethnic identity remains an enigma. They are named in the conventional list of peoples of Palestine before the Israelite occupation, and are there distinguished from the Amorites, who were an important element in ancient Jerusalem on the evidence of the names of the two chiefs of Jerusalem in the Execration Texts Yaqir-ʿammu and Shayzanu (see above p. 65), Melchiṣedeq and Adoniṣedeq of Joshua x, whose natural affinity was with the Amorites of the Southern Highlands. We have already seen how under Egyptian suzerainty in the Late Bronze Age a professional military class including non-Semitic elements from North Syria and South Anatolia and even from the Mediterranean were employed as local commandants and as garrison troops to support loyal vassals and to limit the power of others of doubtful loyalty. In Jerusalem itself the name of the ruler Abdi-Khipa indicates the worship of the Hurrian goddess Khipa. Unfortunately we do not know the nature or the extent of the retinue of those local rulers, but the administrative texts from the palace of Rās Shamrā (ancient Ugarit) give indication that the king was supported by a feudal order invested with hereditary fiefs. In Palestine the order in the city states was but a shadow of that at such an important and wealthy place as Ugarit, but there may well have been behind the local ruler in Jerusalem such a professional military class as, for instance, supported the throne of David. These professional soldiers were recruited irrespective of political or ethnic affinities as we see clearly from the case of Ittai of the Philistine border town of Gath and the unfortunate Uriah the Hittite in David's time, and indeed from the employment of David himself as a feudatory of Achish of Gath with his hereditary fief at Ṣiqlag (Khirbet al-Khuweilefeh about nine miles north-west of Beersheba). To such may have belonged the problematic Jebusites at Jerusalem, to whom the control of the city may have fallen after the defeat of Adoniṣedeq at the Battle of Gibeon.

The situation is possibly elucidated by an obscure passage in the account of David's rule in Jerusalem. In II Samuel xxiv David's acquisition of the site of the Temple from Araunah the Jebusite is described. In II Samuel xxiv. 23 it is stated that the land was conveyed by Araunah to David 'as a king to a king' (so the Authorized Version for the Hebrew 'the king to the king'). So far there has been no suggestion in the passage that Araunah or any other was king in Jerusalem when it was taken by David's kinsman Joab. Now in the administrative texts from the palace of Rās Shamrā the term *'ewir* or *'ewirni* occurs evidently as a title of high feudal barons and is there recognized as a Hurrian word. Hence we submit that Araunah, from whom David acquired the site of the Temple, was not the name but the title of the local ruler or at least one of the feudal aristocracy who had seized control of Jerusalem after the defeat of Adoniṣedeq, this being recognized by the writer of II Samuel xxiv. 23, where 'the king' is a gloss on 'Araunah'. The Hurrian title *'ewir* of course does not necessarily make 'Araunah the Jebusite' a Hurrian, but does suggest the possibility. The presence of Anatolian professional soldiers in Jerusalem is further indicated by Uriah the Hittite in David's service. 'Hittite' in this case, as usually in the Old Testament with reference to the people of Palestine, may be loosely used, denoting Hurrian rather than strictly Hittite.* Uriah, whose name, though patient of a Hebrew etymology, may itself be a corruption of the Hurrian title *'ewir*, meaning 'baron' or the like, may also represent the old feudal aristocracy, with whom we should tentatively identify the problematical Jebusites.

Thus in the last two centuries of the second millennium Jerusalem like other city states of Palestine was being isolated by the expansion of elements which the inhabitants of the Canaanite city states had hitherto despised and exploited. Many of these were those we have already encountered as the Khabiru, displaced persons, probably mostly from the deserts east and south of Palestine and fugitives from the various

* In this case, however, Uriah might be an actual Hittite soldier of fortune, one of many who found employment in the south after the collapse of the Hittite Empire in the early twelfth century.

city states, who always found refuge among such displaced persons.* Some of these were of the kinship of Israel, such as Joseph-el and Jacob-el, whom inscriptions of the Pharaoh Thothmes III mention in the fifteenth century in the Central Highlands of Palestine. Now those were drawn into a powerful confederacy on the impulse of new and aggressive tribal elements who had come to Palestine from Egypt and Sinai fresh from the experience of deliverance from Egypt, which was interpreted to them by their leader Moses as a great creative act of Divine grace which called a religious community into being, as was made explicit by a great act of dedication in the experience of the Covenant at Sinai. This religious experience was now mediated to the members of the confederacy now known as Israel in a regular sacrament at the various central shrines Shechem, Shiloh and Gilgal, and became the basis of Israel's solidarity and consciousness as God's people of destiny and the nerve of her struggle for survival and eventual creation of a national state in Palestine, the capital of which, from the peculiar circumstances of its capture about 1010 B.C., was to be Jerusalem.

* In the sixteenth or fifteenth century the ikng Idri-mi of Alalakh (Tell Atchana in North Syria) in his inscription records how he found temporary refuge among the Khabiru on the border of his kingdom until he was able to establish himself on his throne in Alalakh (S. Smith, *The Statue of Idri-mi*, 1949, pp. 14 ff). Hittite diplomatic texts from the palace of Ugarit also show concern about relations with Khabiru.

NOTES FOR CHAPTER II

1 Macalister and Duncan, *Excavations on the Hill of Ophel, Jerusalem, 1923–1925, Palestine Exploration Annual* IV, 1926, p. 173. For pottery of the period see p. 1

2 K. Sethe, *Die Ächtung feindlicher Fürsten, Völker und Dinge auf altägyptischen Tongefässscherben des Mittleren Reiches* (Abhandlungen der preussischen Akademie der Wissenschaften, Phil. -hist. Klasse), 1926. The date is confirmed by a second lot of such texts somewhat later, the probable archaeological context of which at Saqqara is known. The later texts mention certain chiefs in Syria and Palestine of the next two generations, and the conclusion on the date is confirmed by Egyptian palaeography according to the editor G. Posener, *Princes et Pays d'Asie et de la Nubie Textes hiératiques sur les figurines d'envoûtement du Moyen Empire*, 1940

3 Psalm lxxxv 10. Hebrew text 11

4 Genesis xiv. 18–20

5 So S. Mowinckel, *Ezra den Skriftlaerde*, 1916, p. 109, *n.* 2; *The Psalms in Israel's Worship*, 1962, I, pp. 36, 132; A. Bentzen, *Studier over det zadokidiske praesteskabs historie*, 1931, pp. 8–18; H. R. Hall, *The People and the Book*,

ed. A. S. Peake, 1925, p. 11; H. S. Nyberg, *Archiv für Religionswissenschaft* XXXV, 1938, p. 375; H. H. Rowley, 'Zadok and Nehushtan', *Journal of Biblical Literature* LVIII, 1939, pp. 113–41, cf. R. De Vaux, who after a review of this view and others that Ṣadoq was one of the priests of the sanctuary of Gibeon in the service of the tent-shrine (cf. II Chronicles i. 3) or in the service of the ark when it was at Qiryath-jearim (I Samuel vii. 1), suggests that Ṣadoq may have been of another Levitical family than Abiathar of the House of Eli, whom he supplanted (*Ancient Israel*, 1961, pp. 373–4)

6 I Chronicles v. 29–34; vi. 35–8; xxiv. 3, cf. II Samuel viii. 17, Hebrew Text

7 Cf. Psalms lxxii. 6; cx. 4; Lamentations iv. 20

8 Cf. Psalm ii. 7; II Samuel vii. 14

9 II Kings xi

10 Ezekiel xvi. 3

11 J. A. Knudtzon, *Die el-Amarna Tafeln*, 1905–15, 285, 56

12 Knudtzon 279; 280

13 Knudtzon 286, 5–6

14 So F. M. Abel, *Géographie de la Palestine* II, 1933–38, p. 276, which is a more probable location than that of Zimmer at Beth-shemesh

15 Knudtzon 290, 5–11

16 The most comprehensive statement of the facts with the conclusions here adopted is that of J. Bottéro, *Le Problème des Habiru*, 1954

17 Knudtzon 280, 17 ff.

18 Knudtzon 288, 18–21

19 Knudtzon 287, 55

20 Knudtzon 288, 32–6

21 Knudtzon 287, 71–5

22 Joshua xv. 9

23 Joshua iii-x

24 Joshua x. 11–12

25 B. J. Alfrink, *Studia Catholica* XXIV, 1949, pp. 238–69

26 A. Alt, 'Josua', *Kleine Schriften zum Alten Testament* I, 1953, p. 188

27 Cf. Joshua viii. 30–35; xxiv

28 Joshua ix. 17

29 Joshua ix. 11

30 Joshua x. 1–5

31 II Samuel v. 6; I Chronicles xi. 4–8

32 Joshua xv. 8

33 Genesis xxxviii

34 Ruth iv. 12 ff.

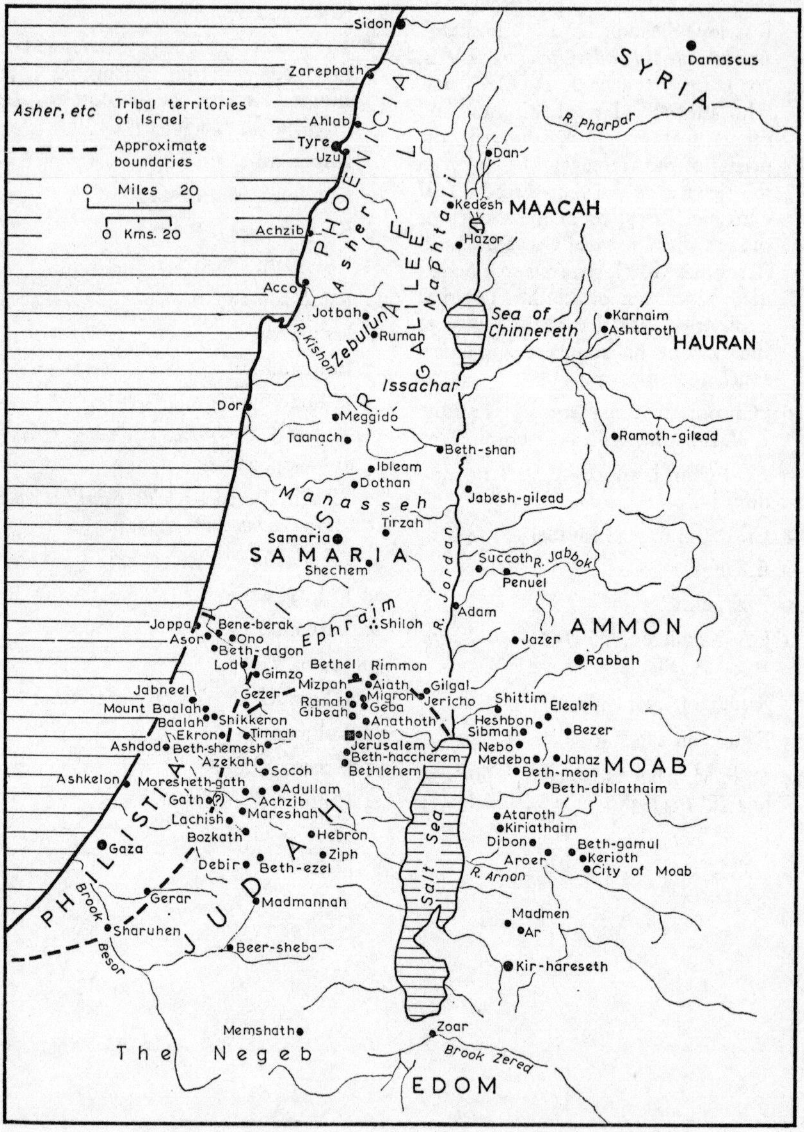

Fig. VII THE HEBREW KINGDOM IN PALESTINE.
(*T. R. Allen after the* Oxford Bible Atlas)

III

THE THRONE OF DAVID

. . . the city of the great King (*Psalm xlviii. 2*)

The emergence of Jerusalem, the obscure fortress on the south-east hill overtopped by the neighbouring heights and on the edge of the Wilderness of Judah, as the capital of a state for half a millennium and the seat of the sanctuary *par excellence* of Judaism and eventually of Christianity was owing to the politic foresight of an individual David, so that the city well merits the designation 'the city of David'.

The solidarity of the various elements of the Israelite kinship in an effective confederacy on the basis of a common faith and belief in their occupation of the land as the Land of Promise by the power and grace of God had provoked the resistance of the people already in the land, and had been strengthened in the conflict. About half a century after the decisive phase of the Israelite penetration other people had established themselves in Palestine. The Philistines and others from the Aegean and Balkans had forced their way along the Syrian coast by land and sea and were halted early in the twelfth century by the Pharoah Ramses III, who claimed 'I settled them in fortresses bound in my name'. That is to say a *modus vivendi* was reached whereby the Philistines settled in the coastal plain, where they are familiar in the Old Testament, particularly south of Jaffa,* in their five great fiefs of Ekron, Ashdod, Gath, Askalon and Gaza, which ensured Egyptian communication with the north. With the penetration of the Israelites and their consolidation in their sacral confederacy, the Philistines had established garrisons in the interior, as at Bethshan at the east end of the great

* The Egyptian papyrus (Golenischeff) regarding the mission of an official Wen-Amon to Byblos in Syria *c.* 1100 B.C. refers to the settlement of a kindred people, the Tkl at the seaport of Dor (at-Ṭanṭūrah *c.* 11 miles south of Haifa). This was incorporated in the kingdom of Solomon, if not of David, and nothing more is known of the Tkl.

6

central plain which carried the trunk highway between Asia and Africa, in which Egypt was so interested. Here their presence is attested by their peculiar anthropoid pottery coffins, which have analogies in the Delta and at Lachish in the foothills south of Judah.[1] They had already garrisons in the hill country immediately north of Jerusalem[2] when Saul arose, and the distinctive pottery associated with the main area and period of Philistine occupation in the south part of coastal plain which has been found at Jerusalem indicates contacts with the Philistines, if not actually a Philistine garrison. The limitations imposed on emergent Israel by these effective garrison forces with the advantages of professional military service and permanent command under a feudal system suggested the counter-measure of a permanent Israelite striking-force under a permanent command. This was partly the origin of the monarchy of Saul, whose palace-fort was thought to have been excavated at Tell al-Fūl (Gibeah of Saul)* four miles north of Jerusalem. Perhaps his tribe of Benjamin, who occupied a narrow strip of stony land barely ten miles wide at the head of two of the main passes from the Philistine plain to the Central Highlands (the Pass of Beth-ḥoron and the Vale of Sorek, see above, p. 21), was designed to form the nucleus of a permanent striking-force such as the Philistines themselves used. But Saul augmented his standing army with men of action and ability wherever they were to be recruited in Israel. Thus David of Bethlehem in the tribe of Judah came into his service. The Biblical narrative[3] relates that David's military successes aroused Saul's jealousy and eventually forced David to seek safety first as an outlaw in the borderland between his native Judah and the Canaanite villages north-west of Hebron[4] and in the land south-east of Hebron[5] which was occupied by the Kenizzites, a kindred Semitic people who worshipped Yahweh, the same God as Israel, at Hebron, and eventually as a feudatory of the Philistine Achish of Gath between the foothills of Judah and the coastal plain (see above, p. 77), who gave him the town of Ṣiqlag (see above, p. 77) as a hereditary fief.[6] David's experience as a feudal vassal with feudal retainers under him is of great significance in his occupation of Jerusalem and in his development of the hereditary monarchy in Israel.

In the campaign of Gilboa David had marched with the Philistines as the feudatory of Achish of Gath, but owing to the suspicions of most of the Philistines he had been spared the embarrassment of fighting against Saul and his men, and retired to his fief at Ṣiqlag. From this base he had been, often surreptitiously, active against the semi-nomad

* Now questioned by Albright, *Cambridge Ancient History*, 2nd ed.

Amalekites, the inveterate enemies of Israel in the southern steppes, and by a judicious distribution of his spoils had been busy courting the support of the Kenizzites about Hebron, among whom he had maintained himself as an outlaw from Saul and from whom he had taken two of his wives. After Saul's defeat and death at Gilboa David moved up to Hebron, the most important place in the Southern Highlands with its shrine of Yahweh, which was sacred both to his own tribe and to the Kenizzites, and here he was anointed king over Judah,[7]* and eventually on the disintegration of the remnants of the authority of Saul and his family he became king also over the confederacy of Israelite tribes north of Jerusalem.

Obviously David's next step would be to unite his dual monarchy over Judah and over Israel, and the Philistines promptly took steps to prevent this effective union. So their army marched up to the vicinity of Jerusalem where the tribal territories of Judah and Benjamin bordered. The present order in the compilation of II Samuel v suggests that this was after David's occupation of Jerusalem.† However this may be, the Philistines failed to prevent David's 'union of the crowns' and their campaign by the Valley of Sorek indicated Jerusalem as

* It is not explicitly said that this transaction was at the shrine, though this may reasonably be inferred from the installation of Saul at the sanctuary of Gilgal, reading 'let us sanctify' (Hebrew *n^{e}qaddēsh*) for 'let us renew' (*n^{e}ḥaddēsh*) (I Samuel xi. 14), and from the statement that the adoption of David as king also of Israel and the agreement which that involved was 'in Hebron before the Lord' (II Samuel v. 3).

† It is stated that 'when the Philistines heard that they had anointed David king over Israel, all the Philistines came up to seek David; and David heard of it, and went down to the hold' (or 'fortress') (II Samuel v. 17). The 'hold' is not located. Since the Philistines in the immediate sequel encamped in the Valley of the Repha'im (II Samuel v. 18) the 'hold' may indicate the fortress on the lowest of the hills of Jerusalem, the south-east hill, but the same word is also used of David's original stronghold when he was an outlaw from Saul, the Cave of Adullam in the tributary wadi, which runs from just north of Hebron to the Vale of Elah, or Wādī 's-Sanṭ (I Samuel xxii. 1, 4, 5), and a similar natural stronghold in the desert of Engedi (I Samuel xxiv. 22, Hebr. text 23). Thus we regard 'the hold' in II Samuel v. 17 as his original refuge, the Cave of Adullam, though the matter is complicated by the apparent conflation of two distinct campaigns in the Plain of the Repha'im by Jerusalem, or at least of two variant versions, one of which culminated apparently in David's victory at Baalperazim and his burning of the Philistine camp (II Samuel v. 20–21), and the other, after 'the Philistines came up yet again and spread themselves in the Valley of the Repha'im', when David defeated them and pursued them from Geba (probably originally 'Gibeah') or 'Gibeon' after Chronicles to Gezer (II Samuel v. 22–5). Possibly David in the first campaign operated from the hills south of Bethlehem and, evading contact, destroyed the camp, like Judas Maccabaeus at Emmaus (see below, p. 134), the battle being fought in the second campaign, the tradition of which influenced that of the first campaign in I Samuel v. 20. We see no compelling reason to place the first campaign before David's occupation of Jerusalem, though the second may be dated then.

David's capital of the united kingdom, if that had not already occurred to him.

Now had the fixing of the capital been simply to anticipate Philistine attack on the weak point where Judah bordered on Israel Saul's fortress of Gibeah (Tell al-Fūl), more directly commanding the pass by the Valley of Sorek and the Ascent of Beth-ḥoron, or even Gibeon four miles to the north-west of Gibeah would have been more suitable. These places, however, were in Benjamin with affinities with the North Israelite confederacy and with the House of Saul, with whom David had been latterly at enmity. So by fixing his capital here he might have alienated the support of the Kenizzites and the tribe of Judah at Hebron and Bethlehem. The most effective capital of the united kingdom would be a fortress hitherto neither in Israel nor Judah. Jerusalem was the obvious choice, the fortress between the ravine of the Qidron and the Central Valley, which Benjamin and Judah in their occupation of their tribal territories had been content to bypass.

Having marked out Jerusalem as his capital because of its neutral status, David proposed to capture it independently of the forces of Israel and Judah. To this end he exploited his experience as a feudal vassal of Achish of Gath, having in turn feudal retainers from his fief in Ṣiqlag who owed him personal allegiance. According to II Samuel v. 6 'the king and his men' invested Jerusalem. This obviously means just what it says, and is more faithful to historical fact than the much later account in I Chronicles xi. 4–6, which attributes the exploit to David and all Israel. Nevertheless the latter passage gives the important addition that it was Joab, who was the kinsman of David, who led the vital onslaught (I Chronicles xi. 6). The account in II Samuel v. 8 indicates that this was in response to a challenge by David to his men, the question being who should 'go first up on the gutter' (Hebrew *ṣinnôr*). Since this probably refers to the watershaft, which would admit only one man at a time, it was an enterprise for the boldest spirit—by common tradition Joab. Already settled around Jerusalem, the local Israelites already knew of the Spring of Giḥon outside the east wall of Jerusalem and the watershaft which gave access to the spring from within the wall (see above, pp. 26–27 and fig. II). So Joab entered the tunnel and climbed up the rough-walled vertical part of the shaft and there presumably mounted guard till others joined him in the gently-sloping gallery. Eventually he and his commando emerged in the city at the strongly fortified north end, 'the stronghold of Zion' proper, and the city was captured. This became David's headquarters[8], and eventually his modest palace[9] and, with a northward extension and much embellishment, the palace of Solomon, part of which possibly lies under the modern road by which the traveller crosses the narrow saddle of the south-east hill before entering the Old City by the modern enlargement of the Dung Gate ('the Gate of the Moors') in the Turkish wall.

Thus David acquired a suitable capital with all the advantages for his peculiar task of forging a united state against possible Philistine aggression. The capture of the Jebusite fortress by his own personal feudal retainers and by his kinsman Joab gave him further advantages. In that rude society Jerusalem was a perpetual reminder of the resolution and energy of David. The city so captured was literally 'the city of David', his crown possession, a state within a state. Here he was free to develop the machinery of government independent of the prejudices or caprices of the tribes of Israel, an important advantage in view of his necessary innovations in the establishment of a permanent government. For it must be remembered that between the Hebrew monarchy established by David and the loose confederacy of the tribes, 'when there was no king in Israel and every man did that which was right in his own eyes', only the unstable reign of Saul intervened, whom Samuel had succeeded in limiting to the status of permanent commander of the striking-force of Israel. From his point of vantage too in Jerusalem as his personal possession, supported by his feudal army, David succeeded in establishing a dynasty. This also was a novel institution in Israel, where men were familiar with the authority of leaders like the great judges, who were moved by the impulse to stand forth and strike in an emergency and were signalized by their initial success as called and endowed by God. The authority of those men was strictly *ad hoc*. In the stern exigencies of tribal history no man was born to the purple. But the feudal order which was the basis of David's rule made it possible for authority to be bequeathed. For this David further provided by securing Jerusalem as a personal possession, a measure which was emulated a century after David by Omri in North Israel, who endeavoured to extricate Israel from chronic civil war by establishing a hereditary monarchy, acquiring the hill of Samaria for two talents of silver[10] as his personal possession, on which he built his capital as the basis of his dynasty. David's assessment of the situation which prompted his seizure of Jerusalem is corroborated by the fact that even in his own lifetime he had to face two revolts, that of Absalom his own son, which obliged him temporarily to evacuate Jerusalem[11] and of Sheba and elements of Benjamin and other northern tribes.[12] Indeed in the last resort the succession was established in the case of Solomon by palace intrigue and by the support of the feudal forces under Benaiah[13] against the more conservative Israelite elements, who supported David's oldest surviving son Adonijah.

Jerusalem, however, under David was not only 'the city of David'; it was the capital of Israel. David effected this by bringing the Ark to Jerusalem. This ancient symbol, a wooden chest or portable shrine, the original contents of which, if any, are quite uncertain,* was the symbol of the presence of Yahweh, the God of Israel, militant among his devotees.† Traditionally originating in Israel's nomadic past in the desert,‡ it was more particularly associated with the tradition of the

* The conception of the Ark at various stages of the literary tradition in the Old Testament reflects the developing theological interpretations of the symbol. In Numbers x. 35 ff. (E, ninth or eighth century) it symbolized the Divine presence and activity in battle, cf. I Samuel iv. 7, 'A god has come into the camp.' Deposited in a built temple in Shiloh and Jerusalem, it was considered the throne of the invisible God (cf. I Samuel iv. 4; II Kings xix. 15) as indicated by the cherubim, the Hebrew analogy to the winged sphinxes which are familiar as the side-supports of thrones e.g. in the Megiddo ivories and on the sarcophagus of Aḥiram of Byblos. In Deuteronomic writings from the end of the monarchy in Judah and in the Exile the Ark, called 'the Ark of Yahweh' in the early sources, is termed 'the Ark of the Covenant', in which the tablets of the Law were reputed to have been kept. Here the Deuteronomists may be reviving an old tradition in treating the Ark simply as a chest, cf. the deposits of agreements in sanctuaries beneath the feet of statues of Hittite and Egyptian gods (R. De Vaux, *Ancient Israel*, 1961, p. 301, also G. von Rad, 'Zelt und Lade', *Gesammelte Studien zum Alten Testament*, 1958, pp. 109–29). The last main source of the Pentateuch (P) associates the Ark as the repository of 'the Testimony' (Exodus xxv. 16) with the Tabernacle, where God was considered to meet man at his own discretion in revelation, as in the Law, and in mercy, the blood of atonement being sprinkled on the lid of the Ark, called in P the 'mercy seat' (Leviticus xvi. 2, 3–16). The only detailed description of the Ark is in Exodus xxv. 10–22, from the late P source with its far-reaching theological developments.

† This is clearly suggested by acclamation (the 'myth') accompanying the ritual of the taking of the Ark on the journeys or expeditions of Israel and of its setting down or return, 'Rise up, Lord, and let thine enemies be scattered; and let them that hate thee flee before thee' and 'Return, O Lord, unto the many thousands of Israel' (Numbers x. 35–6, E).

‡ Here, however, the tradition may not be accurate, since the Ark is only twice mentioned in the older narratives of the desert period (Numbers x. 35 ff.; xiv. 40–45), and not in association with the Tent of Meeting (Exodus xxxiii. 7–11), which properly belonged to the desert tradition. The Ark on the other hand is more particularly associated with the tradition of the occupation of the Promised Land, and is specifically associated with the sanctuary of Shiloh (I Samuel iv. 3 ff.). The Ark has been compared to a litter which is mounted on camel back among the Ruwalla Bedouin of the North Syrian desert, but as this, like the Tent of Meeting, was used in divination, the analogy with the Tent is more apt than with the Ark. Ark and Tent may be associated with two different groups of the progenitors of Israel, those to whom the Ark belonged emphasizing the authority of the hereditary priesthood as the custodians of the Ark, and those to whom the Tent of Meeting belonged emphasizing the ministry of the charismatic prophet, as Exodus xxxiii. 7–11 indicates.

occupation of Palestine and latterly with the central sanctuary of the tribal confederacy at Shiloh about twelve miles south-east of Shechem. From here it had been taken into battle at a critical juncture in the Philistine wars and had been captured on the defeat of Israel.[14] Regarded by the Philistines as the cause of a series of natural disasters, it was sent back to the Israelites with compensatory offerings[15] and was eventually kept near Qiryath-jearim by modern Qiryat al-'Inab, also called Abū Ghōsh (see above, p. 21) seven miles west of Jerusalem. The Ark was now eventually brought to Jerusalem, which thereupon became the new amphictyonic sanctuary, the shrine which was the focus of the faith which was Israel's traditional means of integration. From that momentous occasion when the Ark was installed in or by the city of David with the sacrifice of oxen and fatlings at every six paces and ringing shouts of triumph and horn-blowing and David in a linen loin-cloth dancing with abandon 'before the Lord with all his might' Jerusalem became what it has remained, the Holy City. The Ark in its tent-shelter[16] was the central sanctuary of all Israel and the predecessor of the Temple, which Solomon built on the height of the east ridge north of the fortified city of David. The installation of the Ark became a regular, probably annual, sacrament in Israel[17] till the destruction of city and Temple in 586 B.C.

It has been thought that David retained also the local pre-Israelite cult of Jerusalem, adapting it to the Israelite cult as far as was consonant with the principles of Israelite religion. This view is usually associated with the theory that Ṣadoq, who supplanted Abiathar as the principal priest under Solomon[18] and possibly under David,[19] was really a priest of the local cult before David's occupation of Jerusalem, a view which claims as support the fact that two of the rulers of pre-Israelite Jerusalem have *ṣdq* as a component of their names, namely Melchiṣedeq and Adoniṣedeq (see above, p. 67). Moreover in Psalm cx. 4, which is a prophetic oracle to the Davidic king on the occasion, or anniversary, of his enthronement, it is stated 'Thou art a priest for ever after the manner of Melchiṣedeq'. This seems to associate the Davidic king with the ancient Canaanite conception of kingship, where the king was the servant of God and priest *par excellence*, as in the legends of the ancient kings Keret and Dan'el in the Rās Shamrā Texts, which in their extant state were redacted not later than *c.* 1360 B.C. The image of royalty in the Psalms from Jerusalem under the House of David, where the king is represented as the son of God,[20] whose reign is the reflection of the omnipotence and eternal rule of God[21] and the vital channel of the Divine blessing in nature and society,[22] is certainly something quite novel in Israel and finds its closest parallels in all particulars in the general conception of kingship in the ancient Near East, and particularly in the legends of the ancient Canaanite kings Keret and Dan'el at Rās Shamrā.* It may well be that the local cult at Jerusalem was retained by David, adapted of course to suit the ethos of Israel, in order to foster the mystique of sacral kingship, which would increase his authority and enable him to establish a dynasty. With cult cult-personnel may also have been adopted, including possibly Ṣadoq as the heir of the priestly authority of the ancient kings. Now, however, David and his successors occupied the position of the ancient priest-kings of Jerusalem, and Ṣadoq and his descendants were strictly delegates of the king[23] until, after the liquidation of the state in 586, the priest recovered his ancient authority in the rehabilitation of the Jewish community in the Persian period (539–333 B.C.) until Rome cast her shadow over Judah and the High Priest was nominated by vassal kings and Roman governors.

But the mystical conception of the king as the temporal guarantee of the Sovereignty of God, which was appropriated and developed under David and his successors, survived the collapse of the House of David to become the source of the conception of the Messiah of Jewish eschatology, the supernatural agent of the inauguration of the Divine new order, the Kingdom of God, of which contemporary Judaism and the followers of Jesus of Nazareth were to give such divergent interpretations.

So David succeeded in creating for the first time in the history of Palestine a territorial state which was nearly commensurate with the extent of Palestine, and in making Jerusalem the capital. The city of David was the capital not only of such a state, but of a modest empire. This included Edom north-east of the Gulf of Aqaba with its entrepôts on the incense-road from South Arabia† and the copper-mines of the escarpment east and west of the Araba north of the Gulf of Aqaba,‡

* The writer has discussed the conception of kingship in ancient Canaan in its historical development from the heroic age reflected in the legends of Keret and Aqhat in the Ras Shamra Texts to the actual office of the king as depicted in the administrative texts from the palace of Rās Shamrā in the fourteenth century and in the Amarna Tablets from the same era, *The Legacy of Canaan*, 2nd ed., 1965, pp. 218–230.

† The visit of the Queen of Sheba (I Kings x. 1–13) was probably a trade mission occasioned by Solomon's control of the bottleneck between Edom and Sinai at Aqaba.

‡ The excellent study of copper-mining and smelting in this region from this period and earlier by B. Rothenberg and technical colleagues must here be cited, 'Ancient Copper Industries in the Western Arabah', *Palestine Exploration Quarterly*, 1962, pp. 5–71. David's association with Edom for the control of the mines may be the ultimate source of the Muslim tradition which attributes metal-working to 'the Prophet David', particularly shirts of mail, Qur'an, Surah 21, 80 (Egyptian Royal ed.).

Moab and Ammon east of the Dead Sea and Jordan, which controlled the trade route to Damascus, the lands settled by the Aramaean tribes and tribal confederacies north of the headwaters of Jordan and in the country of Damascus itself, the metropolis of the North Arabian desert and an important emporium of desert-borne caravans. Towards the headwaters of the Orontes the king of Hamath had appreciated the significance of David and had reached an agreement with him.[24] David's control over the Aramaeans at least as far north as Damascus must certainly have increased his prestige among the Aramaeans further north, and this probably bore concrete fruits in trading facilities as far as the Euphrates, which may be the basis of the apparently extravagant claims that the Promised Land extended as far as that river.[25] In any case, with the spoils and tribute of David's reign, Jerusalem and its tent-sanctuary achieved both wealth and prestige.

The time was singularly favourable for the establishment of the kingdom of David and its consolidation under Solomon. Egypt under its feeble priest-kings of the Twenty-first Dynasty had no imperial ambitions; Assyria, soon to dominate the politics of Western Asia, was in temporary eclipse; the Hittite Empire in Anatolia and North Syria had collapsed in the early twelfth century; and the Aramaean tribes, who had settled in Syria shortly after the decisive phase of the Israelite penetration into Palestine, were not yet consolidated, and were in fact subject to David in consequence of their premature and probably ill-organized support of Ammon in David's war against that neighbouring state.[26] The older Canaanite powers on the coast of Syria were already seeking their empire in overseas trade and pursued their interests in Palestine and in the trade with South Arabia from Aqaba* by friendly relations with Israel to the great advantage of both. The Phoenician allies of David and Solomon gave the new state advantage of their technical skill in the building of David's palace and of Solomon's Temple and other buildings in the new capital. In other respects too Solomon was influenced by his Phoenician allies. He exploited the strategic significance of his realm between Africa and Asia and between the Red Sea and the Mediterranean and became an enormously wealthy

* The port of Ezion-geber is now shown by B. Rothenberg to have been not, as was previously supposed, at the exposed northern shore of the Gulf of Aqaba near the Early Iron Age site of Tell al-Khaleifeh, but the island off the north-east shore of the Gulf called Jazirat al-Far'un (Pharaoh's Island), which has, according to an Admiralty report, the only safe anchorage on that coast, which is subject to sudden violent winds. Archaeological remains studied by Rothenberg and a team of Israeli archaeologists in a survey during the Sinai crisis of 1956 support this view, *Bible et Terre Sainte* 72, 1965, pp. 10–16.

merchant prince, like Herod the Great after him. He also organized his fiscal system on the Canaanite model now familiar to us from the administrative tablets from the palace of Rās Shamrā (ancient Ugarit),[27] organizing the population, both Israelite and Canaanite, for fiscal contributions of produce and labour. This measure was so offensive to democratic principles in Israel that it occasioned an abortive rebellion in his own time under Jeroboam the son of Nebat[28] and the secession of the northern tribes from his son Rehoboam under the same Jeroboam, who had returned to Palestine,[29] probably with the support of Egypt, where he had found refuge under the energetic Pharaoh Sheshonk of the Twenty-second Dynasty.[30]

Under Solomon the fortifications of Jerusalem were strengthened[31] and the city extended. It was probably the extension northwards over the narrow saddle at the north end of the ancient fortified settlement on the south-east hill to include his palace with its courts and the Temple and its courts that occasioned Solomon's extension of the terrace and buttress outwork on the eastern slope, which was probably the Millo (lit. 'filling', see above, pp. 31ff.), which may also have provided barracks for his professional soldiers.[32]

The palace he built for his Egyptian queen[33] must have been a conspicuous building, but its location is quite uncertain. It was evidently not in the city of David, but on a higher hill. If it were part of the palace-complex it would be north of the old north wall of the pre-Solomonic settlement, but it may have been independent, possibly on the east spur of the south-west hill projecting towards the site of the Temple, the amenity of which was appreciated by the Hasmonaean princes and Herod Agrippa II, whose palaces stood there. It may even have been higher up on the south-west hill, either on the summit, where the prevailing wind from the west could be enjoyed, or on the east slope, where gardens might be laid out. The conjunction of palace and Temple, as well as the actual plan of the Temple, has a close parallel in a palace and adjoining temple from a ninth-century archaeological station at Tell Taināt in North Syria,[34] but the conception of palace-cum-temple is in the case of Solomon's building probably Egyptian.* The building, however, was by Phoenician masters, but of Temple and palace nothing identifiable remains except perhaps the capital of a proto-Ionic column from the debris on the east slope in the excavations of 1963, which, we think, has a peculiar significance as a symbol of the tree of life in a society where the

* Borchardt (*Klio* XV, 1918, pp.179 ff.) cites cases of palace and temple in the same building-complex from Tell al Amatna, Karnak and Madinat Habu from the fourteenth to the twelfth century.

king was the vital channel of life and vitality for the community.*

It was the Temple, however, that was the most significant monument of Solomon's reign. It stood on the high ground of the eastern ridge above the palace and the city of David in the area at present occupied by the Muslim Ḥaram ash-Sharīf ('the Noble Sacred Precinct'). This present precinct of course with its southward extension and retaining walls perpetuates the work of Herod the Great in his rebuilding of the Second Temple, that which was rebuilt in 516 B.C. Solomon's Temple and precinct was much less imposing. Its site and plan in the Ḥaram ash-Sharīf is quite unknown, but it was intimately related to the rock under the Muslim Dome of the Rock with its cave underneath. One Jewish tradition regards this as the site of Solomon's great altar, which according to II Kings xvi. 14 (cf. I Kings viii. 22), was in the court before, i.e. east of, the Temple, and another as the site of the inmost shrine, or Holy of Holies, where the Mishnah (*Yoma* V, 2) notes 'the foundation stone', on which the high priest set down the censer on the Day of Atonement.†

Solomon's Temple was of relatively modest proportions with an inside measurement of 60 cubits by 20 cubits by 30 cubits in height for the main hall (Hebrew *hēykhāl*) and inmost shrine, which was a cube of 10 cubits, which stood higher than the rest of the building, being reached by a flight of steps. Added to this was a porch which projected 10 cubits along the front of the building and side-chambers of three storeys, each extending 5 cubits from the Temple wall, probably inside measurement. Thus the outside measurement of the ground-plan was probably no more than about 40 by 20 yards.‡ This, however, was but the shrine, and the area for public worship was the great court outside, where the great altar and other cultic installations stood.

* The motif in the capital is the stylization of the spike of a palm-tree or the bud of a lotus with the leaves curling to either side. One may trace the development in Canaanite art from a date-palm natural or stylized flanked by rampant caprids, which reach up to the fruit on Palestinian pottery from the southern part of the coastal plain *c.* 1500–1200 B.C. The significance of the tree is indicated by the mother-goddess (Ashera) between two rampant caprids, to which she offers ears of corn on the fine relief on the lid of an ivory unguent-box from Minet al-Beida by Rās Shamrā (fourteenth century B.C.). The *'ashērāh* in Hebrew signifies both mother-goddess and her symbol, a tree natural or stylized, often mistranslated in AV as 'the grove', which stood in the sanctuary. The tree is more and more stylized in Canaanite art until it develops into the pillar with proto-Ion capital, which is peculiar to palace architecture, as at Samaria and the palace at Ramat Raḥel between Jerusalem and Bethlehem.

† Did Jesus refer to this tradition in his famous declaration 'Thou art Peter, and on this rock will I build my church'?

‡ Allowing for the minimal thickness of the side-walls, which were rebated to hold the ceiling-beams of the side chambers, I Kings vi. 6.

The conception of the shrine in a much larger sacred precinct is familiar in the ancient Semitic world and is admirably illustrated on a larger scale than Solomon's Temple in the present Muslim Sacred Precinct in Jerusalem (Pl. 12).

This was now the central shrine of all Israel, built principally to house the Ark as the symbol of the God of Israel with his people, the God who was particularly known as militant in the cause of Israel, and as revealing himself in the crises of history, in the Great Deliverance from Egypt, which was Israel's genesis, and in the experience of the Covenant, in which Israel was made conscious of the nature of the God who had delivered her and of her peculiar status and purpose in the Divine economy in history, which was summarily adumbrated in the Law. Those articles of faith were now expressed sacramentally in the great festivals in the Temple liturgy in the psalms relating to those occasions. But in the Temple which adjoined the palace the king was, as he had been in ancient Canaan, the priest *par excellence*, the representative of God before the people and the embodiment of the community before God. So under David as part of the mystique of royalty the properly Israelite conception of the Divine Covenant with Israel was developed in the context of the continuance of God's living intervention in the history of Israel to the conception of the Divine Covenant with the House of David. This article of faith, promulgated by David with the support of the prophet Nathan, [35] was expressed in the liturgy of the Temple[36] and survived even the national disaster of the destruction of Jerusalem in 586 and the Babylonian Exile, so that a great prophet in the Exile could anticipate the rehabilitation of Israel as the fulfilment of the 'everlasting covenant', 'even the sure mercies of David'.[37] This novel element, woven now into the faith of the tribes of Israel, was a careful adaptation of the ideology of sacral kingship from the local religion of pre-Israelite Jerusalem, and so well did it serve its purpose that, with the exception of a six-years' usurpation by the queen-mother Athaliah the daughter of Ahab (841–836 B.C.) Judah remained loyal to the House of David as long as the state survived.

The cult of the God of Israel in the Temple was developed in another direction. The Temple was publicly dedicated by Solomon as chief priest 'at the feast in the month of Ethanim'.[38] The name of the month signifies 'the regular rains', 'the former rain' of Scripture, which makes ordered agriculture possible. This was anticipated at the autumnal New Year festival, the most significant religious occasion in the community of ancient Israel. Now as the greatest seasonal crisis in the peasant's year this was also the greatest occasion in the nature-cult in Canaan before the Israelite settlement. As we now know from the Rās Shamrā myths the tension and anxiety for the vital rains, which one may still sense in those parts after the long summer drought, was expressed in the sacred drama of the vicissitudes of the god Baal-Hadad, the Lord of Nature *par excellence*, manifest primarily in the winter storms and rain and secondarily in the vegetation so promoted. His crucial conflict with the floods of Chaos, on which he imposes a 'hither and no further', is dramatically described, and also his conflict with Death, or Sterility (*Mot*), including his death (the passion) and revival and final triumphant conflict with *Mot*. The relation between the myth of Baal's triumph over the unruly waters (Sea-and-River) and that of his conflict with *Mot* is not quite clear, but for our present subject it is highly significant that the result of Baal's triumph is the establishment of his kingship. This is symbolized by the building of his 'house', both palace and temple, which is a major theme of the myth of the conflict of Baal and *Mot*. That this clearly relates to the autumnal New Year anticipating the vital regular rains is plainly indicated in the myth of Baal's conflict with *Mot* by the culmination of the building of the 'house' with the installation of a roof-shutter which is ceremonially opened in an act of imitative magic to prompt the rains:

> 'Let a window be opened in the house,
> A shutter in the midst of the palace.'
> . . . .
> He opens a window in the house,
> A shutter in the midst of the palace,
> 'Open, O Baal, the clouds with rain.'
> (Baal) utters his holy voice. . . .*

In dedicating the Temple at that particular season when the Canaanite myth depicted the completion of the house of Baal, Solomon was surely incorporating elements which had already been adopted into the worship of God and had been regulated *de rigueur* as the Israelites settled as peasants in Canaan, and adopted with the techniques of the Canaanite peasant the rites whereby he enlisted the power of Providence in nature in the seasonal crises.

The adoption of this seasonal festival and its adaptation to the cult of Yahweh the God of Israel was more than the assertion of the extension of the power of the God of Sinai, the God militant of the tribes of Israel, to the domain of fertility in nature in the settled land. The imagery and theology of the related Canaanite mythology was also adapted, to the great enrichment of the faith of Israel. Hence Psalms

* I.e. in thunder, the harbinger of the 'former rains'.

relevant to this occasion accentuate the element of conflict with the powers of Chaos, often depicted, as in Psalms xlvi. 3; lxxiv. 12–19; lxxxix. 10–15; xciii, as the Unruly Waters. Here as in the Baal-myth of Canaan the triumph of God is signalized by his establishment as King. The regular association of the Kingship of God in the Psalms with this sequence of ideas and imagery familiar in the Canaanite Baal-myth leaves us in no doubt that, whatever the Kingship of God came to signify in Hebrew thought, the conception itself of the Divine Kingship established as the result of conflict with the forces of Chaos came into the theology of Israel through their adaptation of the liturgy of the Canaanite New Year festival, the Canaanite expression of faith in the power of Providence in nature, of the power of Cosmos over Chaos.* In the religion of Israel, however, this was adapted in the light of Israel's experience of God in the crises of history rather than in nature, hence the powers of Chaos are identified with Israel's historical enemies, Pharaoh and his chariots at the Sea of Reeds (A.V. 'Red Sea') and later enemies, who are unnamed.[39] So faith in God as Lord of history was fostered in Israel throughout the chequered history of the monarchy when the tides of imperial conquest swirled around the little state in the mountains around Jerusalem and later when the state was engulfed. But the ideology of the day of the Lord's 'show down', 'the day of the Lord' on which the Hebrew prophets animadverted, could also engender a false confidence as in Israel of Amos' time and in the materialistic variety of later political Messianism. Hence Amos and Isaiah of Jerusalem in the eighth century deepened the conception of the conflict of God with the forces of Chaos in nature and history to the conception of the uncompromising Divine conflict with the forces of moral chaos within Israel as well as without. Such, both on the positive and negative side, was the ultimate fruitful result of the incorporation of the Canaanite New Year liturgy into the cult of Israel in Solomon's Temple.

We have already noted that in the expression of faith in the Kingship

* This was but one aspect of the conception of the kingship of God as it was developed in Israel, and concerns what W. Schmidt has aptly termed the dynamic, as apart from the static, aspect of the kingship of God (*Königtum Gottes in Ugarit und Israel*, Beihefte zur *Zeitschrift für die alttestamentliche Wissenschaft* LXXX, 1961), God experienced in action against the menace of Chaos. It was likely that Israel also developed the Canaanite conception of El as the final authority in nature and society beyond all menace of the powers of disorder, God Omnipotent, Schmidt's 'static conception' of the kingdom of God. This was probably already expressed in the pre-Israelite cult of El Elyon ('El the Most High') in Jerusalem, as argued by H. Schmid, 'Jahweh und die Kulttraditionen von Jerusalem', *Zeitschrift für die alttestamentliche Wissenschaft* Neue Folge XXVI, 1955, pp. 169–97.

of God and his ordered government (*mishpāṭ*, which also means 'judgement') the Canaanite theme was adapted to express Israel's distinctive experience of God in the crises of history. The first of these was the Exodus, the Great Deliverance from Egypt. This great creative Divine act was consummated in his adoption of Israel as his covenanted people, the implications of that status in religious and social obligation being expressed in the Law. The sacramental experience of the Covenant with its historical prelude in the Exodus, the experience of God's grace and power as the basis of his absolute claim on Israel, and the endorsement of the Law, was the great religious act which integrated the various elements of the sacral confederacy of the tribes of Israel at their central sanctuaries at Shechem, Shiloh and Gilgal in the days of the settlement in Canaan. This great Covenant-sacrament was transferred to Jerusalem with David's restoration of the Ark of God, and continued to be the essential element in the cult in Solomon's Temple, which, whatever else it may have signified, was built primarily to house this symbol of the presence of God of Israel in the inmost shrine, or 'Holy of Holies'. The occasion of this sacrament was also the New Year festival,[40] or Feast of Tabernacles, also called the Feast of the Ingathering,* one of the three occasions coinciding with vital phases in the agricultural year when pilgrimage to the central shrine was enjoined in Israel in the Ritual Code.[41] Though Deuteronomy xxxi. 10–13 visualizes a full exposition of the Law on this occasion every seven years, there seems little doubt that Mowinckel is right in relating the presentation of the Law in a short compendium such as the Decalogue to this annual occasion.[42] This was most appropriate to the theme of the occasion, which was the triumph of Order over Chaos, the declaration of faith in God as King and in the establishment of his Order, or government (*mishpāṭ*).

The new Year Festival in Solomon's Temple, with what Mowinckel has so felicitously termed the Epiphany of God as King, with all the implications we have noted, gave direction to the life and thought of Israel. While yet the throne of David stood intact men were assured that

* The Ingathering refers to the completion of harvest, which had begun with the grain harvest in April-May and May-June and, with the exception of the olives, which are harvested in September, ended with the vintage. During the summer the grain-crop lay on the threshing-floor to be threshed at convenience, the threshed grain being temporarily stored under thorns. Finally all was brought into storage in pits lined with lime-plaster in the settlements. This was still done in Arab villages under the British mandate, when the bringing in of the produce from the threshing-floor was a public occasion of great solemnity marked by prayer.

The Lord Most High is terrible
A great King over all the earth.
He shall subdue the peoples under us,
Even the nations under our feet.
He shall choose our inheritance for us,
The excellency of Jacob whom he loved.

(Psalm xlvii. 2–4, Hebr. text 3–5)

The great prophet in the Babylonian Exile rallies the scattered remnants of Israel on the same experience with the ringing words:

How beautiful upon the mountains
Are the feet of him that brings good tidings,
That proclaims 'All is well!'
That brings good tidings of good,
That proclaims deliverance, that says to Zion,
Thy God is King!

(Isaiah lii. 7)

In the days when Judas Maccabaeus and his resolute followers fought among the rocks and scrub about Jerusalem for their ancestral faith against the might of the Seleucid Empire they were nerved by the same assurance:

And the kingdom and dominion and the greatness of the kingdom under the whole heaven shall be given to the saints of the Most High, whose kingdom is an everlasting kingdom, and all dominions shall serve and obey him.

(Daniel vii. 27)

And in the fullness of time the consummation of the faith of Israel in the advent of the Lord Jesus is expressed in the pregnant declaration:

The time is fulfilled. The Kingdom of God is at hand.

(Mark i. 15)

After this great article of faith, the Kingship of God, in the cult in Solomon's Temple, which transcends the ages, it seems an anticlimax to describe the clash of arms in the incidentals of history about the walls of Jerusalem, which on the strictly political level is magnified out of proportion now that Jerusalem has become the capital of a small, poor hill-state off the beaten track of history after the disruption of the realm of David and Solomon. Thanks to the intense interest of prophets such as Isaiah, Jeremiah and Zephaniah in the involvement of their people and their God in the crises of contemporary history as they related the conflict to deeper spiritual issues, and to the compiler of the history of Israel in Joshua-Judges-Samuel-Kings, which he presented rather as a philosophy of history, Jerusalem is spot-lighted as the stage of a great cosmic drama, where hope alternates with foreboding, confidence with despair as Israel fulfils or rejects her destiny as the people of God as God and his servants the prophets interpret it. This strange relationship between the sublime and the sordid in the history of Jerusalem must be appreciated as we briefly describe the vicissitudes of Jerusalem under the House of David after the secession of North Israel.

The relative weakness of Jerusalem and Judah in the interplay of politics in Western Asia and even in Palestine itself is emphasized in the gradual impoverishment of Solomon's Temple to buy off threats such as that of the Pharaoh Sheshonk when he showed the flag in Palestine in 926 B.C. and that of Hazael of Syria[43] and of Sennacherib of Assyria[44] or to suborn foreign powers against the rival North Kingdom as in the time of Asa[45] and Ahaz.[46] During this period it was only the involvement of the northern kingdom with powerful foreign enemies that prevented its domination of Judah. Under the House of Ahab, however, Judah was associated with Israel as the junior partner, and eventually Athaliah, the daughter, or perhaps sister, of Ahab, who had married Jehoram of Judah, succeeded in usurping the throne for six years.[47] Though a revolution was carried through, the relative insignificance of Judah as long as Israel remained is emphasized by Amaziah's abortive challenge to Jehoash of Israel, who further despoiled the Temple treasury and demolished about 250 yards of the north wall of Jerusalem between the Corner Gate and the Ephraim Gate.[48] After the liquidation of the rival northern kingdom in 722 the story of Jerusalem continues in like strain, relieved only by Hezekiah's apparent defiance of the emissaries of Sennacherib from the walls of Jerusalem.[49] On this occasion Sennacherib, as his records suggest, stripped Hezekiah of most of the kingdom, leaving him only Jerusalem as his crown possession and Bethlehem as the home of his family.[50] The remote hill-fortress had apparently as little significance in the estimation of the Assyrian king as it had had in the eyes of the Hebrew tribes in the days of their settlement in Palestine. In this period of Assyrian domination Manasseh the son of Hezekiah was evidently the vassal of Assyria, being named in Assyrian inscriptions as present in Nineveh together with the kings of Moab and Edom as supervisors, or perhaps as hostages, while their subjects worked as labour-gangs on Esarhaddon's public works,[51] and in another inscription which records his presence with Esarhaddon on a campaign in Egypt in 668 B.C.[52] Esarhaddon evidently considered Judah a valuable adjunct in view of his domination of Egypt, and it may have been a mark of Assyrian favour that Manasseh was allowed to refortify and expand Jerusalem.[53] On the other hand Manasseh's refortification of Jerusalem may have been specifically connected with the events in the reign of Ashurbanipal the son of Esarhaddon, either with the relaxation of the imperial drive or, more likely, with unrest in the provinces, where his Egyptian vassal Necho I revolted in 655.[54] In the revolt of Shamash-shum-ukīn the brother of Ashurbanipal and his viceroy in Babylon in 652 there was further unrest in the west, complicated by Arab raids into Palestine.[55] As protection against those, Manasseh may have been allowed to refortify Jerusalem, a measure which in any case may have been recommended by the necessity to prepare a base in Judah for operations against Egypt, a situation which later conditioned Persian favour to the Jews in Ezra's mission (see below, p. 108). It is also possible, however, that Manasseh's fortification may have been connected with Judah's part in the rebellion in the west either in 655 or 652, as Albright suggests.[56] This, however, is conjectural and lacks evidence.

The Assyrian domination was symbolized by the admission of Assyrian cults, chiefly associated with star-worship, to the Temple precinct, particularly under Ahaz[57] and Manasseh.[58] These and the fertility-cult of Canaan did not of course exclude the traditional worship of the God of Israel in the large liberality of the ancient world, but they qualified Israel's absolute allegiance to her God. On the decline of the Assyrian power towards the last quarter of the seventh century Josiah as a gesture of defiance cleansed the sanctuary from these alien elements. At the same time the influence of the Canaanite fertility-cult at local provincial shrines was eliminated by the centralization of worship in the Temple at Jerusalem. The completion of the reformation was signalized by a great communal sacrament, the Passover, which was presented as the revival of this festival as a public pilgrimage festival, like the festivals of Unleavened Bread at the beginning of the barley harvest, Weeks (Pentecost) at the end of the wheat harvest, and the New Year festival (Tabernacles). It was probably the traditional association of the Passover, hitherto a domestic, or local, festival with the Exodus as the genesis of Israel as the distinctive people of God and the nucleus of an independent nation that suggested this as an appropriate expression of national independence.

The reformation, which had both a political and a religious aspect, was associated with the discovery of a law-book in the Temple during repairs. This is generally taken to be the nucleus of the present Deuteronomy, comprising the strictly legal portions with at least the outline of historical preliminary as the basis of the absolute demands of God according to the literary convention of the Covenant-sacrament. To be sure the account of Josiah's reformation agrees generally with the principles of Deuteronomy though when we enter into particularities there is little actual agreement. The fact that the theology of Deuteronomy prevails in the prophetic message after that time, in Jeremiah and Zephaniah for instance, and in the compositions of the period and later, such as the historical work Joshua-Judges-Samuel-Kings and the compilation of the traditions of the Prophets, supports the tradition of the influence of the legal nucleus of Deuteronomy in Josiah's reformation.*

Scriptural tradition stresses the influence of the priesthood in the Temple in the reformation, and this cannot be overemphasized. Ṣadoq, the first of the hereditary chief priests, was a royal nominee and a subordinate of the king, who was, according to the Canaanite model, the chief priest. But the priests were on the whole faithful custodians of the ancestral faith, and had vindicated the faith and political independence of Judah against the usurper Athaliah.[59] Now again Hilkiah the priest presented the law-book to Josiah with his support for the reformation. It has been suggested that the discovery of the book with the authority of Moses was a pious fraud. That, however, would not alter the fact that the priests of the Temple were active instigators of the reformation both in its political and religious aspects. We may thus see the priests anticipating the role they were to play under the High Priests as leaders of the community after the Exile. Actually we see no reason to doubt that the law-book, whatever its history, originated in the tradition of the law in North Israel associated with the tradition of the sacrament of the Covenant at the central sanctuaries of the tribal confederacy. It consists as far as the law is concerned in a compendium of religious and social principles in the form of the Decalogue[60] in the context of the Covenant-sacrament, where the Covenant at Sinai is sacramentally appropriated in the present.[61] Legal practices and principles are elaborated in greater detail and greater length, as in the much earlier Book of the Covenant in Exodus xx. 22–xxiii, 33, which is similarly appended to the Decalogue.[62] In comparison to the law in the Book of the Covenant, however, which gives no indication of any institutions in the Hebrew monarchy, the law in Deuteronomy relates to social conditions in the monarchy. It is, as the name suggests, a copy of the Law, or rather an application of the Law to the developing social situation. There is no good reason to doubt that, as it originated in the tradition of the Covenant-sacrament at the central shrines of Shechem,

* The reforms of Nehemiah in the latter part of the fifth century seem also to have been conditioned by the Deuteronomic theology and legislation (see below, p. 114).

Shiloh and Gilgal, all in North Israel, it represents a North Israelite tradition. Its association with the Temple, where traditionally it was found during repairs in the time of Josiah, may perhaps be explained on the assumption that, on the collapse of the north kingdom in 722 just before the accession of Hezekiah, refugees from responsible circles had taken refuge in the south, bringing their legal traditions with them. If they were not already in writing events of 722 would indicate the urgency of committing them to written record. This would probably incorporate more recent matter, and in fact may have been partly the work of the Jerusalem priesthood under Hezekiah, who is also accredited with a reformation like that of Josiah, which was destined to provide also for remnants from North Israel.[63]*

The political designs of Josiah for independence and a revival of the united kingdom of Israel and Judah as in the days of David and Solomon, which the decline of Assyria favoured, did not mature. Josiah had correctly gauged the weakness of Assyria, exhausted by centuries of aggressive imperialism. But Egypt marched north to anticipate the annihilation of Assyria by the Babylonians and their allies from Anatolia and Iran. Josiah correctly assessed the effect of Egypt's success on his political future, and went to intercept the Pharaoh Necho II at Megiddo. But the result was fatal. Josiah fell in 609 B.C., and Judah continued her inglorious history till 586 as the vassal for a brief time of Egypt and then of Babylon under Nebuchadrezzar, and yet more ingloriously as the pawn of Egypt against the Babylonian suzerain. Finally, against the agonized pleading of Jeremiah, first Jehoiaqim and his successor Jehoiachin in 597 and then Zedekiah in 586 were involved by the more violent nationalists in rebellion fomented by Egypt, and the throne of David collapsed when Jerusalem fell and King Zedekiah made his ineffective escape by night with his small retinue down the desolate Qidron Valley by the Gate 'between the two walls'[64] (see above, p. 39, fig. IV, p. 40). But when the walls of Jerusalem were breached, the armed forces scattered, the throne of David abolished and the Temple itself in ruin, the heritage of Israel was preserved by the priests. Those who revised the Law and the tradition of the Covenant not only preserved the tradition of the faith; they interpreted those in

* Hezekiah's purification of the cult may have been connected with his revolt against Assyria in 701 B.C. The great Passover, however, which was the chief feature of Hezekiah's reform according to II Chronicles xxx, is stated in Kings to have been unprecedented since the days of the judges, hence we regard the reform of Hezekiah to be limited, as II Kings xviii. 4 suggests. A revision in the time of Hezekiah of the law brought to Jerusalem by North Israelite refugees as a possible basis of reunion of North and South at some favourable opportunity may be the source of the tradition in II Chronicles xxx.

the light of what had happened as an indication of the will of God, not indeed registered as a final judgement, but with relation to the Divine destiny of Israel in the future. So the Temple of Solomon nurtured a faith which would survive the Temple itself and the monarchy which had created the Temple, and recreate a community which would refuse to be submerged or obliterated, a community which for the usual secular authority and institutions substituted the Law of God.

NOTES FOR CHAPTER III

1 G. E. Wright, *Biblical Archaeologist* XXII, 1959, pp. 54–66
2 I Samuel xiii. 3 ff.
3 I Samuel xviii. 8–9
4 I Samuel xxii. 1–2
5 I Samuel xxiii. 14 ff.
6 I Samuel xxvii. 6
7 II Samuel ii. 4
8 II Samuel v. 9
9 II Samuel v. 11
10 I Kings xvi. 24
11 II Samuel xv-xviii
12 II Samuel xx. 1–22
13 I Kings i
14 I Samuel iv. 11
15 I Samuel v. vi
16 II Samuel vii. 2; I Kings i. 39; ii. 29
17 Psalm cxxxii
18 I Kings ii. 26–7
19 I Kings i. 38–9
20 Psalm ii. 7
21 Psalms ii; lxxii
22 Psalm lxxii; Lamentations iv. 20
23 I Kings iv. 2–4
24 II Samuel viii. 1–14
25 Joshua i. 2–4 etc.
26 II Samuel x
27 J. Gray, *The Legacy of Canaan*, 2nd ed., 1965, pp. 224–5
28 I Kings xi. 26–40
29 I Kings xii. 1–20
30 I Kings xi. 40
31 I Kings xi. 27
32 Nehemiah iii. 19
33 I Kings vii. 8
34 W. M. McEwan, *American Journal of Archaeology* XLI, 1937, p. 9, fig. 4
35 II Samuel vii. 12–17
36 Psalms lxxxix. 1–37; cxxxii. 11 ff.
37 Isaiah lv. 3
38 I Kings viii. 1–2
39 E.g. Psalms ii. 1 ff.; xlvi. 6 ff.
40 Deuteronomy xxxi. 10–13
41 Exodus xxxiv. 22–3
42 S. Mowinckel, *Le Décalogue*, 1927
43 II Kings xii. 17–18, Hebrew text 18–19
44 II Kings xviii. 15–16
45 I Kings xv. 19
46 II Kings xvi. 8
47 II Kings xi. 1–3
48 II Kings xiv. 13–14
49 II Kings xviii. 17
50 The Taylor Prism, D.D. Luckenbill, *Ancient Records of Assyria* II, 1926–27, 240 ff.
51 A. L. Oppenheim, *Ancient Near Eastern Texts*, ed. J. B. Pritchard, 1950, p. 291

52 Oppenheim, *op. cit.*, p. 294

53 II Chronicles xxxiii. 14

54 Oppenheim, *op. cit.*, p. 296

55 R. Kittel, *Geschichte des Volkes Israel* II, 1925, p. 399; W. Rudolph, *Chronikbücher, Handbuch zum Alten Testament*, 1955, pp. 315–17; J. Bright, *A History of Israel*, 1960, p. 290

56 W. F. Albright, *The Biblical Period*, 2nd ed. 1963, p. 79

57 II Kings xvi. 10–18

58 II Kings xxi. 3–5; Zephaniah i. 4 ff.

59 II Kings xi

60 Deuteronomy v. 7–21

61 Deuteronomy v. 2

62 Exodus xx. 2–17

63 II Kings xviii. 4, 22; II Chronicles xxix; xxx

64 II Kings xxv. 4

IV

THE RESTORATION

Let the house be builded, the place where they offered sacrifices, and let the foundations thereof be strongly laid (Ezra vi. 3)

We have already seen how after the reigns of David and Solomon the history of Jerusalem was determined by forces beyond the frontiers of the little hill-state of Judah. So the next phase of her history was heralded by the victories of Cyrus the Great of Persia in the highlands of Iran and Anatolia and in the plains of Lower Mesopotamia.

The power of Babylon, revived under the Chaldaeans, had a short if brilliant career. On the death of Nebuchadrezzar, the strongest of the Neo-Babylonian rulers, it began to disintegrate, and when in 555 the eccentric Nabona'id came to the throne the days of the Babylonian Empire were numbered. This pious antiquarian antagonized the powerful priesthood of Marduk, the city-god of Babylon, and himself sowed the seeds of sedition in the heart of his empire. Meanwhile the star of another potential world-power was on the ascendant in the highlands of Iran.

The Medes from the north part of the Iranian plateau had already played a notable part as the allies of Babylon in the destruction of Assyria. On the fall of the Assyrian capital Nineveh they occupied the Assyrian homeland in North Mesopotamia and under their ambitious king Cyaxares subjugated Asia Minor as far as the Caspian and Black Sea and westwards to the River Halys. Here they came into conflict with the Lydians, then the strongest power in Anatolia, but the combatants shrank back appalled on the occasion of a solar eclipse on 28th May, 585,* and for a generation the Halys was accepted as the boun-

* This was the first solar eclipse to be predicted by a Western scientist, Thales of Miletus, who predicted the year, though not the day. Since he studied astronomy in Egypt it is questionable if this can be claimed as a triumph of European science, cf. J. B. Bury, *A History of Greece*, 1922, p. 227.

dary between the two powers, their agreement being cemented by the marriage of the daughter of King Alyattes of Lydia to Astyages the son of Cyaxares. One of the vassals of the Median emperor was Cyrus, the ruler of a small mountain principality Anshan in South Persia. This astute and vigorous ruler exploited a certain dissatisfaction among the Median nobility, and attacked the forces of Astyages. He was supported by Nabona'id and, defeating the armies of Astyages, had himself declared King of the Medes and Persians. Nabona'id thus had the satisfaction of seeing the elimination of the power of Astyages the Mede, but the success of Cyrus simply meant a change of dynasty, and to his great embarrassment the centre of the Medo-Persian Empire was now much nearer Babylon. Meanwhile Cyrus himself was attacked from the north. Croesus of Lydia, the son of Alyattes and the son-in-law of the defeated Median king Astyages, combined with Nabona'id of Babylon and Ahmes (Greek Amasis) of Egypt to curb the growing power of Cyrus. The alliance was not really effective. The Lydians alone took the offensive, but were soon hurled back on Sardis the capital, which fell in 546, and the empire of Lydia was destroyed, according to the oracle of Delphi, which with studied ambiguity declared that if Croesus crossed the River Halys he would destroy a mighty empire. The empire of Cyrus now stretched from the Persian Gulf to the Bosphorus and the Aegean, including not only the rich metal-bearing mountains of Anatolia but also the arterial trade-routes along which commerce was passing in ever-increasing volume from the East to the awakened West. Cyrus was a power to be dreaded, and well might Nabona'id of Babylon tremble for the part he had played, diplomatically if not actively, in seeking to check his progress.

There were others in the Babylonian Empire who followed the progress of Cyrus with keen anticipation. For the Jewish deportees a new era of hope had dawned; the doom of Babylon was sealed, and once more the voice of Hebrew prophecy was heard. The new hopes are expressed in what is conventionally known among scholars as Deutero-Isaiah (Isaiah xl–lv), the work of the prophetic circle which conserved the tradition of Isaiah of Jerusalem, the contemporary of Ahaz and Hezekiah about two centuries before. The topical significance of this great prophetic outburst is clearly indicated by the fact that Cyrus is explicitly named 'the shepherd' of God who would be the agent of the Divine purpose for Israel[1] and even his anointed one,[2] who, like the king of Israel in days gone past, should be the visible expression of the Kingship of the God of Israel and of his control over the powers of Chaos in nature and history.

The collapse of the Aramaean dynasty of Babylon was swift and complete when Cyrus deemed the time ripe to strike. Actually he exploited the unpopularity of Nabona'id with the powerful priesthood of Marduk in the capital. Well supported by a great number of Nabona'id's subjects and most notably by Gobryas, or Ugbaru, the governor of the district of Gutium on the south-east frontier, Cyrus established himself as sovereign in Mesopotamia with little bloodshed. Automatically the lands of the Babylonian Empire including Syria and Palestine became part of the new Persian Empire, which stretched from the western foothills of the Himalayas to the Mediterranean and from the Black Sea to the Persian Gulf, and after the expedition of Cambyses the son of Cyrus to Egypt in 525 B.C., included the Lower Nile.

The tolerant spirit of the new empire was as broad as its extent. It is definitely known from his inscriptions that Darius I (522–486) was a Zoroastrian. The date of Zoroaster the founder of this ethical faith (see below, p. 143, n.) is not definitely known, but it seems likely that even before the time of Darius in the days of Cyrus and Cambyses the influence of the new faith was felt. It was of great significance in the administration of the new empire that the faith of the ruling power should be ethical and universal rather than nationalist and particularist. Cyrus signalized his assumption of power in the former empire of Babylon by his decree restoring 'gods . . . to their places', housing them 'in lasting abodes' (i.e. restored temples) and restoring also various deported peoples.[3] This refers to his reversal of Nabona'id's policy of concentration of provincial Mesopotamian cults in the capital, but it indicates the general tolerance of the new world-power, from which the Jews among others were to benefit. There is no extra-Biblical reference to a decree which specifically mentions the Jews and the restoration of the Temple as Ezra i. 1–4; iv. 3 and 13–17 state. Indeed it is not difficult to demonstrate on grounds of theology and language that these passages do not cite a genuine decree of Cyrus, but are the reconstruction of the editor of Ezra, which belongs with Nehemiah to the Chronicler's history from the third century B.C. It seems likely that the Chronicler, knowing the *firman* of Artaxerxes to Ezra,[4] took this as the model for a decree of Cyrus in his first year as sovereign of Babylon, which he apparently took as the end of the seventy years' exile predicted by Jeremiah.[5]*

* The matter, if not the verbal authenticity, of the correspondence in Aramaic in Ezra v. 6–vi. 12 is supported by official rescripts regarding the Jewish community in Elephantine regarding the festival of Unleavened Bread and a rescript of Cyrus himself to a fiscal officer Gadatus in Asia Minor regarding the immunities due to an official of the local cult of Apollo near Magnesia (Ed. Meyer, *Die Entstehung des Judentums*, 1896, pp. 19 ff.).

The first company of Jews who ventured to return to the land of their fathers is stated to have come under the leadership of Sheshbazzar, who is designated 'the prince [*nāsī'*] of Judah'.[6] The title may refer to Sheshbazzar's administrative status (cf. Ezra v. 14, where he is styled 'governor', *peḥāh*), but in view of the later appointment of Zerubbabel, a prince of the royal house, the designation may refer to Sheshbazzar's status as the head of the community in the Exile. Actually Sheshbazzar (*Sin-ab-uzzur*, 'May the father [god] Sin succour') may be identical with the Biblical Shenazzar, a son of King Jehoiachin and uncle of Zerubbabel according to I Chronicles iii. 18.[7] These, however, were a minority, the Zionists of the community, perhaps even 'illegal immigrants' as K. Galling suggests.[8]

Certain passages (Ezra i. 1–6; v. 13–17) set before this company the primary duty of rebuilding the Temple, but this, like the official edict of Cyrus in his first year of rule in Babylon, is an idealistic reconstruction of the Chronicler, whose subject is the centrality of the Temple and its cult in the life of the new Israel. A truer picture is presented by the first-hand authorities Haggai and Zechariah, who show that it was eighteen years later than the accession of Cyrus in Babylon that the repair of the Temple was undertaken by the remanent Jewish peasants together with the exiles who had returned with Zerubbabel.[9]

From Haggai i. 11 it is evident that the Jewish community in 520 B.C. was limited in resources, mainly peasants living at subsistence level under the continual menace of ruin, which even one season's drought could bring upon them.[10] The wasting and depopulation of the land after repeated ravages of Assyrians and Babylonians and the recent deportations had encouraged an influx of Arabs and Edomites, who, being forced out of their ancestral home south-east of the Dead Sea by the Nabataeans from the Hejāz, were glad of an opportunity to control the lucrative trade-routes for the South Arabian caravans by way of Aqaba to Egypt[12] now that the branch to Damascus was controlled by the Nabataeans. Thus the former kingdom of Judah was soon occupied by the Edomites from the Gulf of Aqaba to just north of Hebron within twenty-five miles from Jerusalem, so that the Greek sources in the next period refer to the whole district of Hebron as 'Idumaea'. The Book of Lamentations (v. 9) refers to this drastic restriction of Judah:

> We get out bread at the peril of our lives
> Because of the sword of the wilderness,

and again to the hardship of the times (Lamentations v. 10):

Our skin is black like an oven
Because of the terrible famine.

The former kingdom of Judah had shrunk under these encroachments and under Persian administrative reorganization to very small dimensions corresponding to the ancient tribal districts of Judah and Benjamin[13] from about ten miles north of Jerusalem to about twenty-five miles southwards. The limited extent of the district is indicated by the note of the settlements which helped with the rebuilding of the walls of Jerusalem under Nehemiah, namely Jericho, Teqoa, Bethṣur, Qeilah, Zanoah, Jerusalem, Gibeon, Miṣpah and Beth hakkerem. The distribution of stamped jar-handles with the impression YHD in Hebrew or Aramaic characters in excavations in Jerusalem, Jericho, Gezer in the coastal plain, Ramat Raḥel between Jerusalem and Bethlehem and mostly at Tell an-Naṣbeh about nine miles north of Jerusalem confirms this delimitation of the district of Judah. The comparative abundance of pottery stamps at Tell an-Naṣbeh suggests that this was the site of Miṣpah, which is mentioned in Nehemiah iii. 7 apparently as the capital of the district ('which pertained to the seat of the governor of 'Over-the-River").* This district was apparently under the administration of the Persian provincial governor in Samaria in the beginning of the Persian administration. Among the remanent Jewish peasantry there was no hard nationalist core, and soon they intermarried with alien wives, as Nehemiah xiii. 23–4 indicates. Nor was the ruined precinct of the Temple in Jerusalem any longer a distinctive nationalist symbol. Indeed in the last decade of the monarchy Ezekiel had been horrified by the active practice of the cult of Tammuz and the sun in the Temple-precinct, and the prophet in Isaiah lvi-lxvi (Trito-Isaiah), even after the restoration, deplores the various forms of heathen worship and superstition in Jerusalem.[14] Peaceful co-existence with their pagan neighbours and with their less orthodox co-religionists in the province of Samaria, a practical necessity for the remanent Jews about Jerusalem, involved them in the dangers of assimilation, to which the Zionists were particularly sensitive.[15]

In 520 B.C. the prophets Haggai and Zechariah gave a prophetic impulse to the revival of the Jewish community in Jerusalem. It is not clear if these prophets were of a fresh influx of Jews from Mesopotamia who had returned with Zerubbabel of the old royal line and Joshua of

* 'The throne, or seat, of the governor . . .' must define Miṣpah and does not refer to the end of a section of the wall of Jerusalem as AV suggests, cf. RSV, which renders 'the men of . . . Mizpah, who were under the jurisdiction of the governor. . . .' The end of each section of the building is denoted by the preposition *'ad* and not *l^e*, as Simons rightly perceives, *op. cit.*, p. 454.

the priestly line of Ṣadoq in the time of Darius I,[16] or if Zerubbabel and Joshua had been in the land since the time of Cyrus.[17] The settlement of Zerubbabel and his colleagues may have been encouraged by Cambyses the son of Cyrus the Great in conjunction with his expedition against Egypt in 525*, but Zechariah's reference to the movement of Jews from the east as a flight out of Babylon[18] may indicate that either Zerubbabel and his colleagues, or, we think rather, a later contingent including the prophet, withdrew in the troubles that convulsed the Persian Empire when, on the death of Cambyses without an heir in 522, the Magian priest Gaumata claimed the throne by pretending to be Smerdis the brother of Cambyses, who was thought to have been murdered. In the same year there was a revolt in Mesopotamia under Nidintu-Bel, when there might well have been a revulsion of feeling against the Jews, to whom the Persian administration had been favourable. This would admirably account for Zechariah's call to flight from Babylon and his allusion to the servile status of the Jews in the land from which they were called to escape. Those very troubles in the Persian Empire, which prompted the prudent to migrate to Judah, excited ardent nationalist hopes among some elements, including evidently the prophet Haggai, who saw in them a manifestation of the cosmic convulsions where God was shaking heaven and earth before he would emerge triumphant as King with Zerubbabel of the House of David as his earthly vassal.[19]

Zerubbabel, chosen either by the Jewish community in the Exile or by the Persian administration as leader of the immigrants and apparently appointed district governor of Judah in virtue of his birth from the old royal line of Judah, soon found himself thus, probably to his own embarrassment, the centre of nationalist aspirations. These hopes were further stimulated by the building of the Temple.

The Jews who returned with Zerubbabel and Joshua of the old High-Priestly line of Ṣadoq found the Temple still dilapidated,[20] though there had been the intention to rebuild it.[21] In view of the danger of assimilation the Zionists considered the restoration of the Temple, on however modest a scale, imperative in order that the Jews might have a concrete symbol of their faith and a focal point. Enthusiasm was roused by the denunciations of Haggai and by the prophetic visions and oracles of Zechariah, who had perhaps held out the ideal of the rebuilding of the Temple as a stimulus to continued immigration from the east[22] for longer than the dates assigned to his visions in the Book of Zechariah

* We note in this connection the exceptionally good relations between Cambyses and the Jewish garrison in Elephantine (A. Cowley, *Aramaic Papyri of the Fifth Century B.C.*, 1923, no. 29).

suggest.[23] However that may be, the Temple was rebuilt by 516 (the sixth year of Darius I).[24]

As the Temple rose from its ruins and the new community consolidated round Zerubbabel the nationalist hopes of the more sanguine elements in the community intensified. In ancient Canaan and throughout the Hebrew monarchy the building of the house of God had symbolized the Divine Kingship or sovereign rule won after his triumph in the cosmic conflict against the forces of Chaos in nature and, for the Hebrews, in history, which was the theme of the culmination of the New Year festival, the highlight of the religious year in Israel (see above, pp. 92–93). So now the old hope was revived, being reflected in contemporary oracles, notably Haggai ii. 21–3:

I will shake the heavens and the earth,
And I will overthrow the throne of kingdoms,
And I will destroy the strength of the kingdoms of the nations,
And I will overturn the chariots and those who ride in them,
And down shall go horses and their riders,
Each by the sword of his fellow.
On that day, saith Yahweh of Hosts,
I will take thee, O Zerubbabel son of Shealtiel, my Servant,*
And I will make thee as a signet,
For I have chosen thee.

In this oracle, where the internecine strife of the Gentiles surely reflects the civil wars in the Persian Empire between 522 and 518, it is noteworthy that as in the period of the Davidic monarchy the sovereignty of God is temporally guaranteed to the faithful by his vassal, his Servant, who carries out the purpose of the Divine suzerain, his seal, which expresses the Divine will and authority. The Servant-title has indubitably royal implications, and the passage indicates clearly the sanguine hopes of a revival of the royal line of David under Zerubbabel, the Branch[25] which sprouts from the truncated stock of David.[26]

The hopes of a restoration under Zerubbabel of the old royal line of Judah did not materialize, either on account of the sobriety of Zerubbabel, the centre of such hopes,[27] though perhaps unwilling, or because of prompt intervention and his possible removal by Persian authorities, perhaps influenced by the provincial administration at Samaria, which Ezra iv. 8 ff. notes. At any rate the sanguine hopes of the restoration of the house of David under Zerubbabel as an anointed king with the

* 'Servant of God' is a royal title in the Old Testament, e.g. David, and in the Rās Shamrā legends.

High Priest Joshua as his associate[28] were apparently frustrated. Zerubbabel fades from the picture, and only the High Priest sustains the authority in the new Jewish community about Jerusalem,[29] which he was to retain until the authority of the king was separated from that of the High Priest under the will of Alexandra Salome the widow of Alexander Jannaeus (see below, pp. 145–6) and under Rome, when the office was filled by nomination of the vassal kings of Rome. For the meanwhile the district was probably administered from Samaria, where eventually the best-known governor was Sanballaṭ the contemporary of Nehemiah.

The next step in the rehabilitation of the Jewish community was the fortification of Jerusalem. The repair of the walls of Jerusalem, ruined since 586, was the work of Nehemiah, but it had already been begun, possibly as a protection in the insecurity in the provinces in the disturbances in the west of the Persian Empire between 480 and 449.* This work had already advanced as far as the gates before Nehemiah undertook it,[30] but had been frustrated by the delation of the officials, Reḥum and Shimshai,[31] who probably administered Jerusalem from Samaria. At any rate the evidences of destruction were still fresh at the beginning of Nehemiah's mission in 445.[32] As Sanballaṭ, and not Reḥum or Shimshai, was in office in Samaria in Nehemiah's time they had probably been replaced, having possibly been involved in the revolt of Megabyzus, Persian satrap of the province Abarnahra ('Beyond-the-River', i.e. Euphrates), in 450–449. Nehemiah's appointment then and the fortification of Jerusalem may have been part of the re-organization of the provincial administration of the districts in the satrapy of Abarnahra as a counterpoise to Samaria after the part she had played in the recent revolt.

The community in Jerusalem was saved from disintegration through the enthusiasm of the Jews of the Exile, where Jerusalem and the rebuilt Temple had all the compelling force of an ideal as distinct from the contempt born of familiarity with the actual situation. But the enthusiasm and concern of the Jews in the eastern provinces required co-ordination and practical expression. This was given by Nehemiah and Ezra,† both

* J. Bright suggests that the building of the wall before Nehemiah may have been in anticipation of independence in the revolt of Megabyzus the satrap of Over-the-River in 450–449 (*op. cit.*, p. 361). It is in that case unlikely that permission would so soon after have been granted to Nehemiah to undertake his reconstruction.

† A. van Hoonacker first contended for Nehemiah's chronological priority to Ezra, *Muséon* IX, 1890, pp. 151 ff., 317 ff., 389 ff., which has since been maintained by A. Lods, *Histoire de la littérature hébraïque et juive*, 1950, p. 499; N. H. Snaith, *Zeitschrift für die alttestamentliche Wissenschaft* LXIII, 1951, pp. 53–65; H. H. Rowley, *The Servant of the Lord and Other Essays on the Old Testament*, 1952, pp. 131–59; A. Bentzen,

Introduction to the Old Testament II, 1952, p. 207; R. A. Bowman, *Interpreter's Bible* III, 1954, pp. 561–3; H. Cazelles, *Vetus Testamentum* IV, 1954, pp. 113 ff.; L. E. Browne, *Peake's Commentary*, ed. H. H. Rowley and M. Black, 1962, p. 392; O. Eissfeldt, *The Old Testament, an Introduction*, ET P. R. Ackroyd, 1965, p. 553. The chronological priority of Ezra according to the superficial impression of the Books of Ezra and Nehemiah is maintained by E. Sellin, *op. cit.* II, pp. 134–63; R. Kittel, *Geschichte des Volkes Israel* 3rd ed., 1929, III, pp. 567 ff. and R. De Vaux, *Supplément de la Dictionnaire de la Bible* IV, 1949, cols. 763 ff. and J. Wright, *The Date of Ezra's Coming to Jerusalem*, 2nd ed., 1958. T. K. Cheyne, 'Nehemiah', *Encyclopaedia Biblica* iii, 1902, pp. 13 ff.; R. H. Kennet, *Cambridge Biblical Essays*, 1909, p. 123; W. Rudolph, *Ezra und Nehemiah*, *Handbuch des Alten Testaments*, 1949, pp. xxvi–xxvii, 168–71; M. Noth, *History of Israel*, ET. P. R. Ackroyd, 1958, 319–20; J. Bright. *op. cit.*, pp. 375–84; and W. F. Albright, *The Biblical Period*, 2nd 1963, pp. 93–4, regard Nehemiah as prior to Ezra but active in Jerusalem at the same time, which assumes that Nehemiah returned to Palestine after reporting to the Persian capital in 432, no further note of his office or death being recorded. Ezra's mission is dated in the seventh year of Artaxerxes (Ezra vii. 7), and he completed his work apparently after Nehemiah came to Jerusalem (Nehemiah viii; ix; x). Nehemiah's mission is dated from the twentieth year of Artaxerxes to some time after his thirty-second year, when he interrupted his work in Jerusalem to report back to Persia. Since Scripture does not note which of the three kings Artaxerxes is intended we are thrown back on external evidence. The copy of a letter from the Jewish military colonists at Elephantine by Aswan precisely dated in 407 refers to an appeal three years before to Joḥanan the High Priest in Jerusalem, who is probably 'Jehoḥanan the son of Eliashib', the contemporary of Ezra (Ezra x. 6). If this is so Ezra's visit would be in 398 in the seventh year of Artaxerxes II. Nehemiah would then be the contemporary of Eliashib the High Priest, who held office before Joiada the predecessor of Jehoḥanan (Nehemiah xii. 22). This suggests that Nehemiah's mission was in the twentieth year of Artaxerxes I in 445. Nehemiah's mission in 445–432 and Ezra's arrival in 398, however, apparently contradicts Scripture in Nehemiah viii; ix; x, which apparently associates Nehemiah and Ezra in Jerusalem. Those passages in the present Book of Nehemiah, however, are no part of Nehemiah's memoirs (Nehemiah i-vii. 72; xii; xiii), as is indicated by the Greek II Esdras 18.1 ff., with which Josephus (*Antiquities* XI. v. 4–6) agrees, and they have been added with adjustments and a certain telescoping of tradition to the main history of the Chronicler, who compiled Ezra, Nehemiah and Chronicles. It is significant that in Nehemiah viii; ix; x the versions in the Greek II Esdras and Josephus do not actually mention Nehemiah, and the Hebrew Nehemiah viii. 9, which associates Nehemiah and Ezra, is suspect as suffering redactional adjustment. Nor do the Nehemiah memoirs, the most reliable evidence in the Book, mention Ezra except in Nehemiah xii. 26, 36, where 'Ezra' has all the appearance of a scribal insertion. The problem on any evidence is notoriously complex, but the date of Nehemiah's mission in the latter part of the fifth century seems clearly established by the evidence of the Elephantine Papyrus of 407, which names the High Priest Joḥanan the son, or perhaps grandson, of Nehemiah's contemporary Eliashib and also Delaiah and Shelemiah the sons of Sanballaṭ the governor of Samaria, the contemporary of Nehemiah (Nehemiah ii. 10, 19; iv. 7; vi. 1–5, 15). The mainly administrative interests of Nehemiah and his attack on social and religious abuses sporadically and *ad hoc* suggests that the authority of Ezra's law had not yet been publicly endorsed, and we shall treat the work of Nehemiah and Ezra in that chronological order as respectively mainly administrative and religious, leaving open the question of the activity of Ezra coinciding with the men of strong personality and dedicated determination, the Theodore Herzl and the Chaim Weizmann (see below, pp. 275–8) of their day. The former, having received a royal commission to Jerusalem by his influence at the Persian court,* secured a certain political status for the community in Judah with respect to the Persian provincial administration in Samaria. The latter with the support of a new influx of Zionists from Mesopotamia and the introduction of the revised Law, revitalized the community and completed Nehemiah's work of social and religious reform. Through the patience and determination of these men the community was finally rehabilitated after the hiatus since the end of the monarchy under the impersonal authority of the Law, which was to transcend the political limitations of the district of Jerusalem and give coherence to Israel in the ever-widening Dispersion from that day until now, when the authority of the Law transcends the constitution of the revived State of Israel.

There was need for the dynamic force of men like Nehemiah and Ezra, for in spite of the resettlement of Jerusalem and its district and the rebuilding of the Temple and the restoration of the office of the High Priest the life of the community had sunk to a low ebb. In the struggle for survival the iron of materialism had entered into the soul. Those who remained in the land had annexed the lands of the exiles and now that they returned perjured themselves to keep the stolen property (the substance of Zechariah's vision of the flying scroll, Zechariah v. 1–4). There was bad faith in business and exploitation of the labouring classes,[33] who through poverty were forced to borrow on the security of their land and the liberty of their children, with little hope of a charitable settlement and less of repaying their debts.[34] The Book of Malachi, relating to this period, emphasizes the fact that in this disintegration of the community the faith became a dead letter. The poor

latter part of Nehemiah's work after his return (Nehemiah xiii. 6–7), as Albright, Rudolph, Noth and Bright accept. The last view may suggest that the date of Ezra's mission in the seventh year of Artaxerxes is a scribal error for the thirty-seventh year of the same Artaxerxes (I) in whose reign (the twentieth to the thirty-second year) the first term of Nehemiah's office in Jerusalem is dated. K. Galling (*Studien zur Geschichte Israels im persischen Zeitalter*, 1964, pp. 158–61), contends for Ezra's mission in 398, but suggests that 'the seventh year of Artaxerxes' may be prompted by the seven years during which Bagoas the officer of 'another Artaxerxes' subjected the community in Jerusalem to special surveillance after the murder of Jesus by the High Priest Joḥanan (Josephus *Antiquities* XI. vii. 1) and that Ezra may be dated any time between 400 and 397. Possibly his mission was connected with the lifting of the strict control of Bagoas which Josephus mentions.

* Herodotus (III. 34) notes the office of cup-bearer at the Persian court as a high dignity.

could no longer pay tithes, and the rich were too materialistic to care to do so,[35] and even the priests were infected with the mood of the time and practised sordid peculation with inferior sacrifices[36] and dishonest decisions.[37]

The actual circumstances of Nehemiah's appointment, apart from the rather personal account in Nehemiah ii. 1–8, are quite unknown to us. From Nehemiah's commission, his credentials to the satrap of the province Beyond-the-River and to district governors,[38] his armed escort[39] and his official title of Tirshatha ('governor')[40] and *peḥāh* ('governor'), there is no doubt as to his official status in Judah, now a separate administrative district independent of the jurisdiction of Samaria, under which it had probably been since the end of Zerubbabel's office. But, though a Persian official, Nehemiah was primarily a Jew, whose loyalty to ancestral tradition was more ardent because of his absence from Jerusalem. He came to his post in 445, determined to make Jerusalem a bulwark of Judaism. It is symptomatic of his determination and his enthusiasm that three days after his arrival he made an inspection of the ruined walls.[41] The fact that he did so secretly by night with a few familiars[42] indicates the timidity of the local Jewish community, who dreaded the reaction which Nehemiah's particularist policy might provoke from their neighbours such as Sanballaṭ and Ṭobiah, the rulers of Samaria and Ammon, who were incidentally also Jews, but were more liberal. The situation has had its modern parallel in the Zionist movement of our time, which was not cordially supported by assimilationists in Western Europe for the same reason—until the National Socialist genocide left no choice.

The priority in Nehemiah's administration was the building of the walls of Jerusalem. He exploited his royal commission, which had already made materials available from the royal domains for the walls and a residence for the new commissioner,[43] and his recruitment of labour from all classes and quarters of the tiny province itself rallied interest in the focal point of the faith.[44] The lists of those parties and the sections of the wall seem at first glance like another dreary Biblical catalogue, but for those involved it was a veritable roll of honour, and there are few with any sense of the dramatic who can read the chapter with indifference with its list of historic place-names, which the memoirs of Nehemiah here share with our own romantic historical ballads. Nehemiah's work we have described as the restoration of the walls as they were under Manasseh (see above, pp. 37ff. and fig.I), with a significant shrinkage on the east of the south-east hill, where the massive terrace and buttress work on the steep slope to the Qidron was beyond the power of the small community now in Jerusalem, and indeed beyond their needs. The story too of the attempts of the neighbouring provincial governors to frustrate this work is dramatic and familiar in local Levantine history. They endeavoured to enervate the Jews by ridicule;[45] they suborned predatory bands from the nomads of the south, from beyond Jordan and from the coastal plain[46] to divert the Jews by raids on their homes in the provinces and on the working parties on the walls. But Nehemiah organized alternative shifts of labour and armed patrol and defence, and the raids had simply the effect of concentrating the outlying communities for the moment in Jerusalem. A conference with Nehemiah was proposed in the foothills north-west of Jerusalem,[47] but the treacherous purpose was rather obvious. Finally they threatened to denounce Nehemiah for exceeding his commission and aiming at rebellion. Whether the report was actually forwarded or not is uncertain, but probably Nehemiah called their bluff. More subtly the rival governors exploited the timidity and apathy of persons in Jerusalem, suborning one who was to profess an oracle to cause Nehemiah to seek sanctuary in the Temple for fear of his life, [48] and thereby to lose face with his people. This too Nehemiah resisted with the memorable words 'Should such a man as I flee?' The work was completed in fifty-two days.[49] This was rather in the nature of repair of the circumvallation, to be later perfected, as Josephus indicates, stating that the wall was completed after two years and four months.[50] The new capital was manned by an appeal to the provincial Jews in the district supplemented by a selection by lot.[51]

It was not the makeshift walls, however, which was to give character to Jerusalem. Nehemiah had to restore the community sense of the Jews as the people of God, a people of destiny, who were to be the living witnesses to the will and power of God, primarily to Israel and eventually through Israel to mankind. This had been undermined by various abuses. By intercourse with the more liberal Jews of Samaria and beyond Jordan, who were open to syncretism with pagan religion, the community about Jerusalem were losing their distinctive self-consciousness of status and calling, and mixed marriages had a like effect.[52] Within the community men were remiss in their tithes to the sanctuary and to the Levites,[53] and as an orthodox Eastern Jew Nehemiah was horrified to find that the Sabbath was not observed.[54] Debts were incurred by the poor at high interest, and mortgages of land and liberty were remorselessly foreclosed.[55] Nehemiah set himself to rectify those abuses, probably with the authority of the Deuteronomic law, and, with the practical resolution proper to his character and commission, he obliged the community through its representatives to seal a covenant binding them to refrain from those specific social and religious abuses.[56]* This, however, was no more than the foundation of the new community laid by Nehemiah the administrator; the complete reconstruction was the work of Ezra the scribe.

Among the papyrus documents from the military colony of Jews at Elephantine by Asswan there is one[57] dated 419 B.C. subscribed by one Ḥananiah, obviously a Jew, who cites a rescript from the capital to the Persian provincial governor Arsham directing the keeping of the seven-days festival of Unleavened Bread from the 14th to the 21st of Nisan.[58] This has immediate relevance to the missions of Nehemiah and Ezra. It indicates a regular office for Jewish religious affairs staffed by Jews, and, if this was not already operating before Nehemiah's mission, as it may well have been, Nehemiah's work must have done much to suggest its establishment. In any case the position of Ḥananiah and his particular interest authenticates the Biblical account of the appointment of Ezra 'the scribe', or rather here 'the secretary', 'of the law of the God of heaven'[59]† and his mission to promulgate the revised religious ordinances in Judah and in all Jewish communities in the satrapy Beyond-the-River.[60] In particular it increases the probability of the account of Ezra's commission in the Aramaic passage in Ezra vii. 12–26, which preserves the tradition of an imperial rescript.‡ Noth[61] feasibly explains the association of 'the law of God' and 'the law of the king' in Ezra vii. 26 by the suggestion that the Persian authorities endorsed a proposal officially submitted by responsible Eastern Jews, or possibly even, as we have already suggested, by a department for religious affairs in the provinces, and it has even been suggested that Ezra may have been one of these and have himself drafted the document.[62]

Setting out with a company of Jews from Babylon and the vicinity, Ezra travelled northwards and arrived at Jerusalem four months later.[63] Obviously he was busy meanwhile recruiting emigrants and expounding the Law according to his commission to integrate Jews throughout

* In the very free composition of the Chronicler, Nehemiah x at first sight seems to follow Nehemiah viii and ix, which properly belong to the later Ezra tradition. In any case it is not part of the Nehemiah Memoirs, but may nevertheless be a genuine tradition of Nehemiah's activity independent of Ezra, who is, significantly, not mentioned in the list of personalities in Nehemiah x. 1–27. Eissfeldt (*The Old Testament: An Introduction*, ET, 1965, p. 549) feasibly proposes that the account of Nehemiah's covenant in Nehemiah x was drawn not from Nehemiah's Memoirs but from Temple records.

† Later Jewish tradition coloured this official title in the light of the development of the scribal office of interpreter of the Law.

‡ Not necessarily the official document, however, according to H. H. Rowley, who argues that the grammar and orthography of the Aramaic is later than the time of Ezra (*Men of God*, 1963, pp. 217–18).

the Empire and particularly in the province Beyond-the-River.[64] Two months after his arrival in Jerusalem he presented the revised law to the people of Jerusalem assembled in a square by the Water Gate probably, that above the Spring of Giḥon in Nehemiah's restored wall. Obviously he had timed his presentation on the first day of the seventh month[65] in preparation for the formal endorsement of the Law at the Feast of Tabernacles,[66]* the chief festival of the agricultural year, which was a pilgrimage occasion. This had been the great occasion in the days of the Israelite settlement in Palestine when the tribes scattered throughout the land realized their solidarity in the sacramental renewal of the experience of God's power and grace in the Great Deliverance from Egypt and in the Covenant, and when they expressed their distinctive status and calling as the people of God by endorsing the moral and religious principles of the Covenant with solemn adjuration.[67] Probably never since the days of Joshua and the Judges had this sacrament ever had such point, a fact appreciated by the Chronicler, who says with a certain exaggeration 'for since the days of Joshua the son of Nun unto that day had not the children of Israel done so'.[68] There never was such a Covenant-sacrament indeed. For whereas the sacrament in the days of the judges reintegrated a sacral confederacy of the tribes who had never quite lost their sense of solidarity, this sacrament united the broken remnants of Israel, liquidated as a people and as a state in the Dispersion, but now henceforth to be reintegrated throughout the world under the authority of the Law.

There were, however, practical problems. Not all the principles of the Law whereby Israel declared herself the people of God could be immediately endorsed without qualification. The outstanding problem was that of mixed marriages. Nehemiah had already been vexed and frustrated to find that families of mixed marriages were speaking their mothers' tongue and doubtless inheriting their ethos and superstitions. He had inveighed against such unions and had laid the Jews under an oath to contract no more,[69] but had not dissolved existing marriages.

* It is well known that Ezra-Nehemiah and I and II Chronicles is one work from the hands of the Chronicler, generally dated much later than Ezra. In the case of the Books of Ezra and Nehemiah his composition from earlier sources is very free and the order perplexing. Though this passage appears in the Book of Nehemiah, of which about i-vii, xi-xiii is based on the memoirs of Nehemiah, the present passage is not part of these memoirs and really belongs to the tradition of Ezra, immediately following the account of Ezra's arrival in Jerusalem (Ezra vii. 9) in the narrative. The mention of Nehemiah the governor as present on this occasion has been taken as a redactional gloss, but since we do not know the date of Nehemiah's death and final demission of office and since the date of Ezra's mission is also doubtful (see above, n. 13) this must be an unwarranted conjecture.

Now with the sanction of the Law[70] this harsh measure was carried into effect, and the instrument of integration of Judaism now became the symbol of division.

With the hardening of the exclusive attitude of the community about Jerusalem more liberal Jews in the provinces, who included such families as that of Sanballaṭ the governor in Samaria in Nehemiah's time and Ṭobiah the governor of Ammon, were excluded from Judaism. The breach between Jews and Samaritans had begun to open with the antagonism between Sanballaṭ and Nehemiah. The fact that the Pentateuch of orthodox Judaism with no really substantial variations is also canonical Scripture—the only canonical Scripture of the Samaritans—indicates that the great schism is not to be dated in the time of Ezra notwithstanding the hostility of Samaritan tradition to Ezra. This of course begs the question of the extent and identity of the Law of Ezra,* but it cannot have been substantially different in spirit from the Law in the Pentateuch, and is unlikely in itself to have occasioned the schism. Such events are usually the result of more personal factors, which we see already in operation with Nehemiah and Ezra as opposed to the local Jews in Jerusalem, among whom the high priest had a grandson married to the daughter of Sanballaṭ.[71] It was no doubt the fierce patriotism of the returned Eastern Jews, the Zionists of their day, which brought about the Samaritan schism, which left such a bitter legacy both to Judaism and to Christianity (see below, pp. 119–20).

* The view of the older criticism is that Ezra's Law was the Priestly part of the Pentateuch, perhaps even the composite Pentateuch (J. Wellhausen, *Geschichte Israels* I, 1878, p. 421). Eissfeldt believes that P was already combined with the older sources of the Pentateuch by the time of Ezra, who imposed it upon the community in Jerusalem as Nehemiah viii-ix describes, *The Old Testament: an Introduction*, ET, P. R. Ackroyd, 1965, pp. 208, 556–7. The Pentateuch, however, and even the Priestly framework, is composite and very comprehensive, including various self-contained bodies of ritual and social laws such as Leviticus i-vii, xi-xv and the Holiness Code (Leviticus xvii-xxvi) and the narrative framework, itself composite. The whole together with the old sources J, E and D as a composite work was adopted as fixed canonical Scripture probably soon after Ezra's work. What Ezra presented and expounded to the people in preparation for the sacrament of the Covenant at the Feast of Tabernacles may be inferred from previous practice on that occasion in Joshua viii. 30–35; xxiv; Deuteronomy xxvii ff. etc. to have been an epitome of moral and ritual law relating to the integrity of the sacral community prefaced by a historical confession of God's grace and power in the great Deliverance from Egypt and the Covenant as the seal of the Divine election of Israel. On this occasion, however, since exposition and interpretation were involved 'from early morning till midday' (Nehemiah viii. 3), the substance of the tradition of the Law and Covenant with its historical prelude was certainly fuller than in the procedure in the old tradition of the Covenant-sacrament, though the same in substance. By the same token it was not so extensive as the whole canonical Pentateuch.

The sobriety and moral discipline of the Jews in Exile had won them the respect of the highest imperial authority, and by wholly creditable means had made possible the rehabilitation of the faith with Jerusalem as its metropolis. Persian toleration had even invested a scion of the Davidic House, Zerubbabel, with the authority of provincial governor, and though it had been expedient to discontinue that experiment the Jew Nehemiah had been subsequently appointed. But his had been a special commission, though he possibly held office till his death. It has been held that no other Jewish governor, so far as we know, was appointed. By 411, as is known from dated correspondence from the Jewish military colony at Elephantine, a governor Bigvai, rendered Bagoas in Josephus, was in office in Jerusalem. The name, however, though Persian, need not indicate that he was a Persian, and is in fact attested as the name of the head of a Jewish family who had returned with Zerubbabel from the Exile.[72] So Bigvai of the Elephantine papyrus may have been a Jewish governor. This whole matter is now elucidated by fiscal jar-handle stamps of the period. Among those which were stamped with the name of the province YHD (Yehud as in Daniel v. 13 and Ezra v. 1, 8; vii. 14) or with the five-pointed 'star of David', one from Jericho bore the stamp *yhd/'wryw* (Yehud/Uriyo).[73] Here Uriyo was at least the fiscal officer and perhaps even the provincial governor. In this case the orthodox Jewish name Uriyo is noteworthy. This is made much more explicit by the stamp found among a great many in a fourth-century stratum at Ramat Raḥel, the fortress between Jerusalem and Bethlehem, which reads *yhwd/yhw'zr/pḥw'* (Yehud/Yeho'azar/the Governor).[74] Here again the name denotes an orthodox Jew and the title is a variant of one of the titles of Nehemiah. Eventually the name of the province and its governor appears on coinage, as on a small silver coin from the fourth century stamped with the owl of Athene of Athens and the legend YHD, the name of the province, with the name of Hezekiah, who may have been the high priest mentioned by Josephus[75] as an able statesman at the end of the Persian period and the beginning of the Hellenistic age.[76] Whether or not Hezekiah on this coin and the governors Uriyo and Yeho'azar were high priests or secular officers like Nehemiah is of course uncertain, but the political status of the high priest as the successor of the pre-Exilic king from the Hellenistic era until the destruction of the Temple except at the end of the Hasmonaean period and under Herod the Great and Herod Agrippa I indicates that Hezekiah may well have been identical with Josephus' Hezekiah the high priest and that Uriyo and Yeho'azar may also have been priests.

The history of the Jewish community in the little Temple-state in the hills about Jerusalem between its rehabilitation under Nehemiah and Ezra and the end of the Persian period in 333 is, as we should expect, obscure. Jerome, however, retains a tradition, probably derived from Eusebius, that the Jews about Jerusalem were involved in the great revolt in Syria against Artaxerxes Ochus,[77] which Diodorus Siculus (xiv. 40–51) dates 351–349, a number of them being deported to the region of Hyrcania south and east of the Caspian Sea. On this, however, earlier sources are silent, though the fact that one of the Persian generals at this time was Orophernes suggests that the Book of Judith (mid second century B.C.), which records Judith's assassination of Holofernes, may retain a tradition of the revolt. According to the narrative Judith was not a native of Judah but of the great central plain, so that the book contains no reference to the Jerusalem community except a reference to the High Priest's congratulations. The anachronisms, moreover, are blatant, imposing the utmost caution in using the book as a historical source. But it is cast in the Persian period after the restoration of the Jerusalem community, conceivably retaining the tradition of the revolt against Artaxerxes Ochus, to the consequences of which, with evident exaggeration, Hecataeus of Abdera[78] apparently referred in stating 'the Persians formerly carried away many ten thousands of our people to Babylon'.

It has already been noticed that the exclusive Zionists returning to Jerusalem from the east had rebuffed the less rigid devotees of Yahweh in the province of Samaria, with whom the remanent Jews about Jerusalem were evidently disposed to live amicably, as indicated by the marriage of the grandson of Eliashib the High Priest of Nehemiah's time with the daughter of Sanballaṭ.[79] The fact that the Pentateuch, incorporating matter after the reforms of Nehemiah is canonical scripture both for the Jews and their bitter sectarian rivals the Samaritans indicates that the notorious schism must date after the time of Ezra, but probably not much later, since Ezra is an accursed figure for the Samaritans. A recent discovery of Aramaic MS. fragments with clay seals and coins in a cave at Abū Sinjeh in the dry, desolate hills north-north-west of Jericho* may permit us to date the schism more particularly. The dates on the papyri together with the coins carry the evidence down to 335 B.C. and give fuller information about the district governors of Samaria in the Persian period. One document dated in 354 names as governor Ḥananiyah the son of Sanballaṭ. As a child was quite regularly named after his grandfather the son of

* F. M. Cross, Jr., *Biblical Archaeological* XXVI, 1963, pp. 110–21. K. Galling (*op. cit.*, pp. 209–10) suggests that they were brought to the cave for safety when Samaria was menaced by the advance of Alexander in 331 B.C.

Ḥananiyah may well have been named Sanballaṭ. Now according to Josephus[80] Sanballaṭ, the governor of Samaria in the time of Darius III (336–330), gave his daughter Nicaso in marriage to Manasseh the brother of Jaddua the High Priest in Jerusalem, the son of John, or Jehoḥanan, the contemporary of Ezra. Thus the schism did not antedate the beginning of the reign of Darius III (336–330). But feeling already ran high between the two communities and public sentiment at Jerusalem was sufficiently strong to compel Manasseh to sacrifice his wife or his priestly office in Jerusalem. On his hesitating, Sanballaṭ undertook to build a temple to Yahweh on Mount Gerizim and instal him as priest with certain Levites who had contracted similar marriages.[81] We are not further informed about the building of this temple, which was destroyed by John Hyrcanus (134–104) (see below, p. 139), but it may be safely concluded that with its construction, probably between 336 and 330, the schism between Jew and Samaritan was complete.

NOTES FOR CHAPTER IV

1 Isaiah xliv. 28

2 Isaiah xlv. 1

3 The Cyrus Cylinder, A. L. Oppenheim, *Ancient Near Eastern Texts relating to the Old Testament* (ed. J. B. Pritchard), 2nd. ed. 1955, p. 315; T. Fish, *Documents from Old Testament Times* (ed. D. W. Thomas), 1958, p. 93

4 Ezra vii. 11 ff.

5 II Chronicles xxxvi. 21

6 Ezra i. 8

7 Ed. Meyer, *Die Entstehung des Judentums*, pp. 75 ff.; E. Sellin, *Geschichte des israelitisch-jüdischen Volkes* II, 1932, pp. 83 ff.

8 K. Galling, *Studien zur Geschichte Israels im persischen Zeitalter*, 1964, p. 56

9 Haggai i; Zechariah iv. 9; Ezra iii.

10 Haggai i. 6–11; ii. 15–17

11 Obadiah i. 1–9; Malachi i. 3–5

12 Archaeological evidence is adduced by N. Glueck, *Annual of the American Schools of Oriental Research* XV, 1935, pp. 138–40; J. Starcky, 'The Nabataeans', *Biblical Archaeologist* XVIII, 1955, pp. 84–106

13 Ezra i. 5

14 Isaiah lxv. 11; lxvi. 17

15 Haggai ii. 10–14

16 I Esdras iii ff.; v. 1–6. A. T. Olmstead *History of Palestine and Syria*, 1931; K. Galling, *Vetus Testamentum* II, 1952, pp. 18–36; D. W. Thomas, *Interpreter's Bible* VI, 1956, p. 1039

17 Ezra iv. 1–5; I Esdras v. 65–73

18 Zechariah ii. 6–9

19 Haggai ii. 6–8, 21–3

20 Haggai i. 4

21 Haggai i. 2

22 Zechariah i. 12–17

23 Following A. Jepsen 'Kleine Beiträge zum Zwölfprophetenbuch III', *Zeit-*

schrift für die alttestamentliche Wissenschaft LXI, 1945–48, pp. 95–114 and K. Galling, *Studien zur Geschichte Israels im persischen Zeitalter*, pp. 108 ff., who date the various visions and oracles of Zechariah according to their content rather than according to the precise dates assigned to each, which may well be editorial

24 Ezra vi. 15

25 Zechariah iii. 8; vi. 12–13

26 Cf. Isaiah xi. 1

27 Haggai ii. 6–9, 21–3; Zechariah; iii. 8; vi. 9–15

28 Zechariah iv. 3–14; vi. 9–10, 12–15

29 Zechariah vi. 11

30 Nehemiah ii. 17

31 Ezra iv. 7–8

32 Nehemiah ii. 17

33 Malachi iii. 5

34 Nehemiah v. 1–5

35 Malachi iii. 8–10; Nehemiah xiii. 10

36 Malachi i. 6–14

37 Malachi ii. 1–9

38 Nehemiah ii. 7

39 Nehemiah ii. 9

40 Nehemiah viii. 9; x. 1

41 Nehemiah ii. 11–12

42 Nehemiah ii. 12

43 Nehemiah ii. 8

44 Nehemiah iii

45 Nehemiah ii. 19; iv. 1–3

46 Nehemiah iv. 7–12

47 Nehemiah vi. 1–4

48 Nehemiah vi. 10–14

49 Nehemiah vi. 15

50 *Antiquities* XI. v. 8

51 Nehemiah vii. 4; xi. 1

52 Nehemiah xiii. 23–8

53 Nehemiah xiii. 10

54 Nehemiah xiii. 15–22

55 Nehemiah v. 1–14

56 Nehemiah x. 1–27

57 A. Cowley, *Aramaic Papyri of the Fifth Century B.C.*, 1923, No. 21

58 Cf. Exodus xii. 14–20

59 Ezra vii. 12

60 Ezra vii. 25

61 Noth, *History of Israel*, pp. 332–3

62 R. Kittel, *Geschichte des Volkes Israel*, III, part 2, 1929, p. 583; H. Schaeder, *Esra der Schreiber*, 1930, pp. 53 ff.; A. C. Welch, *Post-exilic Judaism*, 1935, p. 255

63 Ezra vii

64 Ezra vii. 25

65 Nehemiah viii. 2

66 Nehemiah viii. 14–18

67 Joshua viii. 30–5; xxxiv; Deuteronomy xxxvii ff. and particularly Deuteronomy xxxi. 9–13. Though this is post-Exilic it refers to practice in the monarchy and probably in the days of the settlement.

68 Nehemiah viii. 17

69 Nehemiah xiii. 23–8

70 Ezra x. 1 ff.

71 Nehemiah xiii. 28

72 Nehemiah vii. 19

73 N. Avigad, *Israel Exploration Journal* VII, 1957, pp. 146 ff.

74 Y. Aharoni, 'Excavations at Ramat Rahel', *Biblical Archaeologist* XXIV, 1961, pp. 110–11

75 *Contra Apionem* I. §§ 187–9

76 O. R. Sellers, *The Citadel of Bethsur*, 1933, p. 73; A. Reifenberg, 'Ancient Jewish Coins', *Journal of the Palestine Exploration Society* XIX, 1939, pp. 59–60, pl. IV, 2

77 Jerome, Olympiad 105; Eusebius (Chronicon, Armenian Version) and other later, and probably derivative, sources cited by E. Schürer, *A History of the Jewish People in the Time of Jesus*

Christ, ET. 1885, II ii. p. 223 *n*., and L. E. Browne, *Early Judaism*, 1929, 202–4

78 Cited by Josephus, *Contra Apionem* i. § 194

79 Nehemiah xiii. 28

80 *Antiquities* XI. vii. 2

81 Josephus, *Antiquities* XI. viii. 2

V

THE DEFENCE OF THE FAITH

. . . and the same horn made war with the saints. (*Daniel vii. 21*)

Darius I of Persia, under whose beneficent despotism the Temple was rebuilt, crossed the Hellespont and at immortal Marathon kindled the spirit of hostility among the Greeks and a morale which, fostered by the victories at Salamis and Plataea, was eventually to find expression in the great Eastern adventure of Alexander the Great. In 334 Alexander crossed the narrow straits and defeated the Persians in open battle at the River Granicus; in the following months, without the co-operation of a fleet, he had seized all the Mediterranean ports of Asia Minor and in 333 met and defeated the Persian army under Darius III at Issus, near which he founded Alexandretta. The Phoenician cities Arad, Byblos and Sidon submitted to the conqueror, and Tyre, confident in her off-shore island rock, was reduced after seven months' arduous siege. Damascus received a Greek governor, and Alexander passed south to Egypt, leaving a Greek governor in the city of Samaria.* In Egypt he was received as a liberator, and with his foundation of Alexandria in 331, the first of many Greek cities in the East, he signalized a new era of Western influence in the East which was to remain without serious challenge for about a thousand years until the conquests of Islam. His empire as a political structure disintegrated at his death.

Alexander's great commanders and governors fought for their claims to succeed their master or to assert their regional independence. Passing over the tedious story of this ignoble struggle, we may note that as far as Palestine was concerned the conflict lay between Ptolemy

* The tradition that Alexander visited Jerusalem before proceeding to Egypt (Josephus *Antiquities* XI. viii; Babylonian Talmud, Yoma 69a), according to Josephus after the fall of Gaza, is quite unreliable, being full of blatant anachronisms. As Alexander was in Egypt seven days after the fall of Gaza a visit to Jerusalem was virtually impossible.

Lagos the governor of Egypt and his descendants and Seleucus the commander of Alexander's heavy infantry, the famous Macedonian phalanx, and his descendants, who had served themselves heirs to the eastern provinces from inland Syria to Lower Mesopotamia. Palestine was desirable to both. Geographically one with Syria, it was a necessary economic adjunct to Egypt, with the seaports and timber of Lebanon. Moreover if Ptolemy wished to keep the advantage for Alexandria which the depression of the Syrian seaports under Alexander had given her and to preserve unchallenged the monopoly of South Arabian trade by the Red Sea and Gaza it was vital for him to control Palestine. He was near enough to do so and, unlike his rival, was unhampered by an enemy in his rear, and so Egypt dominated Palestine until defeated by Antiochus III in 198 B.C. at the Battle of Paneas (modern Banias) among the foothills of Hermon.

At this time Jerusalem, though the metropolis of a far-flung Jewish Diaspora whose most important centres were Egypt and Mesopotamia, was the capital of a small province the utmost limit of which in the western foothills and the southern Highlands reached scarcely twenty-five miles. Throughout this district under the authority of the Law and the priesthood of the restored Temple men were very sensitive to the impingement of the new western humanism on the traditional attitude of faith, or response to revealed religion, the more so as it was apparently welcomed among all the neighbours of the Jews, promulgated by the imperial power and prestige of the Ptolemies and Seleucids and promoted through the Hellenistic institutions in the various Greek cities which proliferated at this time throughout the east including Palestine itself. With the ready assimilation of the gods of the nature-religions of the Near East to those of the Greeks distinctive features in the life of the inhabitants were obliterated, and with the tendency of sophisticated Jews also to assimilate Greek culture the more conservative apprehended a similar obliteration of the traditional faith and way of life. The opposition of Jewish orthodoxy to the prevailing conformity emphasized the inherent particularism of Judaism, which in consequence presented itself to the Seleucid administration as a gesture of stubborn defiance. The tension was accentuated when Judah fell directly under the political power of the Ptolemies and the Seleucids, which she was powerless to resist.

The Jews' first experience of Hellenistic suzerainty was under the Ptolemies, whom the stricter of them resented. So when Antiochus III (the Great) of Syria defeated Egypt at Banias in 198 B.C. they hailed him as a deliverer, and their optimism was for the moment apparently justified since Antiochus requited their cordial reception of him by special favours including remission of taxes, support in an extension of the Temple-precinct and an endowment for the Temple service.[1] The enlargement of the Temple may be noted in the conclusion of the celebrated panegyric of famous men by the Alexandrine Jewish philosopher Ben Sira (Ecclesiasticus l. 1–21), which may be quoted as illustrative of the security of Jerusalem in this halcyon time and of the prestige of the High Priest Simon, probably Simon II, entitled the Just (*c.* 220–198):

Simon the High Priest the son of Onias,
Who in his life repaired the shrine,
And in his days strengthened the Temple.
He laid the foundations of the high double walls,
The high retaining walls of the Temple precinct;
In his days a basin for water was beaten out,
A bronze basin like the sea in circumference;
It was he that took thought for his people that they should not fall,
And fortified the city to withstand a siege.
How glorious was he when the people gathered round him
As he came out of the veiled portion of the shrine [the Holy of Holies]
As the morning star among the clouds,
And the moon when it is full,
Like the sun shining on the Temple of the Most High,
And as the rainbow giving light in heavy clouds,
Like rose-blooms in the day of first-fruits,
Like lilies by a spring of water,
Like a green shoot of Lebanon in summer,
As fire with incense in a censer,
As a vessel of solid beaten gold
Embellished with every kind of precious stone,
As an olive tree budding for fruit,
Yea, as a cypress towering among the clouds!
When he put on his glorious robe
And was proudly and perfectly invested,
Stepping up to the holy altar,
He made the precinct of the sanctuary glorious,
As he received the portions from the hands of the priests,
Himself standing by the hearth of the altar
With a garland of his brethren around him;
He was like a young cedar on Lebanon,
And they surrounded him like palm stems,
All the sons of Aaron in their splendour,
With the offering of the Lord in their hands
Before the whole assembly of Israel;
And finishing the service at the altar,

Arranging the offering of the Most High, the Almighty,
He stretched forth his hand to the libation-vessel
And made libation of the blood of the grape;
He poured it out at the base of the altar,
A sweet-smelling savour to the Most High, the King of All;
Then shouted the sons of Aaron,
They sounded the trumpets of beaten metal,
They made a great noise to be heard
As a remembrance before the Most High.
Then all the people together hastened,
And fell on their faces to the ground,
Doing obeisance to their Lord
Almighty, God Most High.
The choristers also praised him with their voices,
In the whole Temple there was made sweet melody.
And the people besought the Lord Most High
In prayer before the Merciful
Until the worship before the Lord was ended
And they had finished his service.
Then coming down he lifted up his hands
Over the whole assembly of the sons of Israel
To give the blessing by the Lord with his lips
And to glory in his name;
And they bowed down a second time
To receive the blessing from the Most High.

Jewish hopes in Antiochus III were unduly optimistic. Egypt and Syria alike represented the new cultural and political forces released in the Near East, humanism based on confidence in the adequacy of human nature and intellect to solve the problems of life, and the philosophy that man was the measure of the universe. The Hebrews too had already appreciated the significance of human factors in the life of the individual and the community, and this is expressed in their historiography in the first main narrative source of the Pentateuch, in the Story of the Davidic Succession in II Samuel and I Kings i–ii and in empiric moral philosophy in the Book of Proverbs from the early monarchy to the Greek period. But for the Hebrews human factors were governed by, and related to, the purpose of an active God, not to static ideals adduced from human conduct and aspirations, a God who could not be expressed but only addressed in response to his confrontation of his people in history with its recurrent moral challenge or in the moral crises in the life of the individual or of society. God's categorical imperative was apprehended by Israel in the Law, the absolute authority which gave coherence to the community and integrated the

Jews despite political eclipse and the Dispersion. In a small canton in a politically significant area between the Hellenistic states in Egypt and Syria, the Jews were inevitably involved with the new Western culture.

This problem to the Jewish community, all the more acute because it was an ecclesiastical polity under the authority of priesthood and Law, was accentuated by administrative problems. These were not so embarrassing under the Ptolemies, irksome as their rule was felt to be, but under the Seleucids difficulties multiplied and intensified. More and more heavily engaged on their open Eastern frontier, where the Parthians claimed the heritage of Persia in Mesopotamia, the Seleucids exerted an ever closer surveillance over the life of the provinces. They were under indemnity to Rome, who had permanently checked their power short of the Taurus Mountains. Their resources thus limited, taxation was heavy[2] and their attention was focused on Palestine and the Syrian coast and on Egypt and they were very sensitive to disloyalty among the Jews and others so near the Egyptian frontier, which was indeed encouraged by the engagement of the best Syrian troops on the Eastern front. Jewish opposition to the Hellenistic suzerains was motivated by ideological antipathy and administrative grievances. These were not sharply differentiated, and the one accentuated the other.

Adjustment to life in a pagan environment under a pagan suzerain was no new problem to the Jews. After the liquidation of the monarchy in 586 B.C. the prophet Jeremiah saw the possibility of living unobtrusively as a good Jew and a loyal citizen of Babylon, and Nehemiah was no less ardent a Zionist because he was a Persian official. The Book of Daniel reflects this problem of dual allegiance, especially in the first part of the book, which depicts Daniel surviving various menaces for his faith while a prominent servant of the Babylonian state. These stories of Daniel may have originated in more liberal Jewish circles in Babylon as a guide and a stimulus to the exiles in their perplexity in a foreign milieu. The problem was to be ever with the Jews until their establishment in an independent state first under their native princes in the second and first centuries B.C. and then in our own time. Meanwhile the Daniel tradition was adapted to the critical situation under the Seleucid suzerains, to which the second part of the Book of Daniel (vii ff.) is particularly relevant. This book is an important source for the history of the time. It attests not only current events but also the ideological conflict in Judaism itself, forced upon it by the new humanism, and in its apocalyptic, or glimpse beyond historical incidentals, it indicates the strength and confidence of Jewish resistance, grounded in its age-long faith in the Reign of God triumphant over the forces of Chaos.

In the crisis brought to Judaism by the new régime there were various reactions. Some like the High Priest Onias III (*c.* 198–174 B.C.) were prepared to contribute to the development of contemporary society in the new political environment, but as loyal Jews. From the Books of the Maccabees[3] it is obvious that there were many Jews who of their own accord welcomed the new culture and were prepared to compromise in various degrees. Many in all sincerity welcomed the opening of the land to the new influences from the West, anticipating mutual advantage to Jew and Gentile. The priests in general, the old aristocracy of the realm and now the political leaders of the community, effected a statesman's compromise which was to be the policy of their successors, familiar in the New Testament as the Sadducees. But among them some, like Jason and Menelaus the puppet high priests who ousted Onias, promoted the Greek way of life through motives of personal ambition and to ingratiate themselves with their Greek masters and win the support they lacked from their own people. Among the opponents of Hellenism the enthusiasm of men varied in degree from sane and sober patriotism to the most intense fanaticism, from the single-hearted zeal of the Ḥasīdīm ('Those Loyal to the Covenant') to the material nationalism and worldly opportunism which became fully apparent with Jonathan the successor of the heroic Judas the Maccabee. The heritage of Israel, crystallized in the Law hedged about by the ritual provisions of Ezra, was in any case preserved, but in such bitter conflict that the iron entered into the soul of Judaism, resulting in a hard legalism which, though conserving the worthy inheritance of Israel, hindered its fuller development. Yet in this great crisis, which was to bring so many unlovely features to light, the glory of the protagonists of Jewish independence and freedom of conscience cannot be quite obscured.

The rift among the Jews in Jerusalem was opened in the latter part of the third century, when Onias II, or Joḥanan (*c.* 245–220 B.C.) used his high-priestly authority to withhold the tribute due to Egypt. In the crisis so precipitated the Jews were dearly rescued by the diplomatic

---

1. Rock-scarp and fragment of the south wall of pre-Israelite and Israelite Jerusalem on the south-east hill with an irrigation channel originally used to fill the Biblical Old, or Lower, Pool.

2. Scarp on the south-east of the south-east hill prepared for the foundations of the pre-Israelite and Israelite fortifications.

tact of one Josephus of the House of Tobias. In gratitude for his efficient, if rather ruthless, service Ptolemy entrusted him and his family with fiscal office in Palestine. Thus Jerusalem was torn between two factions, the one striving to resist foreign influence in politics and culture, the other ready to submit and compromise. The former rallied round the House of Onias; the latter followed that of Tobias.

This party rancour became acute under the Seleucids, who ransacked the Empire to fill an empty treasury. Now in Jerusalem one Simon of the House of Tobias, the commander of the Temple guard, reported to Apollonius the Syrian governor in North Palestine that the Temple treasury contained great wealth which, not being dedicated to sacred purposes, was at the disposal of the king. The royal chamberlain Heliodorus was immediately dispatched, but learned from Onias III that the money did not amount to what Simon had reported and that in any case it was partly for the relief of widows and orphans and partly deposits. Action was stayed, and Jewish legend has elaborated the incident, relating the deliverance to a miraculous apparition.[4] Whatever actually happened, Simon was foiled. He covered his confusion by denouncing Onias as one disaffected to the royal authority. Onias journeyed to the court at Antioch to clear himself and adjust the affairs of the Jewish community at Jerusalem. His brother Jason (Hebrew Joshua) in his absence supplanted him with the support of the Tobiads and a substantial bribe, which he hoped to recover once he was appointed High Priest, for after the reforms of Ezra in the new ecclesiastical community the priests drew levies from sacrifices, compensation for ritual disabilities and from tithes on the produce of the land. Onias therefore took refuge in the sanctuary at Daphne near Antioch, and the political party he represented in Jerusalem went into eclipse.

In 175 B.C. the Seleucid prince Antiochus assumed the authority of his murdered brother and the title Antiochus IV *Theos Epiphanes*, 'the god manifest'.* Antiochus was, in respect of his grandiose ambitions and his humour, where the grim was mixed with the racy, a character like Nero, though saner. Like him he was a lavish patron of the arts and culture of Greece to the point of obsession, seeing in this a medium

* The king among the ancient Semites including the Hebrews was the temporal guarantee of the Order of God. As such among the Hebrews he was described as the son of God (Psalm ii). In Israel this described the social and moral relationship of the king to Divine authority. But in ancient Canaan and the pagan East it was capable of grosser interpretation.

---

3. Royal tombs at the south of the south-east hill, including tombs of the kings of the House of David, destroyed by quarrying in the Roman period.

of the unification of his empire, which would eliminate such islands of exclusive nationalism as Jerusalem. In this he was supported by the usurper Jason. It is recorded that Jason had a gymnasium built in Jerusalem on the Greek pattern, which was suspect as a seedbed of idleness and freethinking which struck at the traditional roots of Jewish particularism, the home and the sanctuary. The extent of Jason's apostasy from Jewish ideals is indicated by his levy of a special fund as his contribution to the games of Herakles, the Greek adaptation of the old Semitic deity Baal Melqart, the Lord of the City, at Tyre, whom Jezebel had once tried to introduce to Israel in the days of Elijah.

Jason, however, was himself supplanted by Menelaus (Menahem) of the House of Tobias by the same methods as he had used to supplant Onias. He fled to Transjordan, and the Jews had in Menelaus (171–161 B.C.) one who was 'not so much a high priest as a raging wild beast'.[5]

Menelaus soon found that it was easier to promise the amount of tribute he had guaranteed than to raise the sum. Summoned to Antioch as a defaulter, he found the king absent and took the opportunity to procure by bribery the death of Onias, the last High Priest who had been worthy of the office. It was believed that the money for the bribe was procured by the plunder of some of the sacred vessels of the Temple, and a riot broke out in Jerusalem, which, however, was quashed by Menelaus, who enlisted the Syrian help by the usual means.[6]

With Egypt as the only direction in which the Seleucids could expand and recruit their diminished resources, Judah on the flank of the advance into the Delta was more and more closely involved in Syrian politics, and it is from the first expedition of Antiochus IV against Egypt in 170 B.C. that relations between the Jews and the Seleucids deteriorates. Checked in Egypt in 170 B.C., Antiochus returned in desperate need of money, and was admitted by Menelaus to the Temple, where he appropriated sacred vessels of value and offerings. The natural opposition of the Jews was suppressed by violence.[7] Jewish resentment naturally intensified, and in Antiochus' second expedition to Egypt in 168 a rumour spread that he was dead. Actually, with Egypt at his mercy, he was confronted by the Roman ambassador Lucius Popillius Laenas, who presented him with the famous ultimatum, drawing a circle round Antiochus where he stood and defying him to step outside it until he renounced his claims on Egypt or declared for war with Rome.[8] Meanwhile Jason, the expelled High Priest, invaded Palestine with a thousand men. Thanks to support in the city, they took it, but Menelaus had time to take refuge in the 'acropolis'.* Frustrated in

* This may be identical with the *akra*, the citadel on the south-west hill (see above, p. 43 ff).

Egypt, which he had actually invaded in anticipation of an Egyptian offensive in Syria, Antiochus was very sensitive about the loyalty of the Jews, and reinstated Menelaus by force of arms, with reprisals against his opponents. A mercenary Philippos was left with a garrison as military governor of Jerusalem. Throughout the district of Jerusalem sacrifice to the gods of the Greek state was imposed as a test of loyalty on penalty of death. Finally in December 168 B.C. on the site of the altar of God in the Temple precinct an altar was built to Olympian Zeus, to which the Book of Daniel alludes in cryptic language as 'the abomination which makes desolate'.[9] This (Hebrew *shiqquṣ hash-shōmēm*) is a parody of 'the Lord of Heaven' (*ba'al hash-shāmayim*), the Syrian version of Olympian Zeus, an image of which, reputedly with the handsome features of Antiochus, was also erected. Insult was added to injury. The pagan altar was dedicated with the sacrifice of a sow.[10]

But there were those who were determined to defy Antiochus to the death. In anticipation of a struggle they had organized themselves as a party of men and women consumed with a zeal for the Law. They were the Ḥasīdīm, 'Those Loyal to the Covenant', of which the Law was the expression. The Second Book of the Maccabees is full of anecdotes of their fortitude. Two women who had dared to circumcise their sons according to ancestral observance had their children bound hanging from their breasts and were driven thus through the city till they were finally thrown from the wall to end their sufferings on the rocks far below.[11] One woman saw the slaughter of her seven sons before she herself died a martyrs' death.[12] The first son, on refusing to comply with the pagan dictates, had his feet and hands cut off and his tongue torn out. Then he was put into a large cauldron and boiled alive before the eyes of his mother and brothers. But the mother, it is said, stood the ordeal with supernatural calm and when finally the youngest son, of three years, was killed before her eyes she glorified God that they had refused to deny him, and gladly resigned herself to the same fate. It is recorded in the same source how certain Jews, determined to keep the Sabbath, which was now profaned by every type of debauchery, especially in the sacred precinct, crept into some of the limestone caves of the vicinity to keep it there. They were discovered, and the Greek garrison kindled huge fires and roasted or suffocated the victims.[13] It is generally held that the author of this source is guilty of picturesque exaggeration, but our familiarity with the horrors of Buchenwald, Belsen and Auschwitz must qualify this view.

In desperation some sought refuge in Egypt, where a son of Onias III had founded a sanctuary at Leontopolis in the district of Heliopolis near the present Cairo.* Others retired to the Wilderness of Judah. Of the latter we have notice, probably, in the Epistle to the Hebrews (xi. 37–8):

> They were tempted; they were slain with the sword; they wandered about in sheepskins and goatskins, being destitute, afflicted, tormented, of whom the world was not worthy; they wandered in deserts and in mountains, in dens and caves of the earth.

If, as we believe, the Sect of the New Covenant at Qumran, who left the famous Dead Sea Scrolls, came out on the question of the legitimate high-priesthood after the usurpation of Menelaus, this may have been the origin of that community,† though no certain *terminus post quem* can be assigned before the time of John Hyrcanus (134–104 B.C.), whose coins have been found in the excavation of the monastic settlement at Khirbet Qumrān.[14]

One of those who clung grimly to the ancestral faith and ordinances was Mattathias, who claimed descent from Asamoneus, Hebrew Hashmon, of a minor priestly family. Anticipating trouble with the Syrian authorities, he had withdrawn to the home of his family in the village of Modein in the western foothills some six miles east of Lydda. He was marked as an influential person and was offered rich inducements to conform to at least the outward ritual of Hellenistic polytheism.[15] But Mattathias stubbornly and consistently refused to compromise. Indeed one day, on seeing a Jew offering sacrifice according to the royal decree, the old man was so enraged that he rushed upon the apostate and slew both him and the supervising commissioner. This was the impulsive act of an outraged patriot and was no part of any organized resistance, so Mattathias fled forthwith with his sons to the mountains of Judah, where the caves offered them ready refuge, as always in the troubled history of Palestine. But Jewish indignation, provoked by fierce persecution, wanted but a leader and an initial impulse and direction. Now Mattathias and his sons in the hills were joined by Jewish patriots, and the resistance steadily gained strength and organization.

* Josephus *Antiquities* XIII. xiii, 1–3. W. F. Petrie claimed to have found the remains of this temple at Tell al-Yahūdīyeh, which, he claimed, corroborated Josephus' statement that the temple and, Petrie would add, the environment, was a replica of that in Jerusalem though on a smaller scale, W. F. Petrie, *Egypt and Israel*, 1911, pp. 100–10.

† This is indicated in the Habakkuk Commentary, where there are repeated references to the opposition of *mōrēh haṣṣedheq* (possibly 'the True Dispenser of the Law') and 'the Evil Priest' (*hakkōhēn hārāshā'*, which may be a parody of *hakkōhēn haggādhōl*, 'the High Priest').

A Syrian garrison now occupied a strong citadel on the south-west hill of Jerusalem and the ancient city of David on the south-east hill (see above, pp. 43 ff.), and it became increasingly difficult for Jews to observe even the most minute of their ancestral rituals. They would foregather unobtrusively to keep their traditional customs; but Syrian patrols discovered them, and since the Jews forebore to fight on the Sabbath day they were butchered in cold blood. Such incidents won Mattathias the support of the Jewish Pietists, the Ḥasīdīm, and soon the patriots were a considerable force of active guerillas. Bands of them would suddenly appear in Jewish villages, slay the pagan priests without mercy, wreck the heathen altars, circumcise Jewish boys in defiance of the Syrian ban, and regain the cover of the hills before the Syrians could retaliate. Mattathias gave the initial impulse to the movement which was ultimately to secure the independence of his people. The achievement of religious freedom and the foundation of the new Jewish state, however, was the work of his sons, of whom Judas alone, designated by his father as the leader,[16] was named 'the Maccabee'.*

Judas was a man born for leadership and heroic action, one of the many fine guerilla leaders whom Palestine has bred, whom the writer of I Maccabees describes with evident pride in the cadence of Hebrew poetry:

> He did on his breastplate like a giant,
> And girt on his warlike harness.
> He set battles in array,
> And protected his host with his sword.
> He was like a lion in his deeds
> And like a lion's whelp roaring for prey.
>
> (I Maccabees iii. 3–4)

Judas was soon to have his mettle tried. Apollonius, the Syrian commander in Samaria, gathered a considerable force and met Judas just north of Jerusalem. His army was routed and he himself slain. As a personal trophy Judas took his sword, which he carried throughout all his campaigns. Another force under Seron was defeated near Beth-ḥoron by the guerillas of Judas, who were greatly outnumbered. The Seleucid forces to be sure were merely provincial auxiliaries, the main Greek troops being engaged against the Parthians on the eastern front; the maquis in the hills of Judah has always been congenial terrain for brigands and irregulars, especially for natives of the region; but above all the Jews, thanks to their conviction that they fought to preserve

* Meaning either 'the Hammerer' or 'Piercer' (Aramaic *maqq^{e}bhay*) or 'the Quencher' (*makk^{e}bhay*). Both forms are found in Rabbinic literature.

the very spiritual source and expression of their distinctive being, had a coherence which the enemy lacked, and it was soon apparent that the forces of Jewish resistance had effectively coalesced under a fine guerilla leader.

The king being engaged in the East, Lysias as regent directed the campaign in Judah. His general Gorgias, in excess of zeal, allowed himself to be drawn from his camp at Emmaus, modern Amwās, in the Valley of Aijalon, into an expedition against Judas in the mountains. Ever mobile and alert, Judas shifted ground, leaving fires blazing to suggest that the camp was still occupied. While Gorgias and his men swooped on the decoy, Judas was far away sacking the Syrian base at Emmaus.

Early the following year, 164 B.C., Lysias in person led fresh forces to Judah by the Wādī 's-Sanṭ (the Biblical Vale of Elah) to Bethṣur* at the head of the pass north of Hebron (see above, p. 21). The sequel is somewhat obscured by the zeal of the writer of I Maccabees,[17] who claims a victory for his hero Judas, his narrative being obviously coloured by the tradition of David and Goliath, which was localized farther down the pass.[18] Lysias may have avoided a decisive action. At this point I Maccabees (iv. 26 ff.), generally more reliable than II Maccabees, is very laconic in the actual account of the encounter, stating that Lysias withdrew after a loss of five thousand men (34–5). Nothing is said of an agreement, and the writer passes on immediately to the restoration of the Temple worship after due cleansing and rededication (36 ff.). II Maccabees xi on the other hand, though exaggerating the Syrian losses, must be taken seriously in the much fuller communication regarding the agreement between Lysias and the Jews, which the regent undertook to have confirmed by the king (13–14). Strongly in favour of the reliability of II Maccabees xi. 14 ff. is the fact that in the subsequent royal rescript cited in verses 27–33 no mention is made of the restoration of the Temple, and emphasis is laid upon the High Priest Menelaus as an intermediary in the agreement, who would certainly not have been accorded this role in a free composition of the writer of either book of the Maccabees. Here the citation of a communication from the Roman embassy to Antioch (xi. 34–7), which there is no good reason to suspect, is highly significant, since already in 190 Rome had defeated Antiochus III at Magnesia and had subsequently limited his enterprises in Asia Minor by the Peace of Apamea (188) and in 168 had frustrated the progress of Antiochus IV in Egypt, and in 164 a Roman embassy in Antioch reinforced the Peace of Apamea. Know-

* 'Through Idumaea to Bethṣur' (I Maccabees iv. 29). Bethṣur is Khirbet aṭ-Ṭubeiqeh, excavated by O. R. Sellers (*The Citadel of Bethsur*, 1933).

ing that the Jews were not unaware of the power of Rome in the East, and understanding that with her interest in Egypt Rome would not be indifferent to the situation in Palestine and in view of Roman objections to alleged violations of the Peace of Apamea, Lysias could hardly do other than make a truce and withdraw from Bethṣur. His losses may be exaggerated, even at the lowest estimate of five thousand, and may have been largely sustained in his recovery of Idumaean strongholds which had been recently taken by the Jews[19] rather than in a pitched battle, though to be sure Judas' army had grown considerably since his recent successes. At any rate Lysias withdrew from Bethṣur, having provisionally conceded to the Jews liberty of worship, which was apparently confirmed by Antiochus, possibly under Roman pressure.

So the Temple was cleansed from the contamination of paganism and rededicated on the 25th of the month Kislew in 164 at the festival of the winter solstice, thereafter called the Feast of Ḥanukkah, or 'Dedication'.[20] A garrison of Syrian troops, however, still occupied the *akra*, or citadel (see above, pp. 43 ff).

During this period it must be remembered that with the exception of Jerusalem and the surrounding district to a radius of some twenty miles there was no resistance on the part of the natives to assimilation to Hellenism, and the vicissitudes of the times had caused many of the moderate Jews to migrate to those regions, where tensions were not so acute. The aggression of Judas and his party now made the inhabitants of those districts nervous and brought those isolated Jewish communities into jeopardy and occasionally involved them in violence, like the Jews in the Arab states after the Zionist coup in Palestine in 1947–48. This involved Judas and his party in a policy which though essentially defensive might easily give the impression of aggression. As a result the Jews were evacuated under arms by Judas from Transjordan and by Simon from Galilee.[21] But in Judah Joseph and Azariah, left on guard, were emulous and impulsive and, exceeding their commission,[22] were defeated in their offensive in the coastal plain. Accordingly on his return Judas had to restore the situation *vis-à-vis* the neighbouring Idumaeans in the coastal plain and the mountains about Hebron.

Antiochus, who died in Ispahan in 163, had succeeded his murdered brother Seleucus, whose son Demetrius was the legitimate heir. The king on his death-bed complicated the situation by designating his own son his heir and nominating one of his Companions, Philip, as regent in place of Lysias,[23] who already had tutelage of the young prince. Lysias had no mind to relinquish his authority, and commotion was to follow. In view of the unsettled position Syrian troops were not numerous in Palestine, and the Jews took advantage to fortify the Temple precinct and to secure their flank by fortifying Bethṣur.[24] Meanwhile Judas besieged the Syrian garrison and their Jewish sympathizers in the citadel.[25] In 163, however, Lysias, in response to an appeal by the High Priest Menelaus and the Hellenizers, invaded again, bringing the young king with him,[26] resolved on concluding the Jewish affair without the usual distraction from home. Advancing by Bethṣur,[27] he compelled Judas to raise the siege on the citadel and come south to stem his advance on Jerusalem. The Syrians contained the Jewish garrison in Bethṣur and continued their advance to the north with an impressive array of Indian war-elephants, one to each company of a thousand infantry,[28] and a proportionate force of cavalry. A fierce battle was fought at Bethzachariah,* but the Jews were forced to withdraw on Jerusalem, where they were besieged in the Temple precinct. Judas and his followers were in danger of losing all that they had gained, but two circumstances saved the situation. That year was a Sabbatical year, when in accordance with Levitical law the land lay fallow.[29] In the midst of desolation the Syrians suffered more than the Jews they were besieging, who had the advantage of stores. Lysias, moreover, was anxious for a settlement which would release him to encounter his rival Philip, who had returned meanwhile from the East with the main armies of the Empire.[30] So the Jews had their religious freedom confirmed, but the fortifications of the Temple were dismantled.[31] As a gesture to Jewish opinion, and possibly to split the opposition, Menelaus was replaced by Alkimus, who, unlike Menelaus, was of Aaronic descent.[32] The internal disorders of the Seleucid Empire, which had saved Judas in this crisis, were to be henceforth chronic, regularly nullifying any advantage which a successful commander might secure, and were the chief means whereby the successors of Judas rose to prominence.

Now a significant cleavage opened in the ranks of the Jews. The moderates entered into communication with Demetrius, who by this time had secured the Syrian throne. The Ḥasīdīm felt that with the restoration of religious liberty the work of Judas and his party was done. The latter, however, were reluctant to give up their power, and their ambitions seem to be indicated by their opposition to Alkimus (161–159 B.C.), who was installed and maintained by force of arms. On an appeal by the new High Priest and the moderates the general Nicanor was sent down. He was apparently disposed for reconciliation,[33] ready to deal with Judas as one soldier with another, but his hand was

* Bayt Zakāriyeh about 11 miles south of Jerusalem and about 6 miles north of Bethṣur.

forced by the home government, and he was forced to open hostilities with Judas, probably with insufficient forces. At Adasa at the head of the Pass of Beth-ḥoron* he was killed and his army fled. Judas and his men hacked off the head and hand of Nicanor, which they set up as a gruesome trophy before the worshippers in the Temple, and 'the day of Nicanor' passed into the Jewish calendar as a feast-day.

In 161 Bacchides was appointed to the command in Palestine. In face of his large army and the opposition of the Ḥasīdīm as well as the more liberal Jews many in Judas' army withdrew, considering his cause desperate and hopeless. Left with some eight hundred fighting men,[34] Judas attacked courageously between Berea (al-Bīreh between Baytīn and Ramallah) and Beth-ḥoron, and actually carried the Syrian lines. But they were eventually split up and surrounded, and when Judas fell the survivors fled. So Judas died as he had lived, fighting against heavy odds. His brothers recovered his body for burial, probably agreeing to disband their followers.

But the most ardent of the partisans would not accept the situation, and Jonathan, the younger brother of Judas, was easily persuaded to lead them, and indeed the intensifying disorders in the Syrian state encouraged the opposition. Bacchides, the most successful of the Syrian generals, fortified key positions in the approaches to Jerusalem and took hostages from the leading Jewish families, but Jonathan kept the field with his guerillas in the semi-desert region north-east of Jerusalem, reaching eventually an agreement with Bacchides and settling at Michmash on the edge of this region which slopes towards Jericho.

From this point onwards the dynastic disputes of the Seleucids encouraged the growth of the power of Jonathan and his family. Jonathan himself was an unprincipled opportunist, and under him the unashamed material ambitions of his house made the breach with the Ḥasīdīm irrevocable. Competing Syrian pretenders courted the support of this guerilla chief, who was thus able to win recognition and arm forces, to secure the restoration of hostages who had been held against his party, and to occupy and fortify Jerusalem. He was appointed High Priest by one of the rivals, and granted rebate of taxes by another with permission to rebuild Jerusalem out of the royal revenues. Jonathan, however, was over-sanguine in his exploitation of the situation and perished in 142 as he had lived, in an entanglement of worldly intrigue.

* There are four sites Khirbet 'Adasa in the same vicinity, one about 4 miles south-east of Beth-ḥoron, two within half a mile of each other about 7 miles east of Beth-ḥoron, and another about 3 miles south-east of them. The first seems to be indicated as the site of the battle, which Josephus locates 30 furlongs from Beth-ḥoron (*Antiquities* XII. x. 5).

Jonathan's status was inherited by Simon, the wisest of the Hasmonaean brothers. He was equally adept at exploiting the political embarrassment of the Seleucids, but with more finesse and with less offence to the susceptibilities of the Jews. The Syrian usurper Trypho in the days of Jonathan, courting the Jews for party reasons, had appointed Simon commander of the coastal plain 'from the Ladder of Tyre to the border of Egypt'. Simon used this commission to consolidate the influence of his people over that part of the coastal plain adjacent to the mountains of Judah to secure the passes to the interior. His key base was evidently Gezer, which he fortified and put under the command of his son John.[35] But he concentrated on the development of the home territory and on the reintegration of the Jewish community. Under Simon the Jews were granted immunity from taxation. The writer of I Maccabees dates Jewish independence specifically in the beginning of Simon's rule in 141, and Antiochus the brother of Demetrius, who had been captured by the Parthians, granted Simon the right to coin money in his own name.* The rare extant bronze coins of Simon do not indicate his office except to name the year of his rule, presumably as High Priest, an honour which, though already conferred on him by Demetrius,[36] was confirmed by the popular acclaim of the Jews. The legend on Simon's coins—in the archaic proto-Hebraic script expressive of nationalist sentiment—is simply the year of his rule (the fourth) and 'for the redemption of Zion' (Hebrew *ligh*^{e}*'ullath ṣīyyōn*), and the images are correspondingly conservative, the citrus fruit (*'ethrôgh*) and twigs symbolic of the Feast of Tabernacles, the chalice commemorating Simon's refurnishing of the Temple,[37] and the palm-tree flanked by full fruit-baskets. Simon succeeded in holding the coastal plain, and at length in his time the Syrian garrison was expelled, or withdrawn, from the *akra* in Jerusalem, which Simon then occupied.[38]

On Simon's assassination in 134 B.C. at Dokus ('Ain Dūq northwest of Jericho) by his son-in-law Ptolemy Abubus, who apparently thought thus to ingratiate himself with the Syrian suzerain, his son John moved promptly up to Jerusalem from Gezer.[39] There he was accepted as his father's successor by popular acclaim, but was immediately besieged by Antiochus VII, who had no mind to relinquish his claim on the province, especially the coastal plain and the sea-port of Jaffa, and with whom Simon's occupation of the *akra* rankled. After a year John was forced to capitulate, but was confirmed in office. The

* The right was granted in 139 B.C., but the earliest coins of Simon date 138, his fourth year, A. Reifenberg, *Journal of the Palestine Exploration Society* XIX, 1939, pp. 59 ff.

Jews were spared the humiliation of a Syrian garrison in Jerusalem, but remained tributary to Syria. They were allowed to retain Jaffa and its hinterland, also in return for tribute. Indeed when Antiochus marched against the Parthians Jewish troops marched with him under John.

This campaign apparently exhausted the declining power of Syria, for in 128 on the death of Antiochus VII John secured independence. His first gesture was the destruction of the Samaritan capital at Shechem and of the schismatic temple on Mount Gerizzim. He passed over to Ammon and Moab and to the plains of the south-west, called now 'the plains of Idumaea' after the Edomite immigrants who had settled there since the fifth century. This was not a defensive measure on behalf of Jewish minorities there like the campaigns of Judas and his brothers in 164 (see above, p. 135); John's campaigns were signalized by uncompromising rigour, the inhabitants being forced to proselytize on pain of death.

In the latter part of the rule of John relations between his house and the Pharisees broke into open rupture. In the early days of the struggle under Judas the Ḥasīdīm had given moral strength to the resistance. Latterly they grew suspicious of Judas and his brothers, who continued the struggle after religious liberty had been secured. In the appointment of Alkimos as High Priest the estrangement between the Ḥasīdīm and the Hasmonaeans became patent, the former accepting him because of his Aaronic descent and the latter opposing him violently. The suspicions of the Ḥasīdīm were confirmed by Jonathan's material ambitions and worldly diplomacy, but Simon did not offend them. By the end of John's rule, however, they had definitely 'separated'* themselves from his house and policy. Josephus' statement that John's success in the days of the decay of the Syrian power roused the envy of the Jews[40] probably reflects the suspicion of the Pharisees, as we may now call the Ḥasīdīm, that he would prove too popular and that the removal of the Syrian threat might lead to Hasmonaean absolutism.

John as distinct from his father had his own name stamped on his coins, designating himself 'Joḥanan the High Priest and Head of the Community of the Jews'. The images of palm-branch, cornucopia, and poppy-head indicate the blessings of peace; but the image of a helmet reminded men that security was backed by strength. Most of the coins indicate the democratic rule of John in the legend 'Joḥanan the High Priest and the Community of the Jews', but the occasional addition of

* 'Pharisee' is probably derived from the root *pārash*, 'to separate', probably denoting primarily the particularism which characterized their elaboration of the Law. T. W. Manson (*The Servant-Messiah*, 1953, pp. 16 ff.) suggested a derivation from 'Persian' in view of the influence of Persian Zoroastrianism on Pharisaic thought, but on the extent and limitation of this influence see below p. 143, n.

'The Head of the Community of the Jews' indicates the growing power of the Hasmonaean house.

Whatever John's aims and ambitions may have been, he seems, like David, to have known the limits of his authority. He truly gauged the power of Syria, co-operating with the strong Antiochus VII and successfully defying his weaker successors. He augmented Jewish territory until it bore reasonable comparison with the kingdom of Judah after the disruption of Solomon's kingdom, though including different regions. He worthily discharged the office of High Priest, and until latterly had evidently held the allegiance of the Pharisees, and Josephus pays him a glowing tribute:

> He administered the government in the best manner for thirty years (134–104 B.C.) and then died. He was esteemed by God worthy of the three great privileges, the government of his nation, the dignity of the high priesthood, and prophecy. (Josephus, *Antiquities* XIII. x. 7)

He was the last ruler of the Jews to combine in his person the old ideal of sacral kingship, though not having the title of king.

The Pharisees' fears were confirmed on the death of John, when his eldest son Judas, Graecized as Aristobulus (104–103), assumed the authority of High Priest and the temporal power. His jealousy of the supreme power did not spare even his own family. Josephus[41] alleges that he was the first of the Hasmonaeans to assume the royal diadem, but the title on his coins as on his father's is simply 'High Priest'.

With the reign of his brother Alexander Jannaeus (103–76), the Greek form of Jehonathan, the new Jewish state reached its zenith. The Seleucid Empire was now in its death-throes, and Egypt was torn by civil war. Out of these disorders Alexander profited to extend his realm to the north of Transjordan and to the coastal plain from Carmel to south of Gaza, but his Egyptian alliance nearly cost him all that he and his house had gained in Palestine. Alexander's opportunist achievements, however, failed to commend him to the Pharisees. Judas had fought at the head of patriots to preserve the Jewish tradition from the contamination of the Gentiles; now Alexander intrigued with the Gentiles and fought his wars of aggression with foreign mercenaries.[42] Whereas his predecessors John and Aristobulus had been content with the titles 'High Priest and Head of the Community of the Jews', the legend on the coins of Alexander Jannaeus was 'Jehonathan the King' in the archaic Hebrew script and in Greek 'King Alexander'.

A man of action and affairs, he had few of the finer susceptibilities or real sympathy with religion, and on this account he incurred first the suspicion and then the wrath of the Pharisees. Officiating as High

Priest at the Feast of Tabernacles, Alexander offended through indifference or mistake against some small point of ritual,* and the people vented their rage on him by pelting him with lemons from the boughs which it was customary for them to carry on that occasion. Enraged, Alexander turned his mercenaries on the Jews and much blood was spilt. His Pharisaic antagonists lost still more sympathy with him after one of his many military failures, in this case against the Nabataeans beyond Jordan. As a final gesture of defiance they called in the Syrians and defeated him near Shechem.[43] Shechem, however, is but forty miles from Jerusalem, and the Jews, fearing the encroachment of the Syrians, began to desert their unnatural allies. Thereupon Alexander retrieved the situation, expelling the Syrians. He rounded on his rebel subjects. Eight hundred of the most ardent Pharisees were crucified in Jerusalem, and to intensify their agonies their wives and children were slaughtered before their eyes as they hung on the crosses. In full view of this appalling scene, which is probably noticed in the Qumran Commentary on Nahum (from Cave 4), Alexander sat feasting with his harem!

Now Jerusalem was the capital of a realm comparable in extent, if not in stability, with the kingdom of David. Internally the most important feature of Alexander's reign was the growing power of the Pharisees and their conflict with the Sadducees. The Pharisees represented the sovereign authority of the Law in its application to the living needs of the day; the Sadducees represented the traditional authority of the Ṣadoqite priesthood, the executives of the Law and the successors of the ancient kings who represented their people in dealings with foreign powers. The Sadducees as the more conservative party, who resented any interpretation of the Law beyond plain Scripture, and who resented still more the growing authority of the *doctrinaires* who expounded the Law as the paramount authority in the affairs of the community, represented the aristocracy of birth and office and the wealthy and successful, who sought security in co-operation with the ruling power; the Pharisees, as Josephus states, were the popular party. From the time of John Hyrcanus, except for nine years under the widow of Alexander, the dynastic aims of the Hasmonaeans and their relations with foreign lands and peoples drew the rulers more closely to the Sadducees. Thus the controversy between Pharisees and Sadducees, while involving many spiritual and temporal issues, turned largely on that of the constitution of the Jewish state and its foreign policy, the impersonal

* This may be the incident when one of the Sadducee priests spilt some of the sacred libation on the ground and not on the altar, and, according to the Babylonian Talmud, Sukkah 48b, was pelted with citrons by the Pharisees.

authority of the Law or the personal authority of the hereditary High Priest, who was now also the secular ruler, strict concentration on the limited internal interests of an exclusive religious community or adaption as a secular state as well as an ecclesiastical polity to the current political situation, which demanded a statesman's experience of the world and its wisdom as distinct from simple devotion to the Law. Confident in their inherited dignity, the Sadducees treated with contemporary powers as according to their birthright, and as often happens when men have actual experience of personalities rather than of mere politics, they lost their Jewish xenophobia and felt sufficient confidence to adopt such of the external ways of the age as seemed convenient to them. They thus incurred the charge of temporizing, and the charge was often justified. The popular party, the Pharisees, instinctively shunning contact with external powers, often through sheer ignorance, prejudice and inferiority complex, reacted violently. Their intense nationalism under the impulse of fervent piety became the most violent and dangerous fanaticism, the fatal effect of which was yet to be seen in the great revolts against Rome. It was the Pharisees who emerged from this eventful conflict with Hellenism bearing the indelible marks of the struggle. The best of the Sadducees had had their anxious moments when the Jewish faith and worship was jeopardized; but the Pharisees had suffered bitter persecution undaunted and had hazarded their lives without compromise.

In their critical struggle they had been encouraged by such as the writer of the latter part of the Book of Daniel with the assurance that they were concerned with more than the mere incidentals of history. The consciousness of the reality of the situation of Israel, a little nation continuously menaced by the powers of paganism, was no new experience. It had been the theme of the Psalms relating to the liturgy of the New Year, the great crisis in the peasant's year and the high-light of the religious year in Israel during the monarchy. Then was presented the conception of the supreme 'showdown' of God and the forces of Chaos in nature and history, when God would manifest himself as King and establish his ordered rule (Hebrew *mishpāṭ*, usually rendered 'judgement'). For the forces of Chaos and brute materialism there was a 'hither and no further'; God was in his heaven and all was ultimately well with the world. This had also been the theme of the Prophets, though the conception with them became more poignant in so far as they emphasized that the triumph of God as King would involve the discomfiture of all that militated against his ordered rule, evil elements in Israel herself not excluded, and, with the prophetic emphasis on the moral nature of God's order, this rehabilitation was presented as a judgement. After the liquidation of the state of Israel and the reorganization of the people as a religious community on the basis of its ancestral faith the experience of the Jews under pagan suzerainty gave new point to the traditional faith in the establishment of the Reign of God, but it led to the emphasis on the discomfiture of the suzerain powers, the prophetic emphasis on the significance of the day of God's triumph as a day of judgement on Israel herself being decidedly weakened. So in the struggle against the material forces of Greek paganism the permanence of the rule of God is emphasized. The Book of Daniel reviews the rise and fall of empires in the last four hundred years since the Neo-Babylonian Empire[44] and animadverts on the instability of the Empires of Ptolemies and Seleucids as a commentary on this theme. Behind these incidentals of history the Kingdom of the God of Israel is unassailed and unassailable; the Judge of all the Earth is inexorable.

In the fundamental struggle between God's Order and the forces of Chaos manifested in the pagan empires of the day, but often depicted from the second century onwards as marshalled by a personal power of evil, Satan or Belial,* the true Israel, 'the saints of the Most High' in

* *Śaṭan*, primarily a common noun in Hebrew, means 'adversary', e.g. I Samuel xxix. 4, then denotes a kind of angelic public prosecutor (Job i. 6 ff.). A later significance of the word, now without the definite article and so a proper name, is in the later interpretation of II Samuel xxiv. 1 in I Chronicles xxi. 1, where it denotes the superhuman agency of evil which moved David to involve his people in trouble by taking a census. The English 'Devil' is developed from the Greek *diabolos*, which develops the conception of the prosecutor *par excellence*, as in Job i. Belial is probably the Hebrew *ʾbᵉlī yaʿal* ('worthlessness'), personified in the inter-testamental period, though a derivation from the verb *bālaʿ*, 'to swallow' has been suggested. The angelology of Judaism from the third century onwards probably reflects the influence of Persian Zoroastrianism, which was the official religion of Persia from the time of Darius I (521–486). According to this ethical faith the powers of good, truth and light and of evil, falsehood and darkness, respectively under the direction of the good spirit Ahura Mazda ('wise lord') and Angra Mainyu ('hostile spirit') and their respective agents the six Amesha Spentas ('immortal holy ones') and the evil spirits, or Daevas, were engaged in a cosmic conflict (J. H. Moulton, *Early Zoroastrianism*, 1913; R. C. Zaehner, *The Dawn and Twilight of Zoroastrianism*, 1961). The main theme here recalls the traditional Israelite cult-theme of the continued conflict of God and the forces of Chaos, in which the kingship of God is established and sustained (see above, pp. 93 ff. and below, pp. 170 ff.). This rather than the ethical dualism of Zoroastrianism was the source of the conflict and judgement theme in Jewish apocalyptic, though the Persian conception was one which Judaism could well understand in the light of its own ideology of the kingship of God, and from which certain features could be easily borrowed, such as the angelic hierarchy, e.g. 'the seven holy angels' including Raphael 'who present the prayers of the saints and go in before the glory of the Holy One' (Tobit xii. 15) and Asmodaus 'the evil Spirit' (Tobit iii. 8), who is surely Aeshma-daeva, one of the evil spirits attendant on Angra-Mainyu. The Book of Tobit is generally dated *c.* 200 B.C.

Daniel, convinced of her peculiar destiny in the Divine economy, felt an acute sense of involvement and urgency. They were convinced that they were involved in the supreme struggle to which the whole conflict between God the Creator and Lord of History and the powers of Chaos had been trending throughout the ages, and they were prepared to hazard all in the struggle. They had come to accept suffering as the necessary preliminary of the final triumph of God[45] and freely spoke of those ordeals as 'the birthpangs of the Messiah', the specially commissioned vice-regent of God who was to inaugurate the new era. And as they visualized the powers of evil co-ordinated by a personal head, they were assured that they stood not alone, but, like Daniel in the fiery furnace, were in the company of angelic powers including the Archangel Michael.[46] A typical expression of this confidence from beyond the Bible some time between the Book of Daniel and the coming of Jesus are hymns from the Jewish (probably Essene) Sect of the New Covenant at Qumran by the Dead Sea and one of their tracts, concerning the War of the Sons of Light against the Sons of Darkness. This strange document, with all the military organization and etiquette of a veritable Salvation Army, reflects this assurance:

> For Thou, O Lord, art [terrible?] in thy royal glory,
> And the congregation of the Holy Ones is in our midst as an
> eternal succour.
> So we have put shame upon kings,
> Scorn and reproach upon mighty men.
> For holy is our God,
> And the King of Glory is with us together with his Holy Ones.
> Mighty Ones and the army of the angels are in our musterings,
> And he that is mighty is in our congregation,
> The army of his spirits is with our marching and deploying,
> Even as clouds or as banks of dew covering the ground,
> Or as rain-showers watering all that sprouts thereupon.

In this supreme struggle when men were encouraged to look beyond the outward manifestations of history to the eternal order and activity of God a new hope emerges in the belief in the resurrection and personal immortality. This had emerged, but only as a wistful hope and a

---

4. The south part of the west hill of ancient Jerusalem across the Valley of Hinnom (Wādī 'r-Rabābī), surmounted by the Benedictine Abbey of the Dormition of the Virgin by the reputed site of the Upper Room; beyond the Central Valley the Muslim Sacred Precinct on the site of Solomon's Palace and Temple north of the City of David.

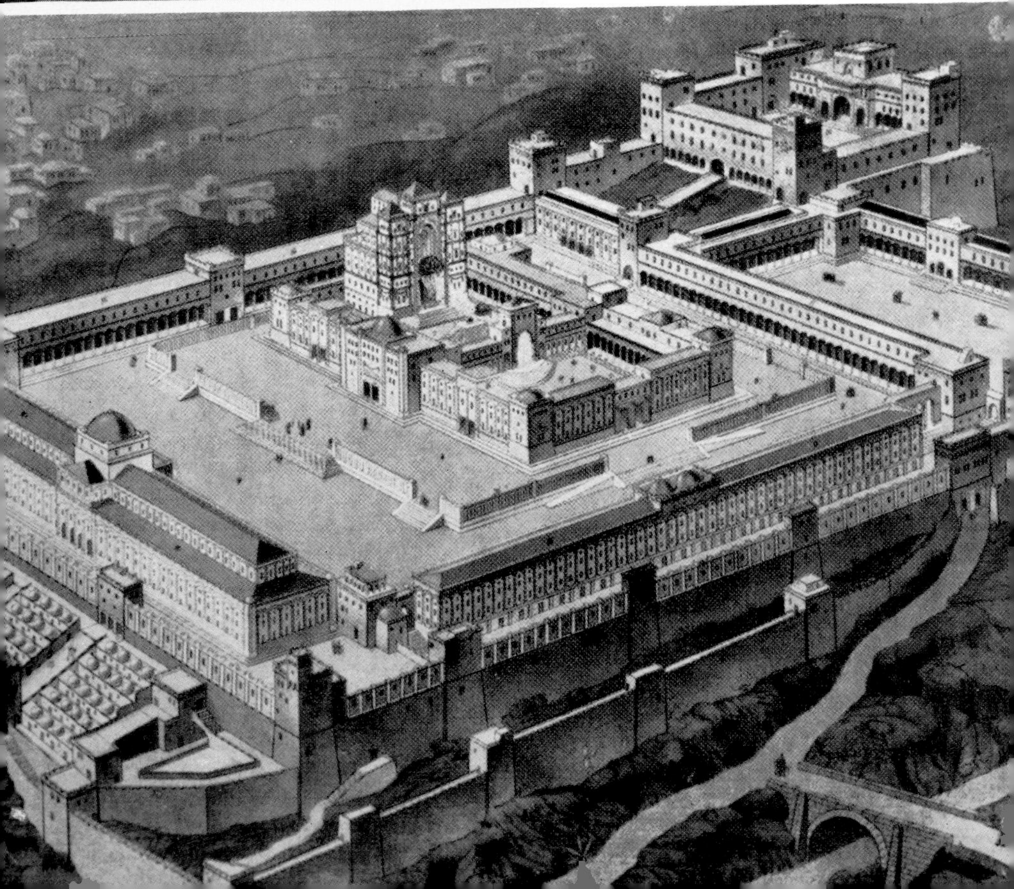

possibility to be immediately discarded, in the posing of the problem of suffering in the Book of Job (xiv. 14 ff.). Now it is asserted that 'Many of those that sleep in the dust shall awake, some to everlasting life and some to everlasting contempt'.[47] This visualized, however, not a general resurrection, but is confined to certain notable saints and sinners. As in the Book of Job this solution is suggested by the suffering of the righteous and the flourishing of their godless persecutors. If there were no prospect of life after death it would surely be a great injustice that the godless should cheat retribution by death and the righteous die in torment and unvindicated. It is perhaps a rather crude solution of the problem, but from this point onwards the hope grows more strong and definite* until it crystallizes in a dogma which was to differentiate the Pharisees from the Sadducees and continue as a cardinal doctrine of the Christian faith.

Thus by the end of the Hasmonaean period just before the middle of the first century B.C. the Pharisees had emerged as the strong popular party, the champions of the absolute authority of the Law against the personal authority of the High Priest, whose worldly experience might too readily lead to compromise of the national ethos. Their resistance toughened in the wars of independence, they firmly believed that they were urgently involved in the Cosmic conflict of God's Order and the forces of Chaos, and ardently anticipated the Divine inbreaking into history and the consummation of the Divine Order through the Messiah. Their loyalty and conviction was strengthened both to do and to endure by the growing conviction that God's Order in which they were involved would transcend sufferings and death itself. Even their bitter enemy Alexander Jannaeus came eventually to realize their political potential, and on his death-bed he bequeathed to his queen Salome (Hebrew Sh^{e}lōm Ṣīyyōn), whose Greek name was Alexandra, the policy of enlisting the support of the Pharisees by special favour,[48] which she carried out so faithfully that Josephus remarks that 'she had,

* Already the resurrection hope in a more general and positive form stimulates the martyrs in II Maccabees (vi. 26; vii. 9; xiv) about the end of the second century B.C. or perhaps a little later (O. Eissfeldt, *The Old Testament: an Introduction*, 1965, p. 581).

---

5. Entrance to the tombs of Herod's family opposite his palace-fort, with a cylindrical blocking-stone (cf. Mark xvi. 3–4).

6. Reconstruction of the sacred area of the Temple of Herod the Great, dominated from the north-west by his palace-fort Antonia on the site of the earlier Hasmonaean fortress (Baris) and the Tower Hananeel of the late Jewish monarchy.

indeed, the name of regent but the Pharisees had the authority'.[49]

Pharisaic tradition is lyrical in praise of the reign of the queen under the influence of Pharisaic counsellors like the Rabbi Simon ben Shetaḥ, believed to be her brother, declaring that 'Under Simon ben Shetaḥ and Queen Salome rain fell on the eve of Sabbath, so that the corns of wheat were as large as kidneys, the barley corns as large as olives, and the lentils like golden denarii'.[50] But the Pharisees, though a wholesome check on the absolutism of the native Jewish princes, used their influence to vindictive ends. They had not forgotten the crucifixion of eight hundred Pharisees by Alexander Jannaeus. So the Sadducees went in fear of their lives and liberties. Their cause was championed by the younger son of Alexander Jannaeus, Aristobulus, who secured the queen's consent to their occupying certain fortresses, thus winning for them a temporary respite from Pharisaic persecution.

At his death Alexander had bequeathed his temporal power to Alexandra-Salome, who had invested her eldest son Hyrcanus with the office of High Priest. The younger son Aristobulus was restless and ambitious, and resented his mother's usurpation of the power to which he aspired. In championing the oppressed Sadducees, Aristobulus probably showed his genuine sympathies, but he also exploited the situation to win their support against his mother and his brother. Josephus represents him as holding over the queen the threat that his party was a strong potential ally of the hostile Nabataeans beyond the Dead Sea and the free Greek cities beyond the Jordan.[51] This menace in fact materialized when the queen lay on her death-bed, when, with a dread of the continued tyranny of the Pharisees as a spur to his innate ambition, Aristobulus and his party seized many strong places and, with support from Syria and the Greek cities of Palestine and Transjordan, he was prepared to fight for supreme authority.

After nine years of political domination and reprisals, the Pharisees grew nervous of the growing power of Aristobulus, who had the support not only of the Sadducees and the neighbouring Gentiles, but naturally attracted the many restless spirits who had been fostered in the wars of Alexander Jannaeus. In their consternation the Pharisees turned to the queen, but Alexandra was now on her death-bed, and such struggles were remote from her interest. So it was left to the High Priest John Hyrcanus to oppose Aristobulus on her death in 67 B.C., and a battle was fought at Jericho. The forces of Hyrcanus deserted, and he was defeated and retired to Jerusalem, where, on Aristobulus' appearance before the Temple, he was content to surrender his secular and priestly authority.

Now, however, the situation was complicated by a new factor.

During the Exile in the sixth century the Edomites, as we have seen, had encroached on South Palestine. They had been forcibly Judaized by John Hyrcanus and Alexander Jannaeus, an action which 'bore bitter fruit to the Jews', since thus came the family of Herod into the orbit of Judaism. Now Antipater, the son of Antipas the governor of Idumaea under Alexander Jannaeus and Alexandra-Salome and the father of Herod the Great, began to exploit the circumstances and personalities of the Jewish community. He persuaded the weak Hyrcanus to take refuge in Petra, the capital of the Nabataean kingdom, whose king he then instigated to invade Judah in support of Hyrcanus. Aristobulus was defeated in battle, and retired, prepared to stand siege in the Temple. The resulting stalemate was broken by the influence of a force now felt in the history of Palestine for the first time and destined to dominate for seven centuries, the power of Rome.

Seleucid decadence had invited the incursion of a young and virile nation, the Armenians, under Tigranes, who swept down on Syria, penetrating apparently as far as Ptolemais (Akko).[52] Having already secured an interest in Asia by the bequest of Attalus of Pergamum in 133 B.C., Rome resented and opposed the rise of Tigranes. The campaigns of the Roman general Lucullus reduced the power of Armenia, but there still remained Tigranes' ally, another aspiring ruler of Asia Minor, Mithradates of Pontus. In 66 B.C. Pompey was appointed Commander-in-Chief in Asia with a commission for three years. While Pompey was engaged against Mithradates in Asia Minor his lieutenant Scaurus was active in the territory in Syria lately over-run by Tigranes. From Damascus Scaurus hastened south on hearing of the dispute between Hyrcanus and Aristobulus, which promised a rich field for exploitation. Hyrcanus and his Nabataean allies were forced to raise the siege of the Temple, and Aristobulus, recovering the initiative. defeated them at a place called Papyron.[53] The action of Scaurus, however, had only kept the issue open, and when in 63 B.C. Pompey came in person to Damascus to settle the affairs of the East in the interest of Rome the contending parties in Judah appealed to his decision. Aristobulus and Hyrcanus through their representatives Nicodemus and Antipater put their case before Pompey, and the Jewish community, significantly, came independently to state their case.[54] Evidently the rule of the Hasmonaean princes, at no time popular, had now become intolerable. Pompey deferred a decision until the settlement of the problem of the Nabataeans,[55] who, expanding like the Jews with the decadence of the Seleucid power, were steadily pushing northwards to Damascus, always the metropolis of the North Arabian desert.

Suspecting an ultimate decision in favour of the innocuous Hyrcanus,

Aristobulus sought to anticipate events. He withdrew to the isolated fortress of Alexandrium (Qarn Sartaba) in the dry badlands sloping east to the Jordan Valley about twelve miles north of Jericho, prepared presumably to defend himself when Pompey returned from the country of the Nabataeans east of Jordan. Pompey, however, divided his forces immediately and marched directly against Aristobulus. Negotiations took place, but Aristobulus kept the shelter of his fortress. Finally when he saw that Pompey was firmly resolved to settle the dispute on his own arbitration Aristobulus occupied Jerusalem, where he continued to negotiate under arms. Pompey advanced on the city by Jericho. Aristobulus now offered to submit to Pompey's proposals, but too late; his prolonged resistance and his occupation of Jerusalem had inflamed the spirit of resistance among his followers, who refused to accept any terms as long as they held Jerusalem.[56] In exasperation Pompey put Aristobulus under arrest.

In the city there was no agreement.[57] Many, appalled at the prospect of war with Rome, clamoured for surrender. The military, however, and those whose status and prosperity depended upon Jewish independence isolated themselves in the Temple, the last strong-hold of suicidal resistance. Pompey pursued the siege patiently and methodically, exploiting the scrupulous Jewish Sabbath observance. He carefully refrained from provoking attack in order to push up the siege-works, and eventually, with little loss of life on the part of the Romans, he captured the Temple after a siege of three months.[58] Among the Jews were many martyrs. Priests were cut down at the altar, and in the streets and Temple courts many were massacred. It is said that often Jew turned sword against Jew, while others set fire to their own houses and perished in the flames. Others leapt to their death over the walls surmounting the precipitous sides of the Qidron ravine, above which the Temple was built. Twelve thousand are said to have perished,[59] and Pompey stood as conqueror in the Temple and, rather in curiosity than in the spirit of sacrilege, he entered the Holy of Holies, or inmost shrine, which only the High Priest entered one day of the year, the Day of Atonement. Men thought of the outrage of Antiochus Epiphanes, 'the abomination of desolation standing where he should not', but Pompey was not aggressive or fanatical. Jerusalem was laid under tribute to Rome, the conquests of the Hasmonaeans in North Palestine beyond the immediate district of Jerusalem were annulled and put under the direct administration of a Roman legate in Syria. Cities in Transjordan and the plains of Palestine, which had been centres of Greek Western culture in the Greek period, were rehabilitated and included in the province of Syria. The personal dispute between the

Hasmonaean princes was finally settled. Hyrcanus was reinstated as High Priest and Aristobulus and his family were taken as prisoners to Rome for Pompey's triumphal procession. In the party struggle between the two Jewish parties Jewish independence had been sacrificed and the way was open for Roman imperialism and the domination for seven hundred years of the political and cultural forces of the West, in resistance to which the power of the Hasmonaean princes had been founded.

NOTES FOR CHAPTER V

1 Josephus, *Antiquities* XII. iii. 3
2 Daniel xi. 20
3 I Maccabees i. 11, 43 ff.
4 II Maccabees iii. 22 ff.
5 II Maccabees iv. 25
6 II Macabees v. 5–16
7 I Maccabees i. 20 ff.
8 Justinus xxxiv. 3
9 Daniel xi. 31
10 Josephus, *Antiquities* XII. v. 4
11 II Maccabees vi. 10
12 II Maccabees vii. 1 ff.
13 II Maccabees vi. 11
14 R. De Vaux, *La Revue Biblique* LXIII, 1956, pp. 565–6
15 I Maccabees ii. 17–18
16 I Maccabees ii. 49 ff.
17 iv. 26–35, cf. II Maccabees xi. 1–26
18 I Maccabees iv. 30 cf. I Samuel xvii
19 II Maccabees x. 15–17
20 I Maccabees iv. 36–59
21 I Maccabees v. 16 ff.
22 I Maccabees v. 19
23 I Maccabees vi. 13–16
24 I Maccabees vi. 26
25 I Maccabees vi. 21 ff.
26 I Maccabees vi. 28–63 regards the expedition as under royal command
27 I Maccabees vi. 28–63
28 I Maccabees vi. 35
29 I Maccabees vi. 49 cf. Leviticus xxv. 2–7
30 I Maccabees vi. 55 ff.
31 I Maccabees vi. 58–62
32 I Maccabees vii. 1–13
33 I Maccabees vii. 28–9
34 I Maccabees ix. 6
35 I Maccabees xiii. 53
36 I Maccabees xiv. 38
37 I Maccabees xiv. 15
38 I Maccabees xiv. 36–7
39 Josephus, *Antiquities* XIII. vii. 4
40 Josephus, *Antiquities* XIII. x. 5
41 *Antiquities* XIII. xi. 1
42 Josephus, *Antiquities* XIII. xiii. 5
43 Josephus, *Antiquities* XIII. xiv. 1
44 Daniel ii, vii
45 Daniel xii. 1
46 Daniel xii. 1
47 Daniel xii. 2
48 Josephus, *Antiquities* XIII. xv. 5
49 *Antiquities* XIII. xvi. 2
50 Babylonian Talmud, Taanith 23a
51 *Antiquities* XIII. xvi. 2
52 Josephus, *Antiquities* XIII. xvi. 4
53 Josephus, *Antiquities* XIV. ii. 3
54 Josephus, *Antiquities* XIV. iii. 2
55 Josephus, *Antiquities* XIV. iii. 3
56 Josephus, *Antiquities* XIV. iv. 1
57 Josephus, *Antiquities* XIV. iv. 2
58 Josephus, *Antiquities* XIV. iv. 3
59 Josephus, *Antiquities* XIV. iv. 4

VI

THE HOUSE OF HEROD

The dominions of Herod were too little for the greatness of his soul
(*Josephus,* Antiquities *XVI. v. 1*)

With Pompey's settlement of the succession to the leadership of the Jews in favour of Hyrcanus, native independence was virtually at an end and the High Priest was again nominated and maintained in office by a foreign power. As this dawned on the consciousness of the Jews opposition to Rome intensified. A movement similar to the rising under Judas Maccabaeus might indeed have materialized had Rome been as weak as the Seleucid Empire had been in the second century.

Jewish resistance found expression in the support given locally to the remaining princes of the Hasmonaean House, Alexander the son of Aristobulus and Aristobulus himself on his return from Rome. Though the Hasmonaeans had been latterly unpopular the Jews now flocked to their standard as leaders against Roman domination, and from their base in the barren, rocky eastern escarpment of Judah and Samaria they embarrassed the Roman legate of Syria in three strenuous campaigns between 57 and 55 B.C.

In the civil convulsions which attended the passing of the republican constitution of Rome Judah like other provinces and vassal states suffered much. The disorders brought men of the grossest type to the front, who sought to turn the uncertain and transient circumstances to their own personal advantage. Crassus for instance in 54 B.C. spared not even the Temple in his systematic plunder of the land. On the actual outbreak of civil war the increasing cost of the maintenance of the rival armies was met by severe taxation of the provinces. Palestine suffered grievously from the extortions of Cassius in 44 B.C., incurring an impost of 700 talents under the penalty of slavery for default.[1]* Another effect of the civil wars of Rome was that influential men in the

* The towns of Gophna (Jifneh about 14 miles north-north-west of Jerusalem), Emmaus, Lydda and Thamna were thus reduced wholesale to slavery.

provinces were often courted with a view to support. On the outbreak of civil war with Pompey for instance Julius Caesar released Aristobulus and sent him to his native land with two legions to counter-act the influence of Pompey.[2] Pompey, however, had a strong party in Palestine, and Aristobulus was poisoned. Alexander too, the son of Aristobulus, was taken off in the interests of Pompey. Thus the Jews, not without some reason, regarded the Romans as merciless exploiters of provincials and, as instrumental in the murder of their native princes, inimical to their national aspirations.

The character of Hyrcanus, whom the arbitration and arms of Pompey had settled as civil and spiritual leader of the Jews, did not attract support. He was apathetic to power, prompt to action only in the cause of his own personal safety, and even then only in response to the stimulus of others. Hyrcanus' unpopularity was shared by the Romans who maintained him in office.

Behind Hyrcanus stood a figure which roused the hatred of all Jewish nationalists, the Idumaean governor of the southern part of Palestine, who became chief minister to Hyrcanus and the real political power in the land. With not the slightest sympathy with Jewish nationalism, Antipater supported Rome both in internal affairs in Palestine and abroad with the Nabataean kingdom and Egypt, and with his support of Rome his influence grew. In return for his support of Julius Caesar in Egypt he was made a Roman citizen with immunity from taxation and authority as procurator over Judaea. In this capacity he appointed his own son Phasael governor of Jerusalem and the vicinity and his second son Herod governor over Galilee. Thus Antipater was triply odious to the Jews. He was despised as a half-Jew;* he was hated as a collaborator with Rome; he was envied as a usurper of the political power of the native princes. Antipater may fairly be condemned as the evil genius of Hyrcanus, who, but for his instigation, would have lived in private obscurity, avoiding all the vicissitudes to which his secular authority exposed him. But as the history of the time unfolds itself Antipater was a power for the public good. He supplied the stabilizing influence which a statesman as distinct from a pretender gives to a nation where the fires of fanaticism are continually smouldering. In 55 B.C., when Gabinius the Roman Legate of Syria was ready to strike at the Jewish rebels under Alexander, Antipater strove hard and not ineffectively for a reconciliation;[3] his substantial support of Julius Caesar in Egypt in 48 B.C.[4] secured for the Jews in Palestine and the provinces the exceptional privileges which they enjoyed by the

* I.e. descended from the Idumaeans in the coastal plain about Askalon, who had been forcibly Judaized by John Hyrcanus (see above, p. 139).

influence of Caesar.[5] In the perilous times following Caesar's assassination on the Ides of March, 44 B.C. he steered the land safely through. No doubt he collaborated with Cassius in his heavy taxation of the land, but it was impossible for any accessible land to escape scot-free in those critical days, and the promptitude of Antipater in entrusting the levy to his sons probably saved bloodshed in addition to extortion. The virtues of Antipater, appreciated in the Jewish communities in Egypt, were lost on the nationalists in Palestine, to whom he fell a victim at last, poisoned by one Malichus, a man whose life he had twice saved.

Antipater's influence and particular politics survived him in his son Herod, whose career is no less notable for its many vicissitudes than for its political and cultural significance in Palestine. Governor of Galilee when his father was chief minister of state in the high-priesthood of Hyrcanus, he distinguished himself by the suppression of a notorious band of brigands, whose leader Hezekias he put to death.[6] He thereby earned the gratitude of the Syrian communities and was noticed by the pro-consul Sextus Caesar. Yet this very service to public security was turned to an occasion against him by the Jews in Jerusalem, who bitterly resented the influence of Antipater and his sons. They brought pressure to bear on Hyrcanus, urging that in putting Hezekias to death Herod had arrogated to himself powers which properly belonged to the Sanhedrin, or Council of Jewish Elders. Accordingly Herod was summoned to stand trial before the Sanhedrin. On the advice of Antipater he appeared, but with a strong force for his security. Herod's potential strength was reinforced by a summary order from Sextus Caesar to clear him from the charge. Thus Herod returned from Jerusalem leaving the Sanhedrin and all his enemies in shame and mortification. Put in command of the army of Syria by Sextus Caesar immediately after his return, Herod marched on Jerusalem and, but for the mediation of his father Antipater, would have exacted summary vengeance. This notwithstanding was the shape of things to come, and Josephus records that of that Sanhedrin only one person survived Herod's eventual vengeance.[7]

Having further recommended himself to the Romans by his expeditious extortion of taxes in the proconsulship of Cassius in Syria between 44 and 42 B.C., Herod secured the authority of Cassius to put his father's assassin to death. Thus we find a precedent set by a civil ruler in Palestine for the administration of internal affairs by direct reference to Rome without any regard for the authority of the Sanhedrin. Jewish independence, so hardly won by the Hasmonaeans, was now in effect a dead letter.

Herod's prompt action prevented a civil war on the emergence of

Antigonus the son of Aristobulus from his refuge in the Lebanon, when he saw his opportunity in the troubled times through which the Roman state was then passing. After his victory over Antigonus in Galilee Herod came to Jerusalem, and Hyrcanus was obliged to countenance the betrothal of the young Idumaean to his grand-niece Mariammē the daughter of Alexander the son of Aristobulus.[8]

The defeat of Brutus and Cassius at Philippi quickened the hopes of the Jews that Herod's support of Cassius would occasion his downfall. Thus they prepared a case against him and brought it before Antony in Asia Minor,[9] but Antony was not convinced that the resentment of the Jews was sufficient justification for suppressing Herod. He had moreover fought in the campaign against Alexander the son of Aristobulus and had seen the activity of Antipater in the interests of Rome. On the repetition of the charge Antony was adamant, and Herod and Phasael were in fact created tetrarchs, or provincial governors.[10]

Meanwhile in his refuge in the Lebanon Antigonus was still a potential rival. In 40 B.C. a great opportunity offered itself for him to realize his ambitions. In that year, while Antony was ingloriously inactive, enslaved by the charms of Cleopatra, the Parthians under Pacorus gathered strength and overran Syria. Antigonus entered into communication with Pacorus, who was to put him on the throne of his fathers at Jerusalem at the price of a thousand talents and five hundred women of noble birth.[11] Antigonus was determined to secure his personal position at any cost. Yet when the Parthian invasion materialized and Herod and Phasael were prepared to resist in the best interests of the people they were shamefully betrayed. Thus the Jews secured Antigonus as 'king' and 'high priest', and Jerusalem was plundered by his Parthian allies as their share of the victory.[12] Hyrcanus and Phasael the brother of Herod were captured, and Phasael took his own life in prison, while Hyrcanus was mutilated to disqualify him from the office of High Priest. It is said indeed that his nephew Antigonus bit off his uncle's ears with his own teeth.[13]

Herod fled with his family and adherents south from Jerusalem, seeking the safety of the desert fortress of Massada overlooking the Dead Sea some thirty-four miles north-north-east of Beersheba. His retreat was harassed by the Jews and he was at least once brought to action some eight miles from Jerusalem at the place he was later to develop as the desert stronghold of Herodium.[14] He beat off their attack and reached Massada, where, in safe isolation, he left his family and his goods which he had salvaged in the care of his brother Joseph. Turning first vainly to the Nabataean king, he reached Egypt and eventually arrived at Rome. Under the patronage of Antony he was introduced to

Octavian, and his case was brought before the Senate. The marked favour shown by the two leaders predisposed the Senate in his favour, and his case was sustained. Herod had intended to petition for the kingship for his young brother-in-law Aristobulus.* So keenly, however, did the Romans feel the treachery of the Hasmonaean Antigonus, and so strongly did Herod's advocates emphasize the loyal services of his father Antipater that by a turn of fortune beyond anticipation the Senate on the suggestion of Antony decreed that Herod should be king. Thus in 40 B.C. Herod became king of the Jews—significantly in Rome—and Antony gave a feast to commemorate the first day of his reign. But even with the support of Rome Herod was able to secure his throne in Jerusalem only after three years.

The Parthians fully occupied Herod's Roman allies; the Jews would not support him; and the situation in Palestine between Herod and Antigonus was too inviting for venal Roman subordinates to resist. Herod's successes in Galilee and the coastal plain were thus nullified and, despairing of an immediate solution of his problem, he went directly to Antony at his headquarters at Samosata on the Euphrates. The cessation of hostilities in the East allowed Antony to detach two legions in Herod's support in Palestine, and Herod himself with one Roman legion and supporters from Lebanon consolidated his position in the provinces and confined Antigonus and his forces to Jerusalem, during the siege of which he consummated his marriage with Mariammē. Eventually he moved up all his auxiliaries to Jerusalem to the number, it is said, of 30,000 infantry and 6,000 cavalry. Antigonus was reduced to grievous straits by the rigours of the siege, aggravated by the fact that 37 B.C. was a Sabbatical year, when the land lay fallow. Yet so keenly were the Jewish nationalists opposed to Herod that the siege lasted several months. When the city actually fell in the summer the intense feeling of the antagonists found expression in desperate resistance on the one hand, and on the other indiscriminate slaughter, which Herod, with the best intentions, could not restrain. Antigonus was captured and sent in bonds to Antony, who put him to death. So perished the last ruler of the House of Hashmon, and Herod ruled as king in Jerusalem three years after he had received the title by decree of the Senate in Rome.

With plain evidence that the Jewish aristocracy and the orthodox party of the Pharisees were implacably hostile, Herod removed many of their number and curbed the power of others by confiscations[15] in

* Josephus calls him Alexander (*Antiquities* XIV. xiv. 5), but Mariammē had only one brother Aristobulus, who became High Priest and was drowned in a bathing party at Jericho (see below, p. 155).

order to preclude the possibility of rebellion. General security and the bloody record of Jewish nationalism might justify those measures, but there were other political murders which were less excusable. Yielding for the moment to pressure from his wife Mariammē and her mother, who had engaged the support of Cleopatra the Queen of Egypt, who was known to have designs on Palestine, which she partially realized, Herod had installed the seventeen-year-old brother of Mariammē, Aristobulus, as High Priest. Of pleasing appearance and of Hasmonaean lineage, he was popular in Jerusalem, and with deep apprehension Herod saw him win that respect and love which he himself could never command from the Jews. So at a feast in Jericho in 36 B.C., under the semblance of horseplay, Herod had him drowned in a swimming-pool.[16] Herod may, however, have had a deeper political motive, as it is alleged that the mother of Aristobulus, who detested Herod as an Idumaean upstart, was in correspondence with Cleopatra, planning to escape to Egypt with Aristobulus,[17] who, it must be remembered, was after Hyrcanus the heir of the Hasmonaean line. With relations as they were between Cleopatra and Antony this might have had disastrous consequences for Herod, and indeed, at the instance of Cleopatra, he was obliged to answer to Antony at Laodicea on the Syrian coast. Antony, however, appreciated Herod's worth as a ruler and a steady ally, and it is likely that a substantial bribe helped to acquit him. Herod had secured the return from captivity in Mesopotamia of the aged Hyrcanus, perhaps to counterbalance the antipathy of the Jews in Jerusalem with popularity among the Jews in Mesopotamia, a most influential centre of the Diaspora, where Hyrcanus had been revered as a former High Priest and King of the Jews. In Jerusalem Herod treated Hyrcanus with great respect, even giving him pride of place on all public occasions. On the downfall of Herod's patron Antony it was alleged that Hyrcanus had entered into treasonable correspondence with Malichus the King of the Nabataens at the instigation of his vindictive and ambitious niece Alexandra, the baneful mother-in-law of Herod. Betrayed by his messenger, it is said, Hyrcanus was convicted on undeniable evidence, and condemned to death by the Sanhedrin. A plea from Herod might have saved his life. It is also alleged that the evidence was forged. However this may be, Herod could not afford to spare a rival to the throne when his own crown was in danger after the defeat of his patron Antony, and so Hyrcanus perished, a poor pawn all his life on the chess-board of political intrigue, and Herod was left the sole man in the land with any claim of power to rule the Jews.

As the clouds of civil war gathered on the Western horizon and the day of Actium approached Herod must have had many misgivings, especially as he saw the deterioration of the character and prestige of his patron Antony in Egypt. Yet he did not swerve in his loyalty to his benefactor, but prepared to assist him in the final struggle,[18] from which, however, he was prevented, it is said, by Cleopatra's jealousy of his growing influence with Antony. Actually he was opportunely engaged on a Nabataean campaign at the time of the Battle of Actium. Herod's future depended upon the grace of the victor of Actium. Accordingly he decided to put himself out of suspense by appearing personally before Octavian. He left his brother Pheroras as regent with the charge to secure the kingdom for his sons if his mission should fail. He sent his wife Mariammē, for whom he had a characteristically jealous Oriental love, to the fortress of Alexandrium in the desolate hills north of Jericho with an order to her guardian Sohaemus that if he should not return alive his beloved wife should not survive him.[19] Securing his mother Kypros and his children in the Dead Sea fortress of Massada, he hastened to meet Octavian at Rhodes. He appeared before Caesar without his diadem. Given leave to speak, he did not conceal his regard for Antony, and emphasized his antipathy for Cleopatra. He pledged himself to be as loyal to Caesar as he had been to Antony. The directness of Herod's appeal commended him; a loyal ally on the flank of Egypt was an advantage, and Herod might be trusted like his father Antipater to be loyal to whatever Roman party was currently dominant. So Caesar restored Herod's diadem and confirmed him in office as a confederate king (*rex socius*), and Herod fully justified his confidence and enjoyed the favour of Rome to the end of his reign.

The triumph of Octavian and the establishment of the Roman Empire brought peace at length to the Mediterranean world. In Palestine Herod's anxieties in the fluctuating fortunes of the contending parties in the passing of the Roman republic were over, and though he reigned as a Roman vassal, organizing his kingdom to keep the Roman peace, to supply the armed support which she expected at need and occasionally to make munificent gifts to the Emperor, the subjects were at least free from the extraordinary levies by the contending parties backed by the brute force of their armies. As *rex socius* Herod's status was 'friend and ally of the Roman people', directly responsible to the Emperor, but usually referring important matters of minor moment to the Imperial legate of Syria, to whom Herod was apparently a trusted and valuable assessor, particularly in financial matters. Such kings as Herod were valuable agents within the Roman Empire, softening the impact of Rome on the provinces and giving the advantage of permanence and of experience and understanding of local problems, which, in the government of an exclusive community like the Jews in Jerusalem, the fortress of their faith, was an exceptional asset. The permanence of the king and his relations with his neighbours and the various elements in his kingdom were of great advantage in the peaceful organization of the province. Thus certain areas infested with brigands such as the region from the foothills of Lebanon eastwards to the lava belt of the Hauran (Trachonitis) and Jebel Druze were added to Herod's realm owing to his proved ability to suppress brigandage. The propagation of Western culture and the Roman adaptation of the Greek way of life was also the responsibility of the *rex socius,* and to further this end Herod received accessions of regions beyond the mountain fastness of Judaea proper in the coastal plain and in Samaria. There he built lavishly and equipped and endowed cities in the Graeco-Roman tradition. The small coastal settlement of Straton's Tower was rebuilt on an extensive scale as Caesarea and by a giant breakwater converted into one of the major ports of the Levant, as Haifa was in our own time. Soon after the death of Herod the Great Caesarea was to supersede Jerusalem as the administrative capital of Palestine. Samaria was rebuilt on a comparable scale and renamed Sebastē (Latin Augusta) in honour of the Emperor. At both cities the most conspicuous feature was a temple to the divinity of the Emperor.

Herod provided for the security of the realm by settling active subjects in various regions of doubtful security or strategic significance throughout the country. Thus in the region north and east of the Sea of Galilee Idumaeans from the south of Palestine and a force gathered by the Babylonian Jewish notable Zamira provided an effective militia, while turbulent mountaineers from this region, who had been inveterate brigands, now found new scope for their energies together with mercenaries from the Balkans and Germany in Herod's standing army in Judaea and the great desert fortresses Alexandrium, Herodium, Massada, Machaerus and Hyrcania, which A. H. M. Jones well characterizes as 'the Bastille of the kingdom'.[20] He settled military colonists on land about Sebastē and was thus able to dominate Jerusalem despite his unpopularity among his subjects in Judaea. In internal administration also Herod as *rex socius* enjoyed great freedom and was able further to curtail the power of Jewish opposition. Not only did he nominate the High Priest, but he now determined the length of his office, which had hitherto been for life. The supreme council of the Jews, the Sanhedrin, with the power of an advisory court in administration and with the judiciary power of life and death, had been constituted by members from the higher priestly orders and others recognized as authorities in the Law. Herod's proscriptions among the old aristocracy and others, both Sadducee and Pharisee, who had supported the last Hasmonaean pretenders between 63 and 37 B.C. had reduced nationalist influence in the court. Now Herod sponsored the promotion to it of men of lower priestly standing who were thus more sensible of his patronage. But in matters of real importance he superseded the Sanhedrin by a privy council, which consisted largely of his own ministers of state, who were not all Jews.

To dominate Jerusalem itself Herod built two great fortresses, the one on the highest point of the west hill, where the Turkish Citadel now stands, and the other at the north-west corner of the Temple area roughly on the site occupied by the Turkish cavalry barracks and more recently used in the British Mandate as a police post and on the site of the present Convent of the Sisters of Zion. This was a development of the Hasmonaean fortress Baris (Aramaic *bir^{e}thā*, 'the Fortress'). Thus from his palace-fort and from the latter fortress, which he called Antonia, which dominated the Temple area (fig. V), Herod could observe any outbreak of hostility in Jerusalem and check it in its inception.[21] In addition he developed the fortification of the famous desert strongholds, formidable in themselves and yet more so from their desert environment at Massada on a lofty crag overlooking the Dead Sea in the south; Herodium, that singular peak like an extinct volcano some six miles south-east of Bethlehem; Hyrcania, modern Khirbet Mird in the Wilderness of Judah between Jerusalem and the Dead Sea; Alexandrium overlooking the Jordan Valley in the dry region sloping eastwards from Shechem; Kypros, named after his mother, dominating Jericho from the South-west; and Machaerus and another Herodium on the Nabataen frontier east of the Dead Sea. Some of these, like Alexandrium, had been fortified in the end of the Hasmonaean period. Others west of the Jordan, like Massada, had been used during the hazardous times during the Roman civil wars and the struggle between Herod and the last Hasmonaean ruling king Antigonus (see above, p. 156).

The impress of Herod is still on Jerusalem. The paved courtyard of the Antonia may still be seen, scored with the wheelruts of chariots and with the 'board' of the games with which the garrison diverted their leisure moments (see above, p. 49). In the Citadel the patient excavations of C. N. Johns of the Mandatory Antiquities Department revealed the foundations of Herod's towers Hippicus and Phasael, which, with Mariammē, the smallest tower to the east, Josephus describes[22] as a notable feature of the palace-fort. In many buildings from later periods in Jerusalem there are distinctive Herodian blocks with their characteristic marginal drafting.

The court of Herod in this palace was imposing and versatile, an enclave of cosmopolitan Hellenistic culture in the mountain fastness of Judaism guarded by a corps of stalwart mercenary lifeguardsmen from the Balkans and Germany and including Cleopatra's former bodyguard of four hundred Galatian Celts, a gift of the Emperor. It is questionable, if even Solomon had had such a court, and it is said that at Herod's funeral five hundred of his slaves and freedmen carried perfumes for his burial. He governed through an efficient bureaucracy, which according to the Roman historian A. H. M. Jones[23] was organized on the model of Ptolemaic Egypt, staffed by liberal Jews and non-Jews alike according to their individual competence. The substantial balance in Herod's budget—in spite of the upkeep of his court, standing army and administration, his fortifications and his sumptuous building in Jerusalem and the provinces and even beyond Palestine, where he found many opportunities to show his zeal in this way for Roman civilization, and his extraordinary gifts to the Emperor and to Greek communities, perhaps motivated by concern for the Jews of the Dispersion*—suggests a meticulous and highly efficient fiscal organization of the realm, the revenues of which would be greatly increased in the security Herod was strong enough to impose. Palestine has always been the nexus of trade-routes between Egypt and Mesopotamia, and his control of Trans-Jordan and the Hauran gave Herod control of the northern, or Damascus, branch of the lucrative caravan trade-route from the South Arabian entrepôts of the trade from India and East Africa. He also controlled the western branch of this trade through Gaza,† and was thus in a very favourable position *vis-à-vis* the merchant princes of the Nabataean kingdom with its capital at Petra. His father Antipater had close connections with the Nabataean nobility, and his fortune from this source probably helped to launch the family on the path of promotion. This substantial source of private income, made yet more productive by Herod's political advancement and territorial additions to the kingdom, made his munificence possible without undue strain on the public resources of his realm.

Like Solomon Herod affected patronage of the arts, or rather, since he was no connoisseur but the essential tycoon and barbarian, he endeavoured like a good *rex socius* to introduce his subjects to the western culture of the Roman suzerain by such characteristic institutions as the

* The remittance of funds from the communities of the Dispersion to Jerusalem was a perpetual grievance of the Greek cities, and in this way Herod secured some return to them.

† The economic significance of Gaza is indicated by the fact that after his capture of the place Alexander the Great sent more than 35 tons of spices to his old tutor Leonidas (Plutarch, *Alexander* XXV. 4).

theatre, amphitheatre and race-course. The hippodrome at Jerusalem is precisely located by Josephus[24] as south of the Temple area, perhaps in the lower part of the Central Valley north of the Pool of Siloam, where Dr. Kenyon attests Herodian paving and building.[25]* His theatre may have been located about half a mile south of the present south wall on the hill beyond the Valley of Ḥinnom under the summit of ar-Rās, where Schick exposed the apparent remains of a theatre with stone-hewn steps and sculptured masonry nearby.[26]† The site of the amphitheatre is located by Josephus 'in the plain', and a location in the Plain of the Repha'im west of the city has been suggested.[27] No trace of this has been found, and 'the plain' may rather be 'the valley of Shaveh' ('the plain') of Genesis xiv. 17, which was the valley-bottom at the confluence of the Qidron, the Central Valley and the Valley of Hinnom, which is a natural amphitheatre. Those institutions were no more popular with the Jews in Jerusalem than the Hellenistic institutions introduced by the Seleucid kings, and indeed the wild beast shows and gladiatorial combats of the amphitheatre were much less edifying. But Rome was more powerful than the Seleucids, and Herod held a firmer grip of the province, in which he had eliminated all potential leaders of the nationalist opposition.

The most notable ornament of Herod's immediate entourage was the Aristotelian philosopher and historian Nicolaus of Damascus, who wrote a history of the world, of which a third was devoted to the eventful times in which he personally lived. He also wrote a biography of his patron Herod, which was one of the main sources of Josephus, and of this, too, considerable fragments have survived.[28] This is a particularly valuable source since Nicolaus, fragments of whose autobiography are also extant, was a trusted confidant and counsellor of Herod, particularly in his domestic complications, and was at least twice an ambassador to the Romans. It is noteworthy that after the

* The Roman hippodrome did not correspond to our race-course, but was confined to two straights with sharp turnings round the centre posts at either end, which made severe demands on driving skill. For such a course there would be sufficient room in the Central Valley.

† In the absence of any legible inscription among the sculptures and with the lack of any report on pottery it is impossible to tell if this belonged to Herodian Jerusalem or Aelia Capitolina, though the distance from the city suggests respect for Jewish prejudice in the Herodian age rather than in the time of Hadrian, when Aelia Capitolina was a Gentile city.

7. The Wailing Wall, the south part of the west wall of the Temple area of Herod the Great.

death of Nicolaus in the reign of Herod's son Archelaus the narrative of Josephus is suddenly markedly meagre in the *Antiquities*.

In Jerusalem Herod's grand conception was his design to rebuild the Temple. In view of the susceptibilities of his Jewish subjects he introduced the idea to them in the eighteenth year of his reign (22 B.C.),[29] and after materials had been prepared and a thousand priests specially trained in building to preserve the ritual purity of the Temple[30] the work began two years later and was finally completed in A.D. 64, only six years before its destruction. The actual shrine was dedicated in 18 B.C. on the anniversary of the inauguration of Herod's reign.[31]

The Temple, that known by the Lord Jesus Christ and described in its complete state by Josephus[32] and the Mishnah (Middoth), was built in a series of terraced courts within a massive boundary wall, which was surmounted by porticoes with Corinthian columns, paved in mosaics and ceiled in carved cedar (Pl. 6). The porticoes on the south side, the Royal Portico, perhaps so called from its situation relative to the old royal palace of the house of David, were particularly imposing, being both deeper and double-storeyed. Access on this side was by ramps through a triple and a double gateway through the solid wall, which the Jews compared to a mole's tunnel.* The porticoes and the paved area inside the boundary wall were accessible to all, Gentiles included, who, however, were excluded from further access on pain of death on notices inset in the precinct wall proper. Two of these notices have survived. Higher and within a higher wall was the Court of the Women, then the Court of Israel, and the highest court, the Court of the Priests, contiguous to the Temple proper. On the highest terrace of all the Temple

* The domed chambers of the triple and double gateway in the south wall could still be seen under the Aqṣa Mosque until comparatively recently (De Vogüé, *Le Temple de Jérusalem*, 1863, Pls. IV and VI), and the vaulted chambers which carried the esplanade out southwards (Josephus, *Antiquities* XV. xi. 3) are still to be seen under the courtyard east of the Aqṣa Mosque.

---

8. North Turkish wall on the line of Josephus' 'third wall' in A.D. 66, running over 'the royal caverns' i.e. Solomon's quarries (see p. 58).

9. Fragment of the Tower Psephinos at the north-west corner of Jerusalem taken by Titus in A.D. 70.

10. The Patriarch's Bath, the pool fed by Herod's aqueduct from south of Bethlehem, for distribution to the upper city of his time including his palace-fort beyond the right corner of the picture. The dome of the rotunda of the Church of the Holy Sepulchre is seen and the minaret of the 'Umarīych Mosque.

was built according to the plan and dimensions of Solomon's Temple, but necessarily modified in accordance with a scribal error in II Chronicles iii. 4, which resulted in the grossly disproportionate height of the porch as 120 cubits. To agree with this detail the porch stood both broader and higher than the rest of the building, an imposing façade, though aesthetically monstrous, despite its gold-plated marble. The building was protected from the droppings of roosting birds by gilded spikes set in the roof. This splendour perished in the great Jewish revolt in A.D.70, and nothing of the Temple itself or its emplacement remains. The present Muslim Sacred Precinct, however, is still defined by the rock-scarp which was the boundary of the outer precinct of Herod's Temple on the north under the hill on which the Antonia was built and by walls which follow the line of Herod's outer precinct on the south and east, where it coincides with the Byzantine and Turkish city-wall, and the fragment of the south part of the west wall, the famous Wailing Wall (Pl. 7).

It was an ironic turn of fortune that Herod, who had preserved and even enhanced his status through the various crises which threatened his utter ruin, should have failed to find peace in his own household. To legitimize his claim on the throne he had married the Hasmonaean princess Mariammē. Herod's passionate love for this beautiful woman was not returned. The death of her brother the popular young High Priest Aristobulus was too obviously contrived by Herod. The prompt execution of the aged Hyrcanus, convicted as he was by the Sanhedrin, could not but touch any scion of the Hasmonaeans, and the extermination of the male branch of the old royal house rankled with Mariammē. With pride of birth and the spirit of youth, she treated Herod and his family with haughty arrogance and scorn, in which she was abetted by her mother Alexandra, who had assumed the role of an avenging Fury, increasing the complications in household and state, while on the other hand Salōmē the sister of Herod requited the contempt of Mariammē and her mother by infamous intrigues, to which the young queen eventually fell a victim. Having put her to death on the suspicion of infidelity in his absence in Rhodes in 30 B.C., Herod was immediately visited with the most violent remorse, which recurred fitfully throughout his life. This tragic event was a perpetual grievance of Mariammē's two promising sons Alexander and Aristobulus, his heirs apparent by whom he hoped to win finally the allegiance of the Jews to his house. They were maligned by the infamous Salōmē and Antipater, Herod's eldest son by the Nabataean Doris, and strangled at Samaria. Antipater in turn met a well-earned death and was consigned to an ignoble grave at the fortress of Hyrcania; Herod's other victims were legion.

In the latter days of Herod, thus clouded by domestic tragedy, orthodox resistance to him intensified, for none of Herod's great benefits to the Jews in Palestine* or the Diaspora could reconcile the die-hards of Jerusalem to his Idumaean origin or to the fact that by the support of Rome he had replaced the native Jewish rulers. Indeed not even the care which he lavished on the new Temple could conciliate the Jews in Jerusalem, but in their mood of hostility it was turned to an occasion against him. Hatred to Herod crystallized in resentment at his use of images in building, particularly in the gold eagle which he had erected above the main gate of the Temple. As the king, now about seventy years old, lay in the agony of his last illness at Jericho two rabbis, Judas and Matthias, roused their young disciples to pull down the image which offended their Pharisaic scruples. On a report that Herod was dead the image was pulled down and cut to pieces. One of Herod's officers, on an exaggerated report of the riot, arrived promptly with his detachment, dispersed the crowd and arrested forty of the culprits together with Judas and Matthias. In the theatre at Jericho sentence was passed. The High Priest was deprived of his office as an accessory to the outrage, and Matthias and his companions, including presumably Judas, were burnt alive. Even on his death-bed the strong hand of Herod held the situation in check, but by this last dramatic assertion of his power a legacy of trouble had been accumulated for his successor. Jewish hostility to Herod and Rome was at the point of explosion.

Tough and tenacious to the last, Herod dragged out the weary days in painful and loathsome illness at Jericho. There is something pathetic in the journey where the invalid was carried to the hot springs of Callirrhoe east of the north end of the Dead Sea, hardly in hope of recovery but of a little ease. He returned to die at Jericho in the spring of 4 B.C., leaving the administration of the kingdom, subject to confirmation by the Emperor, to Archelaus his son by Malthakē of Samaria, with his uterine brother Antipas ('that fox'[33]) and Philip his son by another wife Cleopatra. So Herod passed at length to his rest, and was buried with royal pageantry in the fortress Herodium, which he had built in the Wilderness of Judah. The Emperor confirmed his will, appointing Archelaus over Judaea and Samaria with the title of ethnarch and Antipas and Philip respectively tetrarchs of Galilee and

* In 25 B.C. in the great two-year famine Herod contributed generously and even stripped his palace and melted down his plate to import corn from Egypt and to clothe the people. His organizing ability was shown in his distribution of the corn and in bread baked in public bakeries set up *ad hoc* and in his distribution of seed corn to be sown in the more productive lands of Syria and in the labour force which he drafted there for the harvest and for distribution of the new corn.

Peraea east of Jordan and of Ituraea and Trachonitis north-east of the Sea of Galilee.

Herod inherited his father's opportunism and flair for politics, building up his prestige under the aegis of Rome; his energy and resolution, his frank and engaging personality were his own. Already at twenty-five he had proved himself in the suppression of brigandage in Galilee, and in advancing him to the throne the Roman Senate took a well-calculated risk, which was handsomely justified after Herod had occupied the throne in peace throughout the land and economic development, the fruits of which were seen in his large estate at his death and the greatly increased revenue of his grandson Agrippa I from a realm roughly the same in extent to that of Herod, though with local differences. He promoted Western culture, but rather as a duty to Rome than through intellectual conviction or aesthetic taste. The grandson of one of the Idumaeans forcibly incorporated into Judaism by John Hyrcanus, he could not be expected to be more than a superficial Jew, an attitude encouraged by his early upbringing in the Nabataean capital Petra and by his induction into the intricacies of politics by his father Antipater. He had, however, sufficient appreciation of the vital force of Judaism to realize that as King of Judaea his influence extended far beyond Palestine to the communities of the Diaspora, with whom his relations were much more cordial than, through no fault of his own, with the Jews of the homeland. For those communities, widely scattered but solidly united in faith and a significant economic force within the Roman Empire, Herod showed a statesmanlike concern, and provided the new Temple as a focal shrine of what might reasonably be regarded as his Jewish Empire. But for all his statesmanlike vision he was a robust barbarian, nature's antidote to the suicidal ineptitude of the native nobility and the febrile susceptibilities of the more extreme of the Pharisees, bringing the necessary realism and perspective to the politics of Judaea under the new Roman régime. His interests were the camp, the chase and, with the instinct of his Idumaean fathers, commercial speculation, in which, thanks to his native shrewdness and his political power and control of the vital trade-routes, he was remarkably successful. Quick to appraise men and situations, at least until his mind was poisoned by the intrigues of his family, for which his haughty wife Mariammē was a ready target, and in his latter days, when his own mental deterioration made him even more susceptible to suspicions, he was swift and sure in decision and resolute in action. More than half an Arab, Herod realized most of the essentials of the Arab ideal of 'manhood' or 'humanity' (*murū'a*). He was persistent in revenge, patient and resourceful in adversity, loyal to his kindred, and the protector of the distressed, as in the great famine, to relieve which he sold the palace plate, and his generosity was extravagant. Detested by his Jewish subjects as a vassal of Rome, he nevertheless matched the greatest of the native kings of Israel, and in the political situation of his time was the benefactor of his people, taking the first critical steps in their adjustment to life in the Roman Empire, which bade fair to be happily effected under his grandson Agrippa I, when he prematurely died.

None of the family of Herod who survived his fatal suspicions inherited the strength or ability of their father. Archelaus, his heir in Jerusalem, first excited the hopes of the Jews by facile compliance and later tried to assert himself against popular tyranny by a massacre of three thousand in the Temple precincts at the Feast of Passover in 4 B.C. He left the land in a ferment to go to Rome to have his father's bequest confirmed, and was deposed in A.D. 6, when the province of Judaea on the appeal of a Jewish delegation was put directly under Roman administration by procurators, the best known of whom was Pontius Pilate (A.D. 26–36). Antipas maintained himself in his sombre capital Tiberias till A.D. 37, when he reaped the bitter fruit of his irregular marriage with Herodias his brother's wife* and was deposed by the delation of his brother-in-law Agrippa,† the spendthrift brother of Herodias, and the boon-companion of the Emperor Caligula.

The career of Agrippa is a remarkable instance of the hazards of society in the early Roman Empire, which affected even the provinces. From an early age Agrippa, the son of Aristobulus the son of Herod the Great by Mariammē I, had been brought up in Rome under the tutelage of his mother Berenicē the daughter of Salōmē the sister of Herod, who barely held his extravagance in check. On her death he fell into hopeless debt and, except for a short time when he was placed as market supervisor in Tiberias by Herod Antipas his brother-in-law, his life was dogged by clamant creditors. Eventually at Rome the noble Antonia, the daughter of Mark Antony and sister-in-law of the Emperor

* So Luke iii. 19, not naming the brother, who is named Philip in Matthew xiv. 3 (Codex D, however, omits 'Philip'). Actually according to Josephus (*Antiquities* XVIII. v. 4) Herodias was married to Herod the son of Herod the Great and Mariammē II, who was thus a half-brother of Herod Antipas. Her daughter Salōmē was married to Philip another half-brother of Herod Antipas.

† In emulation of Agrippa, who from dependence on her and Herod Antipas had been made a king, Herodias urged Antipas to go to Rome to seek the same title. He went with some reluctance. Agrippa put in Gaius' hands incriminating evidence of the treachery of his brother-in-law, who had equipment ready for an armed rising and was in terms with the Parthians. Antipas was obliged to admit the charge and was deposed and banished to Lyons in Gaul (Josephus, *Antiquities* XVIII, vii).

Tiberius, out of respect to the memory of his mother, settled his debts and introduced him to the Emperor, and in the court circle he became a close friend of the future Emperor Gaius Caligula. Careless talk to Gaius reported to the Emperor by Agrippa's groom reversed his fortune, and he was loaded with chains and imprisoned. The friendship of Gaius, fatal to most men of rank and worth, proved a blessing to Agrippa. After six months' detention the Emperor Tiberius died and Gaius succeeded. Agrippa was released; in place of his iron chain he was presented with one of gold, and the tetrarchy of Philip the son of Herod the Great being vacant, Agrippa was given this district with that of Lysanias in the neighbouring regions beyond the sea of Galilee with the title of King in A.D. 37. In A.D. 39 he received the forfeited tetrarchy of Herod Antipas in Galilee and regions beyond Jordan.

The presence of Agrippa in Rome on the assassination of Gaius Caligula might well have proved his ruin. However he kept a cool head and by his encouragement—one might almost say patronage—Claudius accepted the onus of Empire.[34] Under the new régime his realm was extended to include Judaea and Samaria. Thus by A.D. 41 the realm of Herod the Great with certain regional modifications was again united under his grandson, and again Jerusalem was the capital of a territorial state as extensive as that of Solomon.

The administration of Agrippa, like his good fortune, confounded those of his own kin and country who had known his unstable career. Lenient but not indulgent, he won the confidence of his subjects, orthodox as well as liberal, and gave the land peace and security, no small achievement in view of the latent forces of violence and fanaticism which had found expression after the death of Herod and were so soon to break out afresh. In Jerusalem he set an example of regular piety and devotion,[35] and though he had spent so much of his youth among the 'fast set' in Rome he now loved to dwell in Jerusalem as the father of his people. He patronized the games in honour of the Emperor in Caesarea and equipped Berytus with public buildings and Western institutions. So his coins minted at Jerusalem bear no human image, so offensive to Pharisaic principles, but simply a sunshade with his name and royal title on the obverse and three ears of barley and the year of his reign on the reverse (Pl. 13). Coins from the provinces, however, are stamped with the images of his imperial patrons Gaius and Claudius and his own—the first likeness of a Jewish king known to us—with the epithet Philokaisar appended to his name and title (Pl. 13). It must be noted that the Pharisaic tradition as expressed in the Talmud is unswervingly loyal to the memory of Agrippa. His reign, lasting only until A.D. 44, must be regarded as a potential rather than as an effective factor in the general history of the Jews. This wise and beneficent ruler died in his fifty-fourth year. Had he ruled another twenty years the Jewish people would have been saved the rule of the procurators in Rome's evil day and the crowning tragedy of civil war and political extinction. Josephus, like the Talmud, is appreciative:

> Agrippa's temper was mild and equally liberal to all men. He was humane to foreigners and made them sensible of his liberality, but was even more charitable and sympathetic to his kinsmen. Accordingly he loved to live continually at Jerusalem and was exactly careful in the observance of the laws of his country. He therefore kept himself entirely pure nor did any day pass over his head without its appointed sacrifice.[36]

In the reign of Agrippa we see what the reign of Herod the Great might have been but for the intrigues of his family and the envy of the orthodox. That Agrippa should have been able to conciliate the latter seems inexplicable until it is remembered that between the two reigns there fell the event which was 'the great divide' of Judaism and indeed of the Western world, the advent of Jesus of Nazareth and the mission which he inspired, the fulfilment of the whole purpose of the history and the faith of Israel or a colossal blasphemy. Agrippa did not spare the infant Church. James the son of Zebedee was martyred in his reign while Peter barely escaped with his life.[37] The reconciliation of the Pharisees to the Roman-sponsored rule of the grandson of Herod the Great probably reflects the impact of the challenge of the new faith in Jerusalem and the provinces, as Acts xii. 3 suggests, in adding to the account of Agrippa's persecution 'because he saw it pleased the Jews'.

Agrippa's son, also named Agrippa, a lad of seventeen at his father's death, was being reared at Rome under the patronage of the Emperor Claudius. The Emperor was quite ready to settle the kingdom on the young man, but, yielding as in most things to the advice of his freedmen, he left the realm of the late king under the care of procurators immediately responsible to the Imperial Legate of Syria, perhaps wisely advised in view of Agrippa's youth, but possibly through the self-interest of his advisers in creating thus another office which might be disposed of and discharged with profit, as in the case of the notorious Felix[38] the brother of Pallas the freedman and factotum of Claudius, who was procurator of Judaea between A.D. 52 and 60. Agrippa II was made king of the Lebanese principality of Chalcis, once the property of his uncle Herod, with subsequent extentions to Galilee and Transjordan, and in addition he was given the right to nominate the High Priest and was appointed guardian of the Temple.[39] He had a suitable residence on the west slope of the south-west hill in Jerusalem, probably the old palace of the Hasmonaen princes (see above, p. 46). but for the most part he was happy in the pleasant capital of his small mountain principality at Caesarea Philippi north-east of the Sea of Galilee. During the Jewish revolt he emerges in a favourable light as mediator between the Jews and Rome. He might well have filled the place of his father and have assuaged the violent passions of his fellow-countrymen. But the affairs of the Jews were moving to a swift and bloody crisis in Jerusalem. Herod Agrippa II was the last of his race to rule over any part of the domains of his fathers, and the polity of Israel itself was soon to vanish beyond recall till our own day.

NOTES FOR CHAPTER VI

1 Josephus, *Antiquities* XIV. xi. 2
2 Josephus, *Antiquities* XIV. vii. 4
3 Josephus, *Antiquities* XIV. vi. 3
4 Josephus, *Antiquities* XIV. viii. 1–2
5 Josephus, *Antiquities* XIV. x
6 Josephus, *Antiquities* XIV. ix. 2
7 Josephus, *Antiquities* XIV. ix. 4
8 Josephus, *Antiquities* XIV. xii. 1
9 Josephus, *Antiquities* XIV. xii. 2
10 Josephus, *Antiquities* XIV. xiii. 1
11 Josephus, *Antiquities* XIV. xiii. 3
12 Josephus, *Antiquities* XIV. xiii. 9
13 Josephus, *War* I. xiii. 9
14 Josephus, *Antiquities* XIV. xiii. 9
15 Josephus, *Antiquities* XV. i. 2
16 Josephus, *Antiquities* XV. iii. 3
17 Josephus, *Antiquities* XV. iii. 2
18 Josephus, *Antiquities* XV. v. 1
19 Josephus, *Antiquities* XV. vi. 5
20 A. H. M. Jones, *The Herods of Judaea*, 1938, p. 76
21 Josephus, *Antiquities* XV. viii. 5
22 *War* V. iv. 3
23 A. H. M. Jones, *op. cit.*, p. 84
24 *War* II. iii. 1
25 K. M. Kenyon, *Palestine Exploration Quarterly*, 1964, p. 14
26 C. Schick, *P.E.F.Q.S.*, 1887, pp. 161–166
27 F. M. Abel, *Histoire de la Palestine* I, 1952, p. 363
28 C. Müller, *Fragmenta Historiorum Graecorum*, iii, 1849, pp. 343–464
29 Josephus, *Antiquities* XV. xi. 1
30 Josephus, *Antiquities* XV. xi. 2
31 Josephus, *Antiquities* XV. xi. 6
32 *Antiquities* XV. xi. 3–7
33 Luke xiii. 32
34 Josephus, *Antiquities* XIX. iv. 1
35 Josephus, *Antiquities* XIX. vii. 3
36 Josephus, *Antiquities* XIX. vii. 3
37 Acts xii. 1–9
38 Acts xxiv
39 Josephus, *Antiquities* XX. i. 3; ix. 7

VII

THE GREAT DIVIDE

The Reign of God has come near! Right about! (Mark i. 15)

With the extinction of the Hasmonaean dynasty and Rome's calculating arrangement for the government of the Jews through the line of the Idumaean Antipater and eventually through her own procurators, the conviction had grown, especially among the Pharisees, that the destiny of the people must be realized otherwise than along the traditional path of historical development. Former experience of political frustration had forced the Jews more and more to seek such a solution of the anomaly of their unique spiritual status and their consciousness of special calling and the indignity of their political subjection to heathen powers, which reflected the cosmic paradox of the power of evil and suffering in a world which was believed to be the creation of Almighty God. The ancient Davidic king had been regarded as the vassal of God and the temporal guarantee of his Divine Order, the sustaining of which against the powers of Chaos was the theme of the great New Year festival, which enabled men to keep their sense of perspective in the perplexities of Israel's actual situation among the nations. When kings no longer ruled in Israel men looked for the establishment of the Eternal Order by more immediate Divine activity through the agency of the supernatural, or at least supernaturally endowed, Messiah. Those hopes encouraged the more sober type of Pharisee to endure the domination of Rome, turning to an intense cultivation of humble piety and social morality implicit in the Law, and their piety and vision were both shared eventually by Jesus of Nazareth and his followers. But the Messianic hopes also inspired bolder spirits to attack Rome and her vassals as the immediate obstacles to nationalist aspirations and indeed to the Reign of God, which they thus sought to precipitate by force.[1] In such conflicts the iron entered into the soul of the most ardent Jews, faith being replaced by fanaticism, superstition, credulity and desperate violence, which culminated in the blind fury of the revolt against the tried and organized might of Rome in A.D. 66–70 and in the later revolt headed by Simon bar Kokhba in A.D. 132–135.

That such forces were gathering head some time before the actual revolt in A.D. 66 was evident from repeated risings throughout the country immediately after the death of Herod the Great. On the imposition of direct Roman rule on the removal of Archelaus in A.D. 6, which was signalized by a new fiscal assessment involving a census, the theocratic ideal with Messianic implications[2] was apparently asserted by Judas of Gamala. In the time of the procurator Cuspius Fadus (after A.D. 44) one Theudas claimed prophetic authority with supernatural powers.[3] He marshalled his forces and, marching down the Jordan Valley, promised a repetition of the miracle of the passing of Jordan dryshod, thereby associating himself with the culmination of Israel's Drama of Salvation[4] and with Elijah,[5] who was regarded at this time as the herald of the Messianic age.[6] In the time of Felix (A.D. 52–59) a certain Egyptian led out four thousand desperate men to the wilderness[7] and mustered his forces on the Mount of Olives in anticipation of the miraculous collapse of the walls of Jerusalem and the overthrow of the power of Rome by supernatural agency.[8] Such movements achieved nothing, but they were symptomatic of the popular mood of expectancy at what men believed was the end of an era.

The same expectancy, though tempered by a more sober and positive faith, is reflected in the case of Simeon and Anna of Jerusalem, who were 'waiting for the consolation of Israel' and were spiritually prepared to receive 'him who would restore Israel'.[9]

The limitations of the ideology of the Kingship of God and the establishment of the Divine Order in his 'showdown' with the forces of Chaos, which had sustained Israel in the vicissitudes of her history, had been noticed by the prophets of the eighth century, and Amos and Isaiah had raised the conception to the moral plane. The day of God's vindication over the powers of Chaos would not be confined to nature or history, where they could be conveniently identified with the political enemies of Israel. In that critical conflict God would triumph over all the forces of Chaos natural, political and moral. There would be no national discrimination; Israel was not bound to triumph with her God; all who promoted the power of moral disorder, whether without Israel or within, would be discomfited on the Day of the Lord, which assumed more and more the character of a great final assize, the Judgement. This tradition was now revived by John the Baptist in the time of Herod Antipas, and his stirring challenge to prepare for the imminent Day of Judgement by true repentance symbolized by baptism gripped many including the more sober type of Pharisee, who believed in the imminence of God's New Order, the Kingdom of God, but were content to prepare themselves, passively enduring the affront of Rome to the Divine Sovereignty and expecting the consummation of the New Order in God's good time and by his own means.

As Israel, reduced by national disasters and genuinely chastened by the Exile and domination by succeeding world powers, continued to hold her faith in the Reign of God it was inevitable that the challenge of the Prophets had less point than the hope and assurance of God's triumph over the foreign oppressors. The establishment of God's government or Order (*mishpāṭ*), which eventually took more and more the connotation of judgement (also *mishpāṭ*), would mean the vindication of Israel, and the doom only of her enemies. This was the ever more sanguine hope of the more extreme type of Pharisee, who emerged towards the end of the reign of Herod the Great. The attitude of traditional Pharisaism is apparent in its attitude to Herod as a Roman vassal whom it regarded as an evil sent by God for the sins of Israel and so to be passively endured. There arose another party who were convinced that it was their duty to speed the coming of the Kingdom of God by active, and even armed, co-operation. The strength of these Zealots, or devoted enthusiasts for the sole Sovereignty of the God of Israel, who were determined to precipitate the Kingdom of God by force, is apparent in the various armed risings soon after the death of Herod the Great, beginning with that of Judas of Gamala east of the Sea of Galilee in A.D. 6. The Zealot party gathered strength until they dominated Judaism, securing their final ascendancy during the great revolt of A.D. 66–70.

The dangers inherent in the narrow, nationalistic interpretation of the day of the Lord were already apprehended at the end of the Babylonian Exile, when on the eve of deliverance Israel's faith in the Sovereignty of God was evoked in the ringing words from the ancient Temple liturgy associated with the epiphany of God as King in the New Year Festival:*

> How beautiful upon the mountains
> Are the feet of him that brings good tidings,
> That proclaims 'All is well!'
> That brings good tidings of good,
> That proclaims deliverance,

* The association of this passage with the liturgy of the New Year festival is clearly indicated by its recurrence in Nahum i. 15 (Hebrew text ii. 1), with the variation of 'Keep thy feasts' for 'Thy God is King'. The word for 'feasts', though possibly of general connotation, means specific New Year festivals.

That says to Zion,
Thy God is King!

Even in the prophetic circle which preserved the tradition of Isaiah in the Exile the time and circumstances conditioned a nationalistic view of the establishment of the Reign of God. To be sure, it lacked the more lurid expectations of the triumph of God and the discomfiture of the political enemies of Israel which characterized later Judaism, partly reflecting the poetic imagery in which the hope was cast in the context of the New Year Festival and partly the bitter experience of foreign domination, in which Israel had always particularized the forces of Chaos over which God's triumph was celebrated. But it might well be asked if this expressed truly the nature of the Reign of God and Israel's destined place in the Divine economy.

Early in Israel's national history in Palestine the purpose and direction of the history of the people, which was implicit in the Divine election of Israel, had been expressed in the oldest of the main literary sources of the Pentateuch, in the promise to Abraham: 'In thee shall all families of the earth be blessed.'

That fair vision of the positive Divine purpose for Israel was obscured in the negative prospect of political Messianism and the interpretation of the Reign of God which was increasingly dominant in Israel after the Exile. This, however, did not pass without protest, which came most effectively and positively from the Isaianic circle in the Babylonian Exile in the famous Servant Songs, particularly in Isaiah xlii. 1–4; xlix. 1–6 and the Song of the Suffering Servant in Isaiah lii. 13–liii. 12, which are clearly separated from their context in thought and sequence of ideas.

The first passage, acclaiming the Servant of God as one who would not raise his voice nor break the bruised reed nor quench the smoking flax, emphasizes his role as the mediator to the Gentiles of the Law, God's distinctive grace to Israel. The second too emphasizes the function of the Servant as the embodiment—perhaps the spiritual core—of the true Israel as a light to the Gentiles, but it is the last passage which states explicitly how this purpose is to be achieved.

Preceded and followed by passages which exult over the material rehabilitation of Israel, the passage is a confession put into the mouths of 'kings and nations', the conventional antagonists of God in his vital struggle with the powers of Chaos in the establishment of his Kingship. In contrast to their discomfiture so luridly depicted in the conventional liturgy proper to the epiphany of God as King and the triumph of his vice-regent the king, 'the servant of God', as for instance in Psalms ii and cx, the 'kings and nations', even at the moment when the suffering and humiliation of the Servant of God seems to indicate their triumph and to invite their gloating, confess that what the Servant suffers was really their due, which they are spared by the mere mercy of God. In the traditional ideology of kingship in Israel and elsewhere in the ancient Near East men were familiar with the vicarious suffering of the king for his people in acts of penance occasioned by public disasters. Now the prophet in Isaiah lii. 13–liii. 12 advances to the conception that the election of Israel and her representative involves vicarious suffering for all mankind. No less is involved in the declaration of the Divine purpose for and through Israel 'In thee shall all families of the earth be blessed'. The hope of Israel was not in a chauvinistic champion who would supplant the domination of the current world-power by an equally repressive Israel, but in the representative of the true Israel and in the true Israel sacramentally identified with her representative, who would, in bearing the sins of mankind, bring them to a sense of the sovereign grace of God.

In the days of the Roman domination when Pontius Pilate was procurator of Judaea (A.D. 26–36) and Herod Antipas ruled in Galilee (4 B.C.–A.D. 39) came Jesus of Nazareth, mediating the grace, power, and truth of God to the people, which was the traditional role of the ancient Davidic king. Quickening the awareness of the urgency of the power of God by his infinite love and sympathy for men and women declared in word and act, by his life-giving acts of healing and restoration and by his trenchant revelations of fundamental truths and the vital ethic which they inspired, he seemed to fulfil current expectations of the popular Messiah who would inaugurate the Reign of God, and indeed Christian tradition summarizes his proclamation as

> The Reign of God has come near. Right about! and trust the good news!

The announcement of 'the good news', or gospel, of 'the Kingdom of God' of course re-echoes the words of the liturgy in Isaiah lii.7 and the whole familiar ideology of the Reign of God. This was a summons to the traditional faith; but in the imperative 'Right about! [A.V. Repent]' there is a challenge to the popular faith in its indiscriminate association of Israel with God in his cosmic triumph over the powers of Chaos. Here the prophet of Nazareth in his proclamation of the Kingdom of God associated himself directly with the moral challenge of Amos and Isaiah, and made the vital break with popular Messianism which so disappointed his contemporaries.

In spite of the repeated refusal of Jesus to be identified with the popular Messianism, men were slow to dissociate him from this ideal, which had become so congenial to most men at that particular time, and indeed it was the natural fear of the priestly, or Sadducee, party that he would involve the people in an insurrection against Rome. The populace of Jerusalem too seemed to voice their disappointment in Jesus as a fulfilment of their own interpretation of the Messianic hope in their final rejection of him and in their demand 'Crucify him!'

The true prophet can never be ignored. His truth may compel a genuine and wholesome response; it always disturbs; it often causes mortal offence. Jesus experienced all reactions. Staunch to the Law according to his Jewish tradition, he would not suffer it to become an unintelligible, fossilized rubric or a mere shibboleth. He appreciated the efforts of the Rabbis to safeguard its application in a changing society where it was often practically obsolete, though he deprecated pedantry and reduced it to absurdity. For him the vitality of the Law was to be conserved not in casuistic safeguarding of its letter but in the application of its spirit towards the positive end for which it was revealed as an expression of the distinctive nature of the people of God and of God's will for his people. But his sharp retorts to his Pharisaic interlocutors were capable of misrepresentation, and it was easy to demonstrate to men who had made a fetish of the Law that he was dangerously liberal. Nor was human nature likely to forgive his dialectic triumphs and his indictments of human conceit which raised Rabbinic authority in the interpretation of the Law to the status of the Law itself.

It is noteworthy that in contrast to his consistent refusal to identify himself with the popular Messiah Jesus regularly refers to himself quite openly as the Son of Man, perhaps a circumlocution for 'I' according to Aramaic idiom, but with eschatological nuances familiar to a few who had keener spiritual perception. To such he identified himself regularly with the Suffering Servant of Isaiah lii. 13–liii. 12, the embodiment of the true Israel, whose mission was the atonement and reconciliation of his people and of mankind. In those who had caught the significance of this protest against popular political Messianism the life and teaching of Jesus made immediate impact, and for them all that he said or did signified the fulfilment of the Divinely-appointed destiny of Israel. Others again, even among the disciples, had to learn slowly and painfully the fuller implications of the life of Jesus. His work, however, was not in vain, and when he was crucified forty years before the destruction of the Temple and the extinction of the Jewish people the spiritual élite which was identified with him in the role of the Suffering Servant was confirmed in the faith that God had been among them reconciling the world to himself and that in them Israel had emerged from the discipline of the old dispensation into the fresh assurance and challenge of the New Covenant.

But all but a minority followed the old ways, perhaps stauncher because of what they were sincerely convinced was dangerous and disloyal liberalism, their nationalist feeling intensifying in proportion as they suspected the broad universalism of the followers of Jesus, who were soon numbering cosmopolitan Jews in their community[10] and eventually even Gentiles.[11] It would be invidious and unscientific to see in the unhappy career of Judaism to the ultimate tragedy of A.D. 70 and 135 the consequence of the rejection of Jesus. We may justly claim, however, that the ruin of the Jewish people was precipitated by their failure to modify the old forms of the faith, the externals of the Law and the material particularism of the traditional faith in the Reign of God, according to his example. From this point the attitude of official Judaism to the external world hardened in contrast to the missionary approach of the Church, which in the first generation, it must be emphasized, was fundamentally Jewish. Here then is 'the great divide' in the history of Jerusalem, when Judaism in self-defence turned in on itself and the Church with a forward look served itself heir to the faith and destiny of Israel. Jerusalem is part of the Jewish heritage of Christendom, appropriated all the more cordially because of the culmination of the drama of man's salvation on the Cross on Golgotha.

Perpetually resenting the limitation on the sovereign authority of the Law by the secular authority and arms of a foreign power, and with eschatological hopes of the Reign of God to excite them, the Jews were awkward provincial subjects. Nor was Rome fortunate in her procurators, by whom the Jews were governed from A.D. 6 to 66 except for the brief reign of Agrippa I (41–44). Offences were given through obtuseness and obstinacy, as when Pilate insisted on bringing his troops into Jerusalem with their standards with the images of the Emperor,[12] which were sure to offend the Jews, and only refrained with a bad grace. Other actions were excusable though tactless, as when Pilate proposed to appropriate a portion of the Temple funds for the wholly laudable purpose of bringing water in an aqueduct from a source south of Bethlehem* to the city, and indeed to the Temple. A riot followed this alleged sacrilege, which Pilate silenced by intimidation and violence resulting in a number of deaths.[13] Pilate appears as a weak, nervous character who on occasion showed an ill-seasoned obstinacy. This

* On this, the development of Herod's, and possibly even of Solomon's, work, see above, pp. 38, 49. A section of Pilate's aqueduct is now conveniently visible beside the new road from Jerusalem to Bethlehem. A later aqueduct in fine joined stone sections built by Septimius Severus in the early third century is also visible at Bethlehem.

estimate is borne out by the Gospel narrative and to a further extent by the incident of the bloody dispersion of a crowd of credulous and ignorant peasants excited by one who claimed to be a prophet at Mount Gerizzim, which was the immediate cause of Pilate's removal. The rule of Pilate is typical of procuratorial rule and the reaction of the Jews, who took advantage of the fact that the procurators, imperial agents of the middle class with administrative rather than political functions and traditions, lacked the authority and strength for their difficult task. The reign of King Agrippa I (41–44) was as we have seen a halcyon season, though the situation was complicated by the attempt of Gaius Caligula, the last and most unworthy Emperor of the Julian House, to set up his imperial image and cult in the Temple in Jerusalem. Josephus[14] suggests that this was incited by certain slanders raised by the Gentile adversaries of the Jews at Alexandria, who sought thus to cover up the insults they had heaped upon the Emperor's friend Agrippa on his return to his kingdom in Palestine. On the other hand Philo, himself a Jew of Alexandria, suggests[15] that the occasion of Gaius' action was the destruction by the Jews of an altar to Gaius set up by the Gentiles in provocation of the Jews in a synagogue at Jamnia. The action of the Jews was easily misinterpreted, and the determination of Gaius to have the statue of Olympian Zeus in his own image set up in the Temple was more than impious caprice. In strict justice to the Emperor, it must be said that he admitted the objections of his friend Agrippa, who at great personal hazard reminded him of the toleration of his predecessors and the loyalty of the Jews of Palestine and the Diaspora. This threat, though happily abortive, united the forces of Judaism, if not in cordial brotherhood, at least in common hatred of Rome.

Thus the task of the procurators after Agrippa was many times complicated. Cuspius Fadus, the first of these men, suppressed a rising under Theudas, whom he captured and executed (see above, p. 170). His head was sent to Jerusalem to be displayed as a grim warning to others who might cherish plans of insurrection. In effect it proved an incentive to vengeance. Tiberius Alexander, a renegade Jew of Alexandria, had to put down a rising headed by Judas and Simon the sons of Judas of Gamala (see above, p. 163), who were eventually crucified. Under the successor of Tiberius Alexander, Ventidius Cumanus, the fire of revolt still smouldered angrily. At Passover, when Jerusalem was

---

11. Inside the Damascus Gate, locally called the Gate of the Pillar, the main north gate of Hadrian's city of Aelia Capitolina from which the main street (*cardo maximus*) ran south. The present work is Turkish from the seventeenth century and the access through the gate is indirect.

thronged with Jews from all over Palestine and beyond, the procurator ordered a standby in the Temple precincts. Weary with the tedium of sentry-duty or provoked by the arrogance of the Jews, a certain soldier let down his breeches and exposed himself in insult to the devotees. A furious riot ensued upon this mischievous action, which Cumanus strove in vain to allay with words. He then ordered his whole force in Jerusalem to occupy the Antonia, which commanded the Temple courts. A panic arose among the Jews, and in a general *sauve qui peut* a great number were trodden to death in the narrow streets of the city. Even admitting Josephus' exaggeration of the death-roll at twenty thousand[16] this fatal Passover must have left mourners all over Palestine. The strict impartiality of Roman justice and consideration for the religious susceptibilities of the Jews, however, is evident in Cumanus' execution of a soldier who in a search in a village had wantonly torn up a scroll of the Law. At this time there was an outbreak of hostility between the Jews and the Samaritans, which in its final settlement involved the removal of Cumanus, suspected of favouring, if not actually abetting, the Samaritans. It foreshadows later developments in the actual revolt that the Jews in this conflict called a notorious brigand Eliezar to the command. Under Cumanus' successor Felix (52–59), a venal freedman, the brother of Claudius' freedman and favourite Pallas, excitement and terrorism rose in crescendo till open rebellion became almost inevitable. Particularly active were bodies of secret Jewish terrorists, who mixed with the crowds in the streets and struck down their victims with a short dagger (*sica*) which they kept concealed under their cloaks, hence the term *sicarii*. Patriotism was generally the motive; the offence was the slightest degree of moderation; but all manner of base and selfish motives were active.[17] Far from mitigating this vice, Felix actually aggravated it,[18] using desperadoes for his own ends, particularly to remove the High Priest Jonathan, who had presumed to give the procurator a sound admonition. Another

---

12. General view from the south-east showing the Muslim Sacred Precinct with the Aqṣa Mosque in the south wall, the west wing of which was the headquarters of the Templars during the Latin Kingdom of Jerusalem. In the centre is the Dome of the Rock with the Dome of the Chain to the east. The walled-up Golden Gate, a Byzantine work, is in the east wall and the north-west was dominated by Herod's fortress Antonia, where the minaret of the mosque is seen. We believe this to be the scene of Jesus' condemnation before Pilate. The Church of the Holy Sepulchre is under the dark dome by the tall square tower of the German Church of the Redeemer towards the top left.

12

symptom of disease in the body of the Jewish community in that evil time was strife between the secular leaders of the people and the High Priests. This was a recurrence of the old controversy which had raged under Seleucid domination between the impersonal authority of the Law and the personal authority of the hereditary priesthood with their inherited experience of secular statesmanship and their prerogatives. Actually since the limitation of the power of the High Priest after the accession of Herod the Great the office became eventually the monopoly of a few families wealthy enough to court the influence of the ruler who had the power of nomination. The High Priest in consequence of his diminished status grew more and more sordid in the exaction of his priestly perquisites, thus alienating the sympathy of the mass of the people and the lower clergy.[19] Eventually casting off the traditional authority of the High Priest, the Jews were at the mercy of the boldest extremists. The impression conveyed by Josephus, who, it must be remembered, was a patrician and a moderate, is that there were forces in the Jewish community itself which made revolt practically inevitable. But those were evil times for Rome also, the age of Gaius Caligula, Claudius and his meddling freedmen and Nero, and the revolt was precipitated in no small measure by the weakness and vice of the procurators. The last factor may be exaggerated by Josephus to palliate the fault of the Jews, but the Roman Tacitus has no such motive in significantly animadverting on them with his own characteristic terseness 'Yet the patience of the Jews held out until Gessius Florus; under him war broke out'.[20]

The actual outbreak of hostilities is particularized by Josephus[21] in the rejection of the daily sacrifice for Rome and the Emperor, which had been offered at his expense in the Temple. Appalled at the prospect of open war with Rome, the moderates in the city together with the chief priests sought vainly to dissuade the multitude while there was yet time, and a last-minute appeal was made to Florus and to Agrippa II, who had nomination of the High Priest and was Temple-guardian. Florus, whom Josephus accuses of seeking the war as a means of covering up the abuses of his administration,[22] did not deign to reply, but Agrippa immediately sent a force of two thousand cavalry from his realm north and east of the Sea of Galilee, hoping to restrain the insurgents by force of arms when persuasion could no longer avail. This force together with a cohort of Roman troops left previously by Florus as a garrison put the Jewish moderates in possession of the Upper City, dominated by Herod's palace-fort on the south-west hill. The nationalists, however, were unbroken in their determination and held the Lower City and the Temple. Force of numbers proved too great for the moderates in spite of the support of Rome and Agrippa. The rebels entered the Upper City, where they burned the residence of the High Priest as well as the palaces of Agrippa and his sister Berenicē.

Now the rebels were strengthened by other extremists, and their first act was to burn the public archives with the records of debts.[23] The Romans and Agrippa's men were thrown on the defensive in the Antonia and in the palace on the south-west hill. The significance of the revolt was brought home to the Romans by the reduction of the Antonia and the slaughter of the garrison. The rebels then invested the palace with its three great Herodian towers of Hippicus, Phasael and Mariammē. The troops of Agrippa anticipated the fall of the fortress by surrendering on terms, and the Romans were left to sustain the siege alone. With gloomy foreboding this small force made its last stand in the great towers. At the end of their resources they sought to save themselves by honourable surrender, and security was promised by Eliezar the son of the High Priest, who then led a strong party of the people. The *Herrenvolk* complex of the Jewish extremists, however, flouted the obligations of common morality, and surrounding the remnants of the Roman cohort, who had surrendered their arms, they fell upon the helpless men, who met their end with true Roman dignity. Only one man, the commanding officer Metilius, asked for mercy and bought his life at the price of becoming a Jew.[24] Though this was no more than the annihilation of a garrison, it was a decisive act of open rebellion.

Already the worst elements among the Jewish people were emerging as protagonists, and Jerusalem had a foretaste of civil strife, which was eventually to prove more pernicious than the assaults of Rome. Now even before the city was cleared of the Romans parties under Eliezer, the governor of the Temple,[25] and Menaḥem, a son of the rebel leader Judas of Gamala (see above, p. 163), fought each other in the streets and desecrated even the Temple in their internecine strife.[26] In those days of terror there was no respect of person or place. The Temple was violated; the party of Menaḥem had killed the High Priest Ananias in the street, and though Menaḥem, who was himself killed, was the greater villain, Eliezer and his party were not innocent.

At this point Cestius Gallus the Legate of Syria moved with two legions and auxiliaries from his headquarters at Antioch. He mustered his forces at Ptolemais (Akko), where he was joined by Agrippa with three thousand foot and four thousand horse. They proceeded to Caesarea, from which a flying column surprised Joppa, plundering and burning the town. Moving forward to Lydda, Gallus penetrated the Pass of Beth-horon (see above, p. 22) to the upland plain by Gibeon (al-Jīb), where he pitched his base camp.* The Legate moved his assault-forces forward to Mount Scopus, where he attacked the city on its vulnerable north side. The northern suburb of Bezetha, not yet enclosed by the outer wall of the city, which had been begun by Agrippa I but had been discontinued by order of Claudius, was destroyed, and the Romans proceeded to mine the wall of the Temple precinct. At this time influential men in Jerusalem would have admitted the Romans.[27] Adequate contact with Gallus, however, was lacking owing to strict security control, and the legate on his part had apparently no suspicion of the uncertainty in which the defenders found themselves. Josephus maintains that a resolute assault would have reduced the city, but this great opportunity passed when Cestius Gallus ordered the withdrawal of his troops.

This move will remain one of the unsolved mysteries of history. Possibly the legate, whose main interest was the security of the whole province of Syria, had satisfied himself on his march through the land to Jerusalem that the situation was generally well in hand and the trouble localized in Jerusalem remote among the mountains, where the conflicting parties already bade fair to cancel each other out. In any case he withdrew his assault forces to Mount Scopus in the middle of October, where they lay all night. Next day he withdrew to Gibeon, which he abandoned after two days. But if Gallus had calculated on the suicidal enmity of the Jewish parties their mutual hatred did not prevent them for the moment uniting in the harassing of the Roman withdrawal. While the Romans were still in the pass before issuing on to the coastal plain the Jews set on them from points of vantage, and the retreat became a rout.[28] The pass was rich in memories for the Jews. Their Scripture told how Joshua had broken an Amorite confederacy here[29] and how in Saul's war of liberation he had pursued the Philistine down the same pass.[30] Here Judas Maccabaeus and his band of patriots had several times harassed the invading Syrians. Yet never was such a victory won as this, and the unexpected discomfiture of the Romans must have fanned the flame of fanaticism in Jerusalem,[31] which to men elated by Messianic hopes seemed inviolable.

This general sortie from Jerusalem may have been the juncture at which the Christian community in the city, who would certainly be suspected of moderation, profited from a relaxation of security measures in the jubilant mêlée to withdraw to the realm of Agrippa beyond Jordan about Pella.

* *Gabao* (Josephus, *War* II, xix, 1), which he gives as fifty furlongs from Jerusalem, corresponds better to Gibeon (al-Jīb) about 6 miles north-west of Jerusalem, than to Gibeah (Tell al-Fūl), which is only 4 miles north of the city.

Though this initial success against Gallus confirmed the power of the extremists, in the necessary organization for resistance to the reprisals which were sure to follow the Jewish moderates were drawn in, possibly because they saw that full-scale war was inevitable. Their influence and experience were exploited. Joseph the son of Gorion and Ananus the High Priest were put in command of the city with especial charge to complete the wall begun by Agrippa (see above, pp. 57ff.). The provinces too were organized for defence under various leaders including the historian Josephus, whose command was Galilee with the region of Gamala east of the Sea of Galilee. The experience of Josephus is typical of that of the moderates in those troubles. He was never quite trusted, but by repeated conciliation, threat and subterfuge, barely held mutiny in check, the towns of Tiberias and Sepphoris (Ṣaffūriyeh) being particularly insubordinate. Josephus may have over-emphasized the situation, since his history was written under Imperial patronage in Rome, but there seems little doubt that he was considered a lukewarm patriot. His chief opponent was John of Gischala (al-Jīsh about five and a half miles north-west of Ṣafad, modern Gush Ḥalav), an inveterate angler in troubled waters according to Josephus and later to become one of the leaders in Jerusalem in the final siege of the city.

Meanwhile Vespasian had been appointed by Nero to the Palestinian command with three legions and local auxiliaries, and under his able leadership operations proceeded throughout the country with a system and organization which foredoomed the ruin of the Jews.

He moved his headquarters forward from Antioch to Ptolemais (Akko), and reduced Galilee. Josephus was eventually isolated with those who had not already deserted him in the town of Jotapata* in West Galilee, where his vivid description of the siege[32] suggests that he defended the place with rather more ingenuity than spirit. Finally after a siege of forty-seven days the place was betrayed and fell to Titus. Josephus and forty Jewish notables took refuge in one of the limestone caves with which the place is honeycombed. Josephus counselled surrender, but was restrained by his fanatical companions, who insisted on a fight to the death. Josephus then proposed that lots should be drawn and the party killed by one another till the last man should commit suicide. By extraordinary chance or shrewd manipulation—for Josephus was a man of many stratagems—only Josephus remained with another

* Jotapata is usually identified with Khirbet Shefāt about 9 miles north-north-west of Nazareth, which corresponds well to Josephus' description. We suspect, however, that this may be the site of 'Japha', taken by Titus in a diversion from the siege of Jotapata (Josephus, *War* III. vii. 31). We propose the location of Jotapata at the village of Kawkab on a steep crest 2½ miles west of Khirbet Shefāt.

companion, whom he had no difficulty in persuading to join him in surrender. Brought before Vespasian, Josephus played the prophet, and foretelling the general's elevation to the purple,[33]* he was reserved as an honourable captive, continuing as an eyewitness of much of the war and ultimately devoting his leisure to its history. The winter was spent in mopping up resistance in Galilee from the base of one of the legions at Scythopolis (Biblical Bethshan) and in the reduction of Jaffa, which was a pirates' nest.

The next phase in the reduction of the Jews was accomplished by the extremists themselves. Jerusalem was now the refuge of all the intransigents who had escaped from Galilee, and the disorders in the city were intensified. Men of note who were suspected of inclining to peace with Rome were struck down by the secret blades of the Zealots and their violent adherents, who from their headquarters in the Temple committed murder and rapine in the city as though in an alien land. Disgusted with their violence and base motives, the High Priest Ananus sought to rally the people to suppress them, but here John of Gischala saw his chance to win the authority for which, according to Josephus, he had long been lusting. Entrusted by Ananus with negotiations with the Zealots in the Temple under their leader Eliezer, John betrayed his trust and encouraged the Zealots in their resistance, hinting that they call in the Idumaeans from South Palestine to their support.[34]

The hint was taken and the Idumaeans came up twenty thousand strong. Excluded by Ananus and his party, who held the Outer City and the walls, the Idumaeans chafed and stormed in exasperation. Then one night under cover of a violent storm a party of Zealots stole out and admitted them into the city. They wreaked a bloody vengeance. When dawn broke 8,500 dead bodies lay in the streets. A reign of terror ensued; no possessions were safe; nothing was sacrosanct. Those of the high-priestly family who were caught were slaughtered and as a last indignity their bodies were thrown out to lie unburied.[35] With them perished the High Priest Ananus, whom Josephus appraises as the natural leader, who had the cause of liberty genuinely at heart yet realized that the struggle was in vain. From this time there was no leader of responsibility or dignity with whom the Romans could negotiate.

* Actually Josephus says that as a leader in the war he was to be sent to Nero in Rome. He states that he raised doubts in the general's mind about the stability of Nero's reign and suggested that Vespasian might aspire to succeed. This may have been intended to suggest to Vespasian the necessity of keeping Josephus alive and in custody in order to check rumours of this kind, which might be fatal to Vespasian, and to discover how far they were current.

The Zealots, supported by the Idumaeans, now indulged in a fresh orgy of slaughter, in which Josephus states that twelve thousand perished by open violence or by judicial murder, for the horror of such tribunals was not spared to Jerusalem in her evil day. Eventually the Zealots persuaded the Idumaeans to withdraw, glutted with plunder and slaughter, and the city lay at their mercy.

A new danger, however, loomed up outside. Simon the son of Gioras, once military governor of Acrabatene, the region between Jericho and Nablus, had been deposed, and had turned to the *sicarii*, who held the desert fortress of Masada. Soon he sought his fortune as a private brigand and maintained himself in the Wilderness of Judah between Jerusalem and Jericho, the traditional refuge of outlaws and saints. His band grew to an army, and partly by a demonstration of his power and partly by intrigue he extended his influence over the Idumaeans of the south and took Hebron. The Zealots, who would be content with nothing short of a monopoly of violence, regarded Simon and his swelling forces with suspicion, though they refrained from open attack. A guerilla conflict of ambushes was waged, and on one occasion the Zealots captured Simon's wife. Simon thereupon marched on Jerusalem. He was not able to carry the wall, but with his desperate following he wreaked his revenge on all without distinction who ventured beyond the wall. The moderates of Jerusalem were now between two fires; whoever went beyond the walls was the prey of Simon and whoever remained was the prey of the Zealots.

John of Gischala was the evil genius of his people. He had been instrumental in the calling in of the Idumaeans; he had occasioned a disruption among the Zealots,[36] of whom a desperate minority under Eliezer held the Inner Court of the Temple,[37] now by his excesses he drove the people of Jerusalem and certain of his Idumaean associates to call in Simon the son of Gioras.[38] Thus Jerusalem was torn by a triple faction. Eliezer and his men maintained themselves in the Inner Court of the Temple; John and his forces stood, besieging and besieged, in the Outer Court and Lower City, while Simon held the Upper City and much of the Lower Town. The streets of Jerusalem ran daily with the blood of Jew shed by Jew, and the factions destroyed supplies of grain which were likely to fall into the hands of their rivals,[39] so that the threat of famine was added to the horrors of war with Rome and civil strife. And meanwhile Vespasian was two days distant at Caesarea poised for his great offensive.

Even admitting the divisions in Judaism, naturally engendered in a community where the religious interest was paramount and where eschatological hopes vied with a more sober sense of practical moral duty both passivist and activist, the suicidal strife of Jewish parties at this juncture is incomprehensible until it is recalled that the Roman Empire, with the assassination of Nero and three other emperors in the year A.D. 68 was in a convulsion, which the Jews, stimulated as they were by the cruder type of political Messianism, might well consider mortal. The confidence of the more desperate Jewish elements was apparently justified; the caution of the moderates was discredited.

The confident expectancy of the extremists was further encouraged by Vespasian's suspension of the campaign while major political issues in the Roman Empire were undecided. But Vespasian lost nothing by his temporary inactivity. By the spring of A.D. 68 Galilee had been pacified; the tribune Placidus had pacified Transjordan, and Vespasian had moved forward from Caesarea to Antipatris (near Rās al-ʿAin), where he secured the neighbourhood and posted the Fifth Legion at Emmaus to cover the approach to Jerusalem by way of the Valleys of Aijalon and Sorek (see above, p. 21). Resuming full-scale operations in the summer of A.D. 69, he secured the passes from Bayt Jibrīn to Hebron and the historic Vale of Elah leading from the coastal plain south of Jaffa past Azekah to Socoh, where it branched, one tributary giving access to Bethṣur north of Hebron and the other by Bayt Neṭṭīf to south of Bethlehem (see above, p. 21), and Jerusalem was thus isolated from reinforcements and Vespasian's lines of communication with his base camp firmly secured. The Wādī Farʿa from Shechem to the Jordan Valley was penetrated and the Tenth Legion marched south to occupy Jericho, which was an important base for patrols in the 'area of refuge' in the Wilderness of Judah.* Garrisons at Bethel and Ophrah (aṭ-Ṭayibeh, 'Ephraim' in Josephus) facilitated patrols in the 'area of refuge' east of the watershed north of Jericho. Thus every pass was sealed off by the Romans, who had perfect liberty to patrol the land. Only Herod's desert fortresses, the Herodium south-east of Bethlehem, Maṣada in the desert north-east of Beersheba, and Machaerus east of the Dead Sea held out, and Jerusalem was completely isolated; and there the factions of the opposition were bleeding themselves to death.

* The coin sequence at the settlement of the Sect of the New Covenant, the Essenes, at Qumran ends in this year, when, or possibly a little before, the famous scrolls were deposited. A coin found at Khirbet Qumrān counterstamped with X is probably a relic of the presence, or perhaps occupation, of a detachment of the Xth Legion. The evidence of destruction by conflagration and the many arrow-heads indicate violent assault and resistance, which may rather suggest that before 68 the Jewish extremists, probably, we think, the party of Simon the son of Gioras, who controlled this whole area (Josephus, *War* IV. ix. 3–5) had taken over the site from the sectaries, who would then have hidden their Scriptures pending their eventual return, which, however, never materialized.

By the early summer of A.D. 70 Titus, now in command since his father's elevation to the purple, was ready for the assault on Jerusalem. His army of four legions with auxiliaries was brought up, three legions occupying a camp on Mount Scopus and a ridge to the north and one encamped on the Mount of Olives. The presence of the Romans over against the city induced an awkward concord between the three rivals, who now faced the Romans with great hardihood. The Tenth Legion, isolated on the Mount of Olives, was attacked before its defence-works were complete, and Titus just succeeded in rushing up reinforcements to relieve the situation. But the uneasy truce between the rival factions was soon broken. At Passover the party of Eliezer, which held the Inner Court of the Temple, opened the gates to the worshippers. John of Gischala took the opportunity to occupy the coveted position, and Eliezer's party was soon eliminated by the sword.

The doomed city was now more closely invested on the north-west, where Titus directed operations from the point of vantage opposite the north-west angle of the wall, reinforced at that point by the tower Psephinus. Another unofficial truce was observed between the parties of John and Simon within the city, which lent some colour to Josephus' statement that 'the Romans destroyed the sedition'.[40] But already 'the sedition had destroyed the city'. Meanwhile the Jews boldly sallied out from the tower of Hippicus in Herod's palace-fort and succeeded in setting fire to the Roman siege-works and engines. On the fifteenth day of the siege, however, the Romans breached the north wall, of which they demolished a great part, taking up new positions in 'the camp of the Assyrians' within the north-west angle of the city.

The Jews retired intact behind the second wall (see above, p. 37). After five days the Romans pierced this barrier and would have held it had they either demolished a large part of it or laid waste the city inside, but Titus strove to leave the door of reconciliation open, and the Romans paid for their moderation. They were beaten back and regained an entrance only after four days of bitter fighting.

Now began the desperate conflict for the inner wall, which coincided in the north-east with the precinct-wall of the Temple, commanded by the fortress of the Antonia. The distress was acute through famine. Many would fain have deserted to the Romans or undertaken the hazard of escape, but they were detained by the fanatical zeal of the extremists. Titus offered terms through Josephus, who was evidently a tactless choice for an intermediary, but these were rejected. In the rigours of famine the desperate followers of John and Simon abused their strength to extort the last crust of bread from the weaker inhabitants of the city, and Josephus reports a case of cannibalism, where a mother killed and roasted her own son.[41] People ate the very refuse of the street, the leather of shields, wisps of old hay, and rubbish from which even animals had turned. Under cover of darkness men stole out of the city to gather what grasses and herbs they could find, but even this meagre supply failed when the Romans built a wall of circumvallation.

Eventually the Romans captured the tower of Antonia, and breached the third wall. Their final assault on the Temple, the last stronghold of the rebels, was mounted from the Antonia. Grim hand-to-hand struggles took place. The Romans having scaled the porticoes of the Outer Court, which they proposed to use as a vantage-ground, the Jews resorted to fire as a means of defence. Titus was still hopeful of bringing the Jews to terms and at the eleventh hour, when the daily sacrifice in the Temple had failed for want of men to minister on the twenty-seventh day of the month Panemus (Hebrew Tammuz), 5th August, A.D. 70, he sent Josephus to parley, with John and Simon in the hope that the Temple at least might be spared.[42] With their arrogant rejection of the offer the assault on the Temple began. The north gate was burnt and the Jews were driven back on the Inner Court. On the night before Titus was about to launch his final attack upon the Inner Court a soldier on his own initiative climbed up, aided by a comrade and set fire to a certain window of the Temple.[43] Titus gave the order to quench the fire, which had spread along the corridor inside, but in the general confusion the order was either not heard or disregarded by men exasperated by the arduous siege or avid for the plunder of the fabulous wealth of this renowned shrine. Thus on the tenth of the month Ab (29th August) in A.D. 70 the Temple of Herod the Great perished in flames six years only after its final completion, which Josephus regards as Divinely ordained because of the contamination of the extremists.

The rebels retired to the Upper City, where many had already taken refuge in the palace-fort, only to be ousted by the more desperate, who butchered and plundered about 8,400 of their own people.[44] Meanwhile the Romans had cleared the Lower City, setting everything on fire as far as Siloam. The extremists were even then prepared to resist, killing all who attempted to surrender. The end was not long delayed. The whole city was taken. The rebels were hunted down mercilessly. Of the survivors all able-bodied men were sent as slaves to the mines in the Egyptian desert or reserved to fight to death in the arena, while all under seventeen years of age were sold as slaves. John and Simon were captured; starved out of the cisterns and subterranean galleries where they had taken refuge, they surrender at last, John to be imprisoned for life and Simon to be led in Titus' triumphal procession and to be executed in Rome.

The cost of the war had been colossal to the Jews. Josephus states that 97,000 were captured and 1,000,000 had perished by famine or sword. In view of population statistics of more recent times under the British Mandate and at the present time we may suspect Josephus here as elsewhere of exaggeration. But after Vespasian's reduction of the land Jerusalem had become the fortress of the whole Jewish people and there were many pilgrims to the Passover from abroad who were not able to return. The city was complete desolation. Denuded of its inhabitants, it was completely demolished with the exception of the three towers of Herod's palace-fort on the south-west hill, which Titus preserved as a memorial of his victory, and a sector of the west wall south of this site, which was kept as a rampart of the camp of the garrison which was left in occupation.[45]

In the dry bad-lands east of the watershed south of Jerusalem Lucilius Bassus reduced the Herodium and mopped up those who had escaped into the jungle-growth of Jordan. It was not until A.D. 73, however, that his successor Flavius Silva reduced Massada, the grimmest of Herod's desert-fortresses. Owing to the natural strength of this place, almost completely cut off by high steep precipices, and approached from the west by a narrow neck of sloping land, it was well supplied with water channelled into cisterns in the rare flash floods. The task was a formidable one in that desert region, but Roman skill and patience prevailed. When the fall of the stronghold became inevitable the defenders with grim resolution slew every man his own family, then one another by lot till the last man took his own life. There was no Josephus among them! The Romans entered the place in awful silence. Eventually two old women and five children crawled out of underground conduits to relate the story of the last stand of their people.

With the destruction of the Temple and the demolition of Jerusalem the Jews were politically extinct. They had now to suffer the indignity of paying a yearly capitation tax of two drachmae to the temple not of the God of Israel but of Jupiter Capitolinus of Rome. The ruin of the Temple meant the passing of the priests, the traditional intermediaries between the people and their God and the heirs of the authority of the ancient kings. The Sanhedrin as a representative and governing body among the Jews passed with the extinction of the priestly caste. The impersonal authority of the Law had outlived the personal authority of king and priest, and now the Pharisees came into their own. At Jamnia (Biblical Yabneel) in the coastal plain a council of Rabbis was convened and constituted under Rabbi Joḥanan ben Zakkai, a moderate,* which assumed the conservation and interpretation of the Law in its application to the living situation. The authority of this Rabbinical council grew until in the life of the Jews in Palestine it took the place, in a very much more restricted degree, of the old Sanhedrin, on the constitution of which it seems to have modelled itself. Here Jewish traditions were kept alive, and it is noteworthy that when a new leader of the people appeared in the person of bar Kokhba in 132 he found support, though not unanimous, among the Rabbis (see below, p. 189). But after A.D. 70 the Jews were more than ever not a nation but a church or sect. The land was under the administration of a Roman governor *pro praetore* independent of the Syrian command. Judaea, probably in the restricted sense of the district round Jerusalem, was the personal estate of the Emperor, and the coins of Vespasian with his image and that of a sorrowing female seated under a palm tree with the legend *Judaea Capta* or *Judaea Devicta* (Pl. 16) fittingly express the status of the Jews in the home of their fathers.

Such sanguine hopes as had inspired the great revolt were not easily extinguished, and violent eruptions occurred throughout the Mediterranean world wherever the Jews were in considerable numbers.† Nor did Palestine escape. Since the repression of the revolt in A.D. 70 a nondescript settlement had grown up around the Roman camp of the Tenth Legion on the south-west hill. Under Hadrian it was proposed to regularize this settlement, which, as an unwalled town of secondary rank, named Aelia Capitolina after the Emperor (Publius Aelius Hadrianus) and Jupiter of the Roman Capitol, was clearly designed 'to decapitate a race which had proved itself to be unassimilable'.[46] The consequence was a war 'neither insignificant nor short' (Dio Cassius lxix. 12).

The insurgents found a leader in Simon bar Kosiba, whose proper name, indicated in Midrash Echa Rabbah II, 2, is so attested in papyrus dispatches in his name‡ to and from his lieutenants and various headmen in regions bordering on the desert of Judah by the north-west of the Dead Sea, that celebrated 'area of refuge' associated particularly with the Sect of the New Covenant at Qumran. The name was parodied for propagandist purposes to Simon bar Kokhba, 'the Son of the

* It is related that the Rabbi, disgusted by the sordid partisan strife in Jerusalem, had himself carried out of the city in a coffin, thus escaping to the Roman camp (Echa Midrash Rabbah, x. i, 5). He was thus trusted by Vespasian and was able to obtain imperial permission to convene and constitute the synod of Rabbis at Jamnia.

† Few of the great public buildings at Cyrene in Libya escaped destruction by the Jews at this time and somewhat earlier in the reign of Trajan as the inscriptions on Hadrian's reconstructions indicate.

‡ See footnote, p. 190.

Star',* expressing the nationalist hopes, now Messianically interpreted implied for contemporary Judaism in the verse:

> There shall come a star out of Jacob,
> And a sceptre shall arise from Israel. . . .[47]

The famous Rabbi Aqiba, who himself died in the revolt under the iron flesh-combs of the Romans, is said so to have hailed Simon, though more sober opinions of Rabbinic circles were expressed in the reply of Rabbi Joḥanan ben Ṭorṭa, 'O Aqiba, grass will sprout between your jaws sooner than the Son of David will appear'.[48] Nevertheless Aqiba represented the popular response, which he must have done much to stimulate, and that curious blend of mystique and material force which was the nerve of the revolt.

At first Jewish resistance took the form of guerilla warfare, to which the rough country, honeycombed with limestone caves, is admirably adapted, and to avoid encirclement the governor Tineius Rufus withdrew from Jerusalem in order to concentrate on the dislocation of communications between the rebels and to strike at them according to their own methods with mobile commandoes. His withdrawal moreover was imperative since after the demolition after A.D. 70 Jerusalem was little more than a camp on the south-west hill, the defences of which had been further weakened by the levelling of the former city in the north in preparation for Hadrian's new city. The site was thereupon occupied by the Jews and fortified, as we may probably infer from the references to the destruction after the suppression of the revolt.[49] Coins in silver and copper were issued with the name of Simon (actually Simeon) and the legend 'For the Deliverance of Jerusalem' (*l^eḥērūth y^erūshālayim*) in the archaic Hebrew script (Pls. 17 and 18). Some of these depict a stylized façade of the Temple and in it a shrine for the rolls of the Law in place of the ancient Ark. A star above the Temple indicates the Messianic claims of the movement and a wavy line symbolizes the cloud which indicated the presence of God in the Tabernacle.[50] Some restoration of the Temple and the traditional cult is certainly implied in the revived authority of the High Priest, one Eliezer, which is attested in the coins of the revolt. The problematic Mayer-Sukenik wall (see above, pp. 57–59), that hasty agglomeration of hewn blocks either from Agrippa's north wall or from his quarries and ill-jointed masses of roughly squared stones levelled often in the first course by small stones, and rubble-cored, may be from this time,

* Another parody of the name with a different purpose was Bar Koziba, 'the Son of the Lie', by the early Christian fathers and possibly by the Ṣadoqite Sect of the New Covenant in the Land of Damascus (M. J. Lagrange, *Le Judaïsme avant Jésus Christ*, 1931, pp. 334 ff.)

possibly having been constructed by the Romans as they isolated the Jewish resistance in the Jerusalem area in the last phase of the Revolt.

The Legate, though he inflicted heavy casualties[51] seems to have failed to engage the fighting men, who were made desperate by the killing of their women and children. The Gentile inhabitants of the land, now in open settlements under Roman administration instead of in the traditional fortified hill-top villages, also suffered at the hands of the rebels, as for instance at Emmaus (Qulūniyeh, from Colonia), where Vespasian had settled a colony of veterans in A.D. 70. Christians also, according to the contemporary Justin Martyr of Neapolis (Nablus),[52] were singled out for terrible torture and slaughter, which we may credit the more since desperate Jewish nationalists would suspect them as moderates and hate them as renegades, whose faith in Jesus the Messiah was an affront to the Messianic pretensions of the movement.

The Roman troops under Rufus were reinforced and, though the sources are tantalizingly meagre,* we may justly conclude that in

* The movement has now been strikingly documented by discoveries of documents—the aftermath of the discovery of the Dead Sea Scrolls—from several caves within a radius of 10 miles from the oasis of Engedi including among certain Biblical fragments dispatches either from Bar Kosiba [*sic*] himself or from his staff to local commanders. One of these from the Wādī Murabbaʿat about 10 miles north of Engedi is to Joshua ben Galgola the commander of a post at Beth Mashekho giving instruction about a party of Galilaeans with the threat of confinement in chains if the command was not carried out. His post may have been one of the few wells at the mouth of the Wādī Murabbaʿat, where there are small settlements, which may have been held to secure communications and supplies by boat from the more fertile region east of the Dead Sea. There are similar dispatches from the Naḥal Ḥeber 3½ miles from Engedi to the officers Joḥanan bar Baʿyan and Masebah (Y. Yadin, *Biblical Archaeologist* XXIV, 1961, pp. 34–50, 86–95), the one possibly military, the other fiscal, with instructions to hand over certain men of Teqoa on the desert edge south-east of Bethlehem and to reap the crop of a certain Eliezer ben Ḥattab at Engedi, and apparently also concerning supplies by boat. Bar Kosiba's control was indeed strict. There are in addition contracts of sale and lease and other domestic archives dated in the administration of 'Shimeon bar Kosiba, Prince of Israel'. These, with an astonishingly well preserved cache of weapons, bronze vessels and a woman's possessions in a cave most difficult of access in the Naḥal Ḥeber near Engedi indicate the last refuge of the insurgents. One letter has a peculiar interest. This, in the name of Simon bar Kosiba to Jehudah bar Menasheh at Qiryath ʿarabaya, which is possibly in the Wādī ʿUrṭas near Bethlehem, concerns two donkey-loads of palm-branches, citrons, willows and myrtles to be transmitted to 'the camp', obviously for the booths, or bivouacs at, the Feast of Tabernacles (Leviticus xxiii. 40). Such scrupulous regard for orthodox Jewish ritual in a political crisis has a curious parallel in the solicitude of the anachronistic orthodox elders in Jerusalem for a supply of myrtles from Egypt in the crisis of the First World War, which Chaim Weizmann records with humour and astonishment in his history of the establishment of the National Home of Israel (*Trial and Error*, 1949, p. 288).

magnitude and duration the revolt was comparable with that of A.D. 66–70, though the rebels were now much more united and used quite different tactics, guerilla tactics, in which the Palestinians have always excelled, with the exploitation of the wilderness of Judah south-east of Jerusalem. In the former revolt Titus had had four legions with native auxiliaries; now various inscriptions indicate that no less than four legions and several cohorts were engaged, while the Syrian fleet also seems to have been engaged along the coast.*

The revolt having reached a critical stage, Julius Severus was transferred from Britain to the command in Judaea, and eventually the movement was localized in the mountain fastness of Battir, which Eusebius describes as near Jerusalem.[53]† There the insurgents were reduced by hunger, thirst and the rigours of the siege. Simon himself fell, and the revolt was suppressed with the utmost severity. The war had devastated the country, and Dio Cassius (lxix, 14) reports that 580,000 Jews had fallen by the sword besides those who had died by famine or pestilence. At the fairs at Mamre by Abraham's Oak north of Hebron and at Gaza there was such a glut of Jewish captives that a Jewish slave could be bought as cheaply as a horse.[54] But Rome too had suffered. The Twenty-second Legion Deiotariana was annihilated, perhaps largely reduced by poisoned wine,[55] and Dio Cassius (lxix, 14) notes that in writing to the Senate Hadrian was obliged to omit the customary assurance of the welfare of the army!

Jewish resistance finally broken, Tineius Rufus symbolically ploughed over the site of Jerusalem, and marked out a new city, no longer Jerusalem, the Holy City of Judaism, but Colonia Aelia Capitolina commemorating its imperial founder Publius Aelius Hadrianus and Jupiter of the Roman Capitol, who with other deities of Greece and Rome was worshipped in the new city. Even the province was renamed Syria Palestina and no longer Judaea. Jews were excluded from the new city on pain of death,[56] a restriction which was eventually so far relaxed as to allow the Jews to come to what remained of the precinct-wall of the Temple to mourn on one day of the year, the ninth of Ab (August),

* A Latin inscription (*Corpus Inscriptionum Latinarum* viii, n. 8934) records military decorations to its commander by Hadrian 'for services in the Jewish war' (E. Schürer, *The Jewish People in the Time of Christ*, ET, 1890, I, ii, pp. 303–4 n.). Possibly the fleet was engaged in preventing traffic in arms and supplies, which would suggest that there was a closer connection between the rising in Palestine and the Jewish insurrection in Egypt, Libya and Cyprus than is generally admitted.

† F. M. Abel (*Histoire de la Palestine* II, 1952, p. 94) feasibly locates it at Khirbet al-Yahūd just west-north-west of the Arab village of Baitīr, where the railway to Jerusalem winds through a rocky gorge about 6 miles south-west of the city.

the day on which the Temple was destroyed.* But even this indulgence was not always to be enjoyed except by a substantial bribe to the Roman sentries, so that Jerome remarks,[57] 'They who once bought the blood of the Messiah now buy their own tears'. So began the history of the famous Wailing Wall, the last remnant of the west precinct wall of Herod's Temple (Pl. 7), the relic of their ancestral sanctuary to which the Jews clung pathetically through the ages until, ironically—and symbolically—they lost it in gaining the status of an independent nation in Palestine in 1948.

Traditional Judaism had failed in its desperate attempt to precipitate the Kingdom of God by force of arms. The destiny of Israel was now to be fulfilled in the Church of Christ.

* The Babylonian Talmud (Berakhoth 3a) mentions Rabbi Jose (fl. A.D. 140–70) praying at the ruins of Jerusalem, and Midrash Shemoth Rabbah ii on Exodus 3.1 (eleventh or twelfth century) states that the Shekhina (Presence) has never moved from the Western Wall, for it is said (Song of Songs ii. 9) 'Behold he standeth behind our wall'. W. M. Christie (*Palestine Calling*, no date, pp. 156–66) presents relevant evidence that until Turkish times the Wailing Wall had the significance of a central sanctuary for orthodox Judaism.

NOTES FOR CHAPTER VII

1 Matthew xi. 12
2 Acts v. 37
3 Josephus, *Antiquities* XX. v. 1
4 Joshua vi
5 II Kings ii
6 Malachi iv. 5, 6; Ecclesiasticus XI. viii. 1–11; Matthew xvii. 10–11; Mark vi. 15; viii. 28; ix. 11; Luke i. 17; ix. 8; John i. 21
7 Acts xxi. 38
8 Josephus, *Antiquities* XX. viii. 6; *War* II. xiii. 5
9 Luke ii. 25–35; 36–8
10 Acts vi. 1
11 Acts x
12 Josephus, *Antiquities* XVIII. iii. 1
13 Josephus, *Antiquities* XVIII. iii. 2
14 *Antiquities* XVIII. viii. 1
15 *Legatio ad Gaium* § 30
16 *Antiquities* XX. v. 3
17 Josephus, *Antiquities* XX. viii. 5
18 Josephus *ibidem*
19 Josephus, *Antiquities* XX. viii. 8
20 *Duravit tamen patientia Judaeis usque ad Gessium Florum: sub eo bellum ortum* (Tacitus, *History* v. 10)
21 *War* II. xvii. 2
22 *War* II. xvii. 4
23 Josephus, *War* II. xvii. 6
24 Josephus, *War* II. xvii. 10
25 Josephus, *War* II. xvii. 2
26 Josephus, *War* II. xvii. 8–9
27 Josephus, *War* II. xix. 5; *Life* vi
28 Josephus, *War* II. xix. 8
29 Joshua x. 1–15

30 I Samuel xiv. 31

31 Josephus, *Life* vi

32 Josephus, *War* III. vi–vii

33 Josephus, *War* III. viii. 9

34 Josephus, *War* IV. iv. 1

35 Josephus, *War* IV. v. 2

36 Josephus, *War* IV. vii. 1

37 Josephus, *War* V. i. 2

38 Josephus, *War* IV. ix. 11

39 Josephus, *War* V. i. 4

40 *War* V. vi. 1

41 *War* VI. iii. 4

42 Josephus, *War* VI. ii. 1

43 Josephus, *War* VI. iv. 5

44 Josephus, *War* VI. vii. 1

45 Josephus, *Antiquities* VI. ix. 1; VII. i. 1

46 M. Join-Lambert, *Jerusalem*, 1958, p. 102

47 Numbers xxiv. 17–19

48 Jerusalem Talmud, Taanith IV. f. 68a; cf. Midrash Echa Rabbah, II, 2

49 Appian, *Syriaca* 50; Jerome, *Commentary on Joel* i. 4

50 Exodus xxxiii. 9–10

51 Eusebius *Historia Ecclesiastica* IV. vi. 1 ff.

52 *Apology* i. 31, 6

53 *Historia Ecclesiastica* IV. vi. 3

54 Jerome, *Commentary on Zechariah* xi. 5; *Commentary on Jeremiah* xxxi. 15

55 A. Harnack, *Texte und Untersuchungen* VIII, 4. 44

56 Eusebius, *Historia Ecclesiastica* IV. vi. 3; Babylonian Talmud, Taanith IV. 26b

57 *Commentary on Zechariah* i. 15 ff.

VIII

THE METROPOLIS OF CHRISTENDOM

And it shall come to pass at the end of days that the mountain of the Lord's house shall be established in the top of the mountains, and shall be exalted above the hills; and all nations shall flow unto it (*Isaiah* ii. 2)

By the Imperial Edict of Milan in 313 Christianity became a legitimate religion and eventually the established religion in Palestine until the Arab Conquest in the seventh century. Thus the Christian period in the history of Jerusalem coincides with the Byzantine period, and most of the material traces of early Christianity in the land are Byzantine. But already by the death and resurrection of the Lord Jesus Christ Jerusalem had become the metropolis of Christendom.

In the early days the status of Jerusalem as the capital of Judaism seems to have affected the infant Church in spite of the fact that such dynamic figures as Peter and the brothers James and John and James the brother of Jesus were provincials from Galilee. Here they may have desired to remain to perpetuate that sacramental fellowship which they had experienced with the Lord on the night that he was betrayed, to be together 'with one accord in one place', as they were on the occasion of the visitation of the Holy Spirit at Pentecost.[1] The time would soon come for dispersal to the mission; at the moment for the strengthening of the faith through corporate fellowship concentration was necessary and believed to be the will of the Lord.[2] These things, moreover, were not done in a corner, and if the new faith was not to be discredited at the outset it must be prepared to meet squarely the challenge of Judaism in its own citadel; how effectively through Peter and Stephen Acts ii–vii describes. Christianity was, further, a missionary faith, and the opportunities for its mission in Jerusalem were unique. Passover, when Jesus was crucified, had become a great pilgrimage-festival, and many of the pilgrims from the provinces and abroad stayed on to the second great pilgrimage-festival, the Feast of Weeks (Pentecost), seven weeks after Passover. The opportunity was not allowed to pass. Jews and proselytes from Persia to the Black Sea, from Rome to Arabia heard the proclamation of the fulfilment of the faith and hope of Israel in Jesus the Messiah,[3] according to the Dominical commission that the Gospel should be preached 'among all nations, beginning at Jerusalem'.[4]

It must be emphasized that the Christian community at this time consisted of devout Jews, worshipping assiduously in the Temple[5] and respecting the ordinances of the Mosaic Law. They shared too the ardent eschatological expectations of the time, though in their deeper and more positive development of the Messianic hope (see above, pp. 172–3) they differed radically from their fellow-countrymen. As a group of believing Jews of one mind they would be ostensibly just another synagogue in Jerusalem, and James (ii. 2) actually refers to their worship in the synagogue (A.V. 'assembly'). Such a place for meeting and synagogual worship for the early Christian community round the nucleus of the disciples, who themselves constituted the necessary quorum of ten,[6] is indicated in the house, probably that where the disciples were staying in Jerusalem after the Crucifixion and the Ascension,[7] which was traditionally located south of the summit of the south-west hill (Pl. 4), being called by Theodosius 'the mother of all the churches'.

Until the outbreak of the Jewish revolt in A.D. 66 there was a Christian community in Jerusalem, a democratic body with a synagogual constitution, in which James the brother of Jesus and the eldest male of the Messianic house held rather an anomalous position of authority, which, however, was far from absolute, as is indicated by the controversy over the demands on Gentile converts, in which Paul carried his point.[8] The community, which endeavoured, not too successfully, to emulate the Essenes of Qumran in practising community of property, was served also by deacons whose chief function was to administer poor relief,[9] the best known of whom is Stephen, who in addition preached in public.

The new faith as well as appealing to local Jews from Jerusalem and the provinces attracted liberal Jews from the Diaspora, who happened to be in Jerusalem for the Passover like the cosmopolitan company addressed by the disciples in their various tongues. It is significant that some of the priests embraced the new faith, revolting perhaps against the gross political Messianism of the extremists, which was more and more dominating the people to the prejudice of the real spirit of the faith and the sobriety of traditional Judaism.

In the intensification of Jewish nationalism in the middle of the first century A.D., when the Law became the symbol of patriotism, the

Christians, who as good Jews honoured the Law, felt an even greater obligation to respect it scrupulously, the more so since Agrippa's persecution had focused public and official attention on them.[10] Indeed while we generally admire the enthusiasm of Paul rather than the caution of James we too seldom appreciate how often and how gravely the evangelic ardour of the cosmopolitan Paul must have jeopardized the Church in Jerusalem, the metropolis of Jewish fanaticism, which knew no scruple in ridding itself of its adversaries and held moderation to be a mortal offence. Thus with the policy of accommodation for Gentile converts a wedge was driven into the Church itself, and evidently the pressure of such circumstances gave rise to the early heresy of the Ebionites, or 'poor men', who were legalists and practically unitarians, their creed being a compromise between the old faith and the new.

Though the Christian faith from its inception and by its very nature had the appeal of a mission to mankind, it was the persecution by Judaism, such as that under Agrippa I, that initially dispersed many active Christians first through Judaea and Samaria[11] to make the first contact with the Gentiles, such as the Ethiopian eunuch[12] and the centurion Cornelius.[13] It was not a missionary urge, however, which forced the decisive break with Judaism, but rather the refusal of the Christian community to share the final ordeal of Jerusalem in the Jewish revolt of A.D. 66–70. This was not motivated by fear or lack of patriotism, but by a wholesome desire to be dissociated from the blind chauvinism of the fanatics who had come to dominate Judaism on the outbreak of the revolt. The Christian disgust was shared incidentally by many Jewish moderates including Rabbi Joḥanan ben Zakkai, who effected his escape from Jerusalem in a coffin, and so survived to labour for the rehabilitation of Judaism on the basis of the Law. Nevertheless the Christian withdrawal to Pella at this time according to a Divine oracle,[14] which may be the Dominical warning in the Little Apocalypse[15] or an oracle of some prophet of the community reflected there, would doubtless help to adapt Christianity to the Gentile mission.

The withdrawal to Pella at the supreme crisis of the Jewish struggle against Rome accentuated the antipathy of Jew and Christian, but when after the suppression of the Jewish revolt a Christian community was again established in Jerusalem it could develop free from persecutions and the inhibitions of Judaism, thanks perhaps to the presence of the Tenth Legion as a security force in its camp by the ruins of Jerusalem after A.D. 70, and the new city built by Hadrian after A.D. 135 was a Gentile city in which no Jew was allowed to settle.[16] From then the Church and its office-bearers were Gentile.

As Gentiles and as Christians the young Church in Jerusalem naturally suffered in the revolt under bar Kokhba, whose Messianic pretensions were sponsored by such a responsible person as Rabbi Aqiba, perhaps as a riposte to the Messianic faith of the Christians. Though we must always allow for a strong anti-Jewish prejudice in the Christian father, we may well credit the statement of the contemporary Justin Martyrs himself a Palestinian, 'Indeed in the war which has just taken place bar Kokhba the leader of the Jews ordered the Christians especially to be singled out for terrible punishment unless they denied the Messiahship of Jesus and uttered blasphemy'.[17] To intense Jewish nationalism the indifference of mere paganism was tolerable, but the conscious supersession of the Law, which was a symbol of nationalism, was infuriating, the serene faith in the atonement already effected for mankind in the crucified Messiah was a cutting rebuke to the militant Messianism which was the nerve of the movement; and the worship of the crucified Jesus of Nazareth as the Son of God was resented as a blasphemy. Whatever the extent of Jewish persecution, the effect was the further dispersal of Christianity to the provinces, where Caesarea, now under Hadrian's policy the capital of the province, came to the forefront as the centre of Christian life and learning under Origen, Pamphilus and Eusebius. It was not until the Council of Ephesus in 431 that Jerusalem, then raised to a patriarchate of the Orthodox Church, was to recover her pre-eminence in Palestine.

The crises of the two great Jewish revolts which occasioned the dispersal of the Christians from Jerusalem occasioned a break in the traditions of the topography of the city of Jesus' day, which was accentuated by the replanning of Hadrian's Aelia Capitolina and its resettlement by a Gentile population, where not even the minority was Jewish. The area of settlement, apparently not yet surrounded by defensive walls, though defined by monumental gateways at the head of its main streets and public places, such as by the present Damascus Gate with its monumental column in honour of Hadrian and Antoninus Pius and the famous *Ecce Homo* triple arch (fig. V) at the head of the transversal street from east to west on the height of the east ridge, roughly coincided with the present walled city, the plan of which it generally reproduced. It was bisected by its main street, or *cardo maximus* from the Damascus Gate southwards on the line of the present Ṭarīq Bāb al-'amūd ('the Street of the Gate of the Pillar') and its southward projection of Khān az-Zayt ('the Olive Market'), Śūq al-'Aṭṭārīn ('the Perfume Market') and Ṭarīq an-Nabī Da'ūd ('the Street of the Prophet David'). This main street was defined by a row of pillars, traces of which in later buildings may be seen today. Another transversal street ran from the present Jaffa, or Hebron, Gate eastwards to the former Temple area along the line of the present David Street and Ṭarīq Bāb aś-Śilśileh ('the Street of the Gate of the Chain'). The Temple area was apparently left as an open square, where statues of Hadrian and Antoninus Pius were noticed by Jerome in the end of the fourth century together with a statue of Jupiter,[18] which was probably related to a temple of Jupiter Olympius or Jupiter Panhellenius.[19] The Forum, or main public place, of the Roman town was in the region of the later Church of the Holy Sepulchre, defined by a wall and monumental gateways best known from a fragment under the Russian Hospice (Hospice Aléxandre), which is often wrongly cited as a fragment of Josephus' Second North Wall (see above, p. 185). According to Roman custom this was the area of the chief sanctuaries to Jupiter Capitolinus and his consort Juno and other temples to prominent Graeco-Roman deities, such as Venus.[20] Here Christian tradition from the early fourth century at least located Golgotha and the Holy Sepulchre, averring that the tomb of the Saviour had been deliberately desecrated by the temple of Venus with its licentious sexual rites. Whether or not this was so,* it certainly indicates a tradition of the site of the Holy Sepulchre earlier than the official location of the place by Bishop Makarius in the early fourth century, since, had there been no such tradition, such a site as that occupied by the temple of Venus would not have been gratuitously selected. Though there is no compelling argument for the authenticity of the site neither is there any valid objection. Rock-hewn tombs of the style of the last half-century B.C. and the first century A.D., one of which is reputedly that of Joseph of Arimathea, whose original tomb was given up for Jesus, indicates that the area was ritually unclean, hence outside the wall at that period. This is supported by recent archaeological soundings[21] just to the south of the Church of the Holy Sepulchre in the compound of the Muristan ('the Hospital', the headquarters of the Knights Hospitallers of St. John), which indicate from pottery fragments that from the Jewish monarchy till the second century A.D. the area was a quarry and not an area of regular occupation till Hadrian's time. A general impression of Aelia Capitolina, though with the later development of the Byzantine walls under Theodosius II (408–450) and his Empress Eudocia on the line of the present fortifications and the addition of the Church of the Holy Sepulchre, is given in the famous

* The fact that the cave at Bethlehem which Christian tradition regarded as the birthplace of Jesus was a shrine of Adonis is an analogous case, and suggests that such deliberate desecration of Christian sites, if not part of Roman policy, was encouraged by local paganism.

mosaic map (sixth century) in the floor of the Orthodox church at Madaba in Transjordan.*

The interest in the scenes of the earthly ministry of the Lord may be traced back to at least the third century and, if we credit Jerome, even to the day of the Ascension. Nor was this merely the naïve interest of pilgrims, which is familiar from the time of the Pilgrim of Bordeaux (333), but is a real scholarly interest. Alexander Flavian, who came from Cappadocia in Asia Minor as a pilgrim to Jerusalem in 212, was persuaded to remain as Bishop, holding office till 251, when he died in prison as a martyr in the persecution under the Emperor Decius. He was a scholar, whose interest was revealed in his foundation of a library at Jerusalem, which Eusebius the father of Church history was to use for source-material.[22] His interest in the origins of the faith and in factual relations is indicated in his five volumes, now unfortunately lost, synchronizing the Biblical history with the general history of the ancient Near East.[23] This tradition was also represented by Julius Africanus (*c.* 170–240), himself a native of Jerusalem, who interested himself in Christian origins, and notably by the great Origen, whose critical research into the text of the Greek version of the Old Testament (the Septuagint), which led him to anticipate the sensational discoveries in the Wilderness of Judah south of Jericho, was a guarantee of his critical investigation of Christian topography.†

The intense interest and critical scholarship of such men must be taken into serious consideration when we assess the probability of local traditions which were now crystallized in commemorative dedications in Jerusalem and throughout the land. In 325 for instance the traditional site of the Holy Sepulchre was well established despite the fact that since the time of Hadrian's rebuilding of Aelia Capitolina the locality had been quite altered by the imposition of a platform on which the temple of Venus stood (see above, p. 198). When in 325 before the end of the Council of Nicaea Makarius, the Bishop of Jerusalem, obtained permission to remove this pagan temple and restore the site of the sepulchre the tomb was found as a matter of course together with others which are still to be seen in their natural state, such as that reputed to be the

* The mosaic map was first brought to the notice of scholars in 1884 and was incorporated in the new church in 1890. The most recent publications of the map are M. Avi-Yonah, *The Madaba Mosaic Map*, publication of *Israel Exploration Society*, 1954 and V. R. Gold, 'The Mosaic Map of Madaba', *Biblical Archaeologist* XXI, 1958, pp. 50–71.

† Origen had the opportunity of familiarity with Jerusalem since his home was latterly in Caesarea and he lectured in Jerusalem by the invitation of Alexander Flavian, who greatly admired him. This roused the envy of Demetrius the Bishop of Alexandria, who was Origen's Bishop, and he insisted on his recall.

actual tomb of Joseph of Arimathea. A valuable eyewitness of the actual excavation was Eusebius of Caesarea the historian.[24] A less reliable discovery was that of what was believed to be the true cross in an adjacent cavern (fig. VIII), which coincided with the visit of Helena the mother of Constantine in 326. Forthwith Constantine commissioned the erection of a worthy building, the Church of the Holy Sepulchre, universally referred to in the Byzantine period as the Anastasis (Resurrection), which better reflects the triumphant assurance of the Christian faith (fig. VIII). This, the work of the architects Zenobius and Eustathius of Constantinople, was contrived to be the most imposing building in Jerusalem. Opening, as the mosaic map of Madaba indicates, from the main street, or *cardo maximus*, of the city as founded by Hadrian, its lofty pillared porch gave access by steps through three doors, denoted in the Madaba mosaic, to a colonnaded atrium before the basilica proper with its four colonnaded aisles and nave leading to the high altar in its apse. The contemporary name of this basilica was the Martyrium. Behind this was a spacious colonnaded court, in one corner of which was the rocky knoll traditionally associated with Golgotha, the place of the actual Crucifixion, which was reached by a stairway from the inner of the south aisles. West of this was the vast rotunda with its open dome supported by two storeys of columns over the sepulchre itself. The sepulchre, hewn originally out of the slope of the rock, was now hewn clear of the surrounding rock, which was then levelled, and was enclosed in a small shrine surmounted by a cupola on small pillars (Pl. 27). The conception of the small shrine with its cupola has been preserved to the present day, though the original building was destroyed in the persecution under al-Ḥākim, the heretic Caliph of Egypt in the tenth century, when the tomb itself in its encasing rock was levelled to the ground. What is now venerated in the present small shrine is at the best the floor of the tomb, the rock of which is paved in marble, being flanked by an altar. The splendid building was dedicated in a great seven-days ceremony from the fourteenth to the twenty-first of September 335 in the presence of the Emperor and a great convocation of Eastern prelates immediately after the Council of Tyre. The plan of this great and magnificent building and even its elevation may be certainly reconstructed, but after the destruction by the Persians in 614 and reconstruction in the period of the Crusades and again after the Orthodox restoration in 1809 little of the buildings except the general conception of the rotunda and the shrine of the tomb and part of the basilica remains (fig. VIII on p. 201 and pl. 26).

Under Helena's stimulus churches were built on the Mount of Olives at the site of a cave traditionally associated with Jesus' instruction

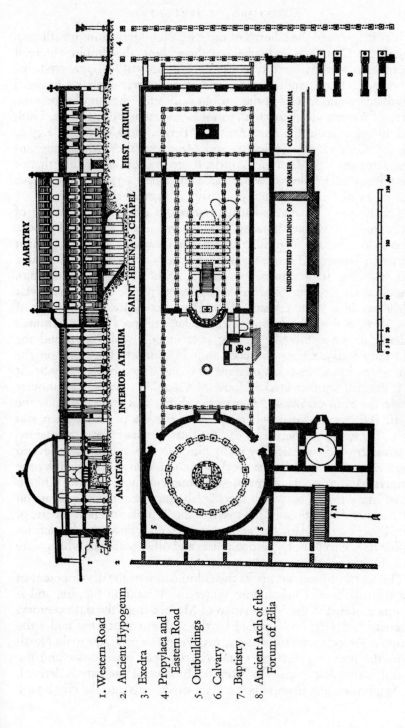

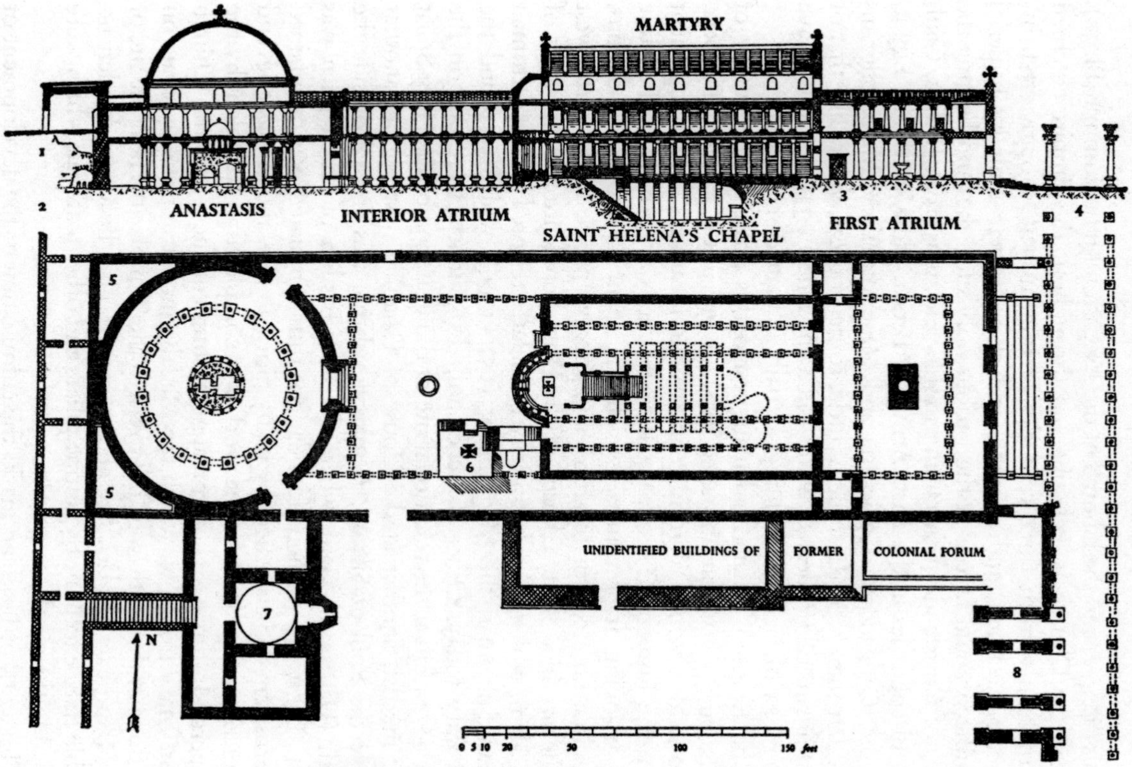

1. Western Road
2. Ancient Hypogeum
3. Exedra
4. Propylaea and Eastern Road
5. Outbuildings
6. Calvary
7. Baptistry
8. Ancient Arch of the Forum of Ælia

Fig. VIII PLAN OF THE CHURCH OF THE HOLY SEPULCHRE OF THE EMPEROR CONSTANTINE. (*Courtesy of the École Biblique and Elek Books Ltd.*)

of his disciples and the Church of the Ascension on the summit (Pl. 32). When the Church in Palestine and throughout the Empire emerged triumphantly from three centuries of intermittent, though often intense, persecution, and churches and chapels were built by Imperial munificence and favour at the various holy sites, the land became the focus of Christendom, attracting monks and nuns from Britain, Gaul, and all countries in the East, Armenia, Persia, India, Ethiopia, Egypt, Pontus, Cappadocia, Coelesyria and Mesopotamia.[25] Many pilgrims have left their records, some of little, some of great, value, like that of the Pilgrim of Bordeaux, who visited the land in 333 and must have seen many of Helena's buildings actually in course of construction.

The Empress Helena had inaugurated this phase of the history of Jerusalem; it was consummated by the work of the Empress Eudocia, who made a votive pilgrimage in 438 and returned after estrangement from the Emperor Theodosius II to end her days governing Palestine and enjoying its revenues, which she spent in pious foundations, churches, hospices for pilgrims, an episcopal palace at the north-west of the precinct of the Church of the Holy Sepulchre and the walls of Jerusalem, which are substantially those later restored by the Ottoman Sultan Sulaymān the Magnificent (1520–1566), which surround the Old City today. Other churches built by Eudocia were one on the south-west hill at the traditional site of the visitation of the Holy Spirit at Pentecost, another at the House of Caiaphas nearby, and another above the Pool of Siloam. A martyr's shrine was erected outside the north (Damascus) Gate, where the later basilica of St. Stephen was built. The work of pious foundations thus stimulated was maintained in Jerusalem and elsewhere by many pious donors, and monasteries and hospices were endowed. The work was completed in Jerusalem by the Emperor Justinian, whose greatest monument there was the Church of St. Mary the New, which the Madaba mosaic appears to locate on the slope of the south-west hill towards the Temple area near the site of the Hasmonaean palace (see above, p. 44). This, however, has left no visible trace except in Byzantine pillars and other materials which were reused in the nearby Aqṣa Mosque.

The work of Justinian marks the culmination of the development of the metropolis of Christendom under the Byzantine Empire, and is commemorated in the Mosaic map of Madaba from the sixth century. The city is depicted as fortified by the wall as constructed under the Empress Eudocia with twenty-one towers and six gates, the main North Gate, the present Damascus Gate with its open place inside and the conspicuous pillar from which the Arab name of the gate is derived, St. Stephen's Gate, from which a main street leads into the city by the first stage of the *via dolorosa*, the Golden Gate in the east wall of the Temple area, now walled up (Pl. 21), the present Dung Gate and the Zion Gate in the south wall and the Jaffa, or Hebron, Gate, in the west wall, from which a main street runs into the city along the line of the present David Street and the Street of the Gate of the Chain. The main street with its double row of pillars running from the Damascus Gate to the Zion Gate is the *cardo maximus* of Hadrian's city. The Church of the Holy Sepulchre is depicted with its porch on the main street, its atrium, inner court, basilica and rotunda stretching in the map nearly to the west wall north of the Jaffa Gate. North-west of the St. Stephen Gate is the Church of St. Anne the mother of Mary, and another building north of it encloses the twin pools with five colonnades.[26] In the south-east of the Temple area there is another Church, evidently that mentioned by the pilgrim Theodosius (*c.* 530) as at the pinnacle of the Temple, where Jesus was tempted.[27] This may be the Church of John the Baptist built by the Patriarch John III (516–525). Justinian's Church of St. Mary the New is depicted with double bronze doors west of the south-west corner of the Temple area. Just within the west sector of the south wall was the great basilica, probably on the site of the visitation by the Holy Spirit at Pentecost on what in Byzantine times was called Mount Zion. This church was called by Theodosius for obvious reasons 'the mother of all the churches'. The detail of the mosaic may be supplemented by the description of the pilgrim Theodosius, who was roughly contemporary with the mosaic artist. In addition to the principal churches just noted in Jerusalem Theodosius mentions also a Church of St. Peter fifty Roman paces from 'the mother of all the churches' on the site of the House of Caiaphas also noted in the Madaba mosaic. A hundred Roman paces further to the north he notes the Church of Holy Wisdom on the reputed site of the Praetorium, here located at Herod's palace-fort on the site of the Turkish Citadel,[28] which does not appear on the Madaba map. He notes also Eudocia's Church of the Virgin by the Pool of Siloam and her church to St. Stephen outside the Damascus Gate, which he calls the Galilee Gate.[29] In the suburbs he notes the Church of St. Mary in the Valley of Jehoshaphat (Pl. 31), where another church commemorates the Last Supper, with four rock-hewn couches each capable of accommodating three men.[30] He counted twenty-four churches on the Mount of Olives including two basilicae on the traditional sites where Jesus taught his disciples, one probably where he spoke of the destruction of Jerusalem and the sequel and the other where he taught the Lord's Prayer.[31]

An impression of Jerusalem as the result of this devotional and commemorative building in the Byzantine period is given by the Patriarch

Sophronius, who negotiated the surrender of the city to the Caliph ʿUmar in 638:

> Then would I ply my steps until I came unto Zion, to the place where the grace of God came down in likeness of tongues of fire; where the Lord of all celebrated the mystic supper and washed his disciples' feet in order to imbue them with his own humility. Mary it is who pours forth salvation for all men like a river, for its fair waters flow forth from that stone whereupon the child of God was laid. Hail to thee, O Zion, thou splendid sun of the worlds; with sighs and groans do I yearn for thee by day and by night. When he the bonds of hell did burst and caught up into his own ascent the dead whom he rescued from thence, it was here that he graciously manifested himself. Now leaving thee, O Zion, and the heights, and embracing the stone whereon my Creator was scourged on my account, I would fain pass into the house and weep with sighs above the stone which marks the spot where the royal virgin was born in her father's house. Entering the holy church of the sheep-pool, where renowned Anna bore Mary, and going into the church, the church of God's Holy Mother, I should embrace and kiss its beloved walls. I would behold the steps whereon the palsied man took up his bed and walked, being made whole at the bidding of the word. I would rejoice with heartfelt joy whenever I sang of the field which received the body of God's mother Mary, the glorious field of Gethsemane, wherein was made a tomb for the Mother of God. O, how sweet thou art, most noble mount of God whence Christ ascended up into heaven.

Here we notice that, in the century since Theodosius, tradition had transferred the site of the Last Supper to the site of the visitation of the Holy Spirit in a church on 'Mount Zion', which since the fourth century had been a kind of Christian museum into which many relics from other sites had been gathered. It is interesting to note that this part of the south-west hill is now again the focus of pilgrimage, for Jews, and houses a museum, not indeed of relics of the antiquity of the faith but of the sad relics of the agony of European Jews under National Socialism.

As one follows the pilgrims from the Pilgrim of Bordeaux (333) to Hesychius (*c.* 600), the last pilgrim before the Muslim Conquest to have left a record, one tends to get a somewhat distorted picture of Palestine. The Edict of Milan did nothing more than secure toleration for Christianity as a *religio licita* in the Roman Empire, tolerated but not established. Indeed despite later edicts which aimed more positively at the suppression of heathen cults throughout the Empire the lusty heathen were the despair of ecclesiastics and were occasionally able to persecute their Christian neighbours as we see plainly from the account by Marcus the Deacon of the journey of Porphyry the Bishop-elect of Gaza to his see and of his incumbency there at the end of the fourth and the beginning of the fifth century, where we learn that in Gaza even after the edict of the Emperor Arcadius (398–406) against heathenism there were eight pagan temples and many private shrines and 280 Christians out of a total population of between 50,000 and 60,000.[32] In Jerusalem, however, one of the seats of the Imperial administration, the influence of the Church predominated, though Cyril of Scythopolis in the *Life of St. Saba*, who lived from 439 to 532, mentions persecutions of the Christians by the Samaritans[33] and this is further attested by Procopius.[34] Both writers record restitution of Christian property, but it is significant that adequate restitution and protection were effected by force of arms. In this case, however, the disorders were occasioned by external politics (see below, p.p. 206 ff).

Nor were the adversaries of the Christian faith only from without. Heresy was a chronic disease in the early Church. The learned Origen of Caesarea was the subject of controversy in Jerusalem, and the African Pelagius, the adversary of St. Augustine, came to Jerusalem and left a legacy of heresy and controversy, which was vigorously combated by Jerome, who had settled in Bethlehem. In the first century of the life of the Church there were many who failed to disengage themselves from the discipline of the old faith of Judaism and ended as the Ebionites practically as unitarians, accepting the ethic of Jesus the Messiah but rejecting his divinity. Others reacted violently against the restrictions of the Law, knowing no moderation or restraint in their newfound spiritual freedom. These heretical tendencies were held tolerably in check as long as the apostles lived to combat them by their personal authority. With the passing of the first generation of those who had known the Lord heretical opinions developed and flourished,[35] not, however, unrefuted, as the voluminous treatises of the early fathers attest. Far from being united in common opposition to heathendom or to the grosser heresies, the Church was divided on all conceivable minor issues, and there is scarcely one of the Church fathers whose pages are not redolent of some campaign against some sect or heresy of greater or less degree. Gregory of Nyssa records[36] that when he was in Palestine at the end of the fourth century he was called in by the heads of the Church there to arbitrate on a matter which had provoked great turmoil and confusion. Cyril of Scythopolis[37] states that St. Saba appealed to the Emperor Justinian to root out the heresy not only of the Arians,*

* Arius, an Egyptian monk, emerged in 318 as protagonist of the doctrine that Jesus Christ the Son was not Divine, but created, indeed the first of God's creation and the essential instrument of the Divine creation and purpose.

but also that of the Nestorians* and the Origenists.† The controversy over the combination or discrimination of the Divine and human natures in Jesus Christ, on which the Council of Chalcedon declared in 451, had fatal repercussions in Jerusalem. There the Empress Eudocia, who was a convert from Greek humanism, espoused the condemned Monophysite doctrine that after the Incarnation there was but one nature in Jesus, the Divine, to the exclusion of the human, and thereby encouraged its protagonists, who actually expelled the Orthodox Patriarch and massacred their opponents. Though Eudocia herself was to recant before her death the conviction was passionately and persistently maintained in the Semitic provinces of the Byzantine Empire. The failure to understand the appeal of this expression of the faith on the part of Semites, whose whole tradition, thought and expression differed so markedly from the philosophic attitude of the Greeks, whose flexibility they lacked, and the heavy-handed efforts to suppress the Monophysite belief by enlisting the armed forces of the Empire really gave an impulse to separatism in Syria and Palestine, which was a potent factor in the Muslim Conquest. Theophanes in his note on the Patriarch Sophronius of Jerusalem[38] presents the same picture of a house divided. Sophronius, who lived to see Jerusalem capitulate to the Muslims in 638, spent the greater part of his mature years in combating the Monothelite heresy,‡ a refinement of Monophysitism much in favour in Palestine and Syria.

Rome's day of ascendancy in the land, and with it the status of Jerusalem as the flourishing metropolis of Christendom, was rapidly setting. In 540 the recrudescent power of Persia under the Sassanian dynasty over-ran Syria and laid Aleppo in ruins. On that occasion they were bought off with much gold, but the trouble broke out again in 570, when the Persians penetrated Arabia as far as Yemen. There was, however, a temporary revival of Roman arms, and the Byzantine general Justinian undertook a punitive raid, penetrating as far as the Caspian. The Emperor Maurice established better relations with the Persians.

* Nestorius, the Bishop of Constantinople, was condemned at the Council of Ephesus (431) for his defence of the doctrine of his chaplain Athanasius that Jesus had two natures combined in two Persons, being born to Mary merely human, but later invested with Divinity.

† Origen was a Christian humanist, emphasizing as well as the force of revealed truth the innate reason and moral conscience of man as against the doctrine of the radical corruption of the natural man, with which Augustine later so impregnated Western theology.

‡ The doctrine that Jesus, though having two natures, Divine and human, 'truly, perfectly, indivisibly, distinctly', had but one will, Divine. The doctrine was finally condemned at the sixth Oecumenical Council at Constantinople in 681.

But at his death in 602 they took advantage of the disorders in the Roman (Byzantine) state which preceded the usurpation of Phocas. Then Syria was over-run under Khosroes II, Purviz ('Victorious'), but the Persian army turned north to Anatolia, where it reached the shores of the Bosphorus. In 613 they turned south from their victories in Anatolia and Armenia and won a great victory over the Byzantine forces and occupied Antioch, Aleppo, Ḥoms and Damascus. Many of the cities whose native Christians had been antagonized by the religious persecution of the Orthodox Church of Byzantium now opened their gates to the Persians. The invaders were further aided and abetted by Jews, whose inveterate hostility to the Christian faith was exacerbated by the prejudices of Christian clergy and the frequent unconscionable calumnies of controversialists, and by the Samaritan sectaries, who were treated by official orthodoxy with the same truculence as the Jews and had retaliated in kind. Only recently the Samaritans had risen in arms, to be savagely suppressed. Now Samaritans and Jews cordially co-operated with the Persian invaders in their march through Palestine, now largely denuded of its garrisons. In 614 Jerusalem fell. The Patriarch Zacharias, on whose totally inadequate resources the government of Jerusalem had devolved, endeavoured to negotiate a surrender, but factions in the city prevented this. The Persians kindled large fires by the north wall, which split some of the limestone blocks, and after twenty days they effected a breach. The city was given over to sack and massacre, encouraged by the pagan Persian priests and intensified by the hatred of Jews and Samaritans. The great churches, the monuments of Imperial piety, monasteries and hospices, which graced in rich profusion the metropolis of Christendom and the Mount of Olives, vanished in an orgy of wanton ruin and flames. The wealthiest of the inhabitants were spared with the prospect of ransom, but it is said that over 33,000 were massacred. It is averred[39] that many of the captives were bought up by the Jews for the sole purpose of being slaughtered in cold blood, a melancholy event traditionally localized at the Mamilla Pool about nine hundred yards north-west of the Jaffa Gate. The decay of the Byzantine provinces in Syria and Palestine is often imputed to alleged Arab neglect, but the real reason is the wanton ravages of the Persians, under whom the stricken land languished for another decade and a half from the sack of Jerusalem in 614, and never fully recovered.

Anticipating the revival of Byzantine power, Khosroes eventually permitted reconstruction, and the work was undertaken by Modestius, the *hēgoumenos* of the Monastery of St. Theodosius, who is still honoured by the Orthodox community in Jerusalem as 'the restorer of

Zion' in an annual memorial service on the anniversary of his death on 17th December. But the sacred buildings of Byzantine Jerusalem never recovered their ancient splendour.

The situation was courageously faced by Heraclius, the son of the Byzantine governor of Africa, who had seized the imperial throne in 610. While the Persians menaced Constantinople in 626 he evaded the besieging army and made a bold diversion through Armenia to Mesopotamia, penetrating as far as Ctesiphon on the Tigris just south of where Baghdad was later built. He was not to meet the Persian conqueror Khosroes in battle, but, with internal dissensions among the enemy just before and after the death of the king, he was able to negotiate a peace, and to obtain the restoration of Syria and Palestine and the release of the captives who were held to ransom. The symbol of the faith, what was considered to be the true Cross, was also recovered and restored with due humility by the Emperor in solemn procession from the Golden Gate in the east wall of the ancient Temple area, now the Muslim Sacred Precinct, to the Church of the Holy Sepulchre on 23rd March, 630 (Pls. 19 and 20).

Heraclius' heroic efforts, however, secured all too brief a respite for Jerusalem. Byzantium and Persia had mutually exhausted each other. Both were to reel before the shock from the desert, when militant Islam in the dedicated impetus of the *jihād* ('holy war') controlled by brilliant generals, so far unknown and undreamed of beyond the inner deserts of Arabia, struck both imperial powers simultaneously in Syria and Iraq, and in three cyclonic years ended their dominion south of Anatolia.

NOTES FOR CHAPTER VIII

1 Acts ii. 1
2 Luke xxiv. 49
3 Acts ii. 4–11
4 Luke xxiv. 47
5 Acts ii. 46; iii. 1 ff.
6 Babylonian Talmud, Sanhedrin ii. 17b
7 Acts i. 13
8 Acts xv. 1–29; Galatians ii
9 Acts vi. 2–6
10 Acts xii. 1–3
11 Acts viii. 1
12 Acts viii. 26–39
13 Acts x
14 Eusebius, *Historia Ecclesiastica* III. v. ed. Migne
15 Mark xiii

16 Jerome, *Commentary on Isaiah* xi. 11–13; Migne; Jerome IV. 100; Jerusalem Talmud, Taanith IV. 6

17 Justin, *Apology* i. 31 Migne

18 Jerome, *Commentary on Mt* xxiv. 15, Migne; Jerome VII, 194–5

19 F. M. Abel, *Histoire de la Palestine* II, 1952, p. 100

20 Jerome (Letter to Paulinus, *Patrologia Latina* [Migne] XXII, p. 321) attests the cult of Jupiter and Venus here

21 K. M. Kenyon *Palestine Exploration Quarterly* 1964, p. 14

22 *Historia Ecclesiastica* VI. 20, Migne

23 Jerome, *De Viris Illustribus* XXIII, 673, Migne

24 *Life of Constantine* III. 25 ff.

25 Jerome, *Letter to Marcella* XLVI, Migne, Jerome I, § 206

26 John V. 1 ff.

27 Theodosius, ed. Tobler, IX

28 Theodosius, ed. Tobler, VII

29 *Ibidem* X

30 *Ibidem* XI

31 *Ibidem* XIII

32 Marcus the Deacon, *Life of Porphyry* xi

33 Cyril of Scythopolis, *Life of St. Saba. Texte und Untersuchungen* 4th series, IV. 70

34 *On the Buildings of Justinians* v. 7

35 Eusebius, *Historia Ecclesiastica* III. xxxii

36 *On the Pilgrimage to Jerusalem*

37 *Op. cit.*

38 *Chronikon*, Migne, CVIII, p. 693

39 Theophanes, *Chronikon*, *Patrologia Graeca* CVIII, p. 632

IX

THE SWORD OF THE WILDERNESS

In the name of Allah the Merciful, the Compassionate.

In the very year when Heraclius recovered Jerusalem events were happening far beyond the southern deserts beneath the notice if not beyond the ken* of the great powers of the world which were to release forces which would break the power of Byzantium in the Levant in six years and deal the Persian Empire its mortal blow at Nehavend in 651, and determine the political, cultural and religious history of the Middle and Near East and of North Africa from that day till our own time.

Muḥammad, a poor member of the Banū Hāshim, one of the weaker clans in the caravan entrepôt of Mecca with its pagan temple the Kaʿba ('Cube'), had come slowly and deliberately, even reluctantly, to the conviction of a prophetic call to summon his people to ethical monotheism. A voice crying in the wilderness, he had encountered the determined opposition of the merchant princes of the powerful clans, and when by patience and persistence and by his earnest conviction and gracious personality he had succeeded in winning a following in Mecca his community had been obliged to withdraw† to the agricultural oasis of Medina, where he joined them in 622, slipping out of his native Mecca by night with his faithful friend and early convert Abū Bakr.

* Muslim tradition maintains that in 627 Muḥammad sent delegations to the Persian and Byzantine Emperors, to the Governor of Egypt, the Negus of Abyssinia and the king of the Christian Arab border state of Ghassān summoning them to embrace Islam. The basis of the tradition may have been his effort to establish his credentials as the head of his politico-religious community with a view to establishing trading contacts now that he had practically isolated Mecca. That the tradition has some factual basis is suggested by the fact that in 629 the Patriarch and Governor of Alexandria actually sent gifts to Muḥammad including three slave-girls, by one of whom, Maryam, he had his only son, who died in infancy.

† From the 'withdrawal' (*hijra*) in 622 the Muslim era is reckoned.

By diplomacy and judicious application of force Muḥammad drew the tribes of the Ḥejāz into the new brotherhood of Islam and gradually isolated his opponents in Mecca till in 630 he was able to occupy the city and cleanse the Kaʿba of the symbols of polytheism and by a master-stroke of diplomacy win over his opponents by preserving it as the central shrine of the new faith.

In spite of its remoteness Mecca with its wells in a desert region and its sacred Kaʿba was a vital link in the trade-route with South Arabia with its incense and seaports from which it tapped the markets of India and East Africa, and the merchant princes of the dominant tribe of the Quraysh, to a clan of which Muḥammad belonged, were great financiers, whose empire had expanded silently and unobtrusively into Syria, Egypt and Iraq. Muḥammad himself had seen the cities of Syria on his humbler trading expeditions, and was evidently aware of, and indeed horrified by, the havoc wrought by the Persian invaders and their Jewish allies in the sanctuaries in Jerusalem.* On these expeditions he encountered Jews and Christians in the oases and cities of Syria and probably also in Mecca,† and it may have been his admiration for the wholesome ethic of these faiths that first quickened his spiritual consciousness. Apparently he understood Judaism better, uncomplicated as it is by the metaphysical difficulty of the doctrines of the Incarnation and Trinity, since he incorporated in the ritual of his new faith the fasts of Judaism and the orientation (*qibla*) in prayer towards Jerusalem before he broke with the Jews of Medina, who threatened all that he had laboured to build by impugning his prophetic authority. Thereafter Islam developed independently, but Muḥammad, in spite of his severe handling of Jews in the Ḥejāz for the reason given, at a juncture when the success of his legitimate mission was in the balance, left a legacy of respect for Jews and Christians as 'people of the book', a fact which is noteworthy in the conquests of Islam. The Jewish legacy to Islam is reflected in the Arab names of Jerusalem, Bayt al-Maqdas ('the Sanctuary') or, as at the present day, al-Quds ('Holiness'), which came to supplant Īlīya, the Arab version of Aelia Capitolina, and in the fact that the Muslims built their chief sanctuary in the area occupied by the Temple of Solomon, whom with David they venerated as a prophet.

No conquests of such consequence were ever undertaken so casually.

* Quran, Surah 3, 114 (Egyptian ed.), 'But who does greater wrong than he who bars the sanctuary of God from having his name mentioned in them and who busies himself to destroy them?'

† A credible tradition preserved in *Kitāb al-Aghānī* (tenth century) associates a phase of the settlement of Jews at Yathrib, later Medina, with the one of the great Jewish revolts of A.D. 66–70 or 132–135.

Muḥammad had looked northwards beyond the Ḥejāz and in fact had sent a force of three thousand northwards in 629 under his freedman and early convert Zayd ibn Ḥārith, ostensibly to avenge the death of a Muslim emissary to the governor of Boṣra. This had been repulsed by a Byzantine army from the frontier posts with Arab auxiliaries, the Muslims fighting a delaying action to Mu'tah about seven miles south of Kerak east of the Dead Sea, where they were extricated by Khālid ibn al-Walīd, who for that exploit acquired the title the Sword of Allah. In the following year, when Heraclius recovered Jerusalem, Muḥammad had himself led a force to Tebūk in the northern Ḥejāz, where he had received the subjection and tribute of Jewish communities and of the Christian community of Ayla, modern Aqaba. At his death the force which was mustered under ʿUsāma ibn Zayd was destined for the north and actually proceeded to just south of Jaffa, but that was an affair of honour to give ʿUsāma the opportunity to avenge the death of his father at Mu'tah. The main purpose of these northern raids was primarily to enhance Muslim prestige and to convince such tribes as Ghaṭafān and the Banū Asad, whose territory lay north and east of Medina and who were disposed to hold aloof from Islam. They may also have aimed at convincing the Christian Arab tribes of the borderland of the strength of Islam. Economic and psychological factors were probably also at work. Since inter-tribal wars and raids were now no longer possible in the security of Islam, the new supra-tribal brotherhood, a new field for the warlike energies of the Arabs had to be found. Deprived of the plunder of inter-tribal raids and increasing in population, the Arab tribes looked northwards to the borderlands of Syria and Palestine as a legitimate source of plunder which they regarded as their birthright. Moreover the merchants of Mecca had a vital interest in the trade-routes from South Arabia to Damascus and to Gaza and Egypt, for which the region round Aqaba was of great importance. These, however, were limited objectives. The sweeping conquests and expansion of Islam beyond the borderlands in Syria and Mesopotamia were not visualized even under the second Caliph ʿUmar, whose aim it was to prevent his general ʿAmr ibn al-ʿāṣ passing from Palestine to Egypt, even though, as it proved, Egypt was a plum ripe for picking.

The economic and psychological necessity for war in the North became even more urgent after the death of the Prophet. The various tribes and regions in the Peninsula which had been held to the new faith by the sword under Abū Bakr the successor (*khalīfa*) of Muḥammad were now offered a share in the glories and in the more tangible spoils of militant Islam, and the historian Balādhūrī hints that this sordid motive was perhaps the main nerve of the common enterprise of the Arabs in their dramatic eruption to the North.[1]

There was much in the international situation to encourage the Arabs in these northern enterprises. In Mesopotamia and in Syria and Palestine there were Semitic populations subject to alien races. In the Byzantine provinces there was bitter resentment at the recent imposition of the official creed of the Greek Orthodox Church on dissident local churches by force of arms. The lot of these provincials was particularly grievous owing to the heavy taxation which the long wars had occasioned. Whereas formerly Persia and Byzantium had carefully fostered client Arab kingdoms on their desert frontier, the policy of both was now much less conciliatory. In the beginning of the seventh century the Persian Emperor had had the last native king of the border kingdom of Ḥīra treacherously assassinated and the state administered directly by a Persian governor, surely an incredible piece of political ineptitude, since the Arab kings of Ḥīra had a wide reputation throughout the Peninsula as liberal patrons of Arab letters. In the West subsidies to Arab border tribes and to the client kingdom of Ghassān had been stopped in 629, and the Muslims were probably well aware of local discontent.*

Apart from ʿUsāma's raid to Palestine in 632 the earliest eruption beyond the Arabian Peninsula was the activity of al-Muthanna, a warlike chief of the Banū Bakr, whose territory lay just north-west of the Persian Gulf and who had a long tradition of raiding into Lower Mesopotamia. Al-Muthanna now continued these raids on a larger scale. The Caliph Abū Bakr appointed Khālid ibn al-Walīd, already signalized for his extrication of the survivors of Zayd's defeat at Mu'ta and for his ruthless success in revolts against Islam after the death of Muhammad, to the command on the border of Iraq with no further aim than to continue the raids of al-Muthanna and if possible to bring the Christian Arab border tribes into Islam. The conduct and extent of the operations here and elsewhere in the conquests of Islam at this time depended apparently on the course of circumstances and the discretion or ambition of the field commander. Soon the Muslims under Khālid and al-Muthanna, who evidently co-operated very cordially, were involved with the Persian army, since the Sassanid capital at Ctesiphon, called by the Arabs Medāin ('Two Cities'), was very near the theatre of war. A series of bloody battles did not detain the Muslims, whose casualties were continually replenished from beyond the deserts in their rear, from the friendly shelter of which they operated, skilfully shifting their

* The King of Ghassān, however, Jabala Ibn al-Ayham and his army actually fought in the Byzantine army at the Battle of the Yarmuk in 636.

point of attack until their complete victory. It is with the campaign in Syria and Palestine that we are more immediately concerned.

Here, as far as we may reconstruct from the most reliable sources,* the campaign lasted from 633 to 636. In 633 the Caliph Abū Bakr sent ʿAmr ibn al-ʿāṣ, the future conqueror of Egypt, northwards by Aqaba to Palestine, and supporting columns followed one after another under Yazīd ibn Abī Ṣufyān, Abū ʿUbaidah and Shuraḥbīl ibn Ḥasanah by Tebuk to operate east of the Dead Sea. The first contact with the Byzantine forces was made, according to al-Balādhūrī, near Gaza, where the patrician Sergius was defeated. This action was probably no more than a skirmish,† and the Byzantines were not prevented from concentrating in the Araba, or depression, towards Aqaba. Yazīd advanced from the east and attacked, either in support of ʿAmr or to secure his rear as ʿAmr advanced deeper into Palestine, and won a victory over a force which al-Balādhūrī states to have been three thousand. ʿAmr was then able to range freely through the coastal plain of Palestine, raiding as far as Caesarea, which, however, remained for the moment intact. It is questionable if the Muslims conceived of their objective as a systematic campaign with strategic objectives rather than as a great razzia, to be joined by whatever tribes might decide to pack up their tents and swarm over the land they had over-run.

The other two Arab columns found their task much harder as they proceeded northwards through Transjordan nearer the seat of Byzantine authority in Syria, where there is a tradition of an initial reverse at Marj aṣ-Ṣuffār ('the Meadow of the Birds') near Damascus.

Meanwhile ʿAmr seems to have encountered stiffer opposition in Palestine, perhaps through the diffusion of his forces, and to have

* The comparative vagueness about the Muslim conquest of Syria arises not so much from want of documented details as from the method of the Oriental historian, who does not trouble to use his sources critically, digesting his evidence and presenting a consistent account with critical footnotes, but simply sets down traditional accounts, citing his authorities, side by side, leaving his readers to sift the evidence and assess the relative merits of the authorities. Thus behind ʿĀlī aṭ-Ṭabarī and al-Balādhūri, who are the main authorities for the Arab invasion, lie Saif ibn ʿUmar and, in the case of at-Ṭabarī, Ibn Isḥāq and, in that of al-Balādhūrī, al-Wāqidī. The authority of Saif, in many points at variance with Ibn Isḥāq and al-Wāqidī, is suspect. It is therefore on the basis of Ibn Isḥāq and al-Wāqidī that Wellhausen proposed the reconstruction of the Syrian campaigns that we follow in our text, which is supported by a small but important Syriac fragment in the British Museum (T. Nöldeke, *Zeitschrift der deutschen morgenländischen Gesellschaft* XXIX, 1876, pp. 76 ff.), which supports mainly al-Balādhūrī and his source al-Wāqidī.

† The Syriac source Michael the Syrian (ed. J. B. Chabot, 1963 XI, iv) gives Sergius' forces as 5,000 infantry. Michael's account seems very circumstantial, but his claim that the Arabs were better armed than the imperial troops seems incredible.

appealed for help. Orders came from Medina transferring Khālid ibn al-Walīd from the Persian front. This brilliant master of mobile strategy threw a force of some five or eight hundred* cavalry across the desert† with remarkable speed and daring, and the situation was saved for Islam.

This dramatic march of Khālid is one of the classics of Arab history. In the version of Ibn al-'Athīr[2] we read:

> Khalid reached Qorāqīr ['Waterholes'] and bethought him how he should proceed to Suwa, a desert journey of five days. He found a guide whose name was Rafi' ibn 'Umeirah of the tribe of Ṭai, who warned him that to travel with horses and baggage was impossible, 'For, by Allah, even single horsemen fear to follow this track'. Khalid replied 'There is no other way if we are to fetch a compass around the Greeks and not let them cut us off from succouring our friends'. So he ordered the leader of each company to take water for five days and to deprive a sufficient number of the best camels of water and let them drink once and again until they could hold no more. Next they must tie up the camels' ears and bind their lips so that they should not ruminate.‡ So haply might the water last. At each stage across the wilderness ten such camels were slain for each troop of a hundred lances. The water drawn from their bodies was mixed with their milk for the horses.§ On the fifth day the supply was at an end. When they had reached the neighbourhood of al-'Alamain ('the Two Waymarks'), where water should have been, the guide cried in despair, 'Look if you see the box-thorn; it is about the height of a man sitting'. They replied that they could not see any. Then he cried, 'To Allah do we belong and unto him do we return. You are lost, by Allah! And I am lost along with you.' His sight had become affected. 'Look again, ill be upon

* Wellhausen (*op. cit.*, p. 65) maintains that this was not so much the transfer of troops as the transfer of the command to Khālid. The personal skill and prestige of Khālid was demanded and perhaps also the prestige and authority of other Medinan notables, who had been associated personally with Muḥammad. Wellhausen seems justified in the assumption of the presence of men of Medina in Khālid's retinue since at-Ṭabarī after Ibn Isḥāq states that before the journey over the desert the wives and children were sent to Medina.

† From a critical study of the sources P. K. Hitti (*History of the Arabs*, 6th ed. 1956, p. 149) maintains that Khālid started from al-Ḥira, south-west of where Baghdad later stood and travelled to Dumat al-Jandal, modern al-Jawf. Since the direct way to Syria lies through the Sirḥan depression, where there is abundant ground-water, Khālid's hazardous desert march must have been up the Eastern side of the Sirḥan, keeping well clear of wells and forts of the Byzantines, with Suwa at the north end as his objective.

‡ A variant tradition states that both lips of the camels were pierced with lances which they had to drag.

§ A similar expedient is recorded of the Arabs of the Syrian desert in the inscriptions of Ashurbanipal (668–626 B.C.), D. D. Luckenbill, *Ancient Records of Assyria and Babylonia* II, 1927, § 827.

you.' So they looked and found one tree; it had been cut down so that only the root remained. Then they shouted, 'Allāhu Akbār, God is most great!' So they dug and found a spring and all drank. 'By Allah!', said the guide, 'I never came before to this spring except once with my father when I was a boy.'

This dramatic incident is commemorated in Arab verse,

How excellent are the two wells of Rāfi'
And how well was he guided!
He crossed the desert from Qorāqir to Suwa
In a five days march which when an army makes it weeps.
Never before had there made it visible mortal.

So appeared Khālid the Sword of Allah with his mobile column in the rear of the Byzantine army in the vicinity of Damascus, and events moved rapidly to a climax. The date of the arrival is indicated by the fact that Khālid surprised and defeated the Banū Ghassān in the Marj Rāḥiṭ about fifteen miles north of Damascus on Easter Sunday, 634.

The Palestine force of 'Amr, which had apparently withdrawn temporarily to the south, was now reinforced by Khālid and his troops three and a half months after his arrival in Syria, and at the Battle of Ajnādain, to be located, we think, in the historic Vale of Elah* near

* The site of this decisive action is controversial. The only guidance we have from the sources is that it was between Bayt Jibrīn and Ramleh. This would point to the depression which runs north-south between the mountains of Judah and the foothills and coastal plain, through which ran a Roman road. More particularly it might be located where a wadi from near Bethlehem and another from north of Hebron join near the Biblical town of Socoh (Khirbet ash-Shuweikeh, or rather a neighbouring mound, see above, p. 21) to form the Wādī 'aś-Śanṭ. This was the Biblical Vale of Elah, and the locality in question where this east-west wadi crossed the north-south depression was one of the most important strategic points in Palestine. Here in 1940 the writer investigated two small Byzantine sites called locally Khirbet Jannābat al-Fawqa and Khirbet Jannabat at-Taḥta, the dual site recalling the dual Ajnādain. P. K. Hitti also favours this location. Corroboration of this location is the statement by Saif ibn 'Umar that 'the battle of the Yarmuk' was fought in Jumada (July) 634. Since Ibn Isḥāq and al-Wāqidī, supported by the Syriac fragment, both date the battle of the Yarmuk in Rajab (August-September) 636, two years after Ajnādain it seems that Saif has made an obvious error. The solution, however, is probably that the battle of Ajnādain was fought in the vicinity of Biblical Yarmuth, which is mentioned together with Adullam, Socoh and Azekah in the Vale of Elah in Joshua xv. 35. That in later times Yarmuth was called alternatively Yarmuk is evident from Eusebius, Onomastica, who speaks of 'Yermous of the tribe of Judah is now the village of Yermochos at the tenth milestone from Eleutheropolis (Bayt Jibrīn) going up to Jerusalem'. About a mile north of the Wādī 'aś-Sanṭ opposite the Byzantine sites we have mentioned is a site called in Arab times Khirbet al-Yarmuq, which would correspond admirably with the Biblical data and the circumstances of the Arab campaign.

where David fought with Goliath (Pl. 22), Byzantine resistance in Palestine was disorganized on 30th July, 634.

The Byzantine forces, beaten in the field, withdrew from Palestine, leaving the land over-run by the Arabs, who as usual in their campaigns were accompanied by their families with all their proverbially mobile effects. The Arabs took no fortress, though the extent of their occupation is indicated by the fact that Sophronius the Patriarch of Jerusalem was not able to go to Bethlehem (some five or six miles distant) that year for his Christmas service for fear of the Arab invaders.[3] The Byzantine forces which had withdrawn from Palestine endeavoured to rally at Fiḥl (Pella) east of Jordan opposite Bethshan, and for their protection against the Muslims breached the dams of the River Jālūṭ at Bethshan, thus making a morass of the low intervening land towards the Jordan. But in vain; neither mud nor flood could thwart the Arabs and early in 635 Fiḥl fell.

Meanwhile Khālid and ʿAmr ibn al-ʿāṣ having joined the armies of Yazīd, Shuraḥbīl and Abu ʿUbaidah in Transjordan, the enemy and his native Christian auxiliaries were harassed by their mobile tactics. Boṣra in the Hauran was first overwhelmed. Damascus was isolated and after being invested for six months[4] capitulated to Khālid in Rajab (August-September), 635. The Muslims pushed north down the Orontes, where the natives as far as Ḥamā and Shayzār submitted, content to procure life and spiritual liberty as 'the people of the book' at the cost of the impost which the Muslims demanded, which was generally lighter than the normal fiscal burdens to the Byzantine administration. Most of this country, however, was temporarily ceded in face of a Byzantine counter-offensive from Antioch. The Arabs depended upon free intercourse with the desert hinterland, being rather like pirates with the desert as the sea, which was entirely at their command, from which they could replenish their forces and switch attack. So the Muslims extricated themselves from the Orontes Valley and withdrew to the vicinity of the River Yarmuk, the largest tributary of the Jordan, a rapid mountain torrent which gushes down a tremendous gorge from the Hauran east of the Sea of Galilee to join the Jordan a few miles below the Sea of Galilee.

There on the plateau north of the gorge the Byzantine army, largely composed of Armenians, came upon the Muslims, but hesitated to attack; the Arabs countered the manœuvres of the Byzantine army, waiting and watching. At last the opportunity came. In the sunless, dry heat, probably a sirocco, of 20th August, 636 the Muslims struck in the vicinity of Yaqūsa about two miles north of the Yarmuk and about six miles north-east of al-Ḥammeh by the river. The enemy was routed and cut down in flight. The Muslim victory was complete, and the Emperor Heraclius resigned himself to the loss of Syria and Palestine.

The country was soon entirely in the possession of the Muslims, who had already overspread it with their black tents. Now the towns, Akka, Saffūriyeh, Tyre, Damascus, Ḥoms, Aleppo and Antioch, Ramleh and, in 640, Caesarea, capitulated to the Muslim generals. Jerusalem, isolated since 634 and strong behind her Byzantine walls, which had been recently repaired, stood out for a year after the Battle of the Yarmuk. The Muslims, who had neither the temperament nor the experience for siege warfare, were content to range the country and leave famine to reduce Jerusalem. At length the inhabitants sued for peace in 638, insisting that the Caliph ʿUmar should come in person to negotiate the treaty. The Caliph, who was already with his troops in their headquarters at Jābiyeh south-east of Damascus, was delighted to visit the Holy City, which even then to the Muslims ranked third after Mecca and Medina, the objective of the orientation in prayer (*qibla*) first observed by Muḥammad before he changed it towards Mecca on his break with the Jews in Medina in 623.

In this complete victory the Muslims behaved with a moderation which is quite exceptional in the bloody history of Palestine and is particularly remarkable in what was after all a war of faiths, where Islam was consciously committed to the *jihād*, or holy war. It is recorded that when the Caliph Abū Bakr sent ʿUsāma northwards from Medina he enjoined him:

> See thou beware of treachery. Depart in no wise from the right. Thou shalt mutilate none; neither shalt thou kill child nor aged man nor any woman. Injure not the date-palm, neither burn it with fire; and cut not down any tree whereon is food for man or beast. Slay not of the flocks or herds or camels, saving for needful sustenance. Ye may eat of the meat which men of the land shall bring you in their vessels, making mention thereon of the name of the Lord.

Somewhat incongruously the Caliph is said to have added: 'And the monks with shaven head smite thou thereupon.' There is no evidence, however, that this last command, if indeed it is really genuine and not a late doctrinal interpolation, was literally carried out by those stern warriors, whose dedication to a higher purpose did not preclude humanity.

Such orders must have done much to mitigate the severity of war, and generally once the victory was won and spoils including slaves were divided the Muslims adhered rigidly to their discipline. Typical of the attitude of the Muslims was the fact that on their temporary withdrawal from Aleppo they cancelled the taxes on the various towns which had previously capitulated, since they could no longer guarantee security. 'The security of Islam' (*'īmān 'al-'islām*) had already become a technical convention, an obligation on the Faithful, and this was the spirit of the agreement which 'Umar made with the inhabitants of Jerusalem:

> In the name of Allah the Merciful, the Compassionate. This is what 'Umar the servant of God, the Commander of the Faithful has offered to the people of Aelia (Jerusalem) by way of security. He has given them security for their persons and for their property, for their churches and for their crosses. . . . It is obligatory on the people of Aelia to pay the poll-tax according to what is paid by the people of Medain (the Persian capital). They must expel from the town the Byzantines and the robbers, but whoever among them goes out is guaranteed in the matter of his life and property until he reaches a place of safety, or whoever stays will be safe and have the same obligation as is upon the people of Aelia with regard to the poll-tax. Again whoever of the people of Aelia prefers to depart with his life and property along with the Byzantines, but giving up their churches and crosses, they will be guaranteed safety for their persons until they arrive at a place of safety. . . . And pertaining to what is in this document there is the covenant of God and the guarantee of his Prophet as well as that of the Caliphs and the Faithful, provided they pay the poll-tax which is imposed on them.[5]

This, which was less of a treaty imposed by a conqueror than a guarantee by a victorious faith confident in its inherent strength and conscious of its responsibilities, well expresses the mood of conquering Islam even in the first flush of victory.

The Greek historians Eutychus and Theophanes record 'Umar's visit to Jerusalem. Riding from Syria on his camel down the Jordan Valley, he appeared with his ragged retinue on the Mount of Olives, where he was met in fear and trembling by the urbane Patriarch Sophronius, who conducted him round the Holy City. His chief interest was in the site of the Temple of Solomon, an-Nabī ('the prophet') Sulaymān, who had commanded the *jann* and the forces of nature, and who had already captured the imagination of Islam, and the first focus of Muḥammad's orientation in prayer. The precinct was encumbered with debris of the recent Persian destruction and with the rubbish of the Christian city to such an extent that the gate at the south-west by which they entered was almost totally filled up. But that presented no obstacle to 'Umar, and the proud prelate felt obliged to crawl in first on all fours and clear a way for his guest. It was then that 'Umar inaugurated the clearing of the famous Rock above its cave. The pollution here apparently prevented its immediate consecration,[6] so that the first sanctuary of Islam in Jerusalem was on the site of the Aqṣa Mosque,* which is still the main Muslim shrine in Jerusalem. In company with the Patriarch he visited the other holy sites. Chancing to be in the Church of the Holy Sepulchre, then called the Church of the Resurrection, at the time for Muslim prayer, ʿUmar was invited by the Patriarch to pray in the church. The Caliph objected that this might authorize the appropriation of the church by Muslims of a later time. So he prayed outside, and his prayer is now commemorated by the Mosque al-ʿUmarīyeh south-west of the precinct of the Church of the Holy Sepulchre. It is recorded that as ʿUmar stood on the site of the Temple in the shabby patched shift of clothes in which he had ridden up from Medina to Syria the Patriarch Sophronius shed tears and muttered into his beard the quotation from the Book of Daniel (xii. 11) about the abomination of desolation standing where he should not, and Theophanes casts an invidious glance at ʿUmar's interest in the holy places also of Christianity. 'Diabolical hypocrisy!' is the venomous remark of the Byzantine chronicler, but this is in itself evidence of the moderation of the great-souled, wise ruler of Islam, who in reverent simplicity regarded Jerusalem as the Holy City of both faiths.

However it may have shaken the power of Byzantium, the Arab conquest made little disturbance in the life of the people of Syria and Palestine. In the matter of the faith, which was the chief point of variance between the Muslims and their new subjects, the conquerors treated the natives of Palestine with enlightened tolerance at the best and at the worst with supercilious indifference, living at first apart as an active military aristocracy in cantonments in Jābiyeh and Ḥoms in Syria and Amwās, Ramleh and Tiberias in Palestine. The Muslims gave the alternative of Islam or the sword, but for 'the people of the book', which included Christians and Jews, there was the concession of toleration and the poll-tax (*jizya*). The Muslim commanders made separate agreements on this principle with the various cities in Syria and Palestine according as these were taken by war (*ʿunwan*) or accommodation (*ṣulḥan*), guaranteeing for their part the security of Islam, and no obligation was ever more scrupulously honoured. The native

* Arculf (ed. Tobler, I) saw a timber shrine in the Sacred Precinct in 670, which Adamnan reports on his authority as 'in the vicinity of the wall on the east', which would correspond rather to the Rock than to the site of the Aqṣa Mosque. On the other hand he reports a large wooden table for alms-offerings to the poor, on which Islam insisted, on the site of Abraham's altar where he was prepared to offer Isaac, which is usually located at the Rock (ed. Tobler, VIII).

Christian communities were locally governed by their ecclesiastical heads and knew at last relief from state persecution. They still had their churches, which continued to attract pilgrims from the West. Arculf visited the Holy Land in 670, only thirty-four years after the Muslim victory at the Yarmuk, and Willibald almost a century later. About 870 Bernard the Wise made his pilgrimage and, like Arculf and Willibald, found the holy sites still covered with churches. At Eṣbaiṭa in the southern steppe as late as the ninth century Christian and Muslim could worship side by side in peace, the mosque being built in an angle of the compound of one of the churches in such a way as to disturb Christian worship as little as possible.

During this period the Byzantine Empire was regarded as the patron and protector of local Christians, and as long as the Umayyad Caliphs ruled in Damascus as neighbours of the Byzantine Empire they were sufficiently realistic to maintain a *modus vivendi*. The Umayyads in fact represented one of the most powerful and wealthy clans of merchant princes and financiers of Mecca, who before Islam had had wide contacts with mercantile cities in the provinces both of the Byzantine and Persian Empires. They were thus keenly appreciative of the material advantages of the foremost cultures of the day, and, independently of religion, utilized the experience of their subjects gained under the Byzantine Empire. Thus Manṣūr ibn Sarjūn, an official of the Byzantine administration at Damascus, was entrusted by the Caliph Muʿāwiyah (661–680) with the control of finance, a post held later by St. John of Damascus, known to Christians for his controversial thesis against Islam. Ibn Uthal, also a Christian, was court physician and fiscal officer at Ḥoms on the Orontes. The poet laureate under ʿAbdu ʾl-Mālik (685–705) was al-Akhṭal, who excelled in the drinking-song, and of whom Muslim wits remarked that the only distinctive Christian element in his life was his cups.

This liberal exploitation of Byzantine culture is best exemplified in architecture of the Umayyad period in the Ḥaram ash-Sharīf, the Sacred Precinct, in Jerusalem (Pl. 23). The Dome of the Rock, completed in 691 according to an inscription in which the Abbasid Caliph al-Maʾmūn (813–833) had his own name substituted for that of ʿAbdu ʾl-Mālik (683–692) without, however, having the date changed, is a Byzantine rotunda and its mosaic work is characteristically Byzantine. These are certainly the work of architects and craftsmen trained in the Byzantine tradition and possibly from the Byzantine Empire as they certainly were under al-Walīd I (705–15) the son of ʿAbdu ʾl-Mālik, who was a great and liberal patron of the arts. The Aqṣa Mosque on the south side of the Sacred Precinct (Pls. 24 and 25), which is developed from a mosque of al-Walīd and is possibly built from the ruins of Justinian's Church of St. Mary the New, which stood in the vicinity (see above p. 202), shows the same Byzantine influence in the pillars at the south end of the mosque. This sacred place incidentally is a classic example of how close the two faiths of Christianity and Islam may be on the level of popular tradition, for the prayer-niche (*miḥrab*) giving the worshippers the orientation towards Mecca is associated in Muslim tradition with the Annunciation to Mary, and a stone basin is reputed to be the cradle of Jesus where he spoke to the people, obviously reflecting a variation of the Presentation of Jesus in the Temple[7] associated with the tradition of his discoursing as a boy with the elders in the Temple.[8] Jesus of course is venerated by the Muslims as a prophet.

The most conspicuous monuments of Arab rule in Jerusalem are the Dome of the Rock and the Aqṣa Mosque in the Ḥaram ash-Sharīf, both developed from works of the Umayyad Caliphs of Damascus. The Dome of the Rock, a Byzantine rotunda on an octagonal base, is built over the rock which was associated in Jewish tradition with Abraham's intended sacrifice of Isaac[9] and with Solomon's Temple (see above, p. 91), both figures being venerated in Islam as prophets. The Dome itself, once covered in gold and protected by skins in winter, was ruined by earthquake in 1016 and, like the familiar exterior of Persian blue glazed tiles and stained glass windows, is of later date, but the interior with the pillars, arches and mosaics is from the time of ʿAbdu 'l-Mālik. From the same time is the Dome of the Chain (*Qubbat aś-Śilśileh*), so called from the tradition that David, also a prophet for the Muslims, used to suspend there a silver chain which he had received from the Archangel Gabriel, when he was to deliver judgement. According to one tradition a bell rang when an innocent litigant pulled the chain; according to another the chain receded beyond the reach of the guilty party.* This building, just east of the Dome of the Rock, is like the latter a dome on a double row of pillars arranged on an octagonal plan. This was originally the treasury of ʿAbdu 'l-Mālik's shrine.

In the Aqṣa Mosque ('the Further Place of Prostration'), the actual mosque of the Sacred Precinct, to the south of the Dome of the Rock, it is less easy to visualize the work of the founder the Umayyad Caliph al-Walīd (705–715) since it underwent frequent repairs and alterations

* An elaboration of this tradition is that a certain Jew who was arraigned for the embezzlement of the pledge of 100 gold dinars melted them down and packed the gold in a walking-stick. Before the ordeal he handed the stick to the plaintiff and swore that he had returned the gold. This upset the mechanism of the chain, which, it is said, was ever after withdrawn beyond reach!

after earthquake damage in the eighth century, an adaptation when it was partially occupied as the headquarters of the Temple Order in the Frankish period, and its more recent repairs. It therefore shows many features of architecture and art from various ages and in its frontage gives a decidedly Frankish impression. The name 'the further mosque, or place of prostration' invites explanation, which elucidates the development of Muslim tradition, to which so much in the Sacred Precinct relates. The term is suggested by a passage in the Qur'an (Surah XII), 'Glory be to him who journeyed by night with his servant from the Sacred Mosque (the Ka'ba at Mecca) to the Further Mosque (or 'place of prostration'), the precinct of which we have blessed, that we might show him some of our signs; verily he is the one who hears and sees'. It is impossible to tell whether Muḥammad was visualizing the Temple in Jerusalem or the highest place of prostration in heaven, a night journey to which he had in vision on the Night of Power, when he won his final prophetic conviction. The immediate sequel to the passage just cited in the Qur'an deals with the revelation to Moses, so that a reference to a concrete Jewish tradition would not be unlikely. In later Muslim tradition the legend arose that Muḥammad was transported on a fabulous winged horse al-Buraq ('the Lightning') from Mecca to the Sacred Precinct in Jerusalem, which was thus regarded as the Further Mosque, where, after worshipping in company of his prophetic predecessors including Abraham, Moses and Jesus, he was escorted up a ladder of light to the presence of God in the seventh heaven, where he received revelation and descended again to the sacred rock now covered by the Dome of the Rock, and returned to Mecca on the steed al-Buraq before dawn broke.

Other parts of this gracious spaced area within the Sacred Precinct have similar associations representing the growth of tradition throughout the ages, and various features have been added to the Precinct, such as schools and colleges, hospices for pilgrims and the more spectacular features of ornamental fountains and the open-air pulpit of the judge Burhān ad-Dīn, but these are monuments of a later date, especially from the Muslim revival under Ṣalāḥ ad-Dīn and the Mamluke sultans of Egypt.

One of the last monuments of the Muslim period before the Crusades was the Mosque of 'Umar, al-'Umarīyeh, built about 935 in the southwest of the precinct of the Church of the Holy Sepulchre. This may seem another case of the assimilation by Islam of Christian, as of Jewish, tradition. But actually it is in commemoration of the prayer of the Caliph 'Umar on his visit to Jerusalem in 638, when he declined the invitation of the Patriarch Sophronius to pray within the Church, preferring to pray outside lest Muslims should later make his prayer a pretext for appropriating the church.

With the supplanting of the Umayyad Caliphate in Damascus by the Abbasid Caliphate at Baghdad, with its interest in the East rather than the West, in the Persian rather than the Byzantine legacy, native Christians in Syria and Palestine found less sympathy, but were nevertheless justly ruled in the main, and Jerusalem enjoyed special favour in the Caliphate of Harūn ar-Rashīd (785–809) in consequence of the diplomatic *rapprochement* between the Caliph and Charlemagne in the first decade of the ninth century, when the Holy Roman Empire was seeking to curtail the power of its Byzantine rival. Apart from a church to St. Mary to the south of the Church of the Holy Sepulchre and one on the reputed site of Aceldama ('the Field of Blood') above the west bank of the Valley of Hinnom (Wādī 'r-Rabābī) and an abbey on the Mount of Olives, the most important contribution of Charlemagne to the Christian community of Jerusalem was large endowments, which were to extricate the native Christians and their buildings from periodic emergencies when rapacious governors or uncontrolled

---

Left to right, top to bottom

13. Coin of King Herod Agrippa I (Reifenberg Collection)

14. Jewish silver shekel with branch with pomegranate fruits and the legend *Jerusalem the Holy* from the third year of the First Revolt against Rome (A.D. 66–70) (Reifenberg Collection).

15. Coin of Titus the conqueror of Jerusalem, as Emperor (A.D. 71–81) (Werner Collection).

16. Reverse of the coin of Titus; a captive Jew and mourning Jewess under a palm tree with the legend *Iudaea Capta* (Werner Collection).

17. Silver tetradrachm from the year 2 of the revolt of Simon bar Kokhba against the Romans (A.D. 132), whose name *Shim'on* is the legend, with the façade possibly of the Temple restored, and a shrine with the rolls of the law (Reinfenberg Collection).

18. Denarius from the Revolt of Simon bar Kokhba with chalice from the Temple vessels and the palm-branch from the Feast of Tabernacles, when the advent of God as King was celebrated with his triumph over the forces of Chaos and the enemies of himself and his people. The legend *Eliezer the Priest* is significant for the question of the restoration of the Temple service (Reifenberg Collection).

19 & **20.** Gold solidus of Heraclius commemorating his recovery of the 'True Cross' from the Persians.

IMP T CAES VESP AVG P M TR P P P COS VIII
IVDAEA CAPTA
SC
CONOB

Bedouin raiders menaced them. He also constructed hospices for pilgrims, which were still functioning, though somewhat dilapidated, when the Breton monk Bernard the Wise made his pilgrimage in 870. Bernard (ed. Tobler, X) locates a hospice and library with fields, vine-yards and a garden in the Valley of Jehoshaphat by the Church of St. Mary, that presumably on the reputed site of her tomb (Pl. 31).

The decline of the temporal power of the Abbasid Caliphate in the ninth century coincided with a revival of Byzantine power, which now took the offensive in Syria, which under Nicephorus Phocas (963–969) and John Zimisces (969–976) assumed the proportions almost of a crusade and apparently was so regarded by both Emperors. This, however, had momentarily the effect of exacerbating feeling between Muslim and Christian in Palestine, which was expressed in the burning by Muslims and Jews of the Patriarch John, who was detected in treasonable correspondence with the Emperor in his campaign in North Syria. The campaigns of John Zimisces were even more menacing for the Muslims in Palestine, now under al-Ḥākim the heretic Caliph of Egypt, who claimed descent from the Prophet through his daughter Fāṭima and his cousin 'Ālī. With the support of the Christian mountaineers of Armenia and native Christians of Syria John defeated the Muslims in Mesopotamia and turned west to Syria and Palestine. The evil effects of Abbāsid-Fāṭimid rivalry were apparent, and he decided to strike at the latter, his more immediate neighbours. In 974 he marched virtually unopposed up the Orontes and on past Damascus to Galilee, where he occupied Tiberias and Nazareth, and penetrated to Caesarea on the coast, where he received the submission of the Muslims from Jerusalem. He did not proceed to Jerusalem, however, but decided on strategic grounds to reduce the seaports on the Syrian coast, but his sudden death two years later and the preoccupation of the

---

21. The Golden Gate in the east wall of the Muslim Sacred Precinct, a Byzantine work of the fifth century A.D., since walled up by the Muslims.

22. The writer's location of the battle of Ajnādain, where the Muslims were victorious in A.D. 634, looking north towards the site of Biblical Azekah on the hill. The valley running from the interior from near Bethlehem and Hebron and northwards, turns westward beyond Azekah to the coastal plain. This was the Vale of Elah, where David fought with Goliath (about half a mile east of the roadway), and was one of the main approaches to the interior, used by the Seleucid forces operating against the Jewish nationalists under Judas Maccabaeus and his brothers.

Byzantine armies in the Balkans precluded an exploitation of these victories.

The campaigns of Nicephorus Phocas and John Zimisces thus in a measure anticipated the First Crusade, and indeed the West was aware of the situation. The great mercantile power of Venice, for instance, had forbidden the transport of raw materials to the Muslims during John's campaign on pain of death. The situation of the Christians in Palestine, however, under the generally tolerant Muslim rule scarcely warranted these expeditions, and, as is indicated by John's seizure of the coastal towns, the objective of the campaign was not so much the liberation of native Christians and the holy sites as the curtailment of the power of Egypt as an imperial rival.

Periodic persecutions in this period were less the policy of Islam than the caprice of individuals, and were not sustained. The Muslim geographer al-Muqaddasī, himself as his name implies a native of Jerusalem, about the end of the tenth century testifies that the Christians still had their churches and liberty of worship, ruefully remarking that those who purchased liberty of worship at the price of the poll-tax were but too numerous; they could presume to hold their heads up in public and even throve, especially in the legal and medical professions.[10] The Persian traveller Nasr-i-Khosrau corroborates the statements of al-Muqaddasī. Writing about the middle of the eleventh century some forty years after the savage outbreak of the mad Fāṭimid Caliph al-Ḥākim, he specifically mentions that the Church of the Holy Sepulchre was rebuilt in 1037 by special agreement between the Byzantine Emperor Michael the Paphlagonian and the Caliph.[11] There was in fact a Christian Patriarch of Jerusalem, Symeon, right up to the eve of the First Crusade, though latterly Symeon and his higher clergy were refugees in Cyprus, and when the Muslims put the city in a state of siege in 1099 the native Christians were evacuated.

In spite of the campaigns of Nicephorus Phocas and John Zimisces the Muslim power in Jerusalem was not seriously menaced until the First Crusade in 1099. The city changed masters, but all were Muslim. A Turkish adventurer 'Azīz ibn 'Abaq occupied Jerusalem and South Palestine and recovered it again after the Fāṭimid forces had retaken it. Eventually in 1079 the city was incorporated in the sultanate of Ṭuṭush the brother of the Turkish Emperor in Central Asia, Mālik Shah, under his governor Ortoq, whose family held it till the eve of the First Crusade, which put a temporary period to Muslim rule in Jerusalem.

NOTES FOR CHAPTER IX

1 Al-Balādhūrī, *Futūḥ al-Buldān*, ed. M. J. De Goeje, 1866, 128

2 After Ibn al-'Athīr, *Al-Kāmil fī 't-Ta'rīkh* (ed. C. J. Tornberg) ii. 1867. We cite the translation of W. M. Muir, *The Caliphate, Rise, Decline, and Fall*, rev. ed., 1915, pp. 67–8, which we hope may serve to introduce the general reader to this notable literary monument on a great theme

3 Sophronius, *Patrologia Graeca*, Migne 32. 10 ff.

4 Al-Wāqidī, cited by aṭ-Tabarī, *Annales*, ed. De Goeje, series I, IV, 2155

5 Aṭ-Ṭabarī, *Annales* ed. M. J. De Goeje, 1964, series I vol. V., pp. 2405–6

6 G. Le Strange, *Palestine Under the Moslems*, 1890, pp. 139–40, after the ultimate authority of al-Walīd ibn Muslim of Damascus who died in 810

7 Luke ii. 22 ff.

8 Luke ii. 46 ff.

9 Genesis xxii. 1–14

10 *Palestine Pilgrims Texts Society*, El-Muqaddasī, p. 37

11 *Palestine Pilgrims Texts Society*, Nasr-i-Khosrau, p. 60

X

THE CRESCENT AND THE CROSS

... come from your place out of the uttermost parts of the north, you and many people with you, all of them riding on horses, a great host, a mighty army (Ezekiel xxxviii. 15)

Among the relics of Empire in Palestine the Crusading castles are particularly impressive, Banias towering among the crags below Ḥermon, Belvoir, called in Arabic Kawkab al-Hawa ('Star of the Wind') soaring high over the Jordan Valley between Baysān and Tiberias, Castra Peregrinorum at ʿAthlīt south of the Carmel Head with its bold front to the Mediterranean breakers, and Kerak in Moab beyond the Dead Sea, the eyrie of Reynald of Châtillon. Many a church besides is still used by native Christians in villages or towns throughout the land, sometimes with comparatively little reconstruction, as the Church of the Holy Sepulchre, St. Anne's, St. James' (Armenian), St. Mark's (Syrian Jacobite), St. Elias' (Elijah) in the Old City of Jerusalem and the Church of the Tomb of the Virgin in the Valley of Jehoshaphat, the twelfth-century Monastery of the Cross,* reputedly the site of the tree from which the wood for the true cross was taken, now on the north-west outskirts of the modern Jewish city of Jerusalem, the Hospitaller fortress church at Qiryat al-ʿInab (Emmaus), the Church of St. George at Lydda, and at Saffūriyeh and ʿAin Kārim, reputedly the birth-place of John the Baptist. Other impressive churches of the period are now adapted as mosques, as at Ramleh, Sebasṭiyeh (Samaria), Hebron, Gaza and Nabī Samwīl on the north-west horizon of Jerusalem. In spite of the vicissitudes of history and natural development the stamp of the Frankish occupation is still strong in Jerusalem and Acre, the capital of the Latin Kingdom of Jerusalem after Ṣalāḥ ad-Dīn's sore truncation of the realm. The Old City of Jerusalem within the walls, in fact, with its citadel—once the palace of the Frankish kings—and distinct Christian, Armenian and Muslim quarters and its general plan, still largely

* This venerable monument was destroyed in the Six Days' War of June 1967.

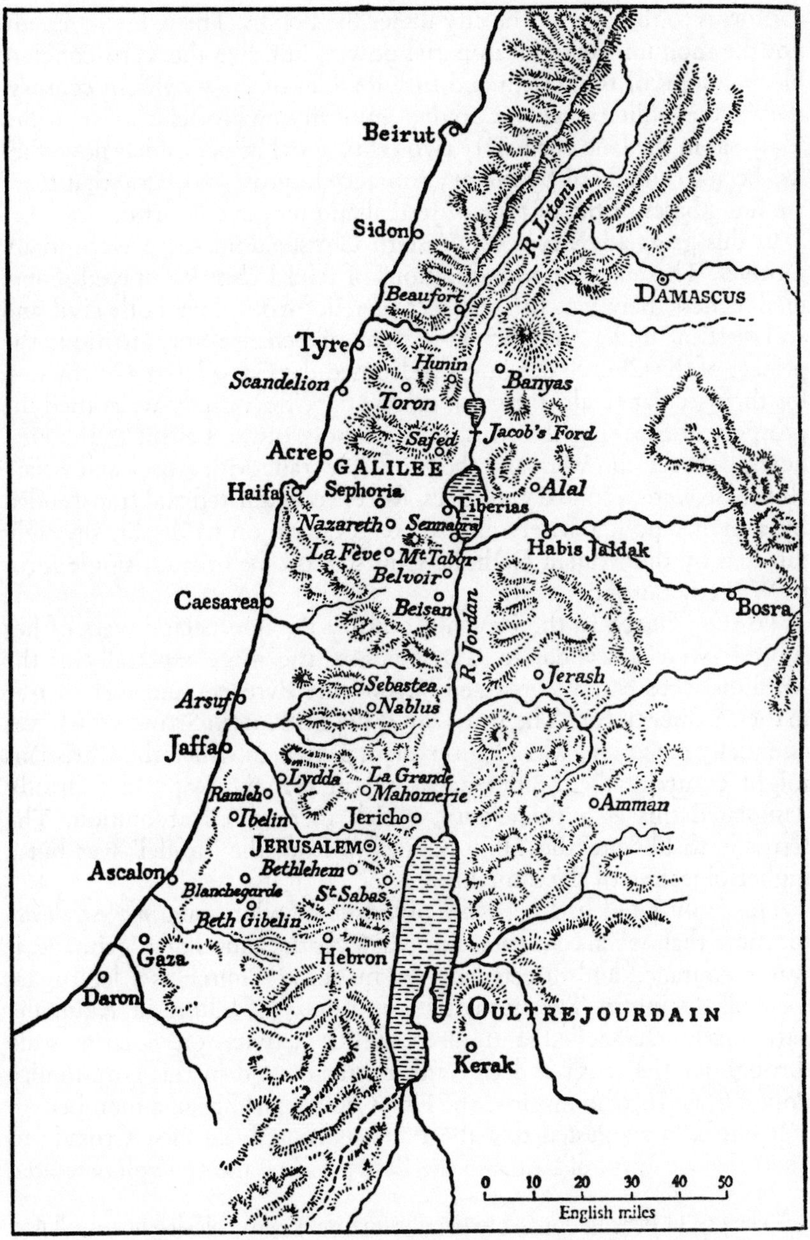

Fig. IX THE KINGDOM OF JERUSALEM IN THE TWELFTH CENTURY.
(*From S. Runciman's* A History of the Crusades
published by the Cambridge University Press)

conforms to the plan of the city under the Franks. These, however, are not the monuments of an imperial power, but, like the ferro-concrete block-houses of the fourth and fifth decades of the twentieth century, they were built by an occupying minority, who held a precarious foothold in the land for barely two centuries. The period has nevertheless been so enhanced by literary romance in prose and verse that there are few phases of the history of Jerusalem quite so colourful.

In this great adventure of Western Christendom there were many motives. The energies and ambitions of feudal chivalry craved scope; in all orders there was the prospect of relief from debt both civil and ecclesiastical under the current system of penance and attrition; the princes of the Church doubtless welcomed the Crusades as a distraction for their secular rivals; the great mercantile cities of Italy welcomed the prospect of breaking the Muslim monopoly of the Levant as the vital nexus between the West and the profitable trade with Africa and Asia.* But these were secondary motives, forces co-ordinated and transcended by a higher policy wisely and, there is no reason to doubt, sincerely directed by the Roman Catholic Church, still the greatest single force in Western Europe.

To the Church in the eleventh century the internecine wars of her subjects were a scandal to Christendom, the more especially as the Muslims were barely contained beyond the Pyrenees and were active in the Mediterranean. The war against the Muslims in Spain, which was essentially defensive, was a legitimate objective, in which the Christians might compose their differences, and in fact the Pope had already designated this as a prior duty, which merited his absolution. The Crusade to liberate the Holy Sepulchre from the 'infidel' was but a higher objective of the same kind.

The Holy Land had been the objective of pilgrimage *par excellence* for more than seven centuries, and whatever the abuses of pilgrimage, it was encouraged and directed by the medieval Church as a legitimate spiritual discipline. The monastic community of Cluny in Aquitaine particularly channelled and directed this activity on a large scale throughout the tenth and eleventh centuries, and in this community Pope Urban II, who inspired the First Crusade, had been a member.

It has been suggested that the Pope sponsored the First Crusade to assert the authority of Rome in the East.† Indeed the Crusaders treated

* The first of these to respond to the situation was Genoa, which sent a small fleet when the Crusaders were investing Antioch.

† W. B. Stevenson (*The Crusades in the East*, 1907, p. 8) attributes this project to Urban's predecessor Gregory VII, Hildebrand, who thus aimed at checking the Turkish advance towards Europe and of extending the influence of the Roman see

Orthodox authority in Constantinople, Antioch and Jerusalem with increasingly scant respect, but that was on the part of the secular orders and minor clergy under their influence, and was not inspired by Rome. This is reflected in the correct and courteous approach of the Papal representative Adhemar the Bishop of Le Puys, the first to respond to the public appeal of Urban II at Clermont and the finest spirit among the leaders of the First Crusade, who unfortunately died soon after Antioch fell. Whatever the pretensions of Rome to authority equal to that of the great Eastern Patriarchates, there is no reason to doubt that Pope Urban II genuinely sought the unity of Christendom and was fully prepared to respect the authority of his Patriarchal colleagues in the East.*

At a council convoked at Clermont in Auvergne in 1095 Pope Urban II at an immense public gathering in the meadows outside the town made his dramatic appeal. In response Bishop Adhemar took the initiative, soon followed by Raymond Count of Toulouse, called also Raymond of St. Gilles after his favourite seat, and by a host of others both gentle and simple. The Pope had known the moment, and the response was infectious. The tradition of the holy war against the Muslims was an essential part of the Western heritage.[1] Many, especially in Provence, like Raymond, had already engaged the Muslims in Spain, while all aspired to ideals familiar to them from the ballad literature inspired by the long struggle between Muslim and Christian in Spain and Southern France, which was often the sum of the liberal education of the medieval nobility. That it played powerfully on the imagination of the Crusaders is obvious from the references in the various Latin chronicles of the Crusades. Many of the lower orders took advantage of the security of the armed forces to perform the pilgrimage; for some it was a relief from the weary monotony of subsistance, for others it was a refuge from justice; many lived by rapine on the road, abandoning all moral restraint beyond their home jurisdiction. Avarice and fanaticism were revealed in the massacres and

---

over the Greek and Armenian Christians of the East. Urban, who succeeded as Pope in 1088, gave the policy of Hildebrand a new orientation in the liberation of the Holy Land. The fact that Pope Urban arranged the concentration of the Crusade at Constantinople suggests that he visualized the enterprise as a common concern and not aimed at the domination of the Orthodox Church, S. Runciman, *A History of the Crusades, The First Crusade*, 1951, p. 115.

* That such was the mind of the papal legate Adhemar is clear from the appeal he addressed from Antioch to the Pope for reinforcements not in his own name but in the name of Symeon the Patriarch of Jerusalem, who was then a refugee in Cyprus. If Symeon had certain doctrinal differences with Rome he was nevertheless cordial in his support and relief of the Crusaders in their grim privations in the siege of Antioch.

looting of Jews in the Rhineland, in which the nobility shared, if not always by direct brigandage at least by blackmail. The vices of mankind were all accentuated in the First Crusade, which Grousset caustically describes as 'a moral alibi for many troubled consciences, adventurers and predatory knights'.[2] Yet many a pilgrim left his cottage or his castle to press on through the swamps and forests of the Danube, the wild mountains of Thrace, through dangers from robber bands, famine and plague, through the chill, bare uplands of Anatolia and the fever-haunted Syrian valleys to storm the walls of Jerusalem and kiss the shrine of the Holy Sepulchre.

In the East conditions encouraged the Crusade. After four centuries the Muslim Empire was disintegrating. In Egypt and North Africa a heterodox Caliph (see above, p. 225) ruled from the wealthy security of the Nile Valley, defying the orthodox Caliph in Baghdad. The political power of the latter was actually in the hands of the Turks, nominally his protectors and executives, but actually the dominating force in orthodox Islam, which, however, was impaired through fragmentation into independent and often hostile secular Sultanates in Asia Minor and the chief commands in Syria and Palestine, such as Mosul, Aleppo, Damascus and eventually Jerusalem. Those were the remote provinces of a Turkish empire the centre of which was in Central Asia, an empire which, moreover, depended precariously on the personal authority of its head. Generally in the eleventh century Palestine was an adjunct of the Fāṭimid Caliphs of Egypt, who held the land by garrisons posted in such key fortresses as Askalon, Acre and Jerusalem and the Syrian ports. Their control, however, was exercised under the constant menace of invasion from the north-east by the Turkish defenders of orthodox Islam, which effectively materialized in 1071, when Jerusalem and the interior passed under Turkish rule under the family of Ortoq, though the Fāṭimid Caliph still held the coast.* In addition certain regions such as Tripoli, Jubail and Tyre on the coast of the Lebanon and Shayzār on the Orontes were ruled by native Arab families.

This multiplication of provinces and the disturbances through local wars hindered pilgrimage to Palestine, which was virtually barred to Christians.[3] But this fragmentation of Turkish authority was the best augury for the success of the Crusade. This was apparent in the first phase of the offensive in Syria. The most serious threat to the Crusaders

* Ibn al-'Athīr (*op. cit.*, p. 191) reports a tradition that the Fāṭimids had actually appealed to the Franks to invade the lands held by the Turks. William of Tyre (*Receuil . . ., Historiens Occidentaux* I, IV, xxiv) attests similar overtures made by the Armenian vizier of the Fāṭimid Caliph, al-Afḍal.

at Antioch apart from famine was the expedition mounted by Kerbogha the Atabeg of Moṣul, but this was impaired mainly by the failure of Ruḍwān of Aleppo and Duqāq of Damascus, the unworthy sons of Ṭuṭush the brother of the Seljuk Emperor Mālik Shah, to support him in time owing to their mutual suspicion. The Arabs moreover, conscious of their older and higher culture, resented the growth of Turkish power in Islam, and it is significant that after the fall of Antioch the Arab families of Munqidh of Shayzār on the Orontes and the Banū 'Amr of Tripoli admitted the Crusaders freely by way of the Buqei'a gap between the Nusairi Mountains and the Lebanon to the coastal plain in the march to Palestine. The failure of Kerbogha's Turkish army to relieve Antioch was also the signal for the Fāṭimids of Egypt at the direction of their astute Armenian vizier al-Afḍal to take Jerusalem from the Turkish family of Ortoq after a siege of forty days.

The secular leaders of the First Crusades were mainly feudal lords or younger sons, comprising various ethnic elements, which largely accounts for their scandalous dissensions. The Franks were represented by Robert Count of Flanders, Godfrey of Bouillon Duke of Lorraine, who became ruler of Jerusalem as Defender of the Holy Sepulchre, and his brother Baldwin of Boulogne, who became Count of Edessa and later King of the Latin Kingdom of Jerusalem. The Normans of France were represented by Robert of Normandy, and those of South Italy and Sicily by Bohemond and his nephew Tancred, who ruled Antioch in turn, while the men of Provence were led by Raymond of St. Gilles, who later laid the foundation of the County of Tripoli. To their standards others of less degree rallied from France, Germany and the Low Countries and from the south of Italy, where the Normans had established their power, and also, incidentally, established themselves as rivals to Byzantium, a relationship which they were to carry over to the Levant. Genoa, Pisa, Venice, Amalfi and Marseilles later sent their fleets with merchants, sailors and pilgrims, and pirates came from both shores of the English Channel and Vikings from Norway under Sigurd Hjorsalfar, brother to the King.

The forces of dissolution of a great enterprise, however, became apparent as soon as the Crusaders crossed the Taurus. Sordid anticipations of loot had been disappointed when the Byzantine Emperor forestalled them in negotiating the surrender of the Sultan Kilij Arslan's capital at Nicaea. Bohemond, the 'wily Odysseus' of the Crusade, broke his oath of fealty to the Emperor in seizing Antioch as his Principality, and Baldwin of Boulogne had already gone off on a privateering expedition which resulted in his foundation of the County of Edessa. Both moves were most important in view of eventual Muslim resistance from Asia, though it is doubtful if this was in the minds of Bohemond or Baldwin.* Actually when the Crusaders invaded Syria they were more sensitive to the danger from Egypt, who occupied Jerusalem and Palestine and with her navy controlled the coast, which was vital to the Crusaders if the minority who would stay behind in permanent occupation were to be reinforced with men and supplies. With this power the Byzantine Emperor and the Franks, whose relations were already strained, had independent diplomatic relations. The discovery from intercepted correspondence that the Emperor was not prepared to support the political aims of the Franks in the East, probably hoping to secure protection for native Orthodox Christians rather through negotiation, opened the rift still wider. As Bohemond's resolution over Antioch hardened Raymond determined to counter the power of the Normans by staking Provençal claims. As the Crusaders proceeded southwards Raymond appeared to be plotting out a domain on the Syrian coast. He endeavoured to reduce certain key fortresses such as Arqa commanding the pass between the coast and the valley of the Orontes near Ḥoms. Popular feeling, however, clamoured against delay and it was not until 1103 that Raymond reduced the region. He was never able to take Tripoli itself, but over against it he built a fortress named Pilgrim Mount, from which the city was eventually taken by his natural son Bertram with the help of a Genoese fleet and King Baldwin I, to whom Bertram did homage for the County of Tripoli in 1109.

In the early summer of 1099 the remnants of the Crusaders, which William of Tyre estimates at the strength of 20,000 effective footmen and 1,500 knights, passed without opposition into Fāṭimid (Egyptian) territory at the mouth of the Dog River just north of Beirut, where a passage is cut in the face of the cliff, which drops practically sheer into the sea.† They occupied Ramleh in the coastal plain of Palestine without opposition, and installed a Latin bishop in the Church of St. George in the vicinity.[4] Raymond of Aguilers, the chaplain of Raymond of St. Gilles, records a council of war, in which in view of the drought of summer, and possibly, though he does not record it, the apparent passivity of Egypt, the question was debated of postponing an attack

* Fulcher of Chartres (*Receuil . . . Historiens Occidentaux* III, XIV), Baldwin's chaplain, mentions the atmospheric apparition of a sword pointing to the East which arrested Baldwin's attention, but he makes no mention of general political strategy at this point. He is obviously appreciative of the significance of the commands of Baldwin and Bohemond in XXXIII, though he implies their selfish motives in his opinion that their diversion to Edessa and Antioch was perhaps providential.

† With inscriptions from the imperial powers of the second millennium B.C. through all ages to soldiers' graffiti from two World Wars, the cliff face here is an interesting record of the pageant of history in Syria.

on Jerusalem and advancing on Cairo and Alexandria. But the risk of invading Egypt with only 1,500 knights and of being cut off from reinforcements from Europe was too great. So on 6th June they passed unopposed on the last lap of their journey to Jerusalem. They penetrated the mountain barrier by Jalo (Biblical Aijalon) and Qiryat al-'Inab (Biblical Qiryath-jearim, which they called Emmaus). There natives of Bethlehem came to invite them to send an occupation force, which was dispatched under Tancred the nephew of Bohemond, and Baldwin du Bourg. They arrived at night and at daybreak the Church of the Nativity in this populous town five miles south-west of Jerusalem was in Christian hands.* The main force proceeded from Qiryat al-'Inab north-east by ancient Gibeon (al-Jīb), which they passed on their left,[5] and they first saw Jerusalem from the village of Nabī Samwīl on its hill-top some seven miles north-west of the city, which on that account they called Montjoie. In their approach they thus followed tradition in attacking the city on its most vulnerable side, and probably anticipated opposition in the approaches. They were unopposed, and by sunset on 7th June they encamped at length before the Holy City.

Jerusalem, garrisoned by Egyptian troops, had been evacuated of its whole Christian population, who were still in the majority in the city, which was put in a state of siege. Water and provisions were conserved, while outside the country was ravaged and the wells poisoned, so that the Crusaders were forced to disperse far and wide for water, being all the while exposed to Muslim raiding bands. The walls, well maintained, followed the line of those round the Old City today, and were accessible only in the north and at the south-west on what has been falsely called since the fifth century 'the Zion Hill'. At all other points the ground falls away too abruptly from the walls for any force with its siege engines to be effective.

The Crusaders in their enthusiasm took up their respective positions at these vulnerable points immediately on their arrival, Godfrey of Bouillon at the north-west angle to the Jaffa, or Hebron, Gate, where he was joined by Tancred from Bethlehem, Robert of Flanders at the Damascus Gate (Gate of the Pillar), called by the Crusaders Stephen's Gate, with Robert of Normandy east of him by the present Herod Gate, called by the Crusaders the Postern of St. Magdalene. The west part of the south wall was invested by Raymond of Toulouse.

Such walls as those of Jerusalem, however, with their firm rock-hewn

* Fulcher of Chartres (*op. cit.*, I, xxv) gives a dramatic account of the response of the natives to the hundred horsemen with Tancred and Baldwin, weeping with apprehension of what they might suffer at the hands of the more numerous enemy, and rejoicing at the token of the rehabilitation of the Christian faith.

foundations, were not to be battered or mined. Assault towers were required, but there was no obvious source of materials for their construction. Guided by native Christians, the Franks procured timber from a wadi some distance from Jerusalem, and providentially certain Genoese ships had put in at the deserted port of Jaffa with provisions and the materials required for siege-engines, and work began on three great assault towers. Added to the great privations of the Christians in the blistering heat and drought of the high summer in that bare, white, glaring, waterless land of Judah was the anxiety lest the Muslim relief force, which they knew to have been summoned from Egypt, should be upon them. For here they were cut off from their base, since the seas were commanded by the Egyptian navy with a strong military base at Askalon. Many indeed renounced the pilgrimage before the walls of Jerusalem. The Arab and Sudanese garrison, though hopelessly outnumbered, defended the city with courage and resource. Both armies used mangonels; bags of chaff and mattresses stuffed with silk were lowered to take the impact of rams and missiles. The assault towers were eventually completed, and after a solemn act of penitence and rededication, signalized by a fast and procession barefoot with crosses and holy relics round the walls of Jerusalem, the Crusaders resumed their posts. Meanwhile the whole host of the Crusaders laboured to fill in the fosse outside the north wall (Pl. 28), and the towers were distributed at points of assault, a little west of the north-east corner of the city at the Tower of the Stork (Burj Abī Laqlaq), at the north-west angle and at Raymond's post on the western sector of the south wall.

The decisive attack began on the night of 13th July a month and a week after the investment of the city. Desperate efforts were made to destroy the assault towers. Flaming arrows were shot into them with sulphur, pitch, oil, and all kinds of combustibles, but their raw-hide coverings and the vigilance of their crews foiled the defenders; nor were sorceresses, who were brought on to the ramparts to bewitch the machines, any more effective. Finally at midday on 15th July after a continuous assault the walls were stormed. Godfrey himself, fighting from a platformed tower, succeeded in throwing a gangway over to the ramparts by the Tower of the Stork,* and his men swarmed over into the city, closely followed by Tancred and the Normans of Sicily. They then opened the Damascus Gate, and the Crusaders rushed in, bent on promiscuous slaughter. Leaders, soldiers and the mob of camp-followers cast humanity to the winds, and the streets of the city ran red with the blood of young and old, men and women alike, and the

* The spot is specifically noted with a cross in the twelfth-century plan of Jerusalem in the Cambrai MS. See pl. 29.

narrow ways were choked with corpses. If the Caliph ʿUmar had distinguished himself by his clemency when Jerusalem capitulated to the Muslims in 638 (see above, pp. 219–20) the piety of Christendom bore a different brand. The defenders of the north wall rushed to the Sacred Precinct, which might with time have been put in a state of defence till the heat of victory had cooled. But Tancred and his Normans were there before defence could be organized, and the refugees were given time only to seek refuge in, and even on the roof of, the Aqṣa Mosque while the Normans looted and desecrated the Dome of the Rock. The refugees in the Aqṣa Mosque promised Tancred a great reward for their lives, which he accepted, but his pledge was ignored by the rabble, now intoxicated with the reek of massacre. Fulcher of Chartres, the chaplain of Baldwin of Boulogne, says that ten thousand were beheaded in the mosque,[6] and Raymond of Aguilers found that next day the paved area of the Sacred Precinct was choked with corpses and blood to the knees.[7]* The Muslim governor and his men, who had been defending the sector assaulted by Raymond in the south-west, withdrew into the citadel by the Jaffa, or Hebron, Gate, which stood on the site of the palace-fort of Herod the Great and the present Turkish Citadel, which the Crusaders regarded as the Tower of David, and surrendered on the promise of a ransom to Raymond. The Count honoured his word and gave them safe conduct to Askalon.[8] But the general fanaticism condemned both clemency and honour. These were the only Muslims who survived.

Such was the triumph of the Cross at Jerusalem on 15th July, 1099, traditionally at the ninth hour, 'when guiltless blood for guilty man was shed', and the perpetrators of this colossal inhumanity went to the Church of the Holy Sepulchre not to seek absolution for their crime but to grovel in mock humility and to render thanks for their victory.

At this juncture a native Christian produced a piece of wood which he claimed to be a piece of the true cross, which, he declared, had been hidden long ago, presumably in the Muslim occupation, in a place which was a secret of his family. This *particula una* was incorporated in a complete cross set in precious metal,[9] which became 'the True Cross' of the Franks, their palladium, which was captured in Ṣalāḥ ad-Dīn's great victory at the Horns of Ḥaṭṭīn in 1187.[10]

In the settlement after the victory conflict of interests again manifested itself. There was none whose authority would not be disputed.

* Raymond of Aguilers applauds the justice of such slaughter in the very precinct which the Muslims had polluted with their 'blasphemies'. Fulcher of Chartres also applauds the indiscriminate carnage, explicitly mentioning that women and children were included. The truculence and fanaticism of these clerics is appalling!

Normally the Greek Orthodox Patriarch of Jerusalem would have been restored, and the Patriarch Symeon, who had organized famine relief to the Crusaders at Antioch when he was a refugee in Cyprus, might have been acceptable to all. But he was now dead, and no other of the higher clergy had returned. Adhemar, Bishop of Le Puys and the Papal Legate, was the one man in the Crusade whose authority all would have recognized. But he too was dead. The clergy claimed that Jerusalem must be a papal state. The warriors, however, by whose energy and courage the land had been won and by whose efforts it must now be kept, were not to be gainsaid, and in this they had the support of the younger clergy, the older men having for the most part succumbed to the fatigues of the Crusade. It is said that the first choice was Raymond of Toulouse, who is reputed to have repudiated the distinction on principle, though perhaps he realized from recent experience at Antioch that his authority was not sufficiently strong. Godfrey of Bouillon was eventually elected Defender of the Holy Sepulchre (*Advocatus Sancti Sepulcri*). The title King was expressly avoided but was used by his brother Baldwin of Boulogne, who succeeded him in 1100.

The hopes of Eastern Christendom in the Crusades were dashed when a Latin patriarch was elected in the person of Arnulf, the chaplain of Duke Robert of Normandy, on whose character the Frankish chroniclers have divided opinions,[11] though freely admitting his popularity. Arnulf showed obtuse disregard for the susceptibilities of native Orthodox Christians and clergy and other branches of Eastern Christendom who had been admitted with their own rites to the Church of the Holy Sepulchre under the Muslims. The Orthodox clergy were actually banned from service in the Church of the Holy Sepulchre. The situation was later modified under Baldwin I, who saw the wisdom of conciliating native Christian opinion. But a legacy of ecclesiastical friction was left to posterity, which is still a notorious scandal in the Church of the Holy Sepulchre. Arnulf did not long enjoy his elevation, however. In the spring of the following year Baldwin of Boulogne Count of Edessa and Bohemond Prince of Antioch came up to Jerusalem for Christmas. By this time Daimbert the papal legate, appointed by Urban II in place of the late Adhemar, had come to the Holy Land with a Pisan fleet. The astute and masterful Bohemond had cultivated the legate,[12] and the countenance of the papal representative secured him much-needed moral support for his tenure of Antioch in face of Byzantine opposition. Now Bohemond in turn had something to offer Daimbert. Present in Jerusalem with a powerful following of Normans at a time when many of the liberators of the city had returned to Europe, Bohemond undoubtedly secured the elevation of Daimbert to the Patriarchate. From him Godfrey and Bohemond received Jerusalem and Antioch as their respective fiefs. Thus Bohemond had won the point for which the clergy had striven, that Jerusalem should be a fief of the Church; he had also secured his own independence of the kingdom of Jerusalem, and had shifted the responsibility for his breach of the oath of fealty to the Byzantine Emperor on to the broad shoulders of the Roman Church. Daimbert, however, was eventually deposed for corruption by a Latin Synod in the reign of Baldwin I, who after certain tensions had eventually the satisfaction of seeing the Latin Patriarchate in the safe hands of Arnulf of Rohea, who was agreeably deferential to his royal authority.

Godfrey and his forces were soon called upon to vindicate themselves in defence of what they had won. Less than a month after the capture of Jerusalem opposition under al-Afḍal, the Armenian vizier of Egypt, began to organize itself with Askalon as a base. The Crusaders concentrated their forces at Ibelin (Biblical Yabneel) in the coastal plain once occupied by the Philistines, and, advancing past Ashdod, they surprised the Egyptian army among the lush orchards of Majdal near Askalon. The victory was complete and the booty enormous, but Askalon was not taken. It was at the mercy of the Crusaders, but a great achievement was frustrated by fatal divisions in their ranks. Among the defenders of Askalon were the sole survivors of the massacre of Jerusalem who had been spared by Raymond, and at their instance the defenders offered to surrender, but to none but Raymond. Godfrey, already suspicious of Raymond, would not agree, and Raymond with Robert Count of Flanders and Robert of Normandy withdrew their troops. This costly quarrel preserved Askalon as an Egyptian bridgehead in Palestine. The menace of this Egyptian base dictated the construction of a ring of powerful fortresses to the north and east: Gibelin (Bayt Jibrīn, now Jewish Beth Guvrīn), Blanchegarde (Tell aṣ-Ṣāfī, Biblical Libnah, or Gath, see above, p. 20) and Ibelin, which was the fief of one of the most powerful families settled permanently in Palestine. The fortifications to contain Askalon were completed ironically in 1143, just a year before the decisive turn in the fortunes of the Frankish kingdom with the fall of Edessa in 1144, so that its capture in 1153 was robbed of much of its value, though, with the unification of the commands in Asia and Egypt under Nūr ad-Dīn and Ṣalāḥ ad-Dīn the capture of this vital Egyptian bridgehead in Palestine was not insignificant. Meanwhile the Egyptian seaports Arsūf, Caesarea, Haifa and Acre were paying tribute to the Franks by 1100, and Jaffa, which had been deserted by the Muslims on the Crusaders' advance on Jerusalem, was refortified by the Crusaders as a vital supply base.

So far the Crusade had been successful in Palestine, but the tenure of the land was precarious. On the fall of Jerusalem many, satisfied that the object of their journey was attained, returned forthwith, and Robert of Normandy and Robert of Flanders, having consummated their Crusade with Baptism in the Jordan and cut their pilgrims' palm-fronds by Jericho, left for home with most of their men less than a month after the victory of Majdal.[13] The interest of other leaders who remained in the East was concentrated on other regions. Baldwin was preoccupied in Edessa and Bohemond in Antioch, while Raymond of St. Gilles had returned to Syria and Constantinople, whence he returned in 1101 to spend the rest of his life until 1104 in reducing the country round Tripoli. Thus of the principal chiefs only Godfrey remained in Palestine with the Norman Tancred, his vassal in Galilee, who, however, went north in 1101 to rule in Antioch in place of his uncle Bohemond, who had been captured by the Muslims in North Syria. Already, however, Tancred had reduced the interior of Palestine, distinguishing himself at Nablus and Baysān (Biblical Bethshan). From his fief in Galilee he had raided beyond Jordan and the Sea of Galilee and exacted tribute for the realm of Jerusalem, which brought Jerusalem into conflict with Damascus, then ruled for the Seljuk prince Duqāq by his atābek, or tutor, Tughtagin. The Franks had so far avoided hostile contact with Damascus, which they had been careful to neutralize during the siege of Antioch with assurances that they had no designs in that direction.[14] The state of Palestine within a year from the fall of Jerusalem is described by William of Tyre.[15] Godfrey and Tancred were left with barely three hundred knights and two thousand foot, a force comparable to the total force of the British Police and native auxiliaries before the rising of 1936–39 inflated the force.* Besides Jerusalem there were few places in the interior larger than large villages, and with Baysān and Tiberias occupied and Hebron, which the Franks called St. Abraham, fortified as a frontier post, this was the limit of the State of Jerusalem, within which Godfrey and his successors granted districts and villages as fiefs to soldiers whose vows or ambitions kept them permanently in the Holy Land. On the coast Jaffa, now refortified, was

* In 1934 the Police Force in Palestine comprised 49 British officers and 650 other ranks with 82 Palestinian officers and 1,607 other ranks to a total of 2,388, H. Luke and E. Keith-Roach, *The Handbook of Palestine and Transjordan*, 1934, p. 314.

---

23. The Muslim Sacred Precinct looking south beyond the Dome of the Rock and the Dome of the Chain with the Aqṣa Mosque to the south, and to the south-east the course of the Qidron Valley past the Mar Saba monastery to the Dead Sea, about three miles south of Qumran.

the port of Jerusalem, while Frankish ravages on Arsūf, Caesarea, Haifa and Acre reduced these places first to tributary status, until after the death of Godfrey they were incorporated in the Kingdom of Jerusalem with wealthy and privileged merchant colonies from Genoa, Venice and Pisa, who played a notable part in the consolidation of the Kingdom, though from the most sordid motives, in transporting men and supplies from Europe and in combating the Egyptian Navy. Nor must the English, Flemish and Scandinavian fleets be forgotten in those vital operations. Communications in the land itself, however, were difficult and brigandage rife. Not even in Jerusalem were the Franks safe, and many were struck down in the night.[16]

This conditioned the establishment of the military order of the Templars to protect pilgrims against brigandage. This order of soldier-monks, organized in classes of knights of the nobility, sergeants of the bourgoisie, and clerics and distinguished by their white habit with a red cross, was founded by Hugh of Payens in 1118 and was named after the headquarters of the Order to the west of, and partly in, the Aqṣa Mosque in the Temple area, their church being the Dome of the Rock. In the same year the Order of St. John was transformed from a purely charitable order to include military brothers. The Order had developed from the staff of a hostel which some citizens of Amalfi had founded in 1070 for the care and entertainment of pilgrims on a site granted by the Muslim governor of Jerusalem south of the Church of the Holy Sepulchre, still called the Mūristān (Hospital) and still belonging to the Order of St. John. This Order of St. John the Almsgiver, an Egyptian saint of the seventh century, was under the authority of the Benedictine Order and functioned until the First Crusade, on the success of which the order was largely endowed, and increased in staff and importance with the great influx of pilgrims, being promoted to the status of an independent order directly under papal authority. When Raymond of Le Puys became Grand Master in 1118 the duties of the Order were divided between its former pacific functions and new military duties like those of the Templars. These two Orders of soldier-monks became the standing army of the Kingdom of Jerusalem, entrusted with the building and garrisoning of castles in key positions, of which the most spectacular is that of the Hospitallers, the renowned

---

24. The façade of the Aqṣa Mosque.

25. The Aqṣa Mosque, interior, facing the prayer niche (*miḥrab*) orientated towards Mecca, with a carved wooden pulpit (*minbar*) to the right of it, which was dedicated by Nūr ad-Dīn Maḥmūd to the capture of Jerusalem and installed by Ṣalāḥ ad-Dīn, whose name it bears.

Crac des Chevaliers, called by the Arabs Ḥuṣn al-Akrād ('Kurds' Castle'), commanding the gap from the coast by Tripoli between the Lebanon and the Nuṣairi Mountains to the Orontes Valley by Ḥoms.

On the death of Godfrey in the summer of 1100 Church and State came into conflict. The Latin Patriarch Daimbert, who had received the homage of Godfrey, found his authority now questioned. The citadel of Jerusalem, called by the Franks 'the Tower of David', was occupied and fortified by a resolute knight Garnier of Gray, who refused to surrender it to Daimbert, but sent an urgent appeal to Godfrey's brother Baldwin of Boulogne, Count of Edessa. Daimbert on his part sent an appeal to his champion Bohemond, Prince of Antioch. His messenger, however, was intercepted by Bohemond's inveterate enemy Raymond of St. Gilles at Laṭakīyeh, and the dispatch was never delivered. Within a month Bohemond was captured by the Turks at Malaṭīyeh, and Baldwin found no effective opposition when he reached Jerusalem in the autumn of 1100, having on his way won a resounding victory over the Turks from Damascus, who ought to have annihilated his small force at the narrow pass at the mouth of the Dog River (see above, p. 234).* He marched forthwith from Jerusalem against Askalon, but the garrison refused to leave the shelter of the walls. Eager to accomplish something, Baldwin undertook operations against the brigands who infested the pilgrim road between Jaffa and Jerusalem, tracking them to their lairs in the limestone caves with which the country is honeycombed and smoking them out relentlessly. Passing through the wild hill-country about Hebron and the desert region towards Engedi, he travelled round the south end of the Dead Sea and returned through Moab to Jerusalem after a patrol of about a month.† Though no contact was made with the organized

* Fulcher of Chartres (*op. cit.* II, ii–iii) describes the jeopardy of the Franks, who would never have passed the Dog River if the enemy had not been over-confident, leaving the pass after the first repulse of Baldwin and coming in force against him in the plain, where the Franks defeated them.

† They went via Hebron and apparently by Engedi and round the south end of the Dead Sea to Petra (Wādī Mūsā), already traditionally associated with Moses' striking of the rock (Numbers xx. 8 ff.). They also visited the reputed tomb of Aaron, which Fulcher (*op. cit.* II, v) describes as occupied by a monastery. If he is referring to Jebel Hārūn, where Muslim tradition venerates a small shrine as the tomb of Aaron, 'monastery' might mean no more than this small building, which would serve also as the cell of the custodian. But Fulcher may be referring to the great tomb with ornamental façade hewn out of the sandstone rock, called ad-Dayr ('the Monastery'), which looks over to the wēlī of Aaron on the summit of Jebel Hārūn. The local Muslims may have thus tried to divert the Franks from the real site, as Sophronius is said to have done with the Caliph 'Umar in the case of the sacred rock at Jerusalem. Fulcher has many interesting personal observations.

forces of the enemy these operations impressed all with the daring and energy of Baldwin. On his return a reconciliation was effected with Daimbert, and on Christmas Day 1100 Baldwin was crowned King of Jerusalem by the Patriarch in the Church of the Nativity at Bethlehem.

Baldwin's immediate task was the reduction of the coastal towns. The arrival of a Genoese fleet at Jaffa in the spring of 1101 gave him his opportunity. A bargain was immediately struck. The Genoese agreed to co-operate in the reduction of the seaports in return for the concession of a third of the booty and slaves and a trading quarter in every town captured. In a few weeks Arsūf was taken and its garrison, according to the terms of surrender, given a safe conduct to Askalon. Caesarea fell and was abandoned to massacre and rapine, this pious work being consummated by the foundation of an archbishopric. With the prospects of commercial advantages, the merchants of Genoa, Venice and Pisa were eager for new enterprises. In 1103, again by the help of a Genoese fleet, Acre was taken. This was of particular importance for the security and material prosperity of the Kingdom of Jerusalem since it was the only secure harbour in Palestine. This provided a convenient port for trade and expeditions from Europe, on which the Kingdom of Jerusalem depended to supplement its exiguous permanent manpower; it further deprived the Egyptian fleet of a base from which to intercept maritime traffic to Jaffa, which is a somewhat hazardous roadstead precariously protected by an offshore reef. The regular plan of campaign at this period of consolidation was to take advantage of the fleets which came from Europe with pilgrims for the Easter festival to capture strongholds on the coast. Thus in 1109 the Genoese fleet helped Baldwin and Bertram, the natural son of the late Raymond, to reduce Tripoli, which became the capital of the County of Tripoli, the fourth Crusading state in the East and of great strategic importance as a seaport and as commanding the gap between the Lebanon and the Nuṣairī Mountains into the Orontes Valley, from which the Turks in Damascus could intercept communications between the Northern Crusader states and Jerusalem. In 1110 Beirūt was taken, and in the same year a Danish and Norwegian fleet under Sigurd Hjorsalfar, brother of the King of Norway, and a Venetian fleet led personally by the Doge helped to take Sidon. In 1123 a powerful and well-equipped Venetian fleet put into Acre, eager for action and trading opportunities. As an earnest of what it might accomplish it sailed boldly against the Egyptian fleet off Askalon and largely destroyed it, sweeping the coast as far as al-'Arīsh. They declared themselves ready to sail against Askalon or Tyre in return for very handsome trading and financial concessions from the Kingdom of Jerusalem. After some dispute the matter was decided by lot, and Tyre fell in July 1124, the last city on the coast to hold out against the Franks with the exception of Askalon.

The conquest of the Holy Land was thus virtually completed, but with the reduction of the ports the rivalries of the Crusaders in the East were complicated by the commercial rivalry of Genoa, Pisa and Venice. The simple ideal of Pope Urban II was already being stifled in a hard shell of worldly realities.

The reign of Baldwin I, under whose leadership all the seaports except Tyre were taken, if outstanding in the line of the most able and energetic kings who reigned in Jerusalem, is typical of the Crusading enterprise in the East, the rule of a minority sustained by occasional support from Europe, but still kept at constant tension, fighting on many fronts, distracted by local interests and defensive demands of the states of Edessa, Antioch, and eventually Tripoli and by the competing interests of parties in the realm. They were, moreover, embarrassed by the reckless zeal of fresh allies from Europe, who were the more eager to precipitate the Kingdom into hazardous enterprises because they had engaged themselves only for a short term in the East. The local rivalries of Turkish amīrs also invited Frankish intromission, and, while the prestige of the Western knights was greatly enhanced and it was highly gratifying to contribute to what Grousset emphasizes as the Muslim anarchy[17] that made their hold on the East possible, this activity inevitably took its toll. Men died young in the Kingdom of Jerusalem, where minority and regency problems were regular. Girls married young, were frequently widowed and as often remarried since the security of the realm under the feudal system demanded fighting men as consorts. Life in the Latin Kingdom of Jerusalem was for the young and virile, a life of action and swift change, where the brave deserved the fair or at least the well-endowed. There were many amenities in the East with its kindlier climate, lighter, gayer clothes, and choice food and seasoning, which Italian merchants took to the West at great profit. All knew the hazard of life, but gaily confident after their initial victories, they were determined to live it to the full, a mood which was recaptured by the two thousand men of the British Mandatory Police Force between the two World Wars.

Space does not permit a full appraisal of the vicissitudes and exploits of the Frankish Kings of Jerusalem, Baldwin I (1100–1118); Baldwin II of le Bourg, his cousin (1118–1131), who was captured and liberated with a king's ransom, which he forthwith raised with a resounding victory over the enemy; and Fulk of Anjou (1131–1144), who completed the ring of fortresses round Askalon, but in whose reign the

Muslim revival began under ʿImād ad-Dīn ('the Pillar of the Faith') Zānghī, the powerful Amīr of Moṣūl. Baldwin III (1144–1162) worthily maintained the Crusading tradition, capturing Askalon in 1153. But under him Edessa, the north-east bastion of the Latin Kingdom, fell, which led to the Second Crusade, with its abortive attack on Damascus[18]—fifty years too late—which drew that pivotal command into the orbit of the influence of Nūr ad-Dīn[19] ('the Light of the Faith') and ultimately into that of Ṣalāḥ ad-Dīn ('the Soundness of the Faith'), his lieutenant in Egypt, whereby the commands of Egypt and Syria were united. Baldwin's brother Amalric I (1162–1173) was induced to intervene in Egypt to counteract the influence of Nūr ad-Dīn under his deputy the Kurd Shirkūh, the uncle of Ṣalāḥ ad-Dīn, with whom he fought successfully. Nor must the gallant leper King Baldwin IV (1173–1183) be forgotten, who governed and fought as long as his fatal disease allowed, and actually forced Ṣalāḥ ad-Dīn to raise the siege of the castle of Kerak in Transjordan, the ancient capital of Moab. Guy, the handsome cadet of the House of Lusignan, who won the heart and hand of Sybilla the sister and heiress of Baldwin IV, led the armies of the Kingdom with more courage than competence, and, always convinced by the last counsellor, cast the die for the fatal encounter by the Horns of Haṭṭīn (1187). Only one more Frankish king ruled in Jerusalem, the German Emperor Frederick II, who won the city as a diplomatic concession from al-Mālik al-Kāmil the nephew of Ṣalāḥ ad-Dīn in 1229, and occupied it to the embarrassment of all Christendom since he was excommunicated by the Pope, and, though his son was the actual heir, himself placed the crown on the high altar of the Church of the Holy Sepulchre and crowned himself.

The reign of Baldwin I may be briefly sketched as illustrative of the life of Frankish chivalry in Palestine. Besides being ever ready to anticipate attack from the Egyptian advance base at Askalon, he anticipated the main threat of the future, that of free communication between Egypt and the further East by Aqaba and Damascus. He penetrated the southern desert, itself no mean enterprise, and left castles at Aqaba, called Aila, and Shōbāk (Krak de Montreal) on the height of the mountains of ancient Edom south-east of the south end of the Dead Sea commanding at once access to Aqaba and the caravan route from Damascus to Medina and Mecca. He also fortified the Island of Pharaoh (L'Île de Graye) off the north-west shore of the Gulf of Aqaba and in the north he secured an advance post against Damascus in his castle Château Baudouin in the plateau north of the River Yarmuk, and Thoron (modern Tibnīn) in the mountains between Tyre and the headwaters of the Jordan. This penniless younger son, the first of the Crusaders to secure a territorial command and eventually the King of Jerusalem, is by far the most colourful of the Crusading chiefs. He never ignored the call to arms, and his stirring adventures are in themselves an epic from the time he rode off with a handful of knights to take the County of Edessa until he was laid to rest beside his brother Godfrey in the Church of the Holy Sepulchre. But he was also a positive and constructive administrator. He solved the problem of the relation of Church and State in Jerusalem to the advantage of the monarchy with its executive potential. He conciliated local Christians and even his Muslim subjects so that both the economic resources and the manpower of his realm were built up. He inspired the respect and even the confidence of his Muslim neighbours, particularly Damascus,[20] and in his reign the Crusaders lost that narrow xenophobia which had characterized the First Crusade, and began to assimilate themselves fruitfully to the Eastern way of life and thought.

The 'Muslim anarchy' which had augured so well for the success of the First Crusade was, as we have seen, accentuated in Syria by the non-co-operative attitude of Aleppo and Damascus, respectively under Ruḍwān and Duqāq, the sons of Ṭuṭush the brother of the Turkish Emperor Mālik Shah. They had inherited from Ṭuṭush a policy of independence of the central authority. For a variety of reasons Ruḍwān was averse to co-operation with any of his neighbours against the Franks. He was apparently addicted to the beliefs of the Baṭanīyeh, the esoteric faith of the Ismailians, or Assassins* in the Nuṣairī Mountains, which was still a novelty. He was thus a sinister figure, suspect to his Muslim neighbours. But he himself was timorous and suspicious, disposed to compromise with the Franks rather to resist by arms. Aleppo, the vital link between Syria and the Muslim East, menacing communications between Edessa and Antioch and commanding the way to Damascus by the Orontes,† was the key to Frankish security in the East, a situation of which the Frankish leaders were apparently

* Lit. 'the *ḥashīsh*-men', so called because of their custom of drugging and kidnapping their recruits, who on awakening found themselves in an environment like the sensuous paradise of Islam. The sect was an off-shoot of the Shi'ah ('the Sect'), which dissented from orthodox Islam after the death of 'Ālī, the Prophet's cousin and son-in-law and progenitor of Muḥammad's descendants through his daughter Fāṭima. The accepted English meaning of 'assassin' is secondary, reflecting political assassination as the weapon of these sinister sectaries. They were particularly inimical to Turkish princes and commanders as Turks as distinct from Arabs and as orthodox (Sunni) as opposed to their sect. Ibn al-Qalānisī (*op. cit.*, p. 58) gives the first of the sect in Syria as al-Ḥakīm al-Munajjim ('the Astrologer'), who was of the entourage of Ruḍwān, whom they supported (*ibidem*, p. 73).

† Aleppo, though a menace to Antioch, was not so significant so long as the Franks occupied only the coast. But so long as they held also Edessa it was vital.

aware,* to judge from their campaign against Maʿarrat an-Nuʿmān and the region just south of Aleppo, from which they were dissuaded by the impatience of the pilgrims, the more so as Ruḍwān was not a formidable enemy. And indeed at that moment the strongest power on the coast and in Jerusalem was Egypt. Soon Aleppo was to be in stronger hands under Ilghāzī the Amīr of Mardīn and eventually under the more aggressive Zanghī the powerful Amīr of Moṣūl and his son Nūr ad-Dīn Maḥmūd, whose aims were apparent in his dedication of a pulpit in Aleppo to the recapture of Jerusalem. The union of the commands of Moṣūl and Aleppo under Zanghī heralded the fall of Edessa, the north-eastern bastion of the Frankish states, in 1144, a year after the Egyptian base at Askalon had been sealed off by a ring of fortresses. Damascus was the remaining weak link in the Muslim offensive against the Kingdom of Jerusalem. By-passed in the First Crusade, when it might possibly have been taken,† it had entered into diplomatic relations with the Kingdom of Jerusalem, and even paid tribute for certain frontier areas east of Jordan and the Sea of Galilee, where Tancred had campaigned in 1100, and enlisted Frankish aid against the neighbouring Turkish commands. Damascus under Duqāq in fact exemplifies *par excellence* the Muslim anarchy at the time of the First Crusade. In the Second Crusade, which was prompted by the fall of Edessa, the impulse of the newcomers from the West overbore the experienced counsel of Raymond of Tripoli, then regent of the Kingdom of Jerusalem in the minority of Baldwin III, and the native barons, who advised an attack on Nūr ad-Dīn in Aleppo from Antioch, and committed the colossal blunder of an attack on Damascus.‡ The attack proved a fiasco, and the net result was the loss of a potential ally, who

* It must be remembered, however, that at this stage the Fāṭimid Caliph of Egypt held the sea and the coastal towns of Palestine and the Lebanon and Jerusalem. In view of the necessity for reinforcements from Europe the first objective was necessarily the command of the ports.

† The inaction of Damascus in failing to oppose the Crusaders at the narrow pass up the cliff face at the Dog River north of Beirut, where they opposed Baldwin in 1100 (see above n. 23), was possibly motivated by their hostility to Egypt, which they wanted to see destroyed by the Franks.

‡ W. B. Stevenson (*The Crusaders in the East*, 1907, p. 160) puts the issue with his characteristic brevity and precision, 'War with Nur ed Din was inevitable for the choice lay between attacking him directly and separately and attacking Damascus with him as its ally'. Stevenson admits, however, that if Nūr ad-Dīn had been attacked in Aleppo he would have been supported by his brother Saif ad-Dīn from Moṣūl, which indicates the strategic significance of Aleppo in uniting the forces of Islam in the East and the West. The fact, however, remains that Damascus was suspicious of Nūr ad-Dīn and conciliatory to the Frankish Kingdom of Jerusalem, and the rashness of the Franks in the Second Crusade made an enemy of a potential ally.

was now drawn into the sphere of influence of Nūr ad-Dīn, who occupied the city in 1154, the year following the Frankish reduction of Askalon. With the extension of Nūr ad-Dīn's influence to Egypt in 1163 the doom of the Kingdom of Jerusalem was sealed. The division between heretic Egypt and orthodox Asia, another manifestation of Muslim anarchy which made possible the success of the First Crusade, was now healed by the energy of Nūr ad-Dīn and his successor Ṣalāḥ ad-Dīn.

By a strange irony the evil day of the Franks was deferred by the very man who was to deal them their death-blow. Egypt was the basis of the power of Ṣalāḥ ad-Dīn. A dynastic dispute over the heretic Caliphate in Cairo gave Nūr ad-Dīn the opportunity of intervention in 1163, when the Franks under Amalric I were also called in by one of the factions, supported by ships and supplies from Byzantium. Nūr ad-Dīn's commander was Asad ad-Dīn ('the Lion of the Faith') Shirkūh, who was eventually successful and ruled as Vizier of the Fāṭimid Caliph in Cairo. On his death in 1169 his nephew Ṣalāḥ ad-Dīn Yussuf succeeded to his power in Egypt and his place was confirmed by the Caliph in Cairo. The heretic Caliph was soon reduced to impotence by Ṣalāḥ ad-Dīn, who soon found an opportunity to root out disaffected elements still disposed to plot with the Franks, and within a year he ruled in Egypt independent of Nūr ad-Dīn in all but name. The action of Ṣalāḥ ad-Dīn in the next few years can only be explained as a course of evasion. He made feint attacks on Palestine and Transjordan, but always retired before Nūr ad-Dīn came up, on the pretext of internal trouble in Egypt. In those years his most significant gain was Aqaba at the head of the Gulf, which was yet to serve him as a vital station on the road to Damascus.

On the death of Nūr ad-Dīn in 1174 events moved swiftly. A council of the Amīrs had appointed the Amīr of Moṣūl guardian of his young son. The Amīr of Damascus, suspecting the ambitions of his neighbours, called in Ṣalāḥ ad-Dīn, who responded promptly. Once established in Damascus with the resources of Egypt, now orthodox, at his command, he was acknowledged by the Caliph in Baghdad as Sultan in Egypt and Syria. He proceeded to vindicate his authority, and in 1183 Aleppo surrendered, which by now was appreciated by the Franks as well as by himself as the key to the whole situation. Having thus united the commands of Muslim Syria* which he personally

* This union of Islam, however, was not easily achieved, Ṣalāḥ ad-Dīn was resented in Mosul and Aleppo as the supplanter of the House of Zanghi and as a Kurd, and all his diplomacy, patience and force backed by the resources of Egypt were needed to overcome this resistance, as H. A. R. Gibb emphasizes, 'The Rise of Saladin', *A History of the Crusades*, vol. I, ed. K. M. Setton, 1955, pp. 566 ff.

ruled from Damascus, and Egypt, which was governed by his brother al-ʿĀdil (Saif ad-Dīn, 'the Sword of the Faith'), Ṣalāḥ ad-Dīn was now free to devote himself to his life's work, the *jihād*, or Holy War, against the invaders of the patrimony of Islam.

In Jerusalem dissensions, intensifying during the last years of the leper King Baldwin IV, now broke out openly. At the King's death Raymond of Tripoli was regent, arrangements having been made that he was to continue in office until a new king, that is to say a husband for the heiress of Baldwin, his sister Sybilla, had been appointed by the Pope. The Templars, however, now a powerful and sinister order in the East, and other impetuous elements such as Reynald of Châtillon, seized control of Jerusalem and had Guy of Lusignan, whom Sybilla had herself chosen as her husband, crowned King by the hand of Sybilla. The elevation of this handsome young French adventurer[21] put the power in the hands of the less responsible elements and eliminated one of the few men who by natural ability and experience might have preserved the delicate equilibrium between Frank and Muslim, namely Raymond (III), of Tripoli.

Under Guy the Kingdom rushed headlong to ruin. Raymond, with the majority of the Frankish barons, had not concealed his resentment at the elevation of the *parvenu*, and now Guy gathered his forces to attack him in his castle at Tiberias. Raymond negotiated with Ṣalāḥ ad-Dīn for help.[22] Thus the weakness of the Kingdom of Jerusalem was made patent to the Sultan, who indeed was always well informed of the situation through his intelligence service. But, however sanguinely he may have anticipated the day of reckoning, there was a truce with the Kingdom of Jerusalem, which ran until 1189, and the Sultan was an honourable man.*

The criminal folly of the Franks nullified the truce in 1187. Reynald of Châtillon particularly is held guilty. This knight, one of the most energetic among the Crusaders of all time, was a colourful personality with rich and varied experience, which included marriage with the heiress of Antioch, a wanton and savage privateering raid on the Byzantine island of Cyprus, and fifteen and a half years in the dungeons of the citadel of Aleppo. He had ability, but neither scruple nor control. This wild spirit had found a home in Kerak beyond the Dead Sea, and from this grim fortress he harried Ṣalāḥ ad-Dīn's communications with

*While his authority in Syria was still insecure Ṣalāḥ ad-Dīn had neutralized the Frankish forces by a number of separate treaties and truces, e.g. with Pisa, Genoa and Venice (who were glad to get access to Egyptian markets), in 1173, with the Byzantine Emperor in 1181, with Raymond III of Tripoli in 1186. The truce with the Kingdom of Jerusalem was made in 1185.

Egypt. His ambition even reached to building ships, transporting them by camel to the Gulf of Aqaba, and projecting an expedition against the Holy Cities Medina and Mecca in 1183. He was frustrated by the Sultan's brother al-'Ādil, though he raided coastal towns including Yenbo the port of Medina and horrified Islam by sinking a pilgrim ship. He raided also the pilgrim convoys on the Pilgrim Road to the east of Kerak and reaped a rich harvest from trading caravans on the desert road between Egypt and Damascus. After a delicate situation the truce with Ṣalāḥ ad-Dīn was renewed in 1186, but Reynauld did not long endure the agony of inaction. In the spring of 1187 he attacked and totally plundered and enslaved a rich caravan. The truce was broken; Ṣalāḥ ad-Dīn decided to strike; he swore solemnly never to spare the life of Reynald.[23]

The tragedy moved dramatically to its climax. Marshalling the largest Muslim army yet encountered by the Franks, who also were most fully represented, Ṣalāḥ ad-Dīn crossed the Jordan south of the Sea of Galilee, captured the town of Tiberias and besieged the castle, which was held by the wife of Raymond, who by now had renounced his truce with the Sultan. The Muslims occupied the high ground above the town under the conspicuous twin peaks known as the Horns of Ḥaṭṭīn. The Franks advanced from Acre to Ṣaffūriyeh, where a counsel of war was held. Raymond of Tripoli passionately urged no advance, a tribute at once to his public spirit and his confidence in the courage of his lady besieged in the castle of Tiberias and in the honour of Ṣalāḥ ad-Dīn, who in fact, on the final surrender, treated her chivalrously and had her escorted to safety. Raymond reckoned that Ṣalāḥ ad-Dīn would not retire with such a great army before engaging the Franks, hence he counselled retiring on Acre, where the Franks might better maintain themselves in the heat of the season, putting Ṣalāḥ ad-Dīn at a disadvantage in advancing through a waterless region.[24] Ṣalāḥ ad-Dīn on his part, with the lake at his back, sent his light mounted archers against the Franks at Ṣaffūriyeh to provoke the Franks to advance at the same disadvantage.[25] After intense debate Raymond's advice was adopted, later to be countermanded on the advice of Gerard de Ridefort the Grand Master of the Templars, and on the morning of 3rd July they left the water and pasture of Ṣaffūriyeh three miles north-north-west of Nazareth. They advanced through ten miles of waterless country to camp at Lūbiyeh on the plateau six miles west of Tiberias and one and a half miles south-west of the Horns of Ḥaṭṭīn, where their guides had promised water. Men and horses arrived, harassed by Saracen skirmishers and in an agony of thirst—to find the well dry. Counsels were again divided between those who in desperation urged that they should attempt to cut a way through to the Sea of Galilee and those who were too exhausted to move from the waterless well. Ṣalāḥ ad-Dīn, meanwhile, had anticipated the Franks and occupied the village of Ḥaṭṭīn just over three miles east of the Frankish camp with abundant water and pasture.

Raymond knew that the army was doomed, and the ghastly truth had dawned even on the most irresponsible. Victory was no longer a hope; even before the battle terrible thirst, aggravated by a sirocco, had made many apathetic even to survival; others defied discipline and tried to slip through the Muslim cordon, but none succeeded. When darkness fell the Franks were completely surrounded, and faced the morrow's battle with gloomy foreboding; according to Ibn al-'Athīr the Muslims 'scented the wind of victory', and 'Allah is Most Great!' and 'There is no god but Allah!' rang throughout their camp all through that fateful night,[26] and 'Malik (the angel of death) and Riḍwān (the angel of paradise) waited expectantly and Riḍwān (the angel of paradise) rejoiced'.[27] On the day of battle on 4th July discipline broke in the Frankish ranks. The infantry tried fondly to break through in mass to the lake, but were headed off, and segregated from the knights, were cut down, finding before them only 'the flames of hell'.[28] The knights fought with the courage of despair, but were borne down exhausted. Raymond and the knights of Tripoli charged the Muslim sector under Tākī 'd-Dīn the nephew of Ṣalāḥ ad-Dīn in good order, but the Muslim general with great presence of mind opened his ranks and let the charge pass innocuously.[29] The ranks were then closed, barring a return to the Frankish army, and Raymond and his followers had no option but to ride for Tripoli. Few were able to break the ring of armed Muslims, which finally closed in upon the King and the survivors, whom they found lying exhausted about the rocky double peaks, the Ḥorns of Ḥaṭṭīn. The battle is described with the vital intensity of high drama by eyewitnesses, Ernoul the squire of Balian of Ibelin, whose personal account is edited by Bernard the Treasurer, and by the Muslim historians 'Imād ad-Din, who was with Ṣalāḥ ad-Din at Ḥaṭṭin and Ibn al-'Athir, who incorporates the eyewitness account of al-Afḍal the son of Ṣalāḥ ad-Dīn. The latter records that his father considered the issue in doubt until the last stand by the Franks around the Cross on the summit of the Horns of Ḥaṭṭīn,* so desperately did the

* Thus Ibn al-'Athīr (*op. cit.*, pp. 685–6), citing al-Mālik al-Afḍal, states that a desperate charge from the summit drove the Muslims back on Ṣalāh ad-Dīn, who changed colour, and another again drove the Muslims back. Both were repulsed, to the joy of the youth, which was checked by the Sultan, who considered the issue in doubt until the tent of the King fell.

Frankish chivalry fight in their hopeless struggle, and such was the reputation of the Frankish knights.

The Latin Kingdom of Jerusalem was in effect liquidated on that fatal field which had brought together such a concentration of Muslim forces as the Franks had never faced since they forced a way to Jerusalem in 1099 and took the city from a divided Islam. The defeat of their own concentration of forces meant that at one stroke Ṣalāḥ ad-Dīn had recovered virtually all Palestine for Islam. The symbol of the Christian domination of the Holy Land, what the Franks believed to be the true cross, was again in the hands of Islam,[30] and the King and practically all the barons were captives.

Ṣalāḥ ad-Dīn, magnanimous as legend has unanimously acclaimed him, was a merciful victor, excepting only the knights of the Orders of the Temple and the Hospital, whom he committed to a company of fanatical Muslims for summary execution, and Reynald of Châtillon, whom he slew with his own hand in quittance of his vow.[31] Gerard de Ridefort, the Grand Master of the Templars, was spared, the Sultan having a part for him to play.

Here we may digress on the career of Gerard, which is interesting as illustrating conditions in the Frankish interlude in the history of Jerusalem. An intimate contact with this personality is lent by a document found in the vicinity of the Aqṣa Mosque, where the Templers had a hall for training in arms. Repairs to the west of the Aqṣa Mosque, where this building stood, revealed a letter which had been secreted between the drums of a pillar. It was a letter expelling a knight who had deserted. This document opens a wide vista on conditions and personalities of the time. Gerard de Ridefort had come out from Flanders in 1173 and had engaged in the service of the Count of Tripoli. He was promised the hand of the first suitable heiress in the County of Tripoli, and confidently expected her estates. But there were others who had something else to offer than a proper person and a strong arm. When the promised heiress was available Gerard had a rival in a wealthy Pisan merchant, who persuaded the Count to dispose of her hand by the argument of gold, to which Gerard had no reply. It is said that, with more purpose than delicacy, the Pisan had the lady weighed in public against gold besants.[32] It has been estimated that if the 10,000 besants which he paid were of full gold standard his bride would have weighed ten stones. In chagrin and disappointment Gerard joined the Order of the Temple, of which he became the Seneschal in 1180—in which capacity he issued the writ already mentioned—and Grand Master in 1184. Taken prisoner at the Battle of Ḥaṭṭīn, which his evil counsel had precipitated, he must have been among the captive knights in the tent of Ṣalāḥ ad-Dīn after the battle, where he experienced the generosity of the Sultan and saw the summary execution of Reynald of Châtillon the Seigneur of Le Crac and Montreal (Kerak in Moab and Shōbak in Edom). Spared from the execution of the Templars and Hospitallers, Gerard was kept in custody and used his absolute influence as Grand Master to induce the Templar garrison at Gaza to surrender, for which he was set at liberty.[33] He fought under Richard Coeur de Lion before the walls of Acre, where he was killed in 1189.

After Ṣalāḥ ad-Dīn's complete victory at Ḥaṭṭīn the denuded fortresses of the land fell one after the other into the hands of the Sultan and his brother al-'Ādil, who now advanced from Egypt into South Palestine. Acre was occupied within a week, and another week sufficed to subdue Haifa, Arsūf and Caesarea on the coast and Nablus, Ṣebasṭiyeh, Nazareth and Ṣaffūriyeh in the interior. al-'Ādil occupied Jaffa, and by the end of August only Gaza, Askalon and Jerusalem in Palestine remained to the Franks, whose position, however, was stronger on the coast of Syria north of Tyre, which was to become the important bridgehead for the temporary revival in the Third Crusade four years later. Askalon fell after a bitter siege on the 4th September. On the same day in Askalon Ṣalāḥ ad-Dīn received delegates from Jerusalem, but to his great surprise they refused to surrender the city, and so the Sultan prepared to take it by force of arms.

In the history of Islam in its finest hours a notable characteristic has been respect for the pledged word. Ṣalāḥ ad-Dīn was scrupulously true to that tradition, and in the case of an honourable enemy or the weak and helpless he was ready to temper strict honour with consideration and mercy. His generosity is well exemplified in the siege of Jerusalem.

One of the few knights who was able to overcome the exhaustion of thirst and the fatigue of battle and to cut a way through to safety when all was lost at the Horns of Ḥaṭṭīn was Balian of Ibelin, one of the great barons of the Kingdom of Jerusalem, who had reached the safety of Tyre. His wife, who was a daughter of the Byzantine Emperor, being with their children in Jerusalem, Balian applied to Ṣalāḥ ad-Dīn for permission to come and convey them to Tyre, and this was granted on condition that he spent only one night in Jerusalem. There Balian arrived to find the Franks, who had been left without a military leader, preparing the city for siege under the direction of the Latin Patriarch. They pressed Balian to assume command. He wrote to Ṣalāḥ ad-Dīn as one soldier to another, explaining his situation, and the Sultan, sympathizing with the call of duty and honour, freed Balian from his obligation and himself arranged a convoy for his lady and family.[34]

Balian organized the depleted resources of Jerusalem and its environs for the siege. After nine days' investment the wall was breached just east of the present Damascus Gate on its vulnerable north side, and though the defenders manned the breach and held out for another three days the cause was lost, and on 2nd October Balian personally surrendered the city to Ṣalāḥ ad-Dīn.

Ṣalāḥ ad-Dīn's occupation of Jerusalem in the name of Islam was another notable triumph of mercy in conscious emulation of the Caliph 'Umar when he received the capitulation of Jerusalem (see above, p. 219). His moderation contrasts strikingly with the vindictive savagery of the soldiers of the Cross in 1099, when the city ran red with the blood of indiscriminate massacre. Accepting the unconditional surrender of Jerusalem and its inhabitants at a great ransom-price, which was defrayed out of a great deposit which the Hospital held for Henry II of England,[35] he agreed to release seven thousand out of the twenty thousand Christians in the city for a greatly reduced price and actually had them convoyed to the Latin towns on the coast. His magnanimity contrasts with the callous indifference and greed of the Christian authorities. The military orders of the Temple and the Hospitallers, who had accumulated great wealth, particularly the former, who were bankers, contributed to the ransom only under extreme pressure, and the Latin Patriarch and clergy had the effrontery to redeem only themselves and leave Jerusalem with a baggage train laden with plate and furniture. al-'Ādil ('the Just') the brother of Ṣalāḥ ad-Dīn was so touched by the sight of poor folk in their masses passing hopelessly to slavery that he craved a thousand of them from the Sultan as a bounty for his services in arms.* Ṣalāḥ ad-Dīn, never impervious to the needs of the weak and helpless, himself freed all the aged, and on the appeal of the ladies whose husbands were in captivity he undertook to release them, and further gave personal gifts to all widows and orphans. Their treatment was much less generous in the Christian communities to which they were convoyed, and indeed it was an open scandal to the faith.

This was the end of the Latin domination in Jerusalem. The Byzantine Emperor intervened with Ṣalāḥ ad-Dīn as one Eastern potentate with another and secured his sanction on behalf of the Orthodox community in the Church of the Holy Sepulchre.† Native Christians,

* Other Muslim leaders went bail for numbers of captives, not all apparently through disinterested motives (Ibn al-'Athīr, *op. cit.*, p. 703).

† The authority of the Greek Orthodox Church in Jerusalem, which claimed episcopal authority deriving from James the brother of the Lord, was vested in the Patriarchs, who now, however, resided not in Jerusalem but in Constantinople. Since the Patriarch Cyrus II took up residence in Jerusalem in 1867 the Patriarchs have

both Orthodox and Syrian Jacobite, did not regret the passing of the Franks and the reversion to Muslim toleration.

So the Crescent triumphed over the Cross. The sacred precinct round the Aqṣa Mosque and the Dome of the Rock was cleansed after Christian worship and occupation by the Templars with their barracks and arms school and their stables by the Aqṣa Mosque, and on the day of public prayer, Friday, seven days after Balian's surrender of the city, Ṣalāḥ ad-Dīn led public worship in the Aqṣa Mosque.

This was the effective end of the Kingdom of Jerusalem which the First Crusade had established, though for another century titular Kings of Jerusalem were to reign in Acre. The most serious menace to Islam in this period was the Third Crusade, more truly an international enterprise than the First and with an even greater potential. This, however, notwithstanding the capture of Acre in despite of terrible famine and the menace of Ṣalāḥ ad-Dīn from his camp nearby at Tell Keisān, was frustrated by the mutual hatred and suspicion of Richard of England and Philip of France and other potentates whom Richard antagonized and eventually by Richard's anxiety for his kingdom under the regency of his brother John. After his failure to relieve Acre and a defeat at Arsūf north of Jaffa, Ṣalāḥ ad-Dīn was thrown back on the defensive. Richard, however, with complications in England under the regency of his brother John, made overtures for peace. Ṣalāḥ ad-Dīn stood firm on his terms, strengthened by the divisions among the

---

resided in the city, with the pastoral cure through bishops of some 50,000 Arab Christians in Palestine and Transjordan. In the interim the most notable event in the history of the Greek Orthodox Church associated with Jerusalem was the Synod of Jerusalem in 1672, when its last official pronouncement of doctrine was made. The effective authority of the Latin Patriarchs of Jerusalem ceased when the city was occupied by Ṣalāḥ ad-Dīn, but was exercised outside Jerusalem at Acre until the fall of that city in 1291. After that time, though there were ten titular Latin Patriarchs of Jerusalem, the Latin interests in Palestine, which were confined to religious establishments at the Holy Places, was represented by the Custodia of Terra Sancta under the Franciscan Order until the re-establishment of a resident Latin Patriarch by Pope Pius IX in 1847. Jerusalem was also a Patriarchate of the Armenian Church from at least a century before the First Crusade. In view of the Armenian affinities of so many of the queens of the Latin Kingdom of Jerusalem the Armenian Church must have flourished, and the present Patriarch can still produce a charter granted by Ṣalāḥ ad-Dīn after the expulsion of the Franks from Jerusalem. Also rehabilitated after the Latin interlude under the Franks was the Syrian Church under a Bishop of Jerusalem, which represents the monophysite tradition (see above p. 206) so congenial to Arab Christians in the sixth century. The headquarters of this community is the church and monastery built around the traditional site of the house of John Mark just south of the present Citadel, now well known through the purchase of the Dead Sea Scrolls from the first cave from the dealer at Bethlehem.

Franks which were made patent to the Muslims by independent overtures made by Conrad of Montferrat, who commanded Tyre. Behā ad-Dīn, the personal secretary of Ṣalāḥ ad-Dīn, expatiates on this situation, in which he was intimately involved.[36] These negotiations were protracted till the winter rains bogged down the armies, and Ṣalāḥ ad-Dīn withdrew from his advance base at Ramleh to Jerusalem. In the summer of 1192 fresh Muslim troops joined the Sultan and Richard moved his army forward to Betenoble (Bayt Nūbā) at the lower end of the pass to the interior by the Wadi Salmān south of Beth-Ḥoron. Meanwhile Jerusalem was put in a state of siege; every well in the neighbourhood was poisoned and every cistern destroyed, precautions which did not escape the notice of Richard,[37] who was well informed of the natural difficulty of laying siege to Jerusalem, where Ṣalāḥ ad-Dīn would be able to concentrate his attack on the Franks at the only two places where the city could be invested, the north wall and the south-west.[38] Little did the Franks realize how critical the hour was for the Muslims.* Ṣalāḥ ad-Dīn in Jerusalem was torn between the alternatives of standing siege with the prospect of his army suffering the fate of the Muslim defenders of Acre, who had been slaughtered in cold blood on surrender on terms, or of hazarding all in a pitched battle outside, which would save his army from complete annihilation but in event of defeat would cost him Jerusalem.[39] So passed three critical days for Islam movingly described by Behā ad-Dīn, who personally shared the excogitation of the Sultan and his agonizing vigils and prayers, and his relief when his military intelligence informed him that Richard's army had withdrawn from Betenoble.[40] The impression that Richard had made on Ṣalāḥ ad-Dīn is indicated by the fear that the Sultan conceived that

* H. A. R. Gibb emphasizes the difficulties of Ṣalāḥ ad-Dīn in the Third Crusade in holding a feudal army of doubtful allegiance in the field for three years in face of repeated defeats, and concludes 'It was by the sheer force of personality, by the undying flame of faith within him, and by his example of steadfast endurance, that he inspired the dogged resistance which finally wore down the invaders' (*op. cit.*, pp. 588–9).

---

26. The entrance to the Church of the Holy Sepulchre, with the Chapel of the Franks on the top of the steps. This is Crusading work. Now the main entrance is from the south, giving access to the choir of the present church, which is very much reduced from its former size and splendour. Calvary is behind the Chapel of the Franks.

27. The interior of the Holy Sepulchre. Once hewn free of surrounding rock and enclosed in a small shrine in the great rotunda, it was later denuded of its rock by a persecuting Caliph, and subsequently enclosed in a shrine and lined with marble.

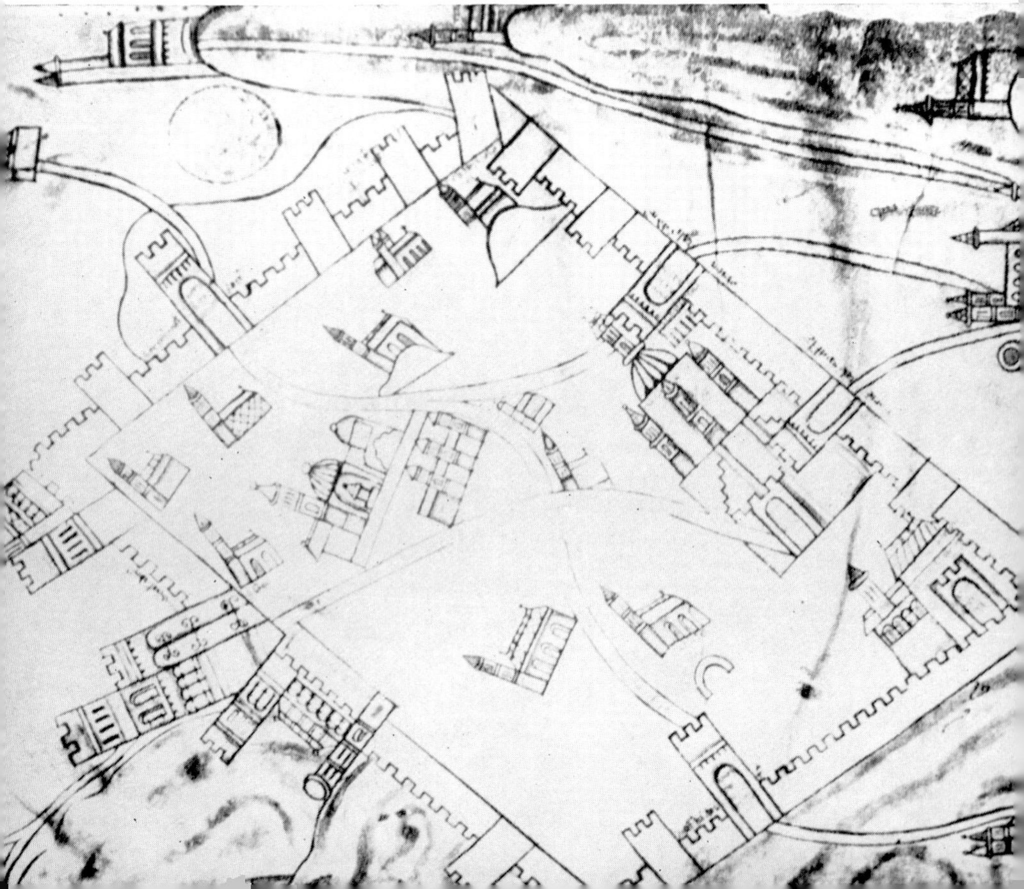

he would now invade Egypt.[41] Richard's retreat, however, which in the words of his confidential Muslim messenger to the Sultan he compared to the retreat of the ram in order to strike harder, was used as an opportunity to continue the negotiations for peace. The Muslim offensive towards Jaffa on Richard's withdrawal to Acre convinced him that the reserves of the Muslim East were too great for the Frankish minority to think of permanent advantage, and, reduced by illness, he concluded peace on Ṣalāḥ ad-Dīn's terms, the Franks retaining the coastal towns from Jaffa to Acre and ceding Askalon, which Richard had rebuilt, now to be again dismantled by Ṣalāḥ ad-Dīn.

So Richard had to renounce the ultimate aim of the Third Crusade, to recapture Jerusalem. It is said that on patrol he actually came within sight of Jerusalem,[42] but in chagrin held his shield before his eyes and turned away from the objective he had had to relinquish. Then and later concessions were won by the Franks from Ṣalāḥ ad-Dīn and his brother al-ʿĀdil until in 1229 al-Kāmil the politic son of al-ʿĀdil conceded Jerusalem to the German Emperor Frederick II, who actually usurped the crown of his infant son, who was the heir to the throne of Jerusalem. Frederick, who was familiar with, and sympathetic to, Islam through his education in Sicily, found the situation a fiasco, having crowned himself King in the Church of the Holy Sepulchre. The kingdom had shrunk to a mere coastal strip; such barons as were left in the realm did not support him as a usurper; as an excommunicate he could not draw support from the Orders of the Hospital or the Temple nor from ecclesiastical, or even secular, powers in Europe, though the less significant Teutonic Order supported him. Even Frederick, who habitually defied convention, found the situation too embarrassing, and left Palestine after six weeks. The Muslim agreement held for Jerusalem, but the Christian community rather existed on toleration, and communications with the coastal region were precarious unless under armed escort. Eventually in 1244 the city fell to the first attack by a band of Khwarizmian Turks, who burned the Church of the Holy Sepulchre, and Jerusalem passed finally out of Christian hands.

The remnant of the Frankish Kingdom of Jerusalem was confined to a

---

28. The eastern extremity of the north wall of Jerusalem, where the Crusaders broke in in 1099, with the Stork Tower at the corner.

29. The map of Jerusalem under the Franks from the manuscript in the Library of Cambrai. The cross in the north wall marks the place where the Crusaders broke in in 1099.

coastal strip from Antioch to Jaffa nowhere more than thirty miles inland, increased by certain isolated strongholds such as the castles at Ṣafad in Upper Galilee and Belfort (Shaqf Arnūn) above a gorge of the Liṭānī River in South Lebanon, which Frankish knights were granted in return for mercenary service in the dreary civil wars between the descendants of Ṣalāḥ ad-Dīn. In one of these actions the effective force of Frankish warriors allied with Damascus met a force of five thousand from Egypt under the Mamlūk Baybars and an army of their Khwarizmian allies at Ḥarbīyeh near Gaza, and only a tenth part of them survived. This sealed the fate of the Franks in Palestine.

There seemed to be a gleam of hope with the Tartar invasions under Hulagu Khan, the grandson of the great Genghis Khan, led by Kitbugha a Nestorian Christian, as were many of the Mongol princes, whose mothers were Christian. The Armenians and Franks in Antioch had made successful alliance with them against the remnants of Ṣalāḥ ad-Dīn's family, but they were embarrassing allies, and men could not forget their hideous sack of Baghdad in 1258. So the Frankish nobles in Acre decided to join Egypt against the Tartars, and Kitbugha was defeated by the Mamlūk Sultan of Egypt Quṭuz in 1260 at 'Ain Jālūṭ at the foot of Mount Gilboa, where once Gideon and his commando had routed the Midianites.[43]

The successor of Quṭuz—and his assassin—Rukn ad-Dīn ('the Pillar of the Faith') Baybars, the victor of Ḥarbīyeh, a slave from the Volga, who had been reared to arms and had risen by ability and unscrupulous resolution from the barracks to the Sultanate, reduced the Frankish holdings to Tripoli, Tyre and Acre. His work was continued by his successor Qalāwūn, whose son al-Khalīl administered the *coup de grâce* at Acre in 1291. The other coastal fortresses fell, not one resisting a single day, and the Templar castle of 'Athlīt (*Castra Peregrinorum*) south of the Carmel Head, from which the last remnants of the Franks made their last embarkation from the Holy Land, was found by the Muslims deserted, an empty shell, to be pounded by the Mediterranean breakers to the ruins in which it stands today, the melancholy symbol of the broken sword of Christendom in arms against Islam, of the shattered ambitions of many adventurers and of the faded ideal of a few.

NOTES FOR CHAPTER X

1 Ibn al-'Athīr (*Receuil des Historiens des Croisades, Historiens Orientaux*, I. 1872, p. 189) begins his history of the Crusades with the fall of Toledo in 1085

2 R. Grousset, *Les Croisades*, 1948, p. 21

3 William of Tyre, *Receuil . . . Historiens Occidentaux*, I, x

4 Raymond of Aguilers, *Receuil . . . Historiens Occidentaux* III, XIX

5 Fulcher of Chartres, *Receuil . . . Historiens Occidentaux* I. xxv

6 Fulcher of Chartres, *op. cit.* I. xxvii

7 Raymond of Aguilers, *op. cit.* XX

8 Fulcher of Chartres, *op. cit.* I. xxx

9 *Ibidem* I. xxx

10 Ibn al-'Athīr, *op. cit.*, p. 685

11 Fulcher of Chartres, *op. cit.* I. xxx

12 *Ibidem* I. xxxiii

13 *Ibidem* I. xxxii

14 Ibn al-'Athīr, *op. cit.*, p.193. A valuable source for the relations of Damascus with the Franks is *The Continuation of the Damascus Chronicle* (ed. H. A. R. Gibb, selections, 1932) by Ibn al-Qalānisī, an official of the chancery in Damascus, who composed his work between 1140 and 1160

15 William of Tyre, *op. cit.* IX. xix

16 William of Tyre *op, cit.* I. x

17 R. Grousset, *Histoire des Croisades et du Royaume Franc de Jerusalem*, 1934–1936

18 Ibn al-Qalānisī, *Damascus Chronicle*, ed. H. A. R. Gibb, 1932, pp. 282–9

19 *Ibidem*, pp. 318–21. Ibn al-Qalānisī, with access to the archives in the chancery of Damascus, in which he was an official, gives 1154 as the date of Nūr ad-Dīn's capture of Damascus

20 *Ibidem*, p. 86. Certain of the lands of Damascus paid tribute to Baldwin, *ibidem*, pp. 93, 113

21 '*Le beau garçon naif*', Grousset, *op. cit.*, vol. II, p. 766

22 Ibn al-'Athīr, *op. cit.*, p. 675

23 *Receuil des Historiens des Croisades, Historiens Orientaux* IV, p. 276 'Imād ad-Dīn like Behā ad-Dīn is a particularly valuable source since he was like Behā ad-Dīn, the secretary of Ṣalāḥ ad-Dīn. Behā ad-Dīn, however, is much more factual, 'Imād ad-Din tending to obscure fact in figurative language, particularly in his description of the battle of Ḥaṭṭīn, where his personal experience was evidently limited to a distant view and a visit to the field after the battle, when he gives a most detailed and gruesome picture of the dead bodies ravaged by wounds and vultures

24 *Estoire de Eracles, Receuil . . . Historiens Occidentaux* II, XXIII. xxxi. Ibn al-'Athir, *Receuil . . . Historiens Orientaux* I, p. 682

25 'Imād ad-Dīn in Abū Shāma, *op. cit.*, p. 264

26 Ibn al-'Athīr, *op. cit.*, p. 683

27 'Imād ad-Dīn in Abū Shāma, *op cit.*, p. 266

28 *Ibidem*, p. 267

29 Ibn al-'Athīr, *op. cit.*, p. 68/, *Estoire de Eracles, op. cit.* XXIII. xli

30 Ibn al-'Athīr, *op. cit.*, p 685, 'the cross of crosses in which they say there is a piece of wood (of the cross) on which the Messiah—upon whom be peace!—was crucified' (see above, p. 237)

31 Ibn al-'Athīr, *op. cit.*, p. 687; Behā ad-Dīn, *op. cit.*, p. 97

32 *Estoire de Eracles, op. cit.* XXIII, xxxiv

33 Ibn al-'Athīr, *op. cit.*, p. 697

34 *Estoire de Eracles, op. cit.* XXIII, liv; *Chronique d'Ernoul*, ed. M. L. de Mas Latric, 1871, pp. 186–7

35 *Chronique d'Ernoul*, pp. 219–20

36 Behā ad Dīn, *op. cit.*, p. 270 ff.

37 *Ibidem*, p. 315

38 Ibn al-'Athīr, *op. cit.*, p. 699

39 Behā ad-Dīn, *op. cit.*, p. 313

40 *Ibidem*, pp. 314–15

41 *Ibidem*, p. 315

42 *Itinerarium Regis Ricardi* (*The Chronicles and Memorials of Great Britain and Ireland during the Middle Ages*, Rolls Series, ed. W. Stubbs, 1864) V. xlix

43 Judges vii

XI

OTTOMAN OBSCURITY

Out of the north evil shall break forth upon the inhabitants of the land (*Jeremiah i. 14*

Western Asia since the tenth century had been more and more dominated by the restless peoples from Central Asia. The Turks had come as slaves and mercenaries and proved their worth as defenders of orthodox Islam. By the eleventh century an Empire under the Turkish House of Seljuk had been established from the borders of China to the Mediterranean, and though it soon disintegrated Turkish dynasties continued to dominate the Near East and to occupy Asia Minor. The Mongols followed, the Christian Hulagu in the thirteenth century and the Shiite Muslim Timur Leng (Tamurlane) in the fourteenth, dreaded by Christian and orthodox Muslim alike, violent like a cyclone but mercifully fleeting. Finally Turks of the House of Osman (Osmanlis, or Ottomans) swept westwards from Central Asia, seeking grazing, plunder and mercenary service. They had been subjects of the great Moghul Khan, but were a turbulent race and, remote from their suzerain, they asserted their independence. They were employed by the Seljuk Sultans of Iconium in Asia Minor to protect their eastern frontier, but they were awkward allies, and, pressing on into the domains of the Sultans, soon became their masters. Turning their attention north, they reduced the decaying remnant of the Roman Empire at Constantinople to desperate straits, and the fall of the Empire was only delayed by the wild, but errant, career of devastation and conquest of the Tartar Timur Leng (Timur the Lame) between 1380 and 1404. The growing power of the House of Osman was eclipsed in Asia Minor, though Timur, having defeated the Ottoman Sultan Bayazid, appointed his son Mūsā as his vassal Sultan of Iconium. After his withdrawal the Ottoman power continued to grow and finally passed into Europe and took Constantinople in 1453.

For fifty years after the fall of Constantinople Palestine was a Debatable Land between the Mamlūks of Egypt and the Ottomans in the north as she had been between Egypt and Assyria in the Hebrew monarchy and between the Ptolemies and the Seleucids in the third century B.C. Eventually Mamlūks and Ottomans met in battle in 1516 at Marj Dābiq north of Aleppo and again the following year near Cairo, when the Turks used their new weapons, firearms, with deadly effect. As a result of these victories the Ottomans under Sultan Selīm I 'the Grim' became the new masters of a Muslim Empire from Africa to Europe and deep into Central Asia, and the Sultan was invested with the spiritual authority of the Caliph by the last of the Abbasid Caliphs in Baghdad.

The repair and building of the walls of Jerusalem as they stand at the present day on the line of the old Byzantine fortifications of the fifth century must be among the first monuments of the Ottomans in Palestine, built by Sulaymān the Magnificent (1520–1566) between 1537 and 1542, but incorporating materials such as Herodian marginal-drafted blocks and indeed whole sections of Byzantine and Mamlūk work, such as the St. Stephen Gate (in Arabic 'the Gate of the Tribes') with the heraldic lions of the Mamlūk Sultan Baybars (Pl. 30) and the Golden Gate in the east wall of the Sacred Precinct (Pl. 21), the work probably of the Empress Theodora, which now, however, was walled up by the Muslims (Pl. 21) owing to the tradition that the Messiah of Judaism and Christianity will make his advent through this gate. The palace of the Frankish Kings of Jerusalem, later rebuilt by the Malmūks, on the site of the palace-fort of Herod the Great by the Jaffa, or Hebron, Gate with its moat and glacis was also incorporated in the defences of Sulaymān.

The fortification of Jerusalem, however, which probably reflects the precautions taken against a resurgence of resistance from Egypt in the early days of Ottoman rule in Palestine, gives a false impression of the political significance of the city in this period. Still the Holy City also of Islam, it sank into four centuries of political obscurity until British sentiment, influenced by Christianity and the romance of the Crusades, rehabilitated Jerusalem as the administrative capital of Palestine under the Mandate.

Not only Jerusalem indeed but the whole of Syria and Palestine sank into obscurity under the Turks. There were various reasons for this decline. With the opening of the New World to the enterprise of Europe and of the Cape route to the Far East, the Levant, from time immemorial the stepping-stone between Asia and Africa and between East and West in commerce, culture and imperial expansion, now became a political and cultural backwater in the Turkish Empire which stretched westwards to Algeria. Having become a European power by the capture of Constantinople, the Turks found that the conquest of the Balkans and their conflict with the Holy Roman Empire with its capital on the Danube was now its major commitment. Having known so many imperial masters, the Semitic communities of the Near East, rarely and only partially integrated in native states and divided by ecology and religion, mutely accepted as their new master the Ottoman Sultan in place of the Mamlūk Sultans of Egypt. The common faith of Islam reconciled the Muslim majority to the Sultan if reconciliation were needed, especially after he was invested with the Caliphate. The bond of Islam in fact accounts largely for the slow development of a pan-Arab consciousness among the subjects of the Ottoman Empire, a fact which is strikingly illustrated even on the outbreak of the decisive Arab Revolt under Ḥusain, which will be one of the major themes of the present chapter. The Arab Near East then presented no problem to the Turkish administration, with the focus of its attention the Balkans and the Mediterranean, and in the dark ages of Turkish domination the natives were abandoned to exploitation both by the hierarchy of the inferior sort of Turkish officials from pasha to gendarme and by their own landlords till the land was well-nigh derelict. The sordid history of this time in Syria and Palestine is barely relieved by local independence movements. Provincial pashas acknowledged a merely nominal allegiance to the Sublime Porte, like Aḥmad al-Jazzār ('the Butcher'), the former Bosnian slave who lived to defy Napoleon from the walls of Acre,* and Muḥammad 'Ālī the Governor of Egypt, whose power in Palestine and Syria was more effective than that of the Sultan until it was checked by the intervention of Britain, Russia, Austria and Prussia in 1840 to prevent the decline of Turkey to the advantage of France in the Eastern Mediterranean.

Characteristic of this period and in a degree portentous of the eventual fall of the Ottoman power in the Levant are various native risings, such as that of the Druze† Fakhr ad-Dīn, who ruled in Lebanon and in

* Aḥmad's resistance was stiffened by the British Navy, supreme since the victory at Abūkīr, which intercepted a French convoy from Egypt and captured Napoleon's heavy artillery.

† The Druzes (Arabic ad-Durūz), who are now settled in the lava region of the Jebel Druze in south-east Syria and the eastern foothills of Hermon, south Lebanon and north Palestine in the hinterland of Acre, are a heretic Muslim sect who profess an eclectic creed formulated by Ismaīl Darāzī, the apostle of the Fāṭimid Caliph al-Ḥākim (996–1020) (see above, p.225). Their tenets and their scripturesare a strict secret, understood only by the initiated among them, but among their beliefs is that in the divinity of the Caliph al-Ḥākim, who claimed succession from Muḥammad through his daughter Fāṭima. As enemies both of orthodox Islam and Christianity they have a tradition of independence, and in the Zionist occupation of Palestine they declared against the Arabs.

the hinterland of Acre in defiance of the Sultan until his death in 1634, and of Dhāhir al-'Umar, an Arab of Ṣafad in Upper Galilee, who was able to establish himself as ruler of Galilee from Tiberias to Acre in 1749 and treat on equal terms, and even conduct war, with the Ottoman pasha in Damascus for a quarter of a century. Napoleon's intervention in the Levant encouraged Arab resistance to Turkish authority, and the son of Dhāhir al-'Umar, now supplanted at Acre by the ruthless and efficient Pasha Aḥmad al-Jazzār, was a steady, if unspectacular, ally of Napoleon. In Lebanon the natives, both as Arabs and as Christians, were ready to rise against the Turks[1] and would have done so had Napoleon suceeded in taking Acre. In fact the Amīr Bashīr of the powerful Shihāb family ruled Lebanon from his palace of Bayt ad-Dīn in South Lebanon for thirty years until 1840.

In this period the weakness of Turkey in Syria was accentuated by the strength of Muḥammad 'Ālī, the former tobacco merchant from Kavala who ruled as Pasha in Egypt from 1805 and as a result of his reorganization of the army and the resources of his province was virtually independent of the Sultan.* On him the Sultan relied to suppress the fanatical Muslim puritans, the Wahhābis, in the Nejd and Ḥejaz, who had shaken the power of the Ottoman Government in Arabia and Iraq and even menaced Syria. By 1811 the prestige of Muḥammad 'Ālī stood very high and was to rise to its zenith when his son Ibrāhīm Pasha swept through Palestine and Syria and by his defeat of the armies of the Sultan at Aleppo in 1832 had Istambul at his mecy. For the next decade, when Ibrāhīm governed Syria and Palestine for his father, the Arabs had a foretaste of independence from the Turks,

* It was under the progressive administration of Muḥammad 'Ālī that Palestine was first really opened to modern Western influence. At this time it was symptomatic of the interest of Europe in Palestine and particularly of the common interests of Britain and Prussia that the origin of the Anglican Bishopric of Jerusalem goes back to 1841. This has a rather curious history. The Lutheran Church in Germany had attempted unsuccessfully to secure episcopal orders from Rome. Hence King Frederick William IV of Prussia sought to attain this objective through the Church of England by the foundation of a bishopric in Jerusalem. This was to be supported jointly by funds from England and Prussia and was to be filled by alternate nomination by Canterbury for the British Crown and by the Prussian Government. The arrangement was suspect to the episcopal scruples of many in the Church of England, and the Lutheran Church did not secure episcopal orders. In consequence the bishopric of Jerusalem lapsed after the death of the first incumbent, Bishop Barcley, in 1851 and was revived as an Anglican bishopric in 1887. The Anglican Church in Palestine was then committed to evangelical and educational missionary work and to fostering and staffing local Anglican communities. The eventual consecration of an Anglican Bishop marks the culmination of this work, and now Jerusalem with its Cathedral Church of St. George is the seat of an Archbishop of the Church of England.

under the policy of Ibrāhīm, who had dreams of an Arab Empire. It was portentous of the frustration of Arab hopes in our own time that the ambitions of Muḥammad 'Ālī and Ibrāhīm in Syria were checked by Britain, Russia, Austria and Prussia in 1840. This, however, anticipates our theme of Arab emancipation, and it would be well that the nature of the Arab subjects of the Sultan in the Near East should be here considered.

We have seen how by the time of his death in 632 Muḥammad had succeeded in creating in the political void of Arabia the religious community of Islam, which was at the same time a vital new state. This Arab brotherhood, confident in its simple, practical faith, was to prove its political potential in one glorious decade in decisively defeating the two great powers of the day, Persia and Byzantium, and establishing itself from Africa to the Taurus and eastwards to the Iranian plateau. In so doing, the Arabs became an aristocracy of arms and of the faith in Palestine, Syria and Mesopotamia. In those regions their advance had been facilitated by their sedentary Semitic kinsfolk, who spoke Semitic dialects cognate with Arabic, thought as the Arabs did and maintained contacts with the Arab border tribes in seasonal grazings and caravan traffic and diplomatic intercourse with Arab border chiefs and kings. Syria and Palestine, the stepping-stone between Africa and Asia, had received the influx of many ethnic elements throughout the ages. Nomads and semi-nomads from the desert edge, Amorites in the end of the third millennium B.C. and Aramaeans from the inner steppes in the end of the second millennium, had settled in the land; Armenoid Hurrians came from the hills of Asia Minor west of the Caucasus in the beginning of the second millennium, and have left distinct traces still in North Syria; Philistines and other Balkan and Mediterranean peoples just before the main Hebrew settlement in Palestine at the end of the second millennium settled in the southern part of the coastal plain, and eventually suggested to the Greeks the name of the land Palestine. Alexander the Great planted colonies of Greek veterans and built and equipped cities after the Greek fashion in the coastal plains and valleys of Syria and Palestine and in Transjordan. These flourished under his successors, who founded dynasties which lasted for almost three centuries in Egypt and Syria and Upper Mesopotamia. Roman veterans were also settled, particularly after the great Jewish revolts in the first and second centuries, when Jerusalem was rebuilt as the Gentile city of Aelia Capitolina. In the imperial age of Rome and Byzantium the natives of Syria and Palestine knew to the full the cosmopolitan influence of the Roman Empire. Europeans served long terms in the East and freely intermarried, and a Roman dynasty, the Severan (183–235), sprang from the union of the Roman (African) general Septimius Severus and Julia Domna the daughter of the chief priest at Ḥoms. Syrian troops served throughout Europe and there were merchant colonies of Syrians in various cities of the West. Meanwhile Syria and Palestine were still frontier provinces open to the desert on their whole eastern front and preserving their age-long contacts with Arabs from the hinterland, by whom the population was continually replenished. Thus in spite of the heterogeneous nature of the population of Syria and Palestine and Mesopotamia also, the Semitic language and ethos predominated, and to the present day the language and life of the people show vestiges of the desert. Thus even in spite of Western influence in politics and religion in the Byzantine period the Greek Orthodox Church in Syria and Palestine, though its highest dignitaries were Greek, was largely native, and able native Semitic officials served in the administration. We have already noticed that the natives, through grievances against official Byzantine policy in administration and particularly in religion, had welcomed the Arabs as liberators in the conquests of Islam.

The Arabs were the latest of several decisive movements from the inner steppes, and like their predecessors the Amorites, Aramaeans and Israel they contributed to the strengthening of the Semitic character of the population. The conquests of Islam welded the whole Semitic world, Arabia, Palestine, Syria and Mesopotamia, into a political, and largely a religious, unity which extended from North Africa to Iran, and eventually further, in spite of the differences of culture and race.

Soon Syria was the capital of the Empire of Islam under the Umayyad Caliphs of Damascus (660–750), under whom the Arabs of the blood came to settle in the sedentary lands. There were no forced conversions in Islam, but the natural burdens of non-Muslim subjects must eventually have encouraged many to adopt the faith of the state, though many native Christian communities, especially about the holy sites and in Transjordan and the Lebanon, have had a long and honourable history under their native bishops, preserving until the present day a sturdy spiritual independence in a plethora of denominations and sects.

With the passing of the supreme power in Islam to the Abbasid Caliphate in Baghdad, in spite of the fact that the ruling family was from the Ḥejaz, the power of the Arabs in Islam, particularly those of Syria and the Ḥejaz, was deliberately curtailed, and Persia became more and more the support of Abbasid power. Eventually as the Empire of Islam was advanced deep into Central Asia the Turkish tribes became Muslim and were eventually the mainstay of the Abbasid rule both in the East and the West, where we have already encountered Turkish feudal commands in Moṣūl, Aleppo and Damascus as the bulwark of the defence of Islam against the Crusades. Up to this time, in spite of sectarian differences, which affected Palestine and Syria but little, Islam had been the bond uniting Turk and Arab, as we may now term the native Semitic majority in Syria and Palestine. The authority of the Qur'ān as the Holy Scripture of Islam imposed also a unity of language, Arabic. This extended to Egypt, where, because of its remoteness from Baghdad, a slave dynasty, the Ṭulūnids, had ruled from 868–915, when they were able for a time to extend their influence to Palestine, to be succeeded by the Shiite ('sectarian') line of the Fāṭimid Caliphs (909–1171). In fact those dynasties in Egypt maintained the distinctively Arab tradition in Islam against the policy of the Abbasids to minimize the Arab element in favour of the Persian. Nor did this tradition suffer under the Mamlūks, the barrack sultans of various provenance, who ruled Egypt from 1261–1517, during which time they expelled the Franks from Palestine and ruled the land until the Ottoman victory near Cairo in 1517. Throughout this period there were notable Arab families, who maintained powerful feudal estate in their ancestral seats, such as the Banū Munqidh of Shayzār on the Orontes in Syria, whose scion 'Usāma, the contemporary of Salāḥ ad-Dīn, has left such valuable and entertaining memoirs of his time.

With the Ottoman victory over the Mamlūks in 1517 the Turks were no longer the servants of the Arab Caliphate isolated in various commands in mutual rivalry, and as such forced to respect the Arab feudal aristocracy in Syria and Palestine. The Ottoman Sultan was soon Caliph, the spiritual head of Islam. There was thus a certain bond of religion between the Turks and the Muslim majority among the Arabs, which was strongest in the days when the canon law based on the Qur'ān and the traditional interpretation of the will of the Prophet was the law of the state. But there was no bond of race or language, except the Arabic of the Qur'ān and of the statutory daily prayers of Islam. With non-Muslim Arabs there was no affinity. The Arabs were justly proud of their historical and cultural heritage; the Turks were arrogant in their military efficiency, which had crushed the Byzantine Empire, and they came to despise the Arabs and their culture, an attitude which hardened as they extended their conquests through the Balkans and North Africa. This lack of sympathy with their Arab subjects increased with the change which was wrought in the Turkish ruling class through the preference of the sultans for Greek and Armenian wives in their harems and through the recruitment of young Christians from the Balkan provinces, who were trained up as Muslims at state expense as an official class and *corps élit*, the famous Janissaries, under the absolute rule of the Sultan. When such men were appointed to a province they ruled with a heavy hand.

The history of Palestine and Syria under the Turks before the end of the nineteenth century would be a long and tedious compilation of minor details with a probable turning-point in the failure of the last Turkish attempt on Vienna in 1683, after which the Ottoman power steadily declined. Its decline in Syria and Palestine was accentuated by the native risings which we have noted from that of Fakhr ad-Dīn in 1634 to the rule of the Amir Bashīr till 1840 and by the virtual independence of provincial governors culminating in that of Muḥammad 'Ālī.

The nine years of Egyptian rule under Muḥammad 'Ālī and Ibrāhīm Pasha may be said to mark the beginning of the modern period in the history of Palestine and Syria. In this region, always appreciated as a valuable economic adjunct of Egypt since the days of the Pharaohs, the decentralized provinces of the pashas were now abolished. Thus at one stroke the opportunity for exploitation of the natives and private adventures and animosities of the pashas and for the ambitions of such local chiefs as Fakhr ad-Dīn and Dhāhir al-'Umar was abolished. The status of the natives improved as they were appreciated for their economic worth in the Egyptian state which Muḥammad 'Ālī was building up within the Ottoman Empire. They were given a share in local government and this was extended even to Christian Arabs. Ibrāhīm Pasha, who had received an Arabic education at Cairo, had an even wider vision of an Arab state, to which he was passionately devoted in the estimation of European observers. Had he been able to realize this ideal his age might have witnessed a revival of Arab power and culture which in Syria and Egypt at least might have recalled the glories of the Umayyad Caliphate of Damascus. It is an indication, however, of the long inuration of the natives to imperial domination that this liberal policy was suspected. The hardy Palestinian peasants resented taxation and conscription for industry and for war. Muḥammad 'Ālī's war with the Sultan-Caliph raised scruples among the Muslims now as later in the Arab Revolt under Ḥusain in the First World War. Opposition to Muḥammad 'Ālī crystallized in a revolt where the peasants maintained a troublesome guerilla war in the mountains of Central Palestine. This is evidence of a feeling of common interest on the part of the natives of Palestine and at the same time of a very important factor which helps to explain the slow emancipation of the Arabs from Turkish domination, namely the strength of the religious bond of Islam. This bound them unnaturally to their Turkish masters and stifled the national development which Muḥammad 'Ālī and Ibrāhīm strove so hard to promote.

More significantly it disrupted the Arab community in Syria and Palestine. It was not for half a century that Muslim and Christian were even to begin to co-operate in their common interest.

Meanwhile during this period the land was opened to Western travel, and, what was more significant, to Christian missions, American Protestant and French Jesuit, who eventually founded the two universities in Beirut, the American University in 1866 and the University of St. Joseph in 1875.[2] Thus by the end of the nineteenth century through schools and universities education was diffused in Syria and Palestine, Arabic books were printed and circulated, a new pride in the cultural and political achievements of the Arabs was engendered and a professional class emerged educated and liberal enough to co-operate with the Muslims in voicing the aspirations of the inarticulate majority. Thanks to this intellectual awakening, movements towards Arab independence, hitherto dependent upon the ambitions of aspiring native chiefs or upon the policy of equally ambitious statesmen like Ibrāhīm Pasha, expressed the aspirations of the people themselves.

Thus when the Turks returned to Syria and Palestine, rehabilitated by the Western powers in 1840, they found a more articulate subject people. The tragedy was that, though the worst abuses of the pashas and their predatory followers was a feature of past history, congenital habits were not so easily lost, and oppression was only slightly mitigated by the presence of European consuls and vice-consuls, who were often Levantine businessmen.

The provinces were organized under a *vālī*, or governor-general, into *vilāyets*, such as Moṣūl, Baghdad and Basra in Iraq, and in Syria Aleppo, Damascus and Beirut, which included Northern Palestine, and smaller districts termed *sanjaqs*, such as the Lebanon. Thus, for instance, in Palestine Jerusalem was an independent *sanjaq* and Akka and Nablus and their districts were *sanjaqs* in the *vilāyet* of Beirut. Each *sanjaq* had its Turkish governor (*mutaṣarrif*) and his staff, troops and gendarmerie. Within the *sanjaqs* there were smaller districts, *qazas*, based on the principal towns. In the *sanjaq* of Akka, for instance, the *qazas* were Akka, Haifa, Safad, Tiberias and Nazareth, each under its *qaimmaqām*, who was responsible to the *mutaṣarrif*. The *qazas* in turn were subdivided into smaller units called *nāḥiyāt* ('districts'), each under a *mudir* ('director'), and the smallest unit was the village with its lands under its headman, or *mukhtār* ('chosen one') and local elders, dignified by the name of 'notables' (*'a'zā'*). Only at the two lowest levels was the subject population represented, and the machinery was ready for intensive exploitation and sudden repression. But the Arabs were subject to conscription, and a military career was open to the officers, and according to the particular policy of the time Arabs might rise in the political service of the Sultan. But these were individuals, who represented their own interests rather than those of the Arab subjects of the Porte. The administrative problem was practically insoluble for the Turks in the Arabian Peninsula under the limitations of nineteenth-century technology. The Ḥejaz was a nominal *vilāyet* with a governor, or *vālī*, in Mecca, but here the local power of the Sharifs of the family of the Prophet secured Arab interest and was eventually to lead a pan-Arab revolt against the Turks. Turkish control over the Arabs of the Peninsula was further hampered by British interest around the coasts in the Indian Ocean and the Persian Gulf.

As the nineteenth century drew to a close old barriers between Muslim and Christian Arabs in Syria and to a less extent in Palestine were gradually being broken down by the renaissance of Arab culture and letters fostered by enlightened Arabs of both faiths, notably in Beirut and Damascus with encouragement from Egypt, long an outpost of Arab culture in the Turkish Empire. This stirring of the spirit among their Arab subjects did not escape the notice of the Turkish administration. Any political hopes which were thereby engendered were blighted by those masters of frustration by force and in some cases by political favour to individuals with the purpose of weakening the movement by depriving it of its important leaders. Nevertheless the Arab awakening continued as an increasing problem to the Turks. Nor did events abroad increase Turkish prestige in the Arab provinces. Great Britain occupied Egypt in 1882, and thereby lent great impetus to Arab nationalism there, with repercussions in Syria and Palestine. In 1830 Algeria had been occupied by the French and in 1881 Tunisia. In Syria the career of Ibrāhīm Pasha and its end in 1840 and the arrest of the Russian invasion just short of Istambul in 1877 by British diplomacy and the resultant Treaty of Berlin had made it clear that the Ottoman Empire was held in existence solely by a policy of equilibrium imposed by the European powers.

Meanwhile Sultan ʿAbdu ʾl-Ḥamīd II (1876–1909) counteracted the loss of his Egyptian and African dominions by stressing his status as Caliph, or spiritual head of Islam. This had the effect of dividing the allegiance of Muslim subjects of France and Russia, while his agents, circulating ostensibly as preachers in the Muslim revival, enabled him to keep a strict check on any resistance movement in his Empire. Among his Arab subjects particularly movements towards independence were checked by all the means characteristic of an unscrupulous despotism. The more venal of the Arabs were recruited to service, and even promoted to honours at Istambul; rival chiefs and their people were set at enmity with one another on the principle *divide ut imperes*; there were secret arrests and political murders, and men too prominent or influential to be so summarily dealt with were 'invited' to reside at the capital, where they were under close espionage. The most notable of those was the Sharif Ḥusain of Mecca and his family, who actually grew up in Istambul.

The revolution of the Young Turks, the Party of Union and Progress, against the absolutism of 'Abdu 'l-Ḥamīd in 1908 seemed to encourage Arab hopes in the declared policy of the recognition of local aspirations and the freedom for cultural and political development in the provinces within the framework of the Ottoman Empire. The new constitution too, which the Sultan was forced to grant, promised Arab representation in the Parliament in Istambul. But in the event Arab representation was disproportionately small. Indeed on the basis of proportionate representation the Arab deputies would have dominated the Ottoman Parliament. Turkish domination continued, and, in alarm at the fires of freedom they had fanned, the Young Turk Party resorted to methods of repression which, however, intensified the Arab hatred for the Turk and drove the independence movement underground. Native aspirations, however, were co-ordinated and voiced articulately by Syrian and Palestinian leaders in the safety of Egypt in the Ottoman Decentralization Party. Now, as one reads the details of the *Arab Awakening* in the excellent study under that title by George Antonius one notices among the personalities involved families such as the Ḥusainī and Nashashībī families of Jerusalem, which are to emerge again in the Arab struggle for independence in the last phase in our study. And among these there is a melancholy galaxy of asterisks which denote martyrdom to the cause.

Meanwhile an Arab Congress convoked in Paris in 1913 made the modest demands for decentralized government for the Arab provinces, more effective Arab representation in Parliament and government and recognition of Arabic as the official language in the Arab provinces. These points were conceded by an official representative of the Young Turk Party, but apparently only with the purpose of blunting Arab opposition, since they were in effect practically nullified. At the same time several Arab secret societies were formed, the most significant being the civilian Young Arab Society (*al-fatat*) and the even more effective society *al-'ahd* ('the Oath') formed of Arab officers serving in the Ottoman Army. Both societies were to play a notable part in the Arab Revolt under Sharīf Ḥusain, and the latter was particularly strong in that it included Arabs from Iraq as well as Syria, all military men who by nature and training were practical men with considerable political and technical experience and by rank and family able to command a following. Up to this point, it must be stressed, the Arabs in spite of their grievances, set themselves the objective not of independence of the Sultan, but of local autonomy in varying degrees within the Empire. As Arab opposition to Turkish domination intensified the Muslims played a larger part in leading Arab opinion, and opposition to Turkish rule was never carried to the extent of the disruption of the Ottoman Empire, in which the Sultan was still Caliph, no matter how much a shadow of earlier reality the Caliphate might be in spite of the political expedient of 'Abdu 'l-Ḥamīd's professed revival of the office. This scruple, coupled with Turkish frustration, now by intensive espionage and violence and now by concessions more apparent than real, retarded the emancipation of the Arabs until the involvement of both Turk and Arab in the larger conflict of the First World War occasioned the final wrench. The last act of the long struggle thus protracted by Turkish prevarication and Arab patience was heralded on the outbreak of the war by the public hanging of leading Arab patriots in 1915 and 1916 in Beirut and Damascus.

The movement for Arab independence wanted a declared leader of acknowledged power and prestige and strong enough to defy the Sultan. As a matter of course it had to be a Muslim. Who then more fitted than Sharīf* Ḥusain of Mecca, nobly descended from the Banū Hāshim, the clan of the Prophet? Unimpeachable in motive and tenacious of purpose, the Sharīf was a strong man in the Holy City of Mecca among his own people, in spite of the Ḥejaz Railway, which brought Medina within five days from Istambul. As one consequence of the constitutional revolution of 1908 Sharīf Ḥusain had been sent back to his native Mecca from the life of patrician inaction to which he had been 'invited' by the Sultan at Istambul.† His office was now Amīr of Mecca, a limited authority, which the Young Turk Government sought still further to limit by the appointment of a *vālī*, or provincial governor. But in this remote province the authority of the representative of the Prophet's clan was more effective among the Arabs, and by virtue of this status and judicious use of force among the tribes under

* Sharīf ('noble') is a courtesy title given to notables of Muḥammad's family in Mecca.

† His sons, notably his second son 'Abdullah, the future King of Jordan, grew to political maturity in Constantinople. Antonius claims that Ḥusain was restored to Mecca by the initiative of the Young Turks in despite of the Sultan (*op. cit.*, p. 103), but 'Abdullah has stated that the appointment was made by the Sultan to the disgust of the Young Turk party (*Memoirs of King Abdullah of Transjordan*, 1950, p. 44).

cover of his Turkish command Ḥusain built up considerable political prestige and was able to resist Turkish efforts towards centralization of authority, though relationships became strained. Here obviously was a rallying point for Arab independence. The future would decide whether Ḥusain would fulfil the hopes of the Arabs by force or diplomacy. This in brief is the general background to the Arab Revolt under the Amīr Ḥusain, which broke out in June 1916, most familiar to Western readers as the theme of T. E. Lawrence's *Seven Pillars of Wisdom*. As the genesis of modern nationalism in the Arab world it is in the context of the present study a necessary part of the background of the Arab-Zionist controversy, the major theme of the last phase of the history of Jerusalem.

The weakness of the Ottoman power in the Levant since the seventeenth century, of which the independence movements of provincial pashas and native leaders alike were symptomatic, encouraged the intervention of European powers, who were increasingly more interested in the Turkish situation since Napoleon's campaign at Acre, particularly on the Syrian coast with its Christian majority and in Egypt and Palestine, where the first European consulate was established in Jerusalem in 1839, representing Her Britannic Majesty. None of the major European powers, however, was interested to see the elimination of Turkey, which would be conducive to rival interests with potential occasion for a major war, and for the same reason none was willing to be involved too closely in Turkish politics. Kaiser Wilhelm II, however, had less compunction or more confidence. In his famous pilgrimage to Jerusalem with the Empress Augusta in 1901 the Kaiser also visited Istambul and secured the concession to build the famous Aleppo-Baghdad Railway as a vital link in the German *Drang nach Osten*. From then there was a remarkable strategic organization of the Levant by German technicians until the outbreak of the First World War, when Turkey declared war on the Allies. During this period Jaffa and Haifa were linked to Damascus by rail through the great central plain of Palestine, the Yarmuk gorge and the Haurān; by 1908 the line was extended from Damascus through the Biq'a, 'the Ḥama approaches' of the Old Testament, and the upper Orontes to Aleppo, and in 1913 to Baghdad. Damascus was linked by mountain railways over the

---

30. The St. Stephen Gate in the north of the east wall of Jerusalem, with the lion, the device of the shield of Sultan Baybars.

31. The Crusaders' arch at the entrance to the crypt of the Church at the Tomb of the Virgin near Gethsemane.

Lebanon to Beirut and Tripoli; even the ancient Pilgrim Road (*darb al-ḥāj*) from Damascus to Medina was covered by rail, and Jerusalem was brought into the network by a line from Jaffa, which pierced the mountain barrier of Judah by the Wādī 'ṣ-Ṣurār (the Vale of Sorek), which it left in the middle reaches to follow a tributary wadi hard by Bettīr, where Simon bar Kokhbā and his desperate followers made their last stand in 134, to debouche on the Plain of the Rephaim in the south-west of modern Jerusalem.

This dark age of the history of Jerusalem was big with the embryo of another significant movement besides the Arab emancipation. With silk hats, court gloves and morning coats in careful storage and court etiquette assiduously rehearsed, certain private gentlemen timed their visit to Istambul and Jerusalem to coincide with the Kaiser's pilgrimage. These were the executives of the Zionist Congress under the president Theodor Herzl,[3] whose vision, determination and energy had convened the First Zionist Congress at Basel in 1887, which had committed itself to the official rehabilitation of the Jews in Palestine on the following principles:

> The promotion, on suitable industrial lines, of the colonization of Palestine by Jewish agricultural and industrial workers,
>
> The organization and binding together of the whole of Jewry by means of appropriate institutions, local and international, in accordance with the laws of each country,
>
> The strengthening and fostering of Jewish national sentiment and consciousness.
>
> Preparatory steps towards obtaining Government consent, where necessary, to the attainment of the aims of Zionism.

The influx of Jews to Palestine was no novelty. Harried by the Inquisition at the end of the fifteenth century, and expelled destitute from Spain and Portugal, a number of Jews after wandering along the coast of North Africa were given a home in Palestine, recently added to the Ottoman Empire in 1517. A number more of the humbler sort of traditionally pious Jews, particularly from Russia and Eastern Europe, cherished the life-long desire to end their days in Palestine, where they were sustained in their life of study in the Law and Rabbinic learning by subscriptions from the Diaspora, requiting their benefactors by prayers and seasonable lamentation or rejoicing at the holy sites,

32. The Mount of Olives with the Church of the Nations in the foreground by the reputed site of the Garden of Gethsemane, and on the summit the Russian Church of the Ascension.

particularly by prayer and lamentation at the Wailing Wall (Pl. 7), that portion of the west wall of the precinct of Herod's Temple which now bounds the Muslim Sacred Precinct (see above, p. 192). Settled in places especially sacred in Jewish tradition, mainly at Jerusalem and Hebron in the south and in the old Talmudic centres of Tiberias and Ṣafad in Galilee, those pietists lived by small trade, maintaining a strict orthodoxy coloured by the medieval ghetto of Eastern Europe and generally oblivious of the intervening centuries of progress and compelling modern realities. In 1837 the Jewish population of Palestine was estimated at eight thousand by the London banker Sir Moses Montefiore in his visit to Palestine. These consisted of Jews from Central Europe, Yemen, Bukhara and were chiefly town-dwellers, who lacked the mental and physical vigour of the later Zionists.

Possibilities of agricultural development had been appreciated by Montefiore, who returned from his visit with an ambitious project which he had the ample means and influence to sponsor. Nor was the problem of the acquisition of land acute, since the revolutionary industrialism and taxation of Muḥammad ʿĀlī had driven many of the inhabitants into Transjordan. In effect Montefiore had to remain content with limited success. He contrived to persuade some fifty families to settle the land near Ṣafad, where they throve rather poorly by small trade and agriculture. In Jewish land settlement in Palestine 1870 is a landmark, the agricultural station of Miqveh Israel being then founded in the plain between Jerusalem and Jaffa. By this time immigration had increased, notably from Russia. The new immigrants, *Ḥōbhᵉbhē Ṣīyyōñ* ('Lovers of Zion') were young and enthusiastic, deliberately seeking refuge from the precarious tolerance of Europe by the commendable measure of helping themselves. From this movement twenty-five agricultural colonies were founded including Rīshōn lᵉṢīyyōn and Petaḥ Tiqvāh in the coastal plain near Jaffa, Zikhrōn Yaʿᵃqōbh on the west flank of Carmel and Rōsh Pinnāh in Upper Galilee. The settlers suffered much owing to their ignorance of local difficulties, but they were saved from ruin by liberal subsidy by the French Jew Baron Edmund de Rothschild. And though they had in the judgement of Weizmann[4] in 1907 eventually lost their initial pioneering impetus and had come to rely on subsidy from abroad they formed an effective bridgehead for later successful Jewish colonization.

The next phase of the Jewish trend to Palestine was that of political Zionism. The concrete expression of the desire for a national home in Palestine is generally ascribed to a German Jew Moses Hess, who wrote on the subject in 1862. The idea germinated in men's minds until a generation later Leon Pinsker from the Jewish Pale in the desolate marsh wastes in south-west Russia urged a national home as a means of self-preservation and security from the caprice of the nations where they sojourned. Pinsker's thought was turned in this direction particularly by the repression of the Jews after the assassination of the liberal Czar Alexander II in 1881, which to be sure was just another of the pogroms of which the Jews lived in constant fear.

Though given articulate expression by such men as Hess and Pinsker and Asher Ginsburg (Aḥad hā-'Ām), the great protagonist of the renaissance of Hebrew culture as a means of national self-expression, the impulse to Zionism was essentially of the people, particularly the repressed masses in the Russian Pale. Condemned to the ghetto, they rallied upon their traditional Jewish faith and culture, which found its ideal focus in Palestine, and they were at once the sure custodians of Jewish tradition and a suspect foreign element to assimilated cosmopolitan Jews of the more tolerant countries. For this reason too they were so strange and enigmatic, not to say repellent, to the British administration during the Mandate. Condemned in towns and villages in the barren wastes of the Russian Pale to poverty relieved only by hard work, thrift and the strict moral discipline of the faith, they developed a strong community sense and an aptitude for labour and endurance and a rural economy,* which eventually bore fruit in the settlement of Palestine.

The impulse to independent status was shared by the Hungarian-born Jew Theodor Herzl, though to be sure he was moved not so much by the desperate urgency of the Russian pogroms as by the social and economic ostracism which were the weapons of anti-Semitism in the urban West. This brilliant cosmopolitan used his influence in the press of Central Europe to rouse interest in the project, of which his book *The Jewish State* (1896) is the classical expression. So far proponents of the idea had relied on individual Jewish financiers to support the immigration scheme; Herzl now turned to the masses of European Jewry, representatives of whom he succeeded in convoking at Basel in 1897 in the first of the Zionist Congresses, which were to be the organ of the opinion of Jewish nationalism in its various degrees until the effective foundation of the National Home in Palestine.

In these congresses the difference in the aims of the Jews of the East and West soon emerged, particularly under Herzl and the opposition represented by Chaim Weizmann among others. The latter were determined on the strategic colonization and eventual domination of Palestine from the outset, while Herzl and the majority of Western Zionists thought in terms of a National Home secured by negotiation

* Weizmann's family in Motol kept two cows.

with the great powers. To be sure a settlement in Palestine was visualized, and to this end Herzl approached the Ottoman Sultan 'Abdu 'l-Ḥamīd, and alluring offers of Jewish financial aid were made in a persistent effort to exploit the known weakness of Turkey at that time, nor was the Sultan averse to Jewish settlement. We have already mentioned Herzl's carefully contrived meeting with Kaiser Wilhelm II in Palestine in 1901. But Palestine was not considered by Herzl essential to Jewish national aspirations,[5] and when after a particularly savage pogrom in Russia in 1903 Lord Lansdowne offered the Jews an autonomous territory in Uganda the Zionist Organization was deeply divided until the offer was formally rejected in 1905. The violent opposition to the Uganda proposition by the delegates from the Russian Pale, the very individuals who in the words of Herzl 'had the rope around their necks', served distinct notice that for the dynamic masses of Eastern Jewry the idea of a National Home in Palestine had developed into something much more positive than a relief measure.

The Uganda proposal was a significant token of the respect in which Herzl's organization was held. It had now made an impact on the great world power which was eventually to burden itself with the responsibility of the establishment of a National Home for the Jews in Palestine—too rashly as the event proved, and with naïve and immoral disregard of the human rights of the indigenous population, who at the time of the Balfour Declaration in 1917 were still subjects of the Ottoman Empire.

Palestine and Zionism, with its political objective in Jewish independence there, now emerged increasingly as a symbol of division among the Jews. For the desperate enthusiasm of the Jews in the ghettoes of Eastern Europe it was a vital element in their faith and hope, fostered even in Exile by a revival of literature in Hebrew as apart from Yiddish, that cant language compounded of Hebrew and Low German in the Hebrew character. In Western Europe on the other hand under more liberal governments there was no need for such defence mechanism. The Jews, even when they remained loyal to their ancestral faith and tradition, found opportunities in assimilation to the culture of the lands of their adoption, and in many cases had even practically renounced their distinctive tradition—of which they were to be forcibly reminded under National Socialism in Germany and the countries she subjugated. Those assimilationist Jews had little sympathy with the xenophobia of the Jews of Eastern Europe. They might indeed favour a Jewish state as a relief measure in the insecurity which all European Jews felt in some measure, but they were not so ardently committed to a full revival of Jewish life in Palestine and in fact they had misgivings about the repercussion of Jewish nationalism there on the policies of the countries in which they had made their homes. This tension extended even to Zionist circles, in which a rift soon developed between theoretical Zionism, which sought a home by arrangement with the great world states as a relief measure, and practical Zionism, the immediate objective of which was to press on by Jewish funds and labour with the colonization of Palestine and the upbuilding of Jewish tradition there and the establishment of a National Home in Palestine, if not indeed of Palestine as the Jewish National Home. The former policy was associated with Theodor Herzl and Western Jews; the latter with Chaim Weizmann and the Jews from Eastern Europe, particularly those of the Russian Pale. Eventually it was Weizmann, the Jew from Motol in the Russian Pale and the scientist with the confidence of the liberal British press and key British statesmen, who effectively bridged the gulf between Jews in Eastern and Western Europe—Weizmann and the insane anti-Semitic orgy of Hitler's Germany.

Herzl's favourable contacts with British statesmen anticipated the official establishment of a Jewish National Home in Palestine, which was the fruit of the determination and phenomenal driving force of Chaim Weizmann, who came to England in 1904 and engaged in chemical research and eventual teaching in the liberal University of Manchester. The career of Weizmann, the real architect of the Jewish National Home in Palestine, is a triumph of determination and single-minded devotion to his avowedly limited interests of his chemistry and practical Zionism. By a remarkable combination of grim purposefulness and happy coincidence the Jew from remote Motol soon had the ear of influential press and statesmen in the highest offices. The Jewish industrialist Charles Dreyfus introduced Weizmann to A. J. Balfour during his election campaign in Manchester in 1906, the recent rejection of the Uganda offer affording a talking point and an opening for Weizmann's exposition of practical Zionism and the settlement of Palestine, which were to germinate in Balfour's mind until finding fruition in the Balfour Declaration. Manchester itself with its influential Jewish community was an admirable strategic centre for Weizmann's Zionist work, though to be sure Jewish sentiment in England lacked the fire and enthusiasm of Zionism in Eastern Europe. Soon Weizmann had engaged the sympathies of the liberal *Manchester Guardian* under the celebrated C. P. Scott. Zionism and the Jewish settlement in Palestine against the background of Czarist pogroms appealed to the pietism of pre-war England as humane and enlightened. It had also spectacular publicity value. In the general ignorance of Arab culture and potential it had even the aspect of a mission, which in the councils of state at that time was a pretext for imperialist expansion, and it must be remembered that Britain did not relinquish her strategic interests in the Levant and the Canal zone until 1947. But, however British patronage of political Zionism may have been presented, the fact that it was so strenuously opposed by the representatve bodies of British Jews suggests that it suited British policy to sponsor Zionism in Palestine, and indeed from the time of the infamous Sykes-Picot agreement in which Great Britain claimed Iraq and France claimed Western Syria as respective areas of occupation the sordid aims of both became increasingly apparent. Britain's sponsorship of Jewish settlement in Palestine was designed as a counterpoise to French claims to the same area and French influence in Syria.[6] The scope which Britain eventually gave France to occupy the eastern part of Syria, expelling Faisal from Damascus, was the price of France's concession on the question of the Jewish national home in Palestine.

Weizmann's great opportunity came with the Great War. Having already made what at the time appeared to be a minor discovery in the production of acetone as a by-product of his experiments in fermentation, Weizmann was able to apply the discovery in the processing of high explosives, for which he was employed by the Admiralty and the Ministry of Munitions, then respectively under Winston Churchill and Lloyd George. It is often loosely stated that Weizmann sold his scientific secret in return for the Balfour Declaration. Actually he had already injected the Zionist ideal into the mind of A. J. Balfour, and his important research work during the war simply gave him further access to high officials. His public service, however, certainly made them more sympathetic to his known Zionist aspirations. In any case Weizmann's claims were admitted at the highest level, and, with what now appears blatant partiality and brutal indifference to local Arab interests, the Zionists themselves were asked to frame the text from which the famous Balfour Declaration was eventually developed. Before the final draft more cautious counsels of English Jews in Government circles had modified the original text, and on 2nd November, 1917 the Declaration was made, the text of which may be quoted:

> His Majesty's Government view with favour the establishment in Palestine of a national home for the Jewish people, and will use their best endeavours to facilitate the achievement of this object, it being clearly understood that nothing shall be done which may prejudice the civil and religious rights of existing non-Jewish communities in Palestine or the rights and political status enjoyed by Jews in any other country.

This, modified by the wisdom of Jewish advisers to the Government, was a decided disappointment to Dr. Weizmann, though it was sufficient to raise the suspicions of Ḥusain, particularly after the shock of limitation of British undertakings to the Arabs in the Sykes-Picot agreement. With characteristic determination, however, Weizmann resolved that the Balfour Declaration was 'no more than a framework, which had to be filled in by our own efforts. It would mean exactly what we should make it mean—neither more nor less.'[7] What this amounted to in the estimation of Weizmann is indicated in his preposterous claim stated to a Cabinet Committee meeting on Palestine policy in 1930 that His Majesty's Government should not endeavour to discharge obligations in Palestine to Jews and Arabs already there but to Jews throughout the whole world as against the 700,000 Arabs in Palestine, asserting that 'The obligation of the Mandatory Power is towards the Jewish people, of which the 170,000 are merely the vanguard'.[8] There is small wonder that the Arabs rose in 1936–39 and that Weizmann found limits to British benevolence and patience! The unhappy history of the British Mandate in Palestine was characterized by the conflict between the Zionists, who were determined on this course, and the Administration, which was determined to fulfil the commitments of the Balfour Declaration strictly to the letter. The tension between the British Government and the local Mandatory Administration military and civil might have been resolved if the more remote sponsors of Zionism had had the Administration's experience of local problems and personnel or even if they had been aware at all of the Arabs in Palestine. Weizmann records the remark of the Welsh Baptist Lloyd George that the place-names in Palestine were more familiar to him than those on the Western Front. Evidently Naboth's vineyard was not one of his chapel memories!

That the Arabs of Palestine and the Levant should have been ignored was doubtless owing to the fact that they were popularly associated with the desert and that they had been long suppressed by their Turkish masters, with whom they had nothing in common but Islam. Even so the considerable number of Arabs who had maintained a long Christian tradition in a predominantly Muslim environment might have been expected to have roused the interest and sympathy of the West rather than Zionism. In fact they suffered even more than the Muslim Arabs under the repressive and corrupt Ottoman provincial administration. The distinctive Arab culture and political aspirations were suppressed; the people were ground to poverty by crippling taxation and corruption at all levels of administration till honest enterprise was killed; and the land fell derelict and was bought up by native landlords, who had learned to thrive under Turkish rule by approved Turkish methods, and by Levantine speculators and moneylenders, who eventually sold the land to the Jews in callous indifference to the fate of the Arab peasantry. Thus while Herzl and Weizmann through the Zionist Congress publicized their cause in the West and gained the ear of the press and statesmen, the Arabs in Palestine were voiceless and negligible in the councils of state and in the consideration of the public. So their case went by default as though they did not exist or were a hopelessly decadent community. Nevertheless when he visited Palestine in connection with the Colonizing Department of the Zionist Movement in 1907 Weizmann became aware of an Arab population of over 520,000 as apart from 80,000 Jewish colonists.[9]

In this general ignorance, unwitting or wilful, of Arab aspirations and potential it was only the knowledge or enthusiasm of a small number of administrators and scholars with actual experience of the Arabs and their culture which appreciated the situation. The chief of these was Lord Kitchener, until the outbreak of World War I British Agent in Egypt. Kitchener's long experience as a soldier and statesman in the Near and Middle East made him keenly sensitive to the threat to British interests in the Persian Gulf and to communications with India in German influence with Turkey, specifically symbolized by the German concession in the Aleppo-Baghdad Railway. The first approach, however, was made by Abdullah, the second son of the Sharīf Ḥusain, the natural statesman of the family, who interrupted his journey from Jidda to Constantinople, where he was Member for Mecca in the Ottoman Parliament, to visit Lord Kitchener in Cairo. As a result of that visit in February 1914 Kitchener was made aware of the strained relations between the Sharīf and the Turks in the Ḥejāz (see above, p. 271) and the possibility of revolt. Though British policy refused to commit itself to support the Arabs against the Turks this was a situation to be exploited when Turkey joined the Central Powers in October 1914.

At that juncture correspondence was opened again on the authority of Lord Kitchener, now Secretary of State for War, between Ronald Storrs, Oriental Secretary at the British Agency in Cairo and 'Abdullah and Ḥusain, but by that time the convenience of an alliance was Britain's and the Sharīf and his sons were naturally cautious. Ḥusain and his third son Faisal were for allegiance to Turkey, partly fearing the immediate consequences of a revolt on the Arab subjects of the Ottoman Empire, who were not effectively prepared, and partly hoping to win the gratitude of Turkey, which they might exploit to the advantage of all Arabs, which was always the objective of Ḥusain. 'Abdullah on the other hand, through his experience abroad, had had his finger on the pulse of pan-Arab opinion, and counselled revolt from Turkey, subject to proper British guarantee in the eventual settlement.[10]

Meanwhile the Sultan as Caliph had proclaimed the *jihād*, or Holy War, as a sacred duty on all Muslims including those, numbering some 126,000,000, in lands controlled by Britain, France and Russia, and bade Ḥusain do the same from Mecca, from which it would be more effective. With great courage and tenacity Ḥusain refused to do this on the pretext that he was vulnerable as long as Britain commanded the Red Sea. This barely allayed Turkish suspicion, and the courage of the Sharīf is the more remarkable when we consider that there was at that time a Turkish *vālī* in Medina with a garrison there and at Mecca. Now Faisal was sent up to Constantinople to explain the difficulties which his father encountered with the Turkish Governor. At Damascus, where he spent some time going and coming, he came into touch with Arab revolutionaries. Till then he had preferred to hope for terms by negotiation with the Turks since he suspected Allied interests in the Levant, which might disappoint Arab hopes of independence, a premonition which was painfully true. The Arab secret societies shared his reserve, and declared themselves to him to be prepared to come over to the Turks if the Allies did not allay those suspicions. This being understood by both Faisal and the revolutionaries, he became a convert to the design to negotiate with Great Britain with a view to revolt, and with the utmost secrecy he took back the terms of the Arab revolutionaries to Ḥusain on his return to Mecca. In further negotiations with Great Britain the Sharīf was fully aware of larger issues than the convenience of the Allies in a diversionary side-show in the Ḥejāz; he was the recognized protagonist of Arab independence, for which he was prepared to work either with the Allies if they gave the necessary guarantee of good faith or, failing that, with the Turks and the Sultan-Caliph. Meanwhile he still would not proclaim the *jihād* from Mecca.

In July, 1915 a more formal correspondence was opened between Sir Henry McMahon the British High Commissioner in Egypt and Sharīf Ḥusain. Correspondence on such a high official level cannot be simple. With Turkish garrisons in Mecca and Medina, the latter now accessible by railway for Turkish reinforcements and supplies, and a total of two Turkish divisions in the Arabian Peninsula, the Sharīf could not immediately commit himself. Moreover, though of the family of the Prophet and as such particularly respected by the Arabs, his status was, nominally at least, impaired by the fact that the Ottoman Sultan was already Caliph, the spiritual successor of Muḥammad, so that the revolt would be formally heresy. But what especially gave the

Sharīf pause was the responsibility he felt for the cause of Arab independence and his demand for adequate British guarantees, no unnecessary precaution as it proved. The Sharīf might well bargain. The initial approach after the Turkish declaration of war had come from Britain, and he had much to offer. Indeed until Ḥusain finally committed himsel, the Allies were on the defensive throughout the East. The Gallipoli expedition had been repulsed with heavy loss; the Turkish troops in Yemen had invaded the Aden Protectorate; the British force working north from Baṣra was encountering increasingly stiff opposition until it was halted at Kut al-Amāra on 28th September, 1915; Turkish incitement to the Holy War was intensifying with the prospect of success in the Sudan and in Libya, where the Senussi chief was an unknown quantity and a potential menace, And meanwhile the Turkish Army in Palestine was still a real menace to the Suez Canal and even to Egypt. In the conflict over the Suez Canal a diversion of Turkish troops in the Hejāz would be welcome, and the revolt of the Prophet's family in the city would certainly neutralize the effect of the proclamation of the *jihād* by the Ottoman Sultan-Caliph, certainly among Arab Muslims. Moreover the alliance of Ḥusain would isolate the Turkish forces in 'Asir and Yemen, with their menace to Aden so long as communications with the north were unbroken.

In his correspondence with McMahon Ḥusain laid down as a condition of the Arab revolt the recognition by the Allies, if victorious, of Arab independence in the area between the Taurus and the Indian Ocean and between the Persian border and the Mediterranean. This most reasonable condition was too direct for Western diplomacy and was met with reserve, which was reciprocated by the Sharīf. Sir Henry McMahon replied that as certain areas in Syria such as the vicinity of Mersīn, Alexandretta and the regions west of the districts of Aleppo, Ḥama, Ḥoms and Damascus were not predominantly Arab, these would have to be exempted from the guarantee of Arab independence. The Sharīf replied that with the rest he would agree, but that in the case of the districts excepted he would reserve the right to raise the matter again. To this in an official note of 1st January 1916 Sir Henry McMahon replied that the British Government accepted all the demands of Sharīf Ḥusain. In June Ḥusain, depending on no more—and assuming no less—than a gentleman's agreement, committed his people to revolt.

The gentleman's agreement as distinct from a legal bond was an expedient convenience in view of the next step, the infamous Sykes-Picot agreement of May 1916, which reserved Lebanon, North Syria and South Anatolia for French administration and South Iraq for

British administration. This agreement, to which Britain, France and Russia were parties, was made without reference to Ḥusain, though in McMahon's second note of 24th October, 1915 McMahon mentions French interests in his exclusion of the area west of the districts of Aleppo, Ḥama, Ḥoms, and Damascus. Nevertheless though Ḥusain met both Sykes and Picot personally, burdened as they were with the guilty secret, in May 1917, he was kept in ignorance until the agreement was divulged by the Bolsheviks in December 1917 after the Russian revolution. The shameful implications were immediately obvious to the Ottoman Government, which forthwith offered Ḥusain all the concessions for the Arabs which he sought; and the guarantee of Germany might have persuaded the Sharīf at this point. But pathetically trusting to British honour, he held fast to his agreement, nor was the war effort under Faisal impaired as it might well have been, though British officers like T. E. Lawrence attached to Faisal's forces were acutely embarrassed and deeply ashamed.[11]

It will have been noticed that in the Ḥusain-McMahon correspondence Palestine was never mentioned. This afforded a legal loophole for Britain to exclude Palestine in later casuistic attempts to reconcile commitments to Ḥusain with patronage to the Jews in Palestine and with the Palestinian Mandate. But that it was included in the area for which Arab independence was claimed is clear from the fact that Ḥusain's original claim for Arab independence from the Anatolian foothills to the Indian Ocean and from the Persian border to the Mediterranean specifies the Western region from Aden to Mersīn. The inclusion of Palestine in the area in which the Arabs were to have independence is certainly implied in McMahon's third note, which defines the reserved areas as the regions 'West of the districts of Aleppo, Ḥama, Ḥoms and Damascus in the two vilayets of Aleppo and Beirut'. Though the northern part of Palestine was in the vilayet of Beirut, the previous mention of the *district*—not *vilāyet*—of Damascus would most naturally exclude Palestine, and so Ḥusain was led to understand. This was certainly the conclusion to be drawn from the dropping of portraits of Sharīf Ḥusain behind the Turkish lines in Palestine with his proclamation to join his war of liberation, to which Allenby refers in a letter dated 3rd October, 1917.[12]

With the publication of the Balfour Declaration on 2nd November, 1917 the possibility of further diminution of Allied commitments to the Arabs was apparent. Though not opposed to Jewish settlement in Palestine, Ḥusain was not satisfied with the vague provision for 'the civil and religious rights' of 'existing non-Jewish communities' in Palestine, and accepted it only when the British agent D. G. Hogarth had given him assurances that *the political and economic freedom of the Arabs* would be safeguarded, an oral assurance to be sure, but one which Ḥusain was shrewd enough to record in writing.[13] The extraordinary liberality of Ḥusain and his family towards the Jewish National Home in Palestine is freely acknowledged by Dr. Weizmann, who actually met Feisal in the end of 1918 at his camp south-east of the Dead Sea, and both then and at the Paris Peace Conference in 1919 the two agreed on the coexistence of Jew and Arab in Palestine. One suspects that Weizmann was discreetly silent on his intention that the Balfour Declaration should mean just what the Zionists intended it to mean, and the suspicions of Faisal at the time of the Paris Peace Conference are revealed in his addendum to the agreement with Weizmann before the Conference:

> If the Arabs are established as I have asked in my manifesto of January 4th addressed to the British Secretary for Foreign Affairs, I will carry out what I have written in this agreement. If changes are made I cannot be answerable for failure to carry out this agreement.

It may be added here that the agreement between Faisal and Weizmann was for their mutual support at the Conference at a time when under the terms of the McMahon correspondence, and despite the considerable retraction of British commitments to the Arabs, Faisal expected to be ruler of an Arab state based on Syria, which might well have absorbed moderate Jewish immigration. In spite of natural caution he was sensible of the possibilities of advantageous co-operation with the Jews. These fair prospects of Arab-Jewish co-operation were bedevilled by French ambitions in Syria, which exceeded her claims in the Sykes-Picot agreement and expelled Faisal from Damascus, and by the British claim to a mandate in Palestine, also in excess of what Ḥusain had admitted in his correspondence with McMahon and even of the Sykes-Picot agreement. So the disunited Arab community was left isolated and headless to shoulder the burden of aggressive Zionism backed by the British Government. The Arab tragedy has been occasioned by the expedient policies of remote powers like France, Great Britain and, after the Second World War, America, and if eventually three sovereign Arab states have emerged in Syria and Palestine this is a triumph of Arab fortitude and perseverance in despite of Western diplomacy.

Meanwhile in the First World War the Arabs kept the Ḥejāz and Transjordan a running sore on the Turkish flank and finally harassed and precipitated their retreat before the victorious army of Allenby. It must be noted that neither the Jews nor the Arabs in Palestine were heavily committed in the First World War, both being Turkish subjects with little opportunity of desertion without reprisals on their kinspeople until Allenby's advance through the land. A regular Jewish battalion served as the Jewish Mule Corps at Gallipoli, and three battalions, mainly of British Jews, were drafted to Allenby's expeditionary force before his final offensive, and about two thousand Arabs from Palestine served as volunteers with Faisal.* Both Arabs and Zionists, however, had secured British undertakings which were to prove more easily given than implemented. Meanwhile the practicality of the British settlement and its problems were still contingent upon an Allied victory.

In 1915 the British Army occupied Egypt, then still at least nominally a Turkish province, though admitting certain foreign interests under concessions, or capitulations. The object was the defence of the Suez Canal against a Turkish attack instigated by the German military staff. Successful in this, the Egyptian Expeditionary Force under General Sir Archibald Murray passed over to the offensive and advanced into Sinai, making history by constructing a railway over the two hundred miles of desert from Cairo to Palestine to facilitate troop movements and supplies and pumping water from the Delta for distribution in pipes to various camps. With over 200,000 effective troops and naval and air support the British invasion was unprecedented in the history of Palestine. History was made also at Jerusalem, which had its first air-raid, by ten British planes, which, however, killed no more than one animal and wounded one man on the Mount of Olives for the loss of five planes and their crews.

The advance was halted before the Turkish lines, which ran from Gaza to Beersheba, with the Turks firmly entrenched on a ridge south of Gaza, from which they swept the open southern approaches with heavy gunfire. Twice the British forces were hurled against this

* Arab support from the natives of Palestine and Syria would have been greater but for brutal repression by Jemāl Pasha the Turkish Commander-in-Chief in Syria, who was informed of two great Arab secret societies, one military, *al-ʿāhd* (the Oath), and the other civilian, *al-fatat* (Youth), with both of whom Faisal was involved in Damascus in April and May 1915 at the hazard of his life, and the dispersal of Arab officers and conscripts from Syria and Iraq to other fronts. In a terrible famine in Syria during the war, the merciless Jemāl Pasha withheld relief from communities he suspected, who must also be reckoned as martyrs to the cause of the Arabs and their allies. After the capture of the Red Sea port of Wejh Lawrence records (*op. cit.*, p. 167) that 'Sir Archibald Murray realized with a sudden shock that more Turkish troops were fighting the Arabs than were fighting him'. Lawrence of course includes all the Turkish troops who were tied up in the Peninsula, many of whom were never actually engaged with the Arab armies until Allenby's victory had rendered their position hopeless.

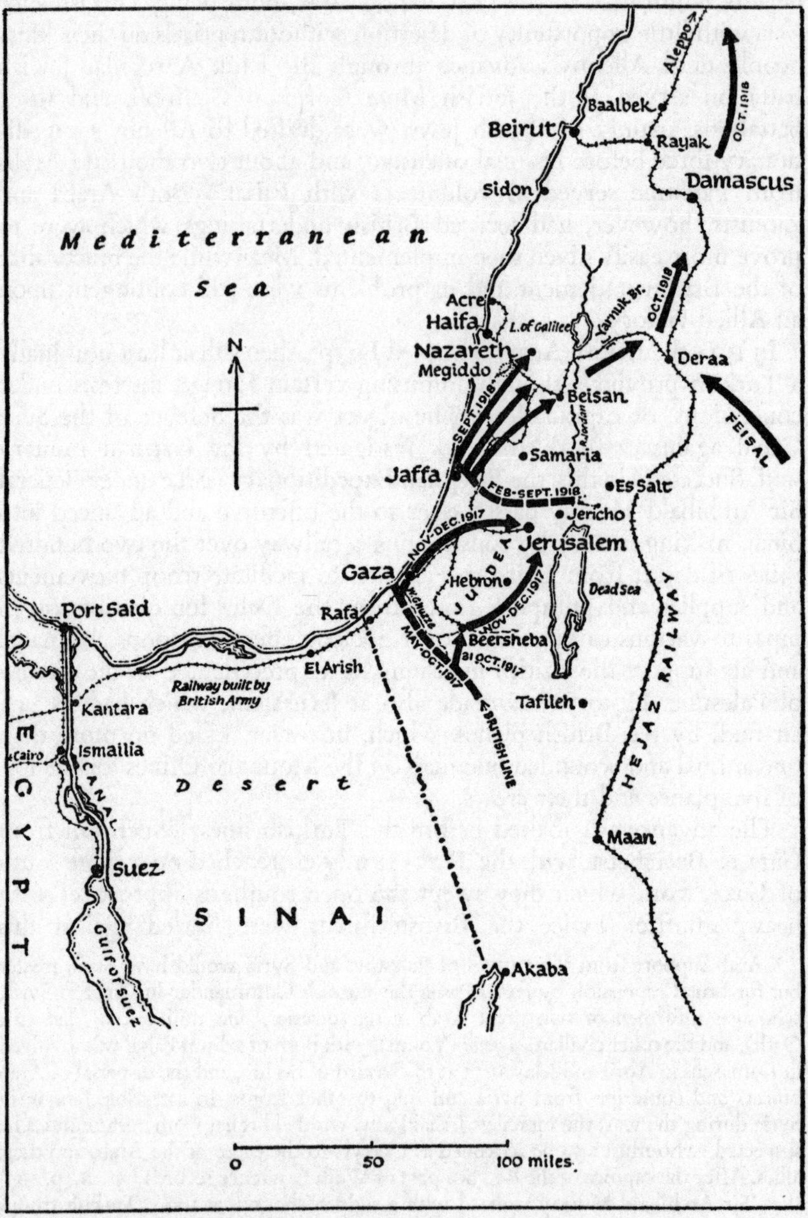

Fig. X. Allenby's Campaigns in Palestine 1917–18.

position and twice they recoiled with heavy losses. Then in 1917 General Sir Edmund Allenby took over the command with reinforcements, and, in a remarkable battle, while Allenby's left wing tied down the mass of the enemy by the bombardment of Gaza, his right wing some twenty-six miles to the east concentrated the main attack on Beersheba, deceiving the Turks by keen intelligence work into believing that this was another of several reconnaissances. By 31st October Beersheba had fallen, and with the flank turned the Turkish position at Gaza was untenable. By 7th November the third Battle of Gaza was won.[14]

Allenby advanced northwards by Majdal, Askalon and the Philistine plain. The Turkish Eighth Army, retreating from Gaza, fought stubborn rearguard actions. It had been Allenby's plan to strike westwards from Beersheba at the flank of the retreat, but the Turks and the German staff had expected an attack up the road from Beersheba to Hebron and Jerusalem and had rushed up reinforcements, which frustrated Allenby's design. Now a Turkish counter-offensive was launched by the Seventh Army from Jerusalem down the Wādī 'ś-Śanṭ, the historic Vale of Elah. Correctly gauging the strength of this counter-attack, Allenby countered it by his flank cover, which fought an action on 11th November near Tell aṣ-Ṣāfī (Blanchegarde of the Crusaders and possible Libnah of the Old Testament), where the Wādī 'ś-Śanṭ debouches on the Philistine plain. Two days later Allenby had captured the rail junction at Lydda, where the line from Jaffa to Haifa is joined by that from Jerusalem, and captured the village of Abū Shūsheh by the site of ancient Gezer, the key fortress on the trunk highway from Egypt to the north in the foothills of Judah, which a Pharaoh had once given as his daughter's dowry when she was married to Solomon.[15] Thus by his capture of the rail junction and Abū Shūsheh, which commanded the approaches to the hills about Jerusalem by the Wādī 'ṣ-Ṣurār (the Biblical Vale of Sorek) and the Wādī Salmān (the Vale of Aijalon and the Ascent of Beth-Ḥoron) Allenby drove a wedge between the Turkish Seventh Army based on Jerusalem and the Eighth Army, which stood now on a strong line north of Jaffa, north of the small but deep Auja River (the Yarkon of Scripture).

The latter was contained by two divisions while three others were directed up the passes, which Allenby now controlled, to the interior, with the major objective of cutting Turkish communications between Jerusalem and Nablus by seizing Ramallah near the highest point of Palestine's Great North Road along the ridge of the hills of the interior. Thus it was hoped that the Turks might be forced to evacuate Jerusalem, which Lloyd George had promised as a Christmas present to the

British people. The 75th Division from the south-west of England advanced up the road from Amwas through the narrow defile of Bāb al-Wād to Qiryat al-'Inab (Biblical Qiryath Jearim), by which the First Crusade had advance on Jerusalem, and like the Crusaders they advanced north-east from here near Nabī Samwīl ('the Prophet Samuel', the Miṣpah of I Samuel vii. 5 ff., which the Crusaders called Montjoie) about six miles north-west of Jerusalem, which they captured. Meanwhile the 52nd Scottish Lowland Division advanced up the Valley of Aijalon and the Wādī Salmān, but in the heavy rains (the 'former rains' of Scripture), which had now begun, the transport of anything but the lightest artillery over a route where the only vestige of a road was occasional patches of the old Roman road from Jerusalem to Antipatris and Caesarea was impossible and the advance of both divisions was halted before al-Jīb (Biblical Gibeon). Further north a Yeomanry Division had penetrated by Beth-Ḥoron the Lower and Upper by a track so bad that it was not adequately defended, and had reached a point only a mile short of the Nablus road. But their artillery also was inadequate and they were forced back to Beth-Ḥoron the Lower.

Meanwhile the enemy launched another counter-attack against the weak link in the British line between the advance force in the mountains and the force containing the Turkish Eighth Army on the Auja River. Like the counter-attack from Jerusalem down the Wādī 'ṣ-Šant it was technically well-conceived according to the rules of German military science, but failed through the weakness of Turkish resources.*

The three exhausted and depleted British divisions in the hills were relieved, and a fresh attack was concentrated on the last stretch of road from Jaffa to Jerusalem, which was commanded from the British position on the height of Nabī Samwīl, while a third fresh division came up from the direction of Bethlehem to which they had advanced from Beersheba and Hebron, covering the right flank of the main attack as Tancred and Baldwin du Bourg had done in the First Crusade (see above, p. 235). By the night of 8th December the western defences of Jerusalem had fallen to the 60th London Division, and on 9th

* There was apparently a conflict also between German purpose and Turkish morale at this moment so soon after the defeat at Gaza, the Turks being temperamentally stubborn defensive fighters behind prepared positions such as the line which they held north of the Auja, which Allenby would have found much harder to force had he not had such overwhelming numerical superiority, having already diffused Turkish resources by his feint towards the East. On the situation see Sir Archibald Wavell, *Allenby*, 1941, pp. 220–1, on which the following account of the Palestinian campaign is mainly based.

December the city was surrendered, the Turkish forces having withdrawn while the roads to Nablus and Jericho were still open. The last capture of the historic hill-fortress came as an anti-climax after its stirring history. A small party of civilians accompanied the Arab mayor of the city along the Jaffa road to the British lines. The mayor offered the keys of Jerusalem to the first troops he met—the staff of a field kitchen who had lost their way, who could not accept them. They were next offered to junior artillery officers, who in turn referred the ingenuous mayor to higher command. Finally General Shea, the commander of the 60th Division, accepted them on behalf of General Allenby.

Two days later Allenby officially entered Jerusalem reverently on foot by the Jaffa, or Hebron, Gate, and standing with his officers and representatives of the various religious communities in Jerusalem on the top of the steps before the Citadel, the site of Herod's palace-fort and of the palace of the Frankish Kings of Jerusalem, had his proclamation read to the people in English, French, Italian, Arabic and Hebrew:

> To the inhabitants of Jerusalem the Blessed and the people dwelling in the vicinity. The defeat inflicted upon the Turks by the troops under my command has resulted in the occupation of your city by my forces. I therefore here and now proclaim it to be under martial law, under which form of administration it will remain so long as military considerations make it necessary. However, lest any of you be alarmed because of your experience at the hands of the enemy who has retired, I hereby inform you that it is my desire that every person should pursue his lawful business without fear of interruption.
>
> Furthermore, since your city is regarded with affection by the adherents of three of the great religions of mankind, and its soil has been consecrated by the prayers and pilgrimages of multitudes of devout people of these three religions for many centuries, therefore do I make known to you that every sacred building, monument, holy spot, traditional shrine, endowment, pious bequest, or customary place of prayer, of whatsoever form of the three religions, will be maintained and protected according to the existing customs and beliefs of those to whose faiths they are sacred.

The Turks with three divisions endeavoured to recapture Jerusalem on 27th December, but were beaten back north and east of the city to a minimum distance of eight miles, When the heavy rains of winter were past Jericho was occupied. Probes along the ridge of the central highlands past Ramallah by Biblical Bethel towards Nablus and over the Jordan towards 'Ammān proved the strength of the Turkish resistance where the broken terrain fragmented the attack. With the withdrawal of troops to the Western Front in the crisis of the spring of 1918, this could not be broken. But if Allenby's two attempts to occupy the plateau about Ammān had failed, he was able to hold a line just north of Jericho and the bridge he had thrown over Jordan, and he succeeded in his objective of drawing a large proportion of the Turkish strength east of Jordan, with results which were to be fully apparent in the final phase of the Palestine campaign.

The summer of 1918 was spent in reorganization after the withdrawal of British units to the Western Front and the transfer to Allenby's army of Indian units. Towards the end of summer the German commander Liman von Sanders made an abortive effort to dislodge the Allied forces from their advance positions just north of Jericho. Allenby apparently decided to exploit the sensitivity of the enemy to the position on this front. Accordingly elaborate precautions were taken to hoax the enemy into believing that a massive offensive was being prepared in the Jordan Valley. But meanwhile with a secrecy which completely deceived the enemy Intelligence the major attack was mounted in the shelter of the orange groves north of Jaffa. The strategy was the same as that at Gaza in reverse, the feint now being on the British right and the main attack on the left.

The great offensive opened at dawn on 19th September in the vicinity of Arsūf, the scene of the victory of Richard Coeur de Lion over Ṣalāḥ ad-Dīn in the Third Crusade (see above, p. 255). The skilful concentration of men and artillery at the crucial point broke the Turkish lines and opened the way directly to the valley which leads from the coastal plain by Ṭūlkarm to Sebasṭiyeh (Samaria) and Nablus. Meanwhile, with a master-stroke of strategy which anticipated the daring sweeps of Hitler's mechanized divisions deep behind the enemy's lines in the Second World War,[16] Allenby threw his two cavalry divisions forward through the passes of Carmel and its south-easterly extension. Less than twenty-four hours after the opening of the offensive the 5th Division had penetrated the most northerly of the passes through the Carmel barrier to emerge on the great central plain by Tell Qaimūn (Biblical Jokneam), which was used by Napoleon in his march on Acre. A brigade dashed on to Nazareth in the foothills of Galilee north of the plain, which they reached at 4.30 in the morning, when the German Commander-in-Chief Liman von Sanders was still in bed quite oblivious of the disaster to the Turkish Eighth Army owing to a highly successful air raid on their headquarters at Ṭūlkarm on the eve of the battle. But the ready response of the natives to the approach of the British cavalry, which in the situation of Nazareth, straggling as it does high up the hillside, could not well be concealed, alerted the

German General, who escaped, it is said, in his pyjamas. Meanwhile the 4th Division had penetrated the historic pass of Megiddo to join up with the 5th Division to take Affūleh and Baysān respectively in the centre and east of the great central plain, here specifically the Biblical Plain of Jezreel, and both on the Damascus railway. They swept on to take the crossings of the Jordan, like the men of Ephraim after Gideon's rout of the Midianites, which took place just south-east of Affūleh.[17] The broken Eighth Army of the Turks was driven eastwards by Samaria and cut off by another cavalry division which had passed later through the pass of Megiddo to turn southward and take Jenīn on the Turkish line of retreat to the north. Two divisions working northwards through the hills towards Nablus under General Chetwode drove the Turkish Seventh Army before them, and when a link up with the victorious British Army Corps from the plain was imminent in Nablus the Turks were forced to seek a retreat through tortuous wadis in the barren hills sloping eastwards to the Jordan. The main escape line was down the Wadi Far'a, narrow and precipitous in its upper course, where the British Air Force did great damage, so much so that the Wādī Far'a was called Death Valley among British service men. So complete was the realization of Allenby's master-plan that, in the words of his biographer General Wavell, 'Only the boldest and most fortunate escaped the fall of Allenby's net'.[18] The most significant of these was Muṣṭafa Kemāl Pasha, the future Ataturk, who commanded the Seventh Turkish Army.

Meanwhile a force under General Chaytor advanced from north of Jericho to the Bridge at ad-Dāmiyeh (Biblical Adam[19] and penetrated by as-Salṭ to Ammān, which fell six days after the opening of the great offensive. Thus the considerable Turkish forces between Ammān and the Ḥejaz were cut off and their fate sealed. The British problem now was not to eliminate this force but to protect it from massacre by Arab tribesmen. Allenby's advance beyond Jordan south of the Sea of Galilee towards Deraa on the Damascus-Ḥejaz railway and over the Jordan north of the lake at Jisr Banāt Ya'qūb (the Bridge of the Daughters of Jacob), which now had Damascus as its objective, encountered only temporary resistance at that bridge and at Irbid south-east of the lake. Within a week of his great breakthrough Allenby had undisputed possession of the whole of Palestine.

The desert hinterland meanwhile was seething with hostile Bedouin spoiling for loot and slaughter but sparingly yet judiciously used by Faisal and Lawrence and their colleagues. With the capture of the railway junction of Deraa at the head of the Yarmuk on 28th September the retreat and the discomfiture of the Turks was complete. Damascus was occupied by the troops of Allenby and Faisal on 1st October, and the victorious army pressed on to occupy Aleppo before 31st October, when the armistice with Turkey was concluded.

So ended the Turkish domination of the Near East, which Lawrence describes, as 'a slow death'.[20] In Palestine new, vital forces were surging up to life: the Arabs uneasy under the strain to which Allied diplomacy had put their friendship, yet still trusting the pledged word of their victorious ally to King Ḥusain; the Zionists, fortified by the Balfour Declaration but more realistic, relying on no one but themselves, resolved to build up a community and material achievements to be seriously reckoned with, and above all determined to exploit the favourable political climate to the full while they might. In this last phase of the history of Palestine and of Jerusalem Great Britain had rashly committed herself to the role of midwife. The result was an abortion and a Caesarean birth.

NOTES FOR CHAPTER XI

1 This was conveyed in a letter from Luigi Malagamba, the secretary of Ahmad, to Sir Sidney Smith dated Acre, 1st March, 1799, *British Admiralty Records*, No. 19, cited by J. H. Rose, *Napoleonic Studies*, 1914, p. 358

2 An excellent appraisal of this movement, of the contribution of individuals, and of the stimulus of education promoted by Christian missions, and of the Turkish reaction is given in George Antonius, *The Arab Awakening*, 1938, pp. 35 ff.

3 *The Diaries of Theodor Herzl*, ed. M. Lowenthal, 1958, pp. 262 ff.

4 Chaim Weizmann, *Trial and Error*, 1949, pp. 161 ff.

5 Weizmann, *op. cit.*, pp. 74, 110–11

6 Antonius, *op. cit.*, p. 264, citing an entry of 13th March, 1915, from *Memories and Reflections* by the Earl of Oxford and Asquith, 1928, concerning a proposal by the British Jew Mr. Herbert Samuel that Great Britain should annexe Palestine and settle three or four million Jews in it, a proposal which had appealed to Mr. Lloyd George

7 Weizmann, *op. cit.*, pp. 161 ff.

8 *Ibidem*, p. 414

9 *Ibidem*, pp. 161 ff.

10 R. Storrs, *Orientations*, 1937, pp. 42. This was the development of certain overtures made personally to Lord Kitchener by Abdullah in 1914 before the war, when relations between the Turkish administration and Ḥusain were strained (*Memoirs of King Abdullah of Transjordan*, ed. P. P. Graves, 1950, pp. 112–13). These, however, concerned the possibility of British pressure on Turkey if the tension amounted to open rupture (*op. cit.*, p. 114)

11 T. E. Lawrence, *Seven Pillars of Wisdom*, 1936, pp. 275–6, 'Rumours of the fraud reached Arab ears from Turkey . . . not being a perfect fool, I could see that if we won the war the promises to the Arabs were dead

paper. . . . Had I been an honourable adviser I would have sent my men home, and not let them risk their lives for such stuff. Yet the Arab inspiration was our main tool in winning the Eastern war. So I assured them that England kept her word in letter and spirit. In this comfort they performed their fine things: but, of course, instead of being proud of what we did together, I was continually and bitterly ashamed.'

12 Cited by B. Gardner, *Allenby*, 1965, p. 141

13 Antonius (*op. cit.*, p. 268) gives a translation of the actual note, one of the many valuable contributions of this rich book, which is as vital to the study of this controversial question as the Arabic sources 'Imād ad-Dīn, Behā ad-Dīn, first-hand authorities and eye-witnesses, and Ibn al-'Athir, who transmits the personal information of Ṣalāḥ ad-Dīn's son, or Ibn al-Qalānisī, the Chancellor of Damascus at the time of the Second Crusade, which foundered at Damascus. Having personally discussed the events with Kings Ḥusain, Faisal and other leading figures, and with access to relevant articles in the Arabic press, Antonius has provided an excellent historical source, which is marked throughout by a critical use of his sources

14 The details of the intelligence hoax of the reconnaissance of Beersheba are told by R. Meinertzhagen (*Army Diary 1899–1926*, 1960, pp. 215 ff.), who was then Chief of Intelligence with Allenby at Gaza. He also tells of the dropping of propaganda leaflets and thousands of packets of cigarettes doped with opium, a plan of his of which Allenby knew but did not sanction. Meinertzhagen claims that the Turkish prisoners brought in for interrogation after the fall of Gaza were so far under the influence of the drug that many were inarticulate (*op. cit.*, pp. 223 ff.)

15 I Kings ix. 16

16 B. Gardner, *op. cit.*, p. 268

17 Judges vii

18 Wavell, *op. cit.*, p. 278

19 Joshua iii. 14

20 Lawrence, *op. cit.*, p. 44

XII

A CITY DIVIDED

Can two walk together except they be agreed? (*Amos* iii. 3)

The British Military Government in Jerusalem was soon to have a foretaste of the problems of administration under the dual commitments to Arab and Jew. As the majority in possession, the Arabs waited expectantly, though the anxiety roused by the shifts of British diplomacy in the Sykes-Picot Agreement and the Balfour Declaration was not quite allayed by subsequent oral assurances. Turkish domination had been peculiarly an Arab burden, and though the Arabs of Palestine had sent only two thousand men to fight in the army of Faisal, their leaders had been active British agents against the common enemy* and there had been Palestinian martyrs to the cause of freedom from the Turk in the long struggle from before the war. They were confident in the support of the solid mass of Arab opinion in the East, though, thanks to their victorious allies, this was not yet effective. The Jewish minority in Palestine, preoccupied with the problem of their still struggling colonies, were apathetic, having known the Ottoman Government as a friend rather than as an oppressor, But the practical and activist section of the Zionist Organization in Europe, now directed by Dr. Weizmann the architect of the Balfour Declaration, was determined to exploit its influence with senior ministers of His Majesty's Government while emotions engendered by the Balfour Declaration and the sense of personal obligation were still fresh in the British mind.

In 1918 under the British Military Government the Arabs received a rude shock, the first of many. The British Military Government was also shocked, for though it was the declared resolution of the Allies to undertake no political measures in occupied countries until military

* The 2,000 Palestinian volunteers were raised mainly by the activity of the future Muftī Ḥāj Amīn al-Ḥusainī. On the assessment of the Arab contribution to the war against the Turks see above p. 285, m.

government gave way to civil administration Dr. Weizmann was allowed to proceed to Palestine and expand Jewish activities and institutions in resolute pursuance of an avowedly political programme, in fact to organize a minority with a programme which in the limited area of Palestine could only result in economic and political domination. By 1920 General Sir Louis Bols, Chief Administrator for Palestine under the Military Government, found his authority virtually nullified by that of the Zionist Commission under Dr. Weizmann, and was forced to appeal for its removal. Actually the Military Government was abolished, and His Majesty's Government committed the supreme folly if not worse, of securing a Mandate for Palestine, where it had already committed itself to the support of one of two parties, which it had foisted on the little country* as an aggressive minority.

The appointment of Sir Herbert Samuel, a Jew and a Zionist, though a moderate and a just administrator, may have been dictated by sentiment, but, brutally tactless or artlessly honest, it certainly served notice of the official policy of Whitehall. This and the specific emphasis on Jewish interests in the terms of the Mandate in contrast to the merely general references to native Arab interests certainly left the Arabs in no doubt as to the policy of the new régime. Nor was such irresponsible commitment fair to the Jews, since it encouraged their most sanguine hopes, which were bound to be disappointed when the local administration first and eventually the British Government realized the practicalities of the situation.

Under the terms of the Mandate (Article IV) a Jewish Agency was provided as an assessor to the civil administration. An Arab Agency with similar advisory and consultative functions was also suggested, but was declined by Arab leaders in Palestine,† as all offers of representation were declined which involved the recognition of an official Jewish party committed to the aggressive Zionist programme and expanding economy‡ which combined to limit opportunities for the economy and labour of the Arab majority. Here there is no doubt that the Arabs committed a major political blunder, however justified they may have been on principle. With a deplorable lack of foresight beyond the immediate situation, they committed themselves to a political limbo and deprived themselves of effective representation, which was

* The settled land of Palestine, as apart from the desert or steppe-land south of Beersheba, is rather less than the area of Wales, and may be covered by car from east to west in two hours and from north to south, 'from Dan to Beersheba', in five hours.

† So the Royal (Peel) Commission in 1936–7 was boycotted until the eve of its departure, when the Arab case was stated in the last five days.

‡ Actually constituted in 1929.

all the more necessary in view of the shameful dissolution of Faisal's Arab State in Syria in 1920.* By contrast the history of the Jewish community in Palestine, largely apathetic at this time except for the political Zionists of Europe, was one of progressive political consolidation based on the status and activity of the Jewish Agency, which refused to be ignored.

Arab apprehension of Zionist aims encouraged by British official policy exploded in riots in 1921 in Jaffa and in attacks on various Jewish colonies, which, however, were not unavenged. Those riots, however, in spite of their apparently local significance and the fact that they were directed against the Jews, had a political as well as an economic significance, as was admitted generally by a Committee of Inquiry.[1] In fact they reflect ultimately the general Arab disappointment in the Mandatory power and its policy and the frustration of Arab aspirations which had been encouraged in the British undertaking to Ḥusain. They must be considered in the general context of the vain resistance to the French occupation of Damascus in 1920 and the Iraqi Revolt in the same year, which is known throughout the Arab East as 'the Year of Catastrophe' (*'ām an-nakba*). The immediate result was the limitation of Jewish immigration in accordance with 'the economic absorptive capacity of the country'. This, the implementation of the Balfour Declaration within the practical limits of Arab interests, was the pattern of the history of Palestine until the end of the Mandate in May 1948.

This period was marked by the refusal of the local Mandatory Administration and by the reluctance of even the British Government to implement the Balfour Declaration beyond the strict letter of the undertaking, notwithstanding the clamant demands of Zionism that it should mean exactly what the Zionists should make it mean. This reasonable policy, as well as being strictly correct, was indeed demanded

* A Syrian Arab Congress at Damascus in March 1920 had proclaimed Faisal constitutional King of Syria, Lebanon and Palestine. On 14th July France, who then occupied the Lebanon, which was all that the McMahon-Ḥusain correspondence and the Sykes-Picot Agreement visualized as a possible area of French influence, presented Faisal with an ultimatum and by 28th July had expelled him by force. Meanwhile 'Abdullāh, relying on the moral support of local Arab opinion, had come up to Ammān in Transjordan, and Winston Churchill, then Colonial Secretary, on his visit to the Near East and Jerusalem in March 1921, probably advised by T. E Lawrence, partially redeemed the situation by provisionally recognizing the authority of Abdullah in Transjordan and persuading him to advise Faisal to put himself forward as candidate for the throne of Iraq under British protection. This was the final settlement of Hashimite claims, which still left the Arabs in Palestine with insufficient constitutional support vis-á-vis Zionist demands under the British Mandate.

in the political and economic situation of the Arab majority in Palestine, now isolated from the rest of the Arab Levant as the result of the cruel frustration of Faisal's hopes of a greater Arab State in the Levant in 1920. From a moral imperative it became a political expediency with the prospect of the growth of Arab unity in Palestine and beyond. Meanwhile local protest against the Balfour Declaration was voiced by Muslim-Christian associations in Palestine, which through the Arab Congress in 1920 demanded an Arab government in Palestine and appointed an executive committee to represent the case of Arab Palestine in London. This *démarche* in 1921 was the first direct contact of Arab leaders with the British Government in the Palestinian question. Solidly supported by Arab sentiment throughout the Near East, the Arabs in Palestine could no longer be ignored as in the era of the Balfour Declaration. In the ultimate event the support of Arab arms and opinion was less effective than the British Government anticipated, and was unable to prevent the establishment of the State of Israel in Palestine.

The failure of the Arabs in Palestine was undoubtedly owing to their failure to speak and act with uniform emphasis to the British Government and to the local Administration and by their persistent refusal to be represented either in an Arab Agency or in an elected Legislative Council which would *de facto* admit Zionist pretensions in Palestine. The comparative Arab unanimity in the Muslim-Christian associations in the early days of the Mandate was soon disrupted by the rivalries of the two great Arab families in Jerusalem, the moderate Nashashībis and the nationalist Ḥusainis, from whom respectively the Administration appointed the Mayor and Muftī of Jerusalem, the latter the celebrated Ḥāj Amīn al-Ḥusainī. The former were amenable to British policy at a time when unanimous resistance was imperative and might possibly have been effective; Ḥāj Amīn as Muftī* of Jerusalem and President of the Supreme Muslim Council was intransigent and the effective leader of Arab armed resistance, but his effort was frustrated by family rivalry, and the net result of his activity was to bring British security forces into action and give the Jewish armed defence force, the Haggannah, a legal status within the Mandatory administration. With the suspension of Ḥāj Amīn at the height of the Arab Rising of 1936–9 and his flight to Syria, co-operative Arab resistance was at an end and, the energies and resources of the insurgents being diverted against moderate Arab

* *Muftī* is a Muslim jurisconsult, who gives a *fatwa*, or formal pronouncement on matters in the community involving canon law, which formerly governed Muslim communities, but is now limited to sacred matters and more intimate social relationships.

rivals, the main objective was never achieved. Ḥāj Amīn and his party were finally discredited with the British Government and the local Administration by his rapprochement with Germany during the Second World War, though to be sure the British record in Palestinian politics had established no claim on his allegiance.

In the uneasy days of the Mandate when Ḥāj Amīn was Muftī and President of the Supreme Muslim Council, Jerusalem was the nerve centre of Arab resistance. Divided within its medieval Turkish walls into Muslim, Christian, Armenian and Jewish Quarters, it had been little disturbed by the tempo of modern Zionism, the impact of which was felt particularly in the coastal plain and the great central plain of Jezreel, or Esdraelon, which stretches from the Mediterranean at Haifa to the Jordan. New Jewish quarters had sprung up outside the city walls, the Bukhāra quarter with its uninspiring tenement houses north-west of the old Damascus Gate and the adjacent ghetto of Mēa Sheārīm, colourful in its own sombre fashion and redolent of the anachronism of the Rabbinic piety of Eastern Europe. This ageing community, consisting largely of pious elders who had come to spend the evening of their days in holy study and meditation in Jerusalem, had, and still has, little sympathy with political Zionism and its aggressive methods, materialistic aims and defiance of cherished conventions, and to be sure Zionism wrote them off as dead weight. This community within and without the Old City, about their petty business or conning over their Hebrew Scriptures and Rabbinic commentaries and pouring out their prayers and lamentations by the Wailing Wall (see above, p. 192), were an institution—and rather a colourful one—of Jerusalem accepted by the Arabs both Muslim and Christian. Even they, however, were to taste the bitter fruits of Zionist ambition and the Arab reaction it provoked. In 1929 a minor incident by the Wailing Wall, the West Wall of Herod's Temple precinct and of the Muslim Sacred Precinct, culminated in a demonstration by Jewish youth, who unfurled the Zionist flag at the wall and sang the Zionist national anthem. This occasioned a wave of Arab violence, in which the old orthodox Jews of Jerusalem, Hebron and Ṣafad were the chief victims, the sporadic and ill-organized attacks on Jewish colonies being beaten off by Haggannah, the Jewish defence force, which was legalized after the riots of 1921.

In the first decades of the Mandate too a great new Jewish quarter spread north-west of the Old City and west of the Mēa Sheārīm and Bukhāra Quarters, and this with its southern extension in residential and administrative buildings towards the Plain of the Rephaim by the Railway Station is the modern Jewish part of the unhappily divided city, the Old City within the Turkish walls, until June 1967, being wholly Arab.

A conspicuous monument of Zionism which was founded at this time was the Hebrew university on Mount Scopus. The project of a Hebrew university had already been mooted at the First Zionist Congress in 1897, not only as a relief measure for young Jews subject to restrictions in universities in Eastern Europe, who were bound to go abroad, but also as the organ and instrument of the cultural and national revival. When Weizmann was in Palestine with the Zionist Commission in 1918 the foundation stone of the Hebrew university on Mount Scopus was laid in July 1918 in the presence of General Allenby and his staff and other prominent persons among the Allies and, significantly at that time, of Muslim, Christian and Jewish notables of Jerusalem. The institution was opened on 1st April, 1925, Lord Balfour presiding. It was already a progressive institution by the end of the Mandate, but, isolated in the Arab-Jewish war of 1947–8, it stands today with the Jewish Hadassah Hospital forlorn on Mount Scopus, its wonderful library, on which the writer has largely drawn in his bibliography, being gradually evacuated by a monthly convoy of the United Nations Organization to the new University Library in the Jewish half of the city. Meanwhile a much more spacious and modern university has been built on the hill dominating the Plain of the Rephaim from the north-west, which is much more adequate to accommodate the large influx of students and scholars since the inauguration of the state of Israel in 1948.

The final phase of the history of Palestine under the British Mandate may be said to be inaugurated by the report of the Royal (Peel) Commission issued in 1937. This was sufficiently realistic to admit that the nationalist feeling of the Arabs and the apparently insatiable ambitions of the Jews, now augmented by refugees from Nazi persecution in Germany to the extent of over 30,000 in 1933, over 40,000 in 1934, over 60,000 in 1935, and over 29,000 in 1936, were irreconcilable within the framework of the Mandate. Partition was accordingly advised, confirming the Jews in possession of those parts of the country they already occupied or had acquired in the coastal plain and Galilee with an international zone from Jaffa to Jerusalem and Bethlehem. This partition was palatable to neither party. It did not satisfy the ambitions of Zionism or sufficiently provide for the refugees from Europe. Moreover, though it allotted to the Jews what they already occupied or had acquired, there was bound to be large-scale eviction of Arab peasants. In assessing the situation in fact the Royal Commission failed to realize that for the majority of the Arab peasants and labouring classes the question was no longer that of nationalist aspiration but of bare survival. The rebels of the great revolt of 1936–9 were not the dupes of political opportunists but a peasant people fighting desperately and enduring great privations for their very existence in the land which was their whole world. How substantial their fears then were is evidenced by the destitution of the half-million refugees from the land now Israel.[1]* In the event the Jews were able in 1948 to annexe in addition the whole region south and west of the mountains of Judah to the Gulf of Aqaba and the south part of the coastal plain with the exception of a strip to just north of Gaza and were able to drive a wedge through to Jerusalem. Here, however, they were halted by the Arab Legion, who held the Old City within its Turkish wall, the open country to the north and north-west and Bethlehem six miles to the south-west. This, however, anticipates the final settlement.

The duration of World War II was a calm before the final storm in Palestine, though for Zionism there was neither relaxation nor compromise. With the war impending, a concession was made to the Arabs by a Government declaration of policy in the White Paper of 1939, which limited Jewish immigration to 75,000 over five years, by which time the Jews should number one third of the population of Palestine. Thereafter further immigration was to be subject to the consent of the Arab majority. Land sales, moreover, were to be restricted. This was a long-standing Arab grievance, justified according to the letter of the law, but a current abuse.† The Jewish occupation of Palestine, it must be remembered, was at this time not a patent usurpation. They had bought the land they occupied, much of it, especially in the coastal

* The situation has, of course, intensified at least twofold since the Six Days' War of June 1967.

†The Report of the King-Crane Commission of 28th August, 1919 notices this in finding that 'To subject a people so minded (against the Zionist programme) to unlimited Jewish immigration, and to steady financial and social pressure to surrender the land, would be a gross violation of the principle just quoted, and of the people's rights, though it kept within the forms of the law'. 'The principle just quoted' is Wilson's principle laid down in his famous address of 4th July, 1918 as one of the four great ends for which the Allies were fighting: 'The settlement of every question, whether of territory, of sovereignty, of economic arrangement, or of political relationship upon the basis of the free acceptance of that settlement by the people immediately concerned, and not upon the basis of the material interest or advantage of any other nation or people which may desire a different settlement for the sake of its own exterior influence or mastery.' The Commission represented by H. C. King and C. R. Crane of America is the truncation of a Commission on which Britain, France, Italy and America agreed to be represented, in March 1919, but from which Britain, France and Italy resiled. The Report was issued in the *Editor and Publisher*, New York, 2nd December, 1922.

plain, neglected and ill-drained, having realized its potential only after the intensive application of Jewish finance, science and above all hard labour. They had, as Weizmann states, covered the soil of Palestine with gold.[2] The injustice was that they bought from landlords, generally absentees, and then relentlessly evicted the Arab peasantry. Though the responsibility for this abuse and its prevention lay undoubtedly with the landlords—often Arabs, but mostly selfish and detached Levantines living the high life in Beirut, Cairo, or in fashionable Mediterranean resorts—the local peasantry had to be protected by this restriction for their own sakes and for the economic and social good of the Arab community in general, for which the Mandatory was responsible. With wholesale massacres of Jews in Europe as the Nazi occupation progressed, the Jews bitterly resented restriction in immigration and land sales; the Arabs, relieved of the apprehension of unlimited Jewish influx, laid down their arms and refrained from embarrassing the Mandatory Power in its major war effort, though the nationalist leader the Muftī Ḥāj Amīn al-Ḥusainī, suspended during the revolt of 1936–9, became a German agent.

In a case involving on the one hand racial persecution and actual genocide on a scale the world had never witnessed and on the other the dispossession of the mute victims of political expediency and diplomatic chicanery, unprincipled speculation and the aggressive use of capital, one can hardly be dispassionate. Much has been written about the 'coffin ships', almost unseaworthy Levantine vessels from the Black Sea ports crammed with Jews fleeing in desperation from the Nazi gas-chambers, and intercepted by the British Navy and Police within sight of the Promised Land and the National Home. The Arab reply was that it was asking too much of the Muslims in Palestine to expiate the crimes of Christendom at the expense of their own homes and livelihood—which for at least half a million Arabs of Palestine is what has actually happened. Actually these 'coffin ships' were derelicts deliberately acquired so as to be expendable on the desolate parts of the coast of Palestine. Nor was the British Government reluctant to provide shelter for these refugees. Only, with the solution of the acute Palestinian problem pending, the home must needs be temporarily elsewhere. Refugee clearance camps were set up in Cyprus, and temporary settlement, not an unpleasant alternative to the gas-chamber, one might reasonably think, was offered. But the Jews were intransigent. The mood of Zionism was illustrated by the incident of the *Patria*, a large *Messageries Maritimes* liner detained in Haifa harbour. A complement of illegal immigrants had been put on board to be settled temporarily in Mauritius, but the Zionists defied the Government and blew the vessel up in the harbour with heavy loss of life owing to a technical miscalculation.*

The policy of the White Paper might have been the basis of a settlement of the Palestine problem after the embarrassment of the war was past but for two factors, namely extreme elements which now became more effective in Israel, and official pressure from America. The bulk of the Zionist community was from Eastern Europe, a particularist community, whom persecution and intense loyalty to their ancestral faith, both in principles and externals, had made congenitally xenophobic, alien both as Jews and Eastern Europeans, not understood by the British administration or by the Arabs nor at pains to make a rapprochement possible. Superstitiously devoted to Palestine as their rightful home, blandly ignoring the passage of History, they arrogantly regarded the British Government and Administration as the mere Gentile agents of Jewish rehabilitation, to be ignored as soon as they had served their turn. Having chosen to put their own interpretation on the Balfour Declaration, they felt an unreasonable resentment that their wildest hopes would not be gratified, and, already feeling their strength in the land, resorted to violence and terrorism against Arabs and British Administration alike. The dastardly activities of *Irgūn Zwai Leūmī* and the notorious Stern Gang were strangely out of accord with Jewish tradition, though in what the Jews felt as the supreme crisis it is difficult to gauge the measure of general Zionist sympathy or disapproval. What is certain, however, is that after 1944 *haggannāh*, the legal Jewish defence force, if not overtly admitting the same methods as the extremist organizations, were equally an embarrassment to the Administration and achieved similar results.

Once again the Arabs in Palestine were to be sacrificed to alien interests. Already after World War I the interests of France had driven Faisal from Damascus and frustrated the hope of an Arab state embracing Syria and Palestine under an enlightened and tolerant Arab king, who had already reached an understanding with the Zionist leader Weizmann. Now on the eve of the expiry of the five-year period prescribed by the White Paper of 1939 American concern for the vote of 4,000,000 Jews in the Eastern states who would tip the

* The design was to explode two bombs simultaneously in the hull on either side of the keel so that the vessel would sink on her keel in the mud of the harbour. One bomb only exploded and the ship heeled over and sank in a few minutes. In contrast to the general *sauve qui peut* two British policemen, British Constables Wilson and Rutland, on board, continued rescue operations until it was too late to escape. These are but two of the British administration in Palestine who gave their lives in dedication to duty during the Mandate.

balance in the Presidential election forced the rescindment of the undertaking of the British Government in the White Paper, though to be sure British opinion in the Commons was divided on this question.

By the time that America had entered the war in 1942 local Jewish opinion in the United States, under pressure of anti-Semitic atrocities in Nazi-occupied Europe, was converted to Zionism and indeed to the conception of an independent Jewish state in Palestine, which found expression in a programme defined by an important conference of an American Emergency Committee for Zionist affairs held at the Biltmore Hotel in New York. From that time Zionist propaganda, sensing the economic and political influence of America in the future settlement of the Near East, was active in all strata of American society, with the more effective approach of Dr. Weizmann to American statesmen at the highest level on the lines of his plan of campaign in England before the First World War and subsequently. Meanwhile, in view of the oil assets of the Near East, American policy was cautious while it had as yet not gauged the political potential of the Arab states. Nevertheless an Anglo-American Commission of Inquiry in 1946 did suggest the rescindment of the White Paper of 1939 and proposed the immediate admission of 100,000 Jewish refugees with further immigration 'under suitable conditions' and the suspension of the restriction on land sales. The only concession to the Arabs was the suggestion that the bar on the employment of non-Jewish labour in undertakings financed by the Jewish national fund should be made illegal, a concession which, even if it were accepted, was more likely to be formal than effective. In its concern about illegal armed organizations and its appeal to the Jewish Agency to co-operate with the Administration in the control of immigration and the suppression of terrorism the Commission revealed its sensitivity to the policy and potential of the now powerful and well-organized Jewish community, which under the leadership of David Ben Gurion and the all-powerful Labour Federation was prepared to wrest by violence what they could not get by negotiation. The British members of the Commission appreciated through experience the difficulty of implementing the recommendations on immigration and land sales without the guarantee of security under the joint responsibility of America and the essential condition of disbanding the Zionist armed organizations. The proposals satisfied neither Jews nor Arabs, and President Truman was not sufficiently realistic to share responsibility for the implementation of the suggestions. American policy was tantalizingly non-committal until 1948, which in the circumstances encouraged trouble in Palestine. The influence of determined Zionist propaganda on the still inexperienced President, however, finally secured the recognition—the first by any foreign power—of Israel's declaration of independence on 14th May, 1948.

As after the First World War now after the Second the fate of Palestine was settled from abroad over the heads of the majority of the inhabitants of the land and their natural confederates in the neighbouring Arab states. In 1947 Great Britain had declared the intention of renouncing further responsibility for the Mandate after 1948, and had referred the problem to a special committee of the United Nations. It was the resolution of the United Nations Assembly after the recommendation of this committee which recognized an Arab and a Jewish state, which in general became effective as the final settlement. The partition of Palestine recommended was very generous to the Jews in that it assigned them the coastal plain from Akka to south of Jaffa, Eastern Galilee and practically the whole of the land south and west of Beersheba except a strip from the Egyptian border to north of Gaza. Under this arrangement Jerusalem was to be an international zone. It is significant that the members of the United Nations Assembly most involved in this settlement, the Arab states, solidly opposed the resolution. This was accepted by the Jews as the basis of the State of Israel, though both Jews and Arabs armed for a final showdown, which the Mandatory Administration, already the target of Jewish terrorism, and perhaps feeling a guilty conscience for the problem with which inconsiderate British generosity to Zionism had burdened the Arabs, did nothing to arrest.

The final round in the struggle for Palestine was war between Jews and Arabs. Early in 1948 the Mandatory Administration prepared to withdraw, leaving security measures in the respective districts occupied by each people to be undertaken by such armed forces and police as each could provide. Arab volunteers from Palestine, Syria and Transjordan numbering about 4,000 concentrated in the central highlands near Nablus under the command of Fawzī al-Kawakjī, who had led the Arab Revolt of 1936–9. Other concentrations were in the coastal plain based on Jaffa and Gaza and in the hills about Jerusalem under the leadership of personalities of the Ḥusainī family. This force was the 'Army of Deliverance', put into the field on the decision of the Arab League to counterbalance the Jewish armed forces already organized in Palestine in readiness for hostilities when the British forces withdrew. The plan was sound, but foundered through lack of organization and the overconfidence of the Arab leaders. The Jewish forces consisted of *haggannāh*, the Jewish militia which had come into being to protect the settlements against Arab attack, *Irgūn Zwai Leumī*, an illegal extremist military organization which had come into being in the Arab

Rising of 1936–9 and was committed to acts of reprisal, and the Stern Gang, which was still more extreme. The last group was an offshoot of *Irgūn Zwai Leumī* in protest against this organization's renunciation of anti-British violence during the war. The latter two groups were thus experts in strategic terrorism, and all their members and those of *haggannāh* were well organized and disciplined. They had moreover taken the measure of the local opposition psychologically as well as physically and had a unity which the Arabs never knew. They had moreover excellent modern weapons, though in limited quantities.

Fawzī, the commander of the 'Army of Deliverance', whose authority was based on his nuisance value as a guerilla leader in the Arab Rising, the success of which had been grossly exaggerated in the Arab press, was rash and irresponsible in a political and military juncture so significant as the present. It was one thing to direct guerilla raids to embarrass the too tolerant Mandatory power and to terrorize Arab moderates; it was quite another to organize a national offensive against a determined and well-organized enemy, who were fighting literally for their very lives. In a country like Palestine, except where an offensive has been undertaken with overwhelming odds, the party on the defensive, where skilled in guerilla warfare, has ample opportunity to counter the moves of the enemy, as Judas Maccabaeus and his men had shown. Now Fawzī's rash attacks without adequate organization of subsidiary services simply exposed his forces as a target for the counter-attacks of a cooler and much more intelligent enemy, which actually had the advantage of internal lines and much more concentrated resources.

The ineptitude of Fawzī was exposed in his first attack on the Jews in the great central plain first at the Jewish colony of Tirat Zwi just south of Bethshan and notably at Mishmar hā'emeq on the south-west edge of the great central plain near Megiddo. Here Fawzī made a bold frontal attack, which failed to make any impression on the strong Jewish defences. But Fawzī had cavalierly neglected his rear, and Jews from the neighbouring settlements fetched a compass round the hills and heavy fire from the rear forced Fawzī to withdraw. The fact that he succeeded in saving his guns, however, was sufficient pretext to the Arab press to claim a victory and encourage Fawzī's fatuous self-delusion. The eventual realization of the failure of the Army of Deliverance in spite of the wishful thinking of the Arab press demoralized the Arabs in Palestine, and injected a fatal hesitancy into the forces of the neighbouring Arab states, most of whom kept a respectful distance from the Jews.

In this ignoble conflict the relief of the Jewish community in Jerusalem and the firmness of the Transjordan Arab Legion are alone worthy of record.

Quite apart from the sentimental significance of Jerusalem in the State of Israel there was already a large Jewish community there, and in fact the city contained a larger cross-section of Jewish life than anywhere else in Palestine. Besides the old orthodox Jews in their south-east quarter of the Old City in the shadow of the Wailing Wall and in the orthodox quarters of the Mēa Sheārīm and the Bukhāra quarters north-west of the Damascus Gate, a large modern open town had developed north-west of the Jaffa, or Hebron, Gate, which was the business quarter of the new city. This was a Jewish enclave so isolated from the colonies in the coastal plain that no partition scheme had ever visualized the city as anything but an international zone. Now with all its traditional meaning for Judaism, Christianity and Islam Jerusalem became a focal point. Though it was the headquarters of the Mandatory Administration and the security forces the city was torn by Arab-Jewish conflicts even before the expiry of the Mandate on 15th May, 1948. The situation was complicated by the fact that there were Jews in their quarter of the Old City held by the Arabs and Arabs inconveniently near the new city, which was held by the Jews, as for instance the village of Deir Yassīn on the outskirts of the new Jewish quarter, where the villagers, a poor sort of Arab peasantry, who had hawked their produce in the new city, were massacred to the youngest child by *Irgūn Zwai Leumī* as an important action in the psychological war against the Arabs, which was but too effective.

In preparation for the war after the withdrawal of the Mandatory Administration and security forces the Arab strategy was to cut communications between the principle towns Tel Aviv, Jerusalem and Haifa and the Jewish settlements in the great central plain. To this end the approaches to Jerusalem through the ravines in the western mountain rampart were occupied, but Jewish initiative and persistence first constructed a new road to by-pass the main point of obstruction where the road climbed through the first defile at Bāb al-Wād, and then fiercely contested strategic heights. The fight raged on historic ground. The by-pass road, called by the Jews 'the Road of Courage', passed south of Gezer and joined the old highway between Jerusalem and Jaffa just north of Bethshemesh, passing between Eshtaol and Ṣorah the home of Samson. At Abū Ghōsh, also called Qiryath al-'Inab near Qiryath-Jearim, the Arab villagers, long in Zionist confidence, offered no resistance, and the key to Jerusalem was Qaṣṭal with its ruined Crusader fort on the high ground between the Vale of Sorek and its tributary which winds past Abū Ghōsh. This position was finally forced and the advancing Jewish forces soon linked up with the Jews in the new north-west suburb of Jerusalem and the city was relieved. The Arab Legion, thrown on the defensive by the refusal of the Egyptian forces a few miles south of Jerusalem to engage the Jews, held the Old City behind the Turkish Wall with the hills northwards to Jenīn on the edge of the great central plain and southwards to twelve miles beyond Hebron.

The support from the neighbouring Arab states Egypt, Iraq, Syria and the Lebanon had had no more than a token value, the contribution of the Arab Legion from Transjordan being a notable exception. A co-ordinated plan of attack failed to materialize, and the ports of Haifa and Akka were allowed to fall into Jewish hands, while Jaffa was overwhelmed and sacked without the Egyptian army being able to approach it. Only the Arab Legion five thousand strong matched the discipline and efficiency of the Jewish armed forces, who numbered some 15,000 representing 600,000 fighting desperately for their existence. The territory of the State of Israel, dearly bought and developed by Jewish labour, within the limits determined by the United Nations Assembly was held and augmented by the whole of Galilee north of Akka, substantially more of the coastal plain down to Askalon and the whole of the Negeb, or Southern Steppe, from twelve miles south of Hebron, including Beersheba, to the north-west extremity of the Gulf of Aqaba, where Israel has built the town of Elath from the desert as an oil-port, now connected with Beersheba by pipe-line. An important salient was driven into Jerusalem, to which the Jews secured access by the railway running precariously near the armistice line as established in the spring of 1949 past Battīr, where the Jews made their last stand against Rome in their last revolt in A.D. 135. If the old Turkish city of Jerusalem with the site of the Temple and the derelict city of David south of the Turkish wall were denied to the Jews by the courage of the Arab Legion, the new town was theirs, and their Parliament, lawcourts, great synagogue and university were still in Jerusalem.

The nucleus of the neighbouring Arab state, the Hashimite Kingdom of Jordan, is the former Amirate of Abdullah, the second son of King Ḥusain of the Ḥejaz, in Transjordan. This region east of Jordan and the Dead Sea to the Eastern steppe with its administrative centre at Ammān had been the eastern region of Occupied Enemy Territory after the capitulation of Turkey in the First World War, and in 1920 after the expulsion of Faisal the brother of Abdullah from Damascus as a sacrifice to French ambitions in the Levant it had been included with Palestine in the British Mandate, but under the separate administration of the Amīr Abdullah with advisers from local tribal sheikhs and British officers. This arrangement was subsequently modified and stabilized by treaty in 1928, whereby the Amīr Abdullah's independent rule of Transjordan was recognized, with a British Resident as assessor and British advisors in the Arab Government. Air bases were provided for the R.A.F., and the Transjordan Frontier Force was locally raised under British command, like the Arab Legion. In Palestine the Amīr recognized British commitments, particularly the establishment of the National Home for the Jews according to the Balfour Declaration. Here it will be recognized that he followed the policy to which his brother Faisal had already committed himself.

Limited in the north by the French occupation of Syria after the expulsion of Faisal from Damascus and on the south by the natural barrier of the deserts and the power of Ibn Saud, Abdullah was naturally involved in the politics of Palestine. Here through his commitment to British Mandatory policy he supported the moderate party under the Nashashībī family. This political alignment, with the suspicion of his personal ambitions in a Palestine where a large and possibly autonomous Jewish community would modify the power of the nationalists under the Ḥusainī family, made Abdullah generally unpopular in Palestine, and eventually on Friday, 20th June, 1951, after the frustration of the Arab defeat in 1948, cost him his life at the hands of an assassin at the door of the Aqṣa Mosque in Jerusalem as he went to his weekly devotions.

Abdullah's career was marked by a steady allegiance to Great Britain even in the darkest days of World War II, which was concretely expressed by his support with the mobile and very efficient Arab Legion under British command against Vichy forces in Syria and in Rashīd Alī's revolt in Iraq in 1941. With the prospect of the end of French power in Syria Abdullah might reasonably have anticipated the eventual realization of an Arab state, which had eluded Faisal in 1920, which might even be the nucleus of an effective confederacy of Arab states.* By this time, however, local nationalist feeling among the Arabs was too strong for such ambitions to be realized. This was made plain by the reaction to Abdullah's proposal at the end of the French Mandate for Syria and the Lebanon in 1945 for a United Syria including Syria, Lebanon, Transjordan and Palestine, the chief antagonist of which was Saudi Arabia. The British Government, however, saw in it the seed not of Arab unity, but of the reverse, and it was not realized. In view of the urgency of the Jewish problem in Arab politics the

* This was certainly visualized by King Abdullah in his instructions to the Transjordan delegates to the conferences of Arab Union in Cairo in 1943 and 1945 (*Memoirs of King Abdullah of Transjordan*, 1950, pp. 254–5).

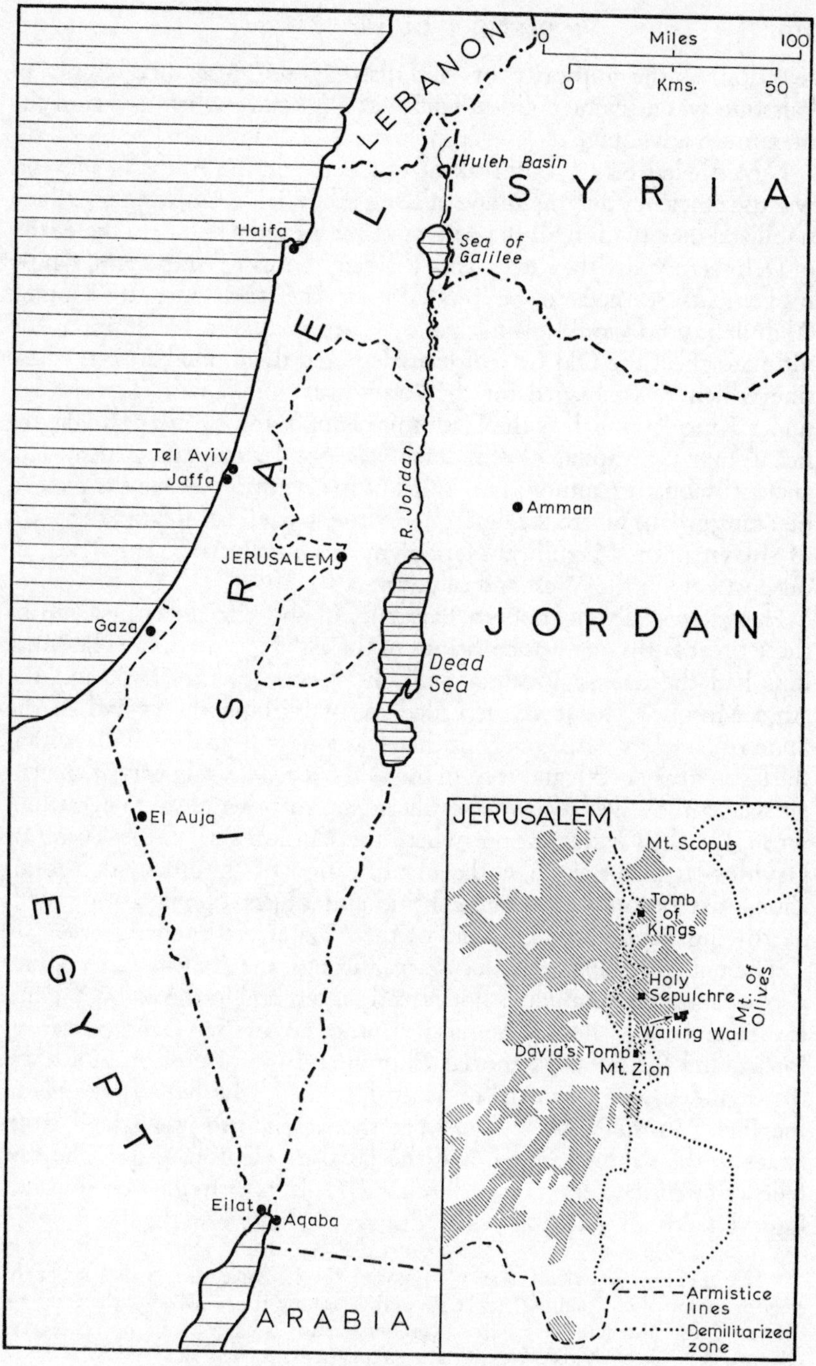

PALESTINE AT THE ARMISTICE, 1948. (*T. R. Allen*)

rejection of the authority of Abdullah by the Arab neighbours of Palestine was a major political failure at a juncture when it was of the maximum advantage to Jewish morale.

Nevertheless on the outbreak of war between the Arabs and Jews it was the efficiency and discipline of King Abdullah's Arab Legion which stabilized the situation for the Arabs in 1948 after the failure of the Army of Deliverance and the forces from the neighbouring Arab states, whose movements seemed to be retarded by the reluctance to support Abdullah, who would plainly gain by any success in Palestine. In the ultimate effect the Old City of Jerusalem and the limited area of Palestine which was salvaged for the Arabs was united with Transjordan under King Abdullah as the Hashimite Kingdom of Jordan. It is significant that the capital of this state was not Jerusalem but Ammān, ancient Rabbath Ammon, the capital of the Ammonites, on the plateau of Transjordan, where the desert meets the sown land. Behind the walls of Sulaymān the Magnificent Jerusalem was not an Arab capital, but an outpost held in the West and of course a sanctuary.

Here, especially in modern Palestine, in this ancient city sacred to three great faiths one was conscious of the unhappy division. The Muslims had the Sacred Precinct with the Dome of the Rock and the Aqṣa Mosque. The Jews succeeded in establishing the capital of the State of Israel in Jerusalem, but that was a new Jerusalem built within the last century north and west of the Old City. The only part of ancient Jerusalem they held was the southern summit of the south-west hill, wrongly called Mount Zion, where the Muslim shrine, the Tomb of David*—as unauthentic as the identification of the hill with Mount Zion—has become a national shrine and object of pilgrimage with harrowing memorials and relics of the Nazi atrocities in Europe.

The unhappy division of Jerusalem through the Arab-Jewish conflict also separated communities not directly interested in the conflict. Thus for instance the noble Anglican Cathedral of St. George was in Jordan and the Scots Memorial Church and Hospice of St. Andrews, the dignified war memorial to Scottish soldiers who fell in Palestine in the First World War, looked over the derelict no-man's-land from Israel to the south-west hill and the Jaffa, or Hebron, Gate. The free fellowship of scholars was also hindered. Objects from the rich archaeological fields of Palestine were distributed between the Rockefeller

* This tradition apparently does not antedate the Crusades, and at the end of the twelfth century Benjamin of Tudela, though indicating the tradition of the tomb on 'Mount Zion' also indicates some uncertainty as to its exact location. The earlier pilgrims Antoninus Martyr (*c.* 570) and Arculf (*c.* 670) attest the reputed tomb of David in a church dedicated to him just north of Bethlehem.

Museum in Jordan and new museums in Israel, while the various learned institutions were similarly separated. The Monastery of St. Stephen with its world-famous *École Biblique*, the home of the learned Dominicans, whom Sir Ronald Storrs called justly 'the intellectual aristocracy of Jerusalem', and the German Archaeological Institute were in Jordan, while the progressive Jesuit Pontifical Biblical Institute and the tremendous intellectual power-house of the Hebrew university were isolated in the Jewish part of the city. There are more tragic divisions of families and homes, and many a poor Arab could actually look over the frontier to the home of which he was dispossessed or to places where he had once met Jewish neighbours in friendly social intercourse. And once a year at Christmas time frontier control was relaxed and Christian pilgrims and the victims of the tragic division could pass freely over to family reunions or to their devotions in the old Byzantine church above the manger of the Holy Child at Bethlehem.

NOTES FOR CHAPTER XII

1 Text cited by Nevill Barbour, *Nisi Dominus*, 1946, p. 100

2 Weizmann, *Trial and Error*, p. 316

Appendix I

CHRONOLOGICAL TABLE

B.C.	
c. 2000	First traces of Amorite occupation in Jerusalem
c. 1850	Jerusalem first named in Egyptian Execration Texts
c. 1400	Jerusalem an Egyptian fief under Abdi-Khipa
c. 1220	Jerusalem isolated in the settlement of Judah and Benjamin
c. 1000	Jerusalem captured by David's men and occupied as 'the city of David', the capital of the Kingdom of Israel
931	The disruption of Solomon's kingdom, thereafter the Kingdoms of Judah and Israel
722	The end of the Kingdom of Israel
622	The reformation of King Josiah in Judah
612	The fall of Nineveh and the end of the Assyrian Empire
612–539	The Neo-Babylonian (Chaldaean) Empire
597	The fall of Jerusalem and the first deportation of Jews to Babylon including King Jehoiachin
586	The destruction of Jerusalem and the Temple, the end of the Kingdom of Judah and the great deportation to Babylon (the Exile)
539	Cyrus the Great captures Babylon
539–333	The Persian Empire in Western Asia
520–516	The rebuilding of the Temple in Jerusalem
445–434	Nehemiah's first term of office as Governor of Judah
397	Ezra's arrival and reform in Jerusalem
c. 335	Schism between the Jews and Samaritans final
333	Alexander the Great defeats Darius III of Persia at the Battle of Issus and the beginning of the Hellenistic period in Western Asia
312	The Battle of Gaza and the beginning of domination of Palestine by the Ptolemies of Egypt
198	The Battle of Paneas and the beginning of the Greek domination of Palestine by the Seleucids of Syria till 128 B.C.

164	Rededication of the Temple under Judas Maccabaeus after its desecration under Antiochus IV (Epiphanes) in 168 B.C.
63	Pompey's settlement of the Near East
A.D.	
63 B.C.–A.D. 636	Roman, later Byzantine, domination of the Near East
20 B.C.–A.D. 64	The Temple rebuilt
66–70	First Great Jewish Revolt
70	Destruction of Temple
132–135	Revolt of bar Kokhba
135	Rebuilding of Jerusalem as Aelia Capitolina
325–335	Building of the Church of the Anastasis (Resurrection), called also the Church of the Holy Sepulchre
614	Sack of Jerusalem by the Persians
630	Restoration of the Cross by the Emperor Heraclius
632	Death of Muḥammad
632–634	The Caliphate of Abū Bakr
634–644	The Caliphate of ʿUmar ibn al-Khaṭṭāb
634	The Muslim victory at Ajnādain
636	The Muslim victory at the Yarmuk
638	The capitulation of Jerusalem to the Caliph ʿUmar
636–1099	The Muslim domination of Palestine
644–656	The Caliphate of ʿUthman
656–661	The Caliphate of ʿAlī
661–750	The Umayyad Caliphate in Damascus
683–692	The Caliphate of ʿAbdu 'l-Mālik, the builder of the Dome of the Rock
705–715	The Caliphate of al-Walīd, the builder of the Aqṣā Mosque
750–1258	The Abbasid Caliphate in Baghdad
785–809	The Caliphate of Hārun ar-Rashid, correspondent of Charlemagne, to whom he made concessions in Jerusalem
963–969	Emperor Nicephorus Phocas, who took the offensive in Palestine
969–976	Emperor John Zimisces, who took the offensive in Palestine
909–1171	The Fāṭimid Caliphate in Egypt
996–1020	The Fāṭimid Caliph al-Ḥākim, under whom the Holy Sepulchre was destroyed
1037	The Church of the Holy Sepulchre rebuilt
1099	The capture of Jerusalem in the First Crusade
1099–1187	Jerusalem the effective capital of the Latin Kingdom
1187	The decisive victory of Ṣalāḥ ad-Dīn at Qurn Ḥaṭṭīn
1191	The capture of Acre in the Third Crusade
1261–1520	The Mamlūk Dynasties in Egypt
1260	The defeat of the Tartars of Hulagu by the Mamlūk Sultan Quṭuz and Frankish allies at ʿAin Jālūṭ

1291	Fall of Acre to the Mamlūk Sultan Qalāwun
1517	Turkish victory over the Mamlūks
1517–1918	The Turkish period in the history of Palestine
1887	First Zionist Congress
1915, 1916	Execution of Arab patriots in Beirūt and Damascus
1915–16	McMahon Correspondence
May, 1916	Sykes-Picot Agreement
June, 1916	Outbreak of Arab Revolt
2nd Nov., 1917	Balfour Declaration
7th Nov., 1917	Allenby's victory at Gaza
9th Dec., 1917	Capitulation of Jerusalem
19th Sept., 1918	Battle of the Auja River
July, 1918	A Zionist Commission in Palestine. Foundation stone of the Hebrew University on Mt. Scopus laid
1920	'The Year of Catastrophe' in the Arab world. The French occupation of Damascus, Arab risings against occupying Allied forces throughout the Near East
1920–48	Palestine under British Administration
1925	The Hebrew University at Jerusalem opened
1936–39	The Great Arab Rising in Palestine
1937	Publication of the Royal (Peel) Commission recommending the partition of Palestine
1939	British Government White Paper limiting Jewish immigration until 1944
1942–	Zionism intensifies in America. Jewish terrorism intensifies in Palestine
13th May, 1948	Expiry of British Mandate
14th May, 1948	Declaration of the Independence of the State of Israel
1948–49	The Arab-Jewish War

Appendix II

GENEALOGICAL TABLES

Table I

THE HOUSE OF DAVID

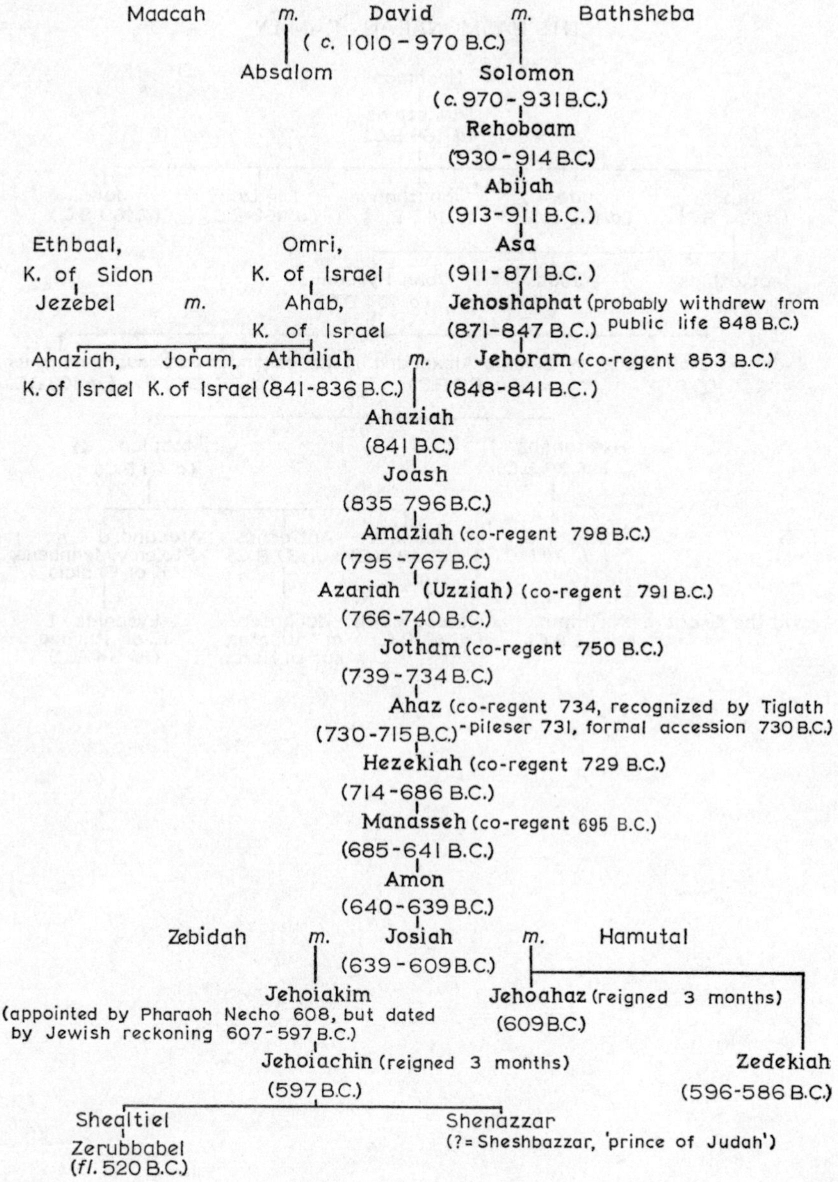
Maacah m. David m. Bathsheba
(c. 1010 – 970 B.C.)
Absalom
Solomon
(c. 970 – 931 B.C.)
Rehoboam
(930 – 914 B.C.)
Abijah
(913 – 911 B.C.)
Ethbaal, K. of Sidon
Omri, K. of Israel
Asa
(911 – 871 B.C.)
Jezebel m. Ahab, K. of Israel
Jehoshaphat (probably withdrew from public life 848 B.C.)
(871 – 847 B.C.)
Ahaziah, K. of Israel
Joram, K. of Israel
Athaliah (841-836 B.C.) m. Jehoram (co-regent 853 B.C.)
(848 – 841 B.C.)
Ahaziah
(841 B.C.)
Joash
(835 796 B.C.)
Amaziah (co-regent 798 B.C.)
(795 – 767 B.C.)
Azariah (Uzziah) (co-regent 791 B.C.)
(766 – 740 B.C.)
Jotham (co-regent 750 B.C.)
(739 – 734 B.C.)
Ahaz (co-regent 734, recognized by Tiglath-pileser 731, formal accession 730 B.C.)
(730 – 715 B.C.)
Hezekiah (co-regent 729 B.C.)
(714 – 686 B.C.)
Manasseh (co-regent 695 B.C.)
(685 – 641 B.C.)
Amon
(640 – 639 B.C.)
Zebidah m. Josiah m. Hamutal
(639 – 609 B.C.)
Jehoiakim
(appointed by Pharaoh Necho 608, but dated by Jewish reckoning 607 – 597 B.C.)
Jehoahaz (reigned 3 months)
(609 B.C.)
Jehoiachin (reigned 3 months)
(597 B.C.)
Zedekiah
(596 – 586 B.C.)
Shealtiel
Zerubbabel
(fl. 520 B.C.)
Shenazzar
(? = Sheshbazzar, 'prince of Judah')

Table II

THE HASMONAEAN FAMILY

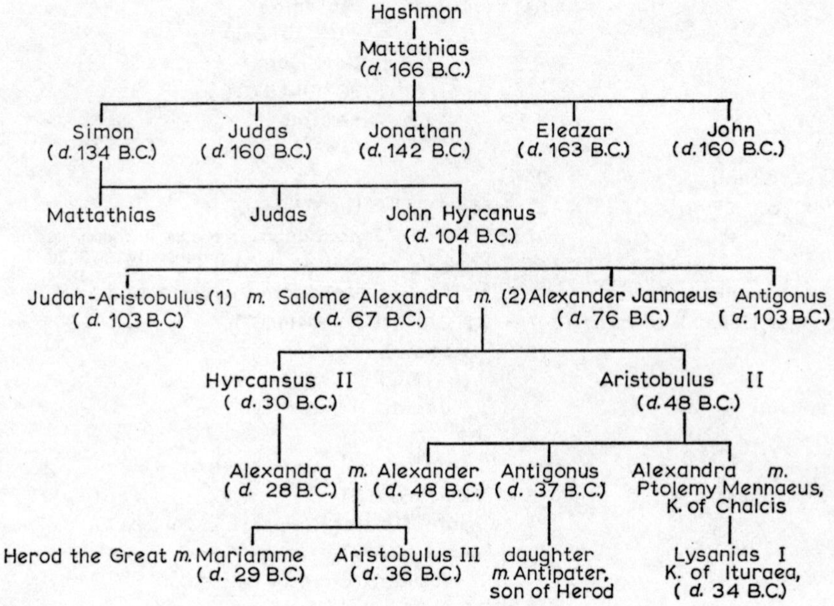

Table III

HEROD'S ANCESTRY AND KIN

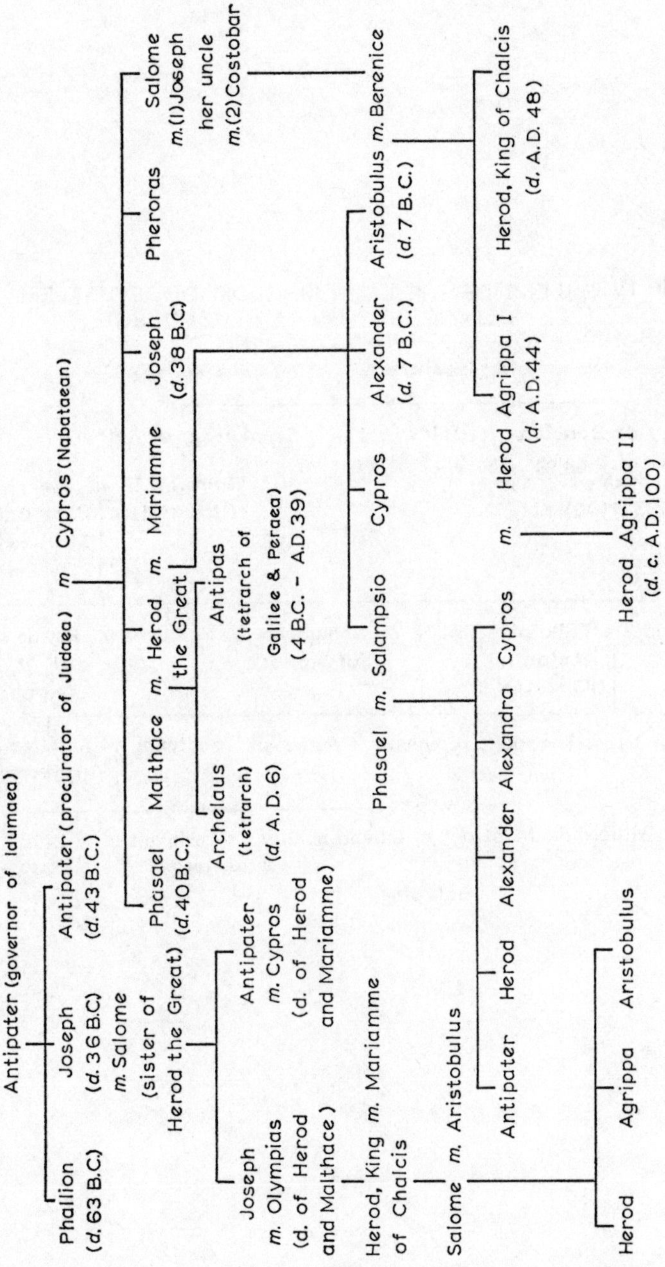

Table IV RULERS OF THE LATIN KINGDOM OF JERUSALEM BEFORE THE MUSLIM RECONQUEST

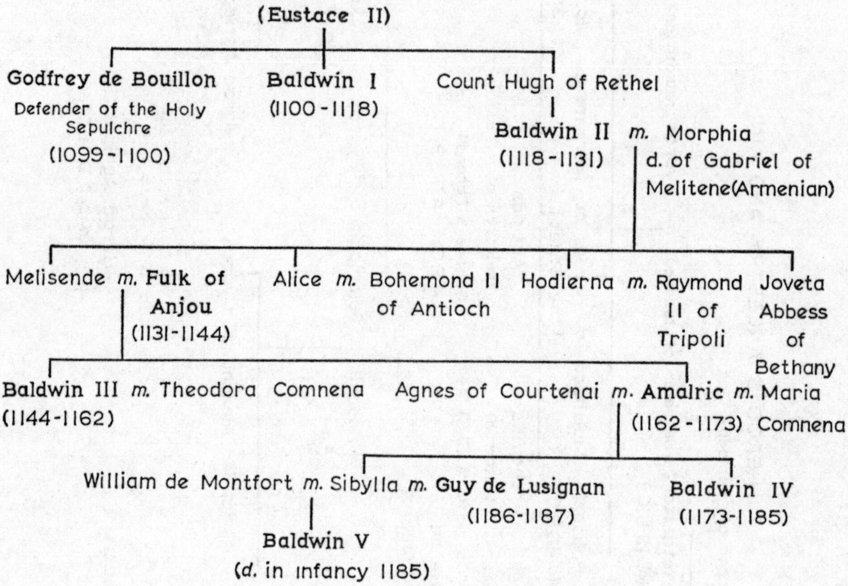

Appendix III

THE HOUSE OF ZADOK

Jaddua	*c.* 350–320 B.C.
Onias I	*c.* 320–290 B.C.
Simon I	*c.* 290–275 B.C.
Eliezer	*c.* 275–260 B.C.
Manasseh	*c.* 260–245 B.C.
Onias II	*c.* 245–220 B.C.
Simon II	*c.* 220–198 B.C.
Onias III	*c.* 198–174 B.C.

APPOINTED BY SELEUCID KINGS OR PRETENDERS

Jason (*brother of Onias III*)	174–171 B.C.
Menelaus	171–161 B.C.
Alkimos	161–159 B.C.
Interregnum	159–152 B.C.
Jonathan the Hasmonaean	152–143 B.C.
Simon the Hasmonaean	143–140 B.C.

APPOINTED BY POPULAR DECREE, OR POPULARLY CONFIRMED: THE HASMONAEAN DYNASTY

Simon	141–134 B.C.
John Hyrcanus	134–104 B.C.
Aristobulus I	104–103 B.C.
Alexander Jannaeus	102–76 B.C.
Hyrcanus II	76–67 B.C.
Aristobulus II	67–63 B.C.
Hyrcanus II	63–40 B.C.
Antigonus	40–37 B.C.

APPOINTED BY HEROD THE GREAT (37–4 B.C.)

Hananel	37–36 B.C.
Aristobulus, last of the Hasmonaeans	Spring-Autumn 36 B.C.
Hananel (*restored*)	*c*, 36–30 B.C.
Jesus son of Phabes	*c*. 30–23 B.C.
Simon son of Boëthus	*c*. 23–5 B.C.
Matthew son of Theophilus	*c*. 5 B.C.
Joseph son of Ellem	*c*. 5–4 B.C.
Joazar son of Boëthus	*c*. 4 B.C.

APPOINTED BY ARCHELAUS, ETHNARCH OF JUDAEA (4 B.C.–A.D. 6)

Eliezer son of Boëthus	*c*. 4–3 B.C.
Jesus son of Seë	*c*. 3 B.C.–A.D. 6
Joazar son of Boëthus (*second time*)	A.D. 5

APPOINTED BY QUIRINIUS, LEGATE OF SYRIA (A.D. 6–9)

Annas son of Seth	A.D. 6–15

APPOINTED BY VALERIUS GRATUS, PROCURATOR OF JUDAEA (15–26)

Ishmael son of Phabi	A.D. 15–16
Eleazar son of Annas	A.D. 16–17
Simon son of Kami	A.D. 17–18
Joseph Caiaphas, son-in-law of Annas	A.D. 18–36

APPOINTED BY VITELLIUS, LEGATE OF SYRIA (35–39)

Jonathan son of Annas	A.D. 36–37
Theophilus son of Annas	A.D. 37–41

APPOINTED BY HEROD AGRIPPA I, KING OF JUDAEA (41–44)

Simon Cantheras, son of Boëthus	A.D. 41–42
Matthias son of Annas	A.D. 42–43
Elioenai son of Cantheras	A.D. 43–44

APPOINTED BY HEROD OF CHALCIS (44–48)

Joseph son of Kami	*c.* A.D. 44–47
Ananias son of Nedebaeus	*c.* A.D. 47–58

APPOINTED BY HEROD AGRIPPA II (50–100)

Ishmael son of Phabi	*c.* A.D. 58–60
Joseph Kabi son of Simon	A.D. 60–62
Annas II (Ananus) son of Annas	A.D. 62
Jesus son of Damnaeus	c. A.D. 62–63
Jesus son of Gamaliel	*c.* A.D. 63–65
Matthias son of Theophilus son of Annas	*c.* A.D. 65–68

APPOINTED BY THE PEOPLE DURING THE WAR

Phinehas son of Samuel	A.D. 68–70

Appendix IV

RULERS OF JUDAEA UNDER ROME

Herod (king)	37–4 B.C.
Archelaus (tetrarch)	4 B.C.–A.D. 6

PROCURATORS

Coponius	A.D. 6–9
Marcus Ambivius	A.D. 9–12
Annius Rufus	A.D. 12–15
Valerius Gratus	A.D. 15–26
Pontius Pilatus	A.D. 26–36
Marcellus	A.D. 37
Marullus	A.D. 37–41

Herod Agrippa I (king)	A.D. 41–44

PROCURATORS

Cuspius Fadus	A.D. 44–46
Tiberius Julius Alexander	A.D. 46–48
Ventidius Cumanus	A.D. 48–52
Antonius Felix	A.D. 52–59
Porcius Festus	A.D. 59–62
Albinus	A.D. 62–65
Gessius Florus	A.D. 65–66

Selected Bibliography

CHAPTER 1

Abel, F. M. *Géographie de la Palestine* I, 1933; II, 1938
Baly, A. D. *The Geography of the Bible*, 1957
Bliss, F. J. and Dickie, A. C. *Excavations at Jerusalem* (Palestine Exploration Fund publication), 1898
Dalman, G. *Jerusalem und seine Geländer*, 1930
Sacred Sites and Ways, ET by P. Levertoff, 1935
Dickie, A. C. *see* Bliss, F. J.
Duncan, J. G. *see* Macalister, R. A. S.
Jeremias, J. *Die Wiederentdeckung von Bethesda*, 1949
Johns, C. N. 'The Citadel of Jerusalem', *Quarterly Statement of the Department of Antiquities of Palestine* XIV, 1950, pp. 139–47
Join-Lambert, M. *Jerusalem*, ET by C. Haldane, 1958
Kenyon, K. M. 'Excavations in Jerusalem, 1961', *Palestine Exploration Quarterly* 1962, pp. 72–89
'Excavations in Jerusalem, 1962', *ibidem* 1963, pp. 7–21
'Excavations in Jerusalem, 1963', *ibidem* 1964, pp. 7–18
'Excavations in Jerusalem, 1964', *ibidem* 1965, pp. 9–20
'Excavations in Jerusalem, 1965', *ibidem* 1966, pp. 73–88
Kopp, C. *The Holy Places of the Gospel*, 1963
Macalister, R. A. S. and Duncan, J. G. *Excavations on the Hill of Ophel 1923–25* (Palestine Exploration Fund Annual IV), 1926
Simons, J. *Jerusalem in the Old Testament*, 1952
Smith, G. A. *Jerusalem, The Topography, Economics and History from the Earliest Times to A.D. 70*, I, 1907; II, 1908
The Historical Geography of the Holy Land, 26th ed., 1935
Stève, A. M. *see* Vincent, L. H.
Vincent, L. H. and Stève, A. M. *Jérusalem de l'Ancien Testament* I, 1954; II, 1956
Weill, R. *La Cité de David* I, 1920; II, 1947

CHAPTER 2

Bottéro, J. *Le Problème des Habiru*, 1954
Bright, J. *A History of Israel*, 1960

Gray, J. *The Legacy of Canaan*, 2nd ed. 1965, pp. 218–30
Knudtzon, J. A., *Die El-Amarna Tafeln*, 1908–15
Noth, M. *The History of Israel*, Revised English Translation, 1960
Posener, G. *Princes et pays d'Asie et de Nubie, textes hiératiques sur des figurines d'envoûtement du Moyen Empire*, 1940
Sethe, K. *Die Ächtung feindlicher Fürsten, Völker und Dinge auf altägyptisichen Tongefässscherben des Mittleren Reiches* (Abhandlungen der preussischen Akademie der Wissenschaft, Phil. hist. Klasse) 1926

CHAPTER 3

Albright, W. F. *The Biblical Period from Abraham to Ezra*, 1963
Bright, J. *Op. cit.*
Noth, M. *Op. cit.*
Robinson, T. H. and Oesterley, W. O. E. *A History of Israel* I, 1932
Schmid, H. 'Jahweh und die Kulttraditionen von Jerusalem', *Zeitschrift für die Alttestamentliche Wissenschaft* XXVI, 1955, pp. 168–97
Schmidt, W. *Königtum Gottes in Ugarit und Israel*, Beiheft zur *Zeitschrift für die Alttestamenliche Wissenchaft* LXXX, 1961

CHAPTER 4

Albright, W. F. *Op cit.*
Aharoni, Y. 'Excavations at Ramat Rahel', *Biblical Archaeologist* XXIV, 1961, pp.
Albright, W. F. *Op. cit.*
Bright, J. *Op. cit.*
Browne, L. E. *Early Judaism*, 1929
Galling, K. *Studien zur Geschichte Israels im persischen Zeitalter*, 1964
Meyer, E. *Die Entstehung des Judentums*, 1896
Noth, M. *Op. cit.*
Oesterley, W. O. E. and Robinson, T. H., *A History of Israel* II, 1932
Olmstead, A. T. *History of the Persian Empire*, 1948
Rowley, H. H. 'Nehemiah's Mission and its Background', *Men of God*, 1963, pp. 211–45
'Sanballat and the Samaritan Temple', *op. cit.*, pp. 246–76
Schürer, E. *A History of the Jewish People in the Time of Jesus Christ*, ET, 1885–1890
Sellers, O. R. *The Citadel of Bethsur*, 1933
Welch, A. C. *Post Exilic Judaism*, 1935

CHAPTER 5

Abel, F. M. *Histoire de la Palestine depuis la conquête d'Aléxandre jusqu'à l'invasion arabe* I, 1952

Allegro, J. M. *The Dead Sea Scrolls*, 1956
Barthélemy, D. and Milik, J. T. *Discoveries in the Judaean Desert* I: *Qumran, Cave I*, 1955
Bevan, E. R. *The House of Seleucus*, 1902
Jerusalem under the High Priests (rev.), 1952
Bright, J. *Op. cit.*
Burrows, M. *The Dead Sea Scrolls*, 1955
More Light on the Dead Sea Scrolls, 1958
Dupont-Sommer, A. *Aperçus préliminaires sur les manuscrits de la Mer Morte*, 1950
Gaster T. H., *The Scriptures of the Dead Sea Sect*, 1957
Milik, J. T. *see* Barthelemy, D.
Ten Years of Discovery in the Wilderness of Judah, 1957
Noth, M. *Op. cit.*
Oesterley, W. O. E. and Robinson, T. H. *Op. cit.*
Reifenberg, A. *Israel's History in Coins*, 1953
Schürer, E. *Op. cit.*
Sellers, O. R. *Op. cit.*

CHAPTER 6

Abel, F. M. *Op. cit.*
Bright, J. *Op. cit.*
Jones, A. H. M. *The Herods of Judaea*, 1938
Noth, M. *Op. cit.*
Oesterley, W. O. E. and Robinson, T. H. *Op. cit.*
Perowne, S. *The Later Herods*, 1958
Schürer, E. *Op. cit.*

CHAPTER 7

Abel, F. M. *Op. cit.*
Bright, J. *Op. cit.*
Noth, M. *Op. cit.*
Schürer, E. *Op. cit.*

CHAPTER 8

Abel, F. M. *Op. cit.*
Avi-Yonah, M. *The Madaba Mosaic Map* (Israel Exploration Society Publication) 1954
Gold, V. R. 'The Mosaic Map of Madaba', *Biblical Archaeologist* XXI, 1958
Molinier, A., Tobler, T. *Itinera in Terra Sancta*, 1879, pp. 50–57
Tobler, T. *see* Molinier, A.

CHAPTER 9

Abel, F. M. *Op. cit.*
Glubb, J. B. *The Great Arab Conquests*, 1963
The Empire of the Arabs, 1963
Hitti, P. K. *History of the Arabs*, 1956
Muir, W. *The Caliphate, Rise, Decline and Fall*, rev. ed. 1915
Le Strange, G. *Palestine under the Moslems*, 1890

CHAPTER 10

Atiya, A. S. *Crusade, Commerce and Culture*, 1964
Chabot, J. B. *Michael the Syrian, Chronicle*, 1963
Gibb, H. A. R. *The Continuation of the Damascus Chronicle* (Ibn al-Qalānisī 1932
Grousset, R. *Les Croisades*, 3 Vols., 1934–6
Setton, K. M. and Baldwin, M. W. *A History of the Crusades* I, 1955
idem, Wolff, R. L. and Hazard, H. W. (ed.) *A History of the Crusades* II, 1962
Runciman, J. C. S. *A History of the Crusades* I, 1956; II, 1952; III, 1954
Stevenson, W. B. *The Crusaders in the East*, 1907
Recueil des Historiens des Croisades, Occidentaux, 1844–1895
Recueil des Historiens des Croisades, Orientaux, 1872–98

CHAPTER 11 AND 12

King Abdullah. *Memoirs of King Abdullah*, ed. P. P. Graves, 1950
Antonius, G. *The Arab Awakening*, 1938
Barbour, N. *Nisi Dominus*, 1946
Herzl, T. *Diaries*, ed. Löwenthal, M., 1958
Gardner, B. *Allenby*, 1965
Lawrence, T. E. *Seven Pillars of Wisdom*, 1936
Marlowe, J. *The Seat of Pilate*, 1959
Meinertzhagen, R. *Army Diary, 1899–1926*, 1960
Wavell, A. *Allenby*, 1941
Weizmann, C. *Trial and Error*, 1949

INDEX